Pelican Books

Working for Ford

Huw Beynon was born in 1942 in Ebbw Vale. He studied economics and sociology at the universities of Wales and Liverpool. Since 1966 he has been involved in research related to the changing nature of work and industry in the U.K. He is the author of several books and pamphlets including *Perception of Work* (with R. Blackburn), *Living with Capitalism* (with Theo Nichols), *The Workers Report on Vickers* (with Hilary Wainwright), *Born to Work* (with Nick Hedges) and *What Happened at Speke?* He currently teaches at the University of Durham.

WORKING FOR

Huw Beynon

Second edition

Penguin Books

Penguin Books Ltd, Harmondsworth, Middlesex, England
Viking Penguin Inc., 40 West 23rd Street, New York, New York 10010, U.S.A.
Penguin Books Australia Ltd, Ringwood, Victoria, Australia
Penguin Books Canada Ltd, 2801 John Street, Markham, Ontario, Canada L3R 1B4
Penguin Books (N.Z.) Ltd, 182–190 Wairau Road, Auckland 10, New Zealand

First published in Penguin Education 1973
Second edition published in Pelican Books 1984

Printed and bound in Great Britain by
Cox & Wyman Ltd, Reading
Set in 9/11pt Linotron Times

Contents

Abbreviations

EEF The Engineering Employers' Federation, which covers firms in the engineering and motor vehicle industries. The Federation negotiates national rates of pay with the constituent unions and it has its own procedure for dealing with disputes, the final stage ending at the York Conference.

NJNC The National Joint Negotiating Committee. Ford has never been a member of the EEF, preferring to conduct its own company-wide agreements with the trade unions. The NJNC is Ford's equivalent to the York Conference. It is the last stage of procedure and the place where national negotiations on rates of pay etc. are conducted between the Company and the unions. Until 1969 the 'trade union side' of the NJNC was entirely composed of full-time, national officers of the various unions. Now, all plant convenors sit on the committee with the officials.

JWC Joint Works Committee. This is the senior negotiating committee at plant level, where it parallels the NJNC. It consists of representatives of management and shop stewards. The shop stewards' committee elects a convenor and a number of supporting senior stewards who serve as JWC members for a year.

JSSC Joint Shop Stewards' Committee. The workers in each plant of the Ford Motor Company elect shop stewards who form a shop stewards' committee. The committees of the three Halewood plants are linked to form the Halewood JSSC, and those of all the Ford plants in Britain to form the Ford JSSC.

As a result of a series of mergers that took place during the 1960s, several unions changed their names, and their initials, several times in the space of a few years. For the purposes of this book their titles have remained constant as:

TGWU The Transport and General Workers' Union. The main organizer of unskilled and semi-skilled workers. Largest union in the country with the largest membership at the Ford Motor Company. Amalgamated with the NUVB in 1972.

AUEW The Amalgamated Union of Engineering Workers. An ex-craft union, the major union in the engineering industry and second largest union in Britain, with the second largest membership in the Ford Motor Company. Once known as the AEU and the AEF.

NUVB National Union of Vehicle Builders. Traditionally a craft union but in the 1960s recruited almost exclusively from semi-skilled workers in the car plants. Now amalgamated with the TGWU.

GMWU The General and Municipal Workers' Union. Once the NUGMW. The third largest union in Britain with a large membership at Ford's until 1969 when over 2000 of its members at the Company's Halewood plant withdrew their membership and joined the TGWU.

EPTU The Electrical and Plumbing Trades Union.

TUC Trades Union Congress. The central congress of the British trade union movement to which most British unions are affiliated.

AFL/CIO The American Federation of Labour and the Committee for Industrial Organisation. The USA equivalent of the TUC but with stronger, more centralized control over its constituent members. The split between the AFL (skilled workers/craft unions) and the CIO (semi and unskilled workers/industrial unions) derives from conflicts in the inter-war period.

UAW The United Automobile Workers in the USA. Leading group within the CIO.

Preface to the First Edition

C. Wright Mills started his book, *The Sociological Imagination*, with the words: 'Nowadays most men feel their ... lives are a series of traps.' That was fifteen years ago. Mills is now dead and people are increasingly bewildered by the events that punctuate the path of their lives. Their minds are dominated by recrimination and regret. Little has happened, since Mills wrote his book, to suggest that the imagination of sociologists has helped matters. That these 'scientific' examiners of society have failed to make clear the issues that so deeply affect people's lives is a condemnation of them and their art. At best, they have written with 'the profession' over their right shoulder, and produced sociology for sociologists: an absurdity which cuts the writer off from the subjects of his writing.

In writing *Working for Ford* I have tried to overcome this contrived isolation. I have never worked for Ford. I have told the story of other people's experiences, some of which I shared, as an outsider. An outsider who was accepted inside. These pages are the product of that hesitant mutuality. They are made up of the activity and conversation of men and women in the pub, the factory, on the picket-line or in their homes, combined in an attempt to describe the lives that people lead when they work on the shop floor of a large car factory; to outline the crises they encounter and the way in which they try to make sense of them and the world they live in. The names are their names and the book is written for them in the hope that they, and others like them, will be able to identify parts of themselves in the story and perhaps, thereby, see more clearly the way they are going.

It remains for me to acknowledge those who have helped. A lot of people helped me; a lot of people got in the way. Many did both at some time during the five years that it took to complete this book. My greatest debt is to the lads at Halewood who befriended me with their hospitality and conversation. They, and the many other people who gave up their time to talk to me, have my gratitude.

Preface to the Second Edition

Soon after *Working for Ford* was published in 1973 I went to talk to an old man to whom I had given a copy of the book. He had retired after working in a variety of different jobs – a factory here and there, a shop, on the roads, in Liverpool. 'It was good', he said, 'to read a book that's written in *our* language for a change. It was a pleasure to read it.' It was good for me to have that conversation, because, at the time, the book was causing something of a stir. Many people *didn't* like it. Lord McCarthy, for example, thought that it demonstrated:

that it is impossible to write a completely uninteresting book about shop stewards – though not for the want of trying . . . Paragraph after paragraph of shop-floor chat is spatchcocked into the text. To judge from this evidence, Ford's must employ some of the most conceited and foul-mouthed stewards in the country! (*Oxford Mail*, 4 June 1973).

Similar kinds of criticism were voiced by Peter Paterson, then deputy editor of the *New Statesman*:

This is a curious piece of work by a sociologist who appears to have experienced a prolonged love affair with a group of militant Merseyside shop stewards. He has produced a catalogue of bloodymindedness that will make most readers wonder how the car industry – or the Ford share of it – possibly survives. If shop stewards are really as ignorant, obstructive and stupid as this book makes out, then the British working man certainly qualifies for Ludendorff's description of the British Expeditionary Force in World War One – 'Lions led by donkeys'. This is a horror story of Dickensian proportions, an industrial Dotheboys Hall, luridly described in the picturesque language of Billingsgate.

Again severe distaste: for the language and for the workers themselves, linked with a disapproval of the method which allowed it all to surface into print.

The tragedy of this book is that Mr Beynon, an academic with the training to analyse and interpret, has instead indulged a fantasy that he is a *Sunday Times* 'Insight' reporter.

This message is clear: Beynon should stick

to the statistical tools of his trade rather than depend on the cryptic direct quotation ushered in and out by his own subjective comments (*Liverpool Post*, 31 May 1973).

McCarthy agreed, commenting on the book's 'persistent naivety' and concluding: 'as it progresses, its factual content gets smaller and smaller, as its stories get taller and taller'. All in all there was a deal of support for the assessment of the book given in *The Times Educational Supplement* by Mike Thomas, then prospective Labour party member of Parliament:

> This book is of doubtful value as an objective sociological study, partly because Beynon comes so much to identify himself with the stewards and partly because it is written in a confused, chatty, repetitive and even ungrammatical style which creates an impression rather than reports facts.

This worry over 'objectivity' and 'facts' also coloured the response that came from the popular press, and the Ford Motor Company. To the press the book had to be seen as a series of partly established 'allegations' about union meetings, sabotage, management attitudes and the like. Referred to as 'The Beynon Report', headlines like this one from the *Daily Mail* were typical: 'The Four Letter Ford Underworld: Shop Floor Study Spares No-one'. The spokesman for the Ford Motor Company in Liverpool, while interested most of all in playing things down and treating the 'report' as irrelevant, was particularly concerned to refute accounts of incidents that had taken place in the plant. For example, he found 'particularly unpleasant' the account of a man lying dead on the factory floor for ten minutes while the line continued to run:

> It is really quite monstrous to suggest that any supervisor should, in any way, jeopardize the health of an employee ... we have no recollection of the particular incident ... But it does seem appalling that someone who is not named should be making a serious allegation of this kind, suggesting that the men are being exploited (*Liverpool Echo*, 30 May 1973).

While agreeing that there 'have been incidents of vandalism and sabotage in the plant', he felt that such behaviour was, 'of course, intolerable and is deplored by everyone at all levels'. Echoing support, a spokesman in London described the book as 'extreme left-wing propaganda ... we don't think it merits serious discussion as it's not a serious attempt at sociology or education'.

Given all this, the reader may well wonder whether it's worth reading any further. Perhaps the book should be returned to the shelf. On the other hand, perhaps the criticisms and comments do seem a bit shrill. Perhaps it's worth bearing with the story a little longer while I try to explain how it was that I came to write the book and what I thought I was doing.

I visited the paint and trim assembly plant (the PTA) on the Ford Motor Company's Halewood estate on a regular basis throughout 1967. At that time I was a research student at the University of Liverpool. After some negotiations, the Ford Motor Company agreed that I could visit the assembly plant and that while I was there I could interview each of the shop stewards who represented assembly-line workers as well as a selection of workers from each of the four main production departments. Before approaching the Company, I had had a series of discussions with the local officials of the trade unions on Merseyside. They were happy to help me, as were the shop stewards in the Ford plant. Having spent some time interviewing *me* to work out what I thought I was doing, and ensuring that it was 'something worthwhile', they agreed to talk to me, and to allow me to attend their meetings. While I was in the plant I spent a day each week with the shop stewards' convenor or his deputy, moving with him throughout the plant, and sitting in on his discussions with workers, stewards and supervisors. This period in the plant allowed me to obtain detailed information from each of the shop stewards and also to observe and listen to them as they negotiated, argued and discussed issues amongst themselves and with their members. I sat at tables in the canteens and at benches around the coffee-vending machines at break times. I talked with workers as they queued up for their dinner, for buses or to clock their cards at the beginning and the end of every day. While I was in the plant several small, sectional disputes erupted into strikes. I observed these events and talked with the people as they decided upon their course of action. I listened, remembered and took notes. Mostly I listened.

This process continued over a period of five years, for after my permitted time in the plant, I kept in regular contact with several of the workers and with the shop stewards' committee. During that time the Company was hit by two major national strikes and was brought to the verge of another. I attended the strike meetings and sat in on the daily discussions involved in the organization of strike action. Throughout all this (these conversations and interviews, these observations at meetings and on picket-lines) I wrote in my notebook. I kept a record. The book emerged out of, and was developed by, this process. On one occasion in 1968 I wrote an account of a strike that had appeared as a spontaneous outburst by the assembly-line workers.

This was published as an article in *New Society* and some of the stewards' committee met with me to discuss and evaluate both the strike and my interpretation of it. The dialogue proceeded. Drafts of chapters were duplicated and distributed for comment and discussion.

At the time of publication, therefore, I was reasonably confident that the account I had offered of life in the Halewood plant could stand up to close inspection. I was, as it were, sure of my facts. I knew that the book wasn't above criticism, and that other interpretations were possible (I didn't have a closed mind or any idea that I had produced a final statement) but I knew that I hadn't produced a *false* account. This confidence was confirmed in a number of ways. Soon after the book's publication Radio Merseyside organized a half-hour discussion programme with several of the Halewood shop stewards. One or two of them were eager to back up the accounts contested by the Company. The incident involving the dead man was expanded as the anonymous steward – Frank Banton – came forward, named the foreman involved and pointed out that it hadn't been ten, but eight minutes that the man had spent lying dead on the floor. He knew this for certain because he had timed it with his stopwatch from the moment when the foreman insisted that work continued. There was no doubt about that.

The 'facts' were supported in other ways too. People wrote me letters. One man, who had worked at the Dagenham plant for thirty years, wrote saying that:

> Many of my colleagues employed at Halewood, Dagenham and elsewhere in the company, plus several journalist friends of mine found your book extremely good. What you submit is quite factual . . . At Dagenham a man lay dead on the lines for *thirteen minutes*. It was I who took up his case with management. Tommy Turner of Hornchurch dropped down dead on the lines in the PTA on the Saturday morning . . . of course they hushed up this scandal. But Tommy Turner was not the only death.[1]

The truth of statements like this came through in *Car*, the magazine for the auto trade, which noted that 'the book is more accurate than most observers seem to think. Ford workers *have* been drubbed and brutalized for too long.' Other writers concurred; some of them generously. The book, they said, had 'got under the skin' of life in a car

---

1. With these incidents in mind, it is perhaps worth noting that in 1973 Dr James Allardice, a medical officer at the Ford Motor Company in Britain, produced a report based upon his investigations into the effects of stress upon assembly-line workers. He planned to present his findings at a medical convention. The report, in fact, was never published. The Company refused Allardice permission to give his lecture, arguing that 'the risk involved in exploring the problem far outweighed the good that might come of it'.

factory in Britain. And I continued to receive letters from car workers who told me that the book describes factory work, just as it is, not only at Ford but throughout the industry. One man put it like this:

> The farmer was asked by an interviewer, 'What is the most important thing in pig keeping?' He replied, 'Why! the bloody pig of course.' So with 'man-u-facture'. The word speaks for itself. I have spent a working life of forty-five years in engineering, from foundry to fabrication of steelwork and the motor trade. Everywhere I have seen the repercussions of the incoherent feeling at the back of working people's minds that they are of less importance than the machine. This is, of course, an utter fallacy but, sad to relate, industry or society does little in its day-to-day functioning to correct this idea, which many give the vague name of progress.

All this was very reassuring for me at the time. Humbling too, because it was clear that, given the chance, many of the people who had written to me were quite capable of providing their own, richly detailed, accounts of factory life. Here it helps settle the balance. But in doing so it raises further questions. If the book is accurate why were people so upset? To begin an answer, we need to look a bit more closely at this relationship between man and machine, and go back in time – to the 1960s.

At the time when *Working for Ford* was published in Britain, other accounts of factory life were appearing in Europe and the USA. These books were also based on time spent talking with workers mostly by students, poets and journalists who had gone into the factories and worked on the jobs themselves. In Germany, the journalist Gunter Wallraff worked anonymously in a variety of different workplaces and wrote graphically about what he saw and experienced. His writings were vilified by the Employers' Association of the Federal Republic, who argued: 'When he describes an industry on the basis of his "research", his writing is characterized by a constant scale of social values which could be fashioned only by a conscious ideologist of class struggle ... His methods of investigation and demonstration must be categorically condemned.' Göran Palm did the same in Sweden and while his critics were not as severe they were equally dismissive – 'The author's method of collecting, structuring and analysing his data does not conform with any scientific standards of objectivity and thus the data presented do not warrant comment.'

Without raising questions about the 'scientific standards' adopted by companies in establishing the evidence for *their* regular contributions to debates on the nature of work, workers and the working environment, what is most noticeable here is the consistency of the response. It comes across again in Hungary where Miklos Haraszti was tried and convicted on the charge of 'incitement to subversion'. Haraszti, like Palm, had worked in a factory and written about it. The authorities claimed that he had 'falsified the facts and generalized on the basis of this false picture'.[2] Everywhere, or so it seems, detailed descriptive accounts of factory conditions and the subjective experience of workers became the centre of controversy. And there was a reason for this.

In the 1960s and early 1970s, working-class people in Europe (East and West) and the USA were reacting in a variety of ways to the tedium of monotonous repetitive work in authoritarian factories. 'Wildcat strikes' were one way; others were absenteeism, lateness and 'job hopping' from firm to firm; yet another was the increased incidence of industrial sabotage. These diffuse, yet related, actions became meshed into the folklore of popular culture. Jokes about absenteeism were commonplace (the manager asks miners why they only work four shifts out of five; they reply, 'Because we can't survive on three'), as were graffiti (the slogan 'Be at peace with yourself, peace is within' drew the reply 'Not if you're on piece work' in one Liverpool lavatory), and the generalized hope that you didn't buy a car that was made on Monday or Friday. The response found one of its highmarks in the 'Paris Revolution' of 1968 when posters proclaimed, 'Work: it will make you ugly'. Here was the root of the problem. Books which recorded such reactions and attitudes, recognizing them as authentic, human (and intrinsically liberating) responses to the new factory conditions, implicitly threatened many of the social and political arrangements that had become taken for granted since the war. In particular they challenged 'industrial relations' orthodoxy, which associated industrial 'maturity' with the recognition of trade unionism, and the establishment of collective bargaining arrangements with

2. A collection of Gunter Wallraff's articles has appeared as *The Undesirable Journalist*, Pluto Press (1977). Göran Palm's account was published in Britain as *The Flight from Work*, Cambridge University Press (1977). The quotation is taken from the foreword by Peter Doherty. Miklos Haraszti's book *Piece Rates* was published in Britain as *A Worker in a Workers' State*, Penguin Books (1971), and contains an account of his trial in the appendix. In France, Robert Linhart's account *The Establishment* was published in Britain as *The Assembly Line*, John Calder (1981). For the USA see especially Bill Watson, 'Counter Planning on the Factory Floor', *Radical America*, vol. 5, no. 3 (May/June 1971) and Richard Pfeffer, *Working for Capitalism*, Columbia University Press (1979). In Japan, Satoshi Kamata's account, *Factory of Despair: Diary of a Seasonal Worker* was published in 1973. See also Matsuo Kei, 'Nissan Motors: Hell's Battlefield', published in Britain in *Solidarity Motor Bulletin*, no. 3 and available from 123 Latham Road, London E 6.

written procedures and the like. They opened up the suggestion that workers, in their experience of the new arrangements, found them wanting. This in turn posed major questions both for companies' personnel policies and the employment policies of governments.[3] It also raised questions about the future of the trade union movement.

The British trade union movement developed during the nineteenth century. Its slow growth and development mirrored the gradual way in which capitalist expansion punctuated the various trades and industries over a period of 150 years. Over this time, men in the skilled trades established union organizations based upon those trades. These unions have been termed craft unions and they protected the interests of the worker principally by restricting entry into the trade. They achieved this through rules and regulations and a form of organization that was based not upon the workshop but upon the *locality*. Much of this remains true today. The Engineering Union, for example, continues to have local branches (to whose secretary members pay their union contributions) which draw their membership from a variety of different factories. At the factory the workers elect *shop stewards* who need not be officials of the branch. In the craft unions, therefore, there has always been a dual power-structure based upon workshop and branch. This was the organizational root of the syndicalist-inspired shop steward movement which reached its high point during the 1914–18 war, and put forward demands for workers' control of the workshops (see Hinton, 1973 and Murphy, 1972).

In contrast, unskilled and semi-skilled workers had their strength not in skill but numbers, and in Britain these people became organized into *general unions* which included all grades of workers from all industries. It is these unions, their strength increased through amalgamations, which came to dominate the union movement in the post-war period. The 'transport workers' (TGWU) and the 'municipal workers'

3. It was in this period, for example, that General Motors established a Director for Employee Research, and the *Harvard Business Review* carried numerous articles on the problem of employee motivation. In the USA the Department of Health, Education and Welfare published its survey, *Work in America*, MIT Press (1974), in which it concluded that 'absenteeism, wildcat strikes, turnover and industrial sabotage have become an increasingly significant part of doing business'. In the UK, an incoming Labour government established a 'Work Research Unit' at the Department of Employment. Its director, Gilbert Jessup, commented: 'Low motivation exists in a lot of firms in British industry because people are not involved in their work. This leads to a lot of real problems such as low productivity, absenteeism, high labour turnover and industrial unrest. We are predicting that these things will get worse if changes are not thought about now.'

(GMWU) expanded into the new growth industries of the late fifties and sixties, and today their combined membership approaches three millions. With this, the shop steward system (for so long the preserve of skilled men in their engineering workshops) became a general feature of industrial life in Britain, presenting the possibility of an alternative, workplace-based locus for trade union action. It was this 'structural gap' between the trade union 'official' organization and organizations on the factory floor which (together with the other disturbances) was seen by many commentators to threaten the stability of the 'industrial relations system' as a whole.

In the 1960s the car plants were to lie at the centre of that instability. It was in the motor sector that unofficial (shop steward led) strike action had escalated more steeply, and there, too, workers seemed more often to be in dispute over the general conditions of their work. The Labour government set up a special 'troubleshooter' – Jack Scamp – to keep tabs on the car industry, and the Royal Commission which it set up on the unions (and for which McCarthy directed research) took a special interest in automobile production. In 1969 industrial journalists were still predicting that the car plants would be the 'Flashpoint of the Seventies' (*Sunday Times*, 21 December 1969). In the popular press generally (and in the public views of leading politicians) these outbursts were most often explained by the malevolence of the shop-floor leaders. Militancy was explained by the fact that 'militants' had captured key positions within the shop-floor organizations. During the 1950s this notion of the 'agitator' had become entrenched in public consciousness as films like *The Angry Silence* and *I'm All Right Jack* portrayed the mindless militant feeding off working-class irrationalism and stupidity at the expense of fair-minded men. So it was in the 1960s. The fact that 'militants' were *followed* was not seen as needing too much explanation; where it received attention at all, car workers were depicted as sheep-like or cowed in the face of bombastic leadership. To many this seemed unlikely. What newspapers as distinct as the *Financial Times* and the *Socialist Worker* had in common was a belief that those strikes represented *real* struggles which had to be taken seriously. Rather than the product of a conspiracy, the struggles in the car plants and the activities of shop stewards needed to be seen as an important political development. To some, the fact that strikes in these plants were increasingly over managerial prerogatives – over discipline, sackings, shop steward facilities and the like – rather than over straight 'wage issues' was seen to mark the potential for a grass-roots, extra-Parliamentary, socialist movement within the working class. The Institute of Workers' Control, for example, argued that the syndicalist demands of the *first* shop steward movement were finding their expression again in the 'explicit demand for control' which was now coming from workers in all sectors of industry. In their view these demands had ignited a spark that was spreading 'right across the international socialist and trade union movements' (Topham, 1964 and Cliff and Barker, 1966).

This was the political phenomenon which lay at the centre of my research at the Ford factory. At one level my concern was to offer an account of the process whereby people became shop stewards; the way they understood the job, the kinds of pressure they were under and how they reacted to them. It was my strong suspicion that this process was rather more complicated than was allowed for in the popular press. Also, in as far as the shop stewards' committee related, in a rather direct way, to the experience of the people who worked on the assembly lines, an account of its operations must face up squarely to the question of control demands from below: both to the extent of it, and to the potential of and problems faced by this kind of 'industrial politics'. It clearly raised, in an immediate way, a whole range of questions about the nature of working-class thinking and working-class action. For example: in what ways did the trade union organization in the factory express (enlarge or modify) the feelings of the workers it represented? How did the people who worked on the assembly lines understand their own interests (as employees of Ford and as workers generally) and how did this fit into their direct experiences of work in the plant? How, and in what ways, did unregulated, spontaneous struggles relate to more organized campaigns of action?

However, it is one thing to pose questions, quite another to find satisfactory ways of answering them. In truth there is no entirely satisfactory solution. For my part, in 1966, I chose to focus upon the shop stewards' committee as it operated within one plant of the Ford Motor Company. I felt such a focus to be justified, given the importance of these committees, and it was a view which was reinforced throughout the period of the research, a period which saw the stewards at Halewood struggling to establish their position both within the plant and the trade unions. In addition I had the hope (and this too was borne out to some extent) that the central position of the committee within the factory would allow it to serve as a prism through which the other relationships could be examined. There are obviously problems with this. In the social and the physical world, focusing involves distortion, and in this case there is the worry that the views and experiences of managers and foremen, as well as workers, union officials and shop stewards from other Ford plants may not be truly represented here. (People who have mentioned this, incidentally, differ enormously in their assessments of the nature and consequence of such possible distortion!) To this, I can only respond by saying that I was aware of the dangers; that I tried to allow for any possible distortion and was careful not to exaggerate it. Ultimately, of course, these issues can only be resolved by more writing and more discussion.

A further problem has to do with the setting of the study within one plant. During the research, it became clear that many of the forces which generated the action within the Halewood factory derived from 'outside' the factory, and that somehow, however awkwardly, relationships within the PTA needed to be located within wider frameworks. Several things were involved here. Take 'work' to begin with. Factory conditions have certainly changed since the war and in Liverpool in the 1960s workers were more likely to be involved in work which fitted Sartre's description of a 'vigilance without content, a captive consciousness kept awake only the better to suppress itself' (Sartre, 1969). But to understand these changes (the development of 'life on the line' in Liverpool) plants like the Halewood PTA need to be located within the transnational organization of companies like Ford and through this to constraints imposed by the capitalist organization of vehicle manufacture. This seemed all the more important in a period when the international division of labour within manufacturing was undergoing a dramatic reorganization. What happened within one plant was increasingly influenced by the position of the plant within the structure of the company and the industry. To understand this it was important to be in the factory, yet to be able to see beyond the direct day-to-day experiences contained within it. This was one 'widening' of the relationships. Another (achieved even more clumsily) involved placing Halewood, and the people who worked there, within the Merseyside context – its economy, and the cultural, political and social traditions of its working class. Much of this was learned as I carried out the research; as I talked to people and listened. And throughout this process I learned something else.

Regularly, and with some feeling, I heard men complain of being treated 'nothing better than a number' by the Company. They resented it, and all the implications that, as line workers, they weren't capable of thought: 'thickos', failures at school, established in their station on the moving line. Here the mass production of vehicles and the mass production of workers through the school system came together. The new meritocratic education system (still powerful in its biases against working-class children) legitimized 'success' while making the judgement of 'failure' more total. As these arrangements developed so did 'working-class values' – the culture, behaviour and standards of working-class people came to be seen as a primary block upon educational achievement.[4] Yet listening to these people talk, hearing them argue and discuss (swear even!), it was hard to escape the realization that in these 'failures' something had been denied. For as they coped with the line, with late buses, with the rain and the lay-off, they managed to take life for what it was while adding a bit more to it – through humour and jest, sometimes pathos.

It was these qualities (and not the baser ones implied by Paterson and McCarthy) which I hoped to demonstrate in my account. Some people were, I know, offended by the use of swear words. I am sorry for this, but would say that my hope, always, was that by constructing the rhythms of the book out of the actions of the people who worked for Ford, and by allowing the account to develop through their words, I would produce a lasting and authentic statement of their experience. In this I was strongly influenced by Edward Thompson's book *The Making of the English Working Class*. There Thompson talks of rescuing past struggles fought by workers from 'the condescension of posterity' (Thompson, 1970, p. 12), and in contemporary analysis the need was no less acute, as educationalists, industrial relations pundits and politicians seemed to devote their professional lives to the task of diminishing (rather than encouraging and developing) the horizons of human experience and ability. Furthermore, Thompson's approach to 'class' (as involving relationships, struggle and action) and 'class consciousness' (as being culturally determined and therefore relative) had an attractive looseness. Perhaps today there is a need to tighten it up a bit, but in 1968 it offered the possibility of a theoretical framework which didn't impose itself upon the detailed experiences of workers but rather responded to those experiences and developed out of them. To that extent, I was quite clear about what I was doing, and maybe at this point I can return briefly to another review of the book, this time in *The Times Literary Supplement*. There it was observed that:

4. Perhaps a view, expressed by the then editor of Britain's biggest selling daily newspaper, the *Daily Mirror*, gives some indication of what's involved here. Writing in his autobiography, Cecil King argues that 'only the people who conduct newspapers and similar organizations have any idea quite how indifferent, quite how stupid, quite how uninterested in education of any kind the great bulk of the British people are'.

Most academic sociologists will probably be critical of *Working for Ford* because it is not explicitly 'theoretical' . . . Mr Beynon formulates no initial hypotheses and spends little time discussing the theoretical contributions made by previous writers as a prelude to demolishing or revising them. But the book is not the less 'theoretical' in the best sense: the discussion of what is actually done by managers, foremen, regional and national trade union leaders, shop stewards and the men themselves is used for a series of analyses which produce useful generalizations about the roles – and the pressures upon – these respective groups of people (7 August 1973).

My hope, in 1973, (with all due modesty) was that the book would be read in this way. While I wanted people to follow and relate to 'the story', I also wanted the book to raise and encourage questions about 'story telling' in general. Put baldly, I hoped that *Working for Ford* might help encourage workers to write themselves, and sociologists to write differently. That, in spite of some significant changes, is still my hope.[5]

So much for the *first* edition. Perhaps I should also say something about this second one. Most of the book remains as it was in 1973. I have made the occasional alteration and deletion (many of these to save space) but I have resisted the temptation to rewrite and add to the sections. Mostly then the same faults remain. What I have done is to expand the book by way of a new introduction, an additional chapter (Chapter Twelve, 'Ford's Global Strategy') and a new concluding chapter ('What Strategy for Labour?'). There are a number of reasons for this. Over the past ten years, I have kept in touch with events in Ford and in the motor industry generally. Many people have shown great kindness in writing to me and sending me documents, and for some time people have been asking me to 'up-date' the book. However, such a task would be impossible. As one man put it: 'You'll need more than a chapter to cover what's happened. Things have changed that much you'll need another bleeding book.' Also, since 1973, a number of books and pamphlets have been written which, taken together, document many of the changes that have affected the British motor industry generally and Ford in particular (see Appendix 2). And so, this new edition is not an 'up-date', I have made no attempt at charting all the main events at Ford since 1972. What I have

5. Within the study of history, the development of 'oral documentation' and the importance of a 'people's history' have seen significant changes. See for example, *The History Workshop Journal*, available from 25 Horsell Road, London N5 1XL. So too, the success of projects like Centerprise in Hackney, and the Federation of Worker Writer. For details write to 136 Kingsland High Street, London E8.

attempted, in 1982, is to explore a theme which, although evident ten years ago, has become a more pronounced feature of the motor industry since then. In 1972 it was possible to see, in 'Ford Europe', the rise of a continental production system within the motor industry. Equally the battle over 'market share' was developing the competitive edge of corporate business. Both these tendencies were accelerated by the oil crisis of 1973. Plants were closed down, companies have faced bankruptcy, sold up or amalgamated with their competitors. What has emerged in this 'crisis' has been increasingly sophisticated continental and global organization of vehicle production. It is this which this edition of *Working for Ford* attempts to take account of, and with it all the attendant problems and issues it poses for car workers and their trade union organizations.

ESTABLISHMENT AND REVISION OF WORK STANDARDS

Step 6, Part B – Check Element Time for Consistency

The Industrial Engineer next checks each individual value and compares it with the rest of the values in the same element group to see whether they are consistent. For example, time values computed for element 1 are ·05; ·04; ·04; ·05; ·04; ·05; ·05; ·03; ·05; ·05. Note that the average is between ·04 and ·05 and that these time values are consistent. Element 2 values are ·07; ·06; ·06; ·07; ·07; ·06; ·07; ·05; ·07; ·06. These also appear consistent. However, in element 3 where the time values are ·08; ·09; ·09; ·10; ·09; ·15; ·09; ·10; ·08; ·08; the sixth cycle element is ·15. This value ·15 is not consistent with the others. Noting the small 'T' in the recorded column, the engineer is reminded that the operator talked to another employee after completing the element, which raised the element time. Because of the fact that the time for the foreign element occurred during element time, it is deleted from the calculations of the standard time because talking to another employee is not essential to the job.

From a Ford Training Manual.

Introduction

As you read this book, workers across the country (and around the world) will be making motor cars. In Britain, most of them work for Ford or BL at four massive production estates in London (Dagenham), Liverpool (Halewood), Birmingham (Longbridge) and Oxford (Cowley). Here, tens of thousands work around the moving assembly line. One man has just fitted a petrol tank into the shell of the car, and is starting to fit another. Another man – on the engine dress – is fitting gears into engines. He will have consulted the shipper which tells him the specifications of the next engine due on the line and the appropriate gear box. It's all computerized. Now: select the gear box, lift it with the hoist and stick it in the hole in the middle of the engine. It is quicker if you do it without the hoist – but watch your back. Screw down the top bolts and it's finished – secured to the engine. Back to the shipper. No time to waste. Forty engines an hour; forty gear boxes; forty operations.

At Halewood, Dagenham and Longbridge, men in the body plants work alongside the robots producing the shells of the Escort, Sierra and Metro. Here the speeds are faster: ninety and a hundred operations an hour. Sweating, keeping up with the robots, feeding the machines. For automation hasn't got rid of machine-paced, assembly-line work. If anything it has intensified it. And especially now, when 'competitiveness' is the key word, and European workers are fed with warnings of the Japanese. It is here 'on the line' that the first Henry Ford created one of the most powerful images of the twentieth century. An image which combined 'efficiency' with 'tedium'; the twin pillars of modern life. People who benefit from the 'efficiency', at a distance, often convince themselves that the pressures of assembly-line work aren't so bad. Those who have experienced it know different. As one journalist noted in 1972:

> At the end of the first fortnight, the sheer monotony of the work was turning me into a zombie. I stopped reading books, and slumped in front of the telly at night without selecting the programmes (*The Times*, 3 March 1972).

Two companies dominate the British motor industry – Ford and BL. One a giant, US-owned corporation producing round the globe, the other now a state-owned and relatively small domestic producer. Over the past two decades the fortunes of these companies (and the people who work for them) have been in sharp contrast. After its formation BL entered the 1970s as the only surviving British motor corporation of any size. It was a clear market leader in Britain with 40 per cent of sales; well ahead of Ford on 25 per cent. Today, Ford is in the lead: in the market and in other ways. The chairman at the CBI and the Institute of Personnel Managers (Terence Becket and Bob Ramsey) were together as the 'top men' of Ford UK. In Britain and Western Europe 'Ford' now stands for 'success'. Ford Europe has emerged as an increasingly powerful centre of profit within the Company. BL has contracted to being a domestic producer of less than 500,000 vehicles; Ford entered the 1980s as the clearest example of an organized transnational producer: 'the most global of the global corporations'. In 1981 the Company stood sixth in Fortune's list of large US corporations: producing around five million units, selling at $38,247,000,000, its assets stood at $23,021,000,000. With plants organized around the world (from South Africa to Brazil, from Mexico to Japan), it confirmed itself as an integrated worldwide production and marketing organization. And at the head of Ford, still, the Ford family.

Forbes magazine described the Ford family in this way in 1982:

> *Ford*: Detroit area. Descendants of *the* Henry Ford. Base of the fortune 12·8 million shares class B stock Ford Motor Company (10 per cent of outstanding common shares but 40 per cent of the votes) held by three surviving grandchildren (Henry II the present patriarch, William Clay . . ., Josephine C) and thirteen great grandchildren. Henry II would pass mantle to son Edsel but watch Benson Jr coming up outside the lawsuits. Family's Ford stock, other assets, readily exceeds 250 million.

The Ewings of *Dallas* are small fry compared with this. The Fords are in the major league, and it is with good reason that *Forbes* talks of Henry II as a patriarch. He – as representative of the family – continues to exercise a powerful and direct control over the operations of the Company – *their* company. Thus, in 1977, he could say that 'somebody called Ford has to be in top Company echelons' (*The Times*, 14 February). At that time, while writing of the ten-man Ford of Europe policy committee, the *Sunday Times* noted that while this 'European cabinet' has responsibility for overall European strategy:

it is not all powerful. The main constraint is that decisions on investment of over twenty-five million dollars must be referred back to the main board in Detroit. This rule, laid down by Henry II personally, indicates where ultimate power lies (9 October 1977).

It lies with the boss. And throughout the 1970s this was made clear at the twice-yearly meetings of the European branches of the Company:

> He sat at the same seat at every meeting, first place at the head of the table ... Smiling, strong, jovial, he goes round the table before sitting down. To everyone he is 'Mr Ford', just like grandfather Henry I, the founder of the dynasty and the inventor of democracy on wheels. No one would presume to call him 'Henry' ... When he has shaken hands with everybody, Mr Ford goes back to his chair, takes off his jacket, spreads his various files on the table, places his packet of Benson and Hedges – later to be replaced by small cigarillos – in front of him, makes sure that everyone is present and then: 'Nice to be here, gentlemen. Let's get down to business ...' (Seidler, 1976, p. 31).

The man on the engine dress has fitted his second gear box and is on his third. In the next six hours or so, he will have had a coffee break (coffee from a machine) and a dinner break in the canteen. And he will have installed another 200 gear boxes. Forty an hour; three hundred and twenty a shift. Another forty if they ask him to work on another hour's overtime. We know nothing about this man. While Henry Ford is a public figure, the lives of the men and women who work for him rarely take on a public significance. Strikes and occasional incidents of loafing or sabotage sometimes make the front pages. Sometimes too they are badgered publicly by politicians and senior managers. Mostly, though, people like these work out their lives in the plants unnoticed and anonymous. And there, in endless ways, in Britain and throughout the world, the managers and machines combine to establish a world in which 'you don't count'.

It is important to make good this deficiency. To offset the balance. And in doing so to explore how the public grandeur of Ford, and the continuance of the family fortune, is dependent upon the regulated tedium endured by the men and women who work for the Company. For they are – in a real and fundamental sense – part of the same world. During this century, millions of people have worked for Ford. Today they are scattered around the globe. This book deals with the experiences of just a few of them: those who worked on the Halewood estate in the 1960s and 1970s. It attempts to show, however, that their lives are linked with other workers (in the present and the past) through the operations of the Ford Company. It is a truth they clearly recognize. On many separate occasions, Ford workers have asked me questions about the Ford family. They *know* the power wielded by Henry Ford and they have wanted to know about him and about the 'first Henry'. 'How did he make his pile?' 'Wasn't Harry Bennett a hoodlum?' 'One of Capone's crowd wasn't he?' 'Whose son is *this* Henry, the one who's screwing us now?' 'Henry two-stroke.' In 1968 they'd read Upton Sinclair's *The Flivver King* and hadn't been greatly impressed by it. They'd also read the UAW pamphlet *We Work for Ford*. They'd seen the pictures and they wanted to know *more*. They made me realize that a book, written about Halewood, needed to begin in the USA. It needed to start in Dearborn, Michigan.

There is no longer anything to reconcile, if there ever was, between the social conscience and the profit motive. Improving the quality of society – investing in better employees and customers for tomorrow – is nothing more than another step in the evolutionary process of taking a more far-sighted view of return on investment.

Henry Ford II, 1969

The advance publicity for US Ford's new Mustang showed the company President Lee Iacocca, standing proudly beside the bonnet ... At this week's unveiling of the latest model his forceful personality was absent yet keenly remembered. Iacocca was heir apparent to Henry Ford II, now 63, and connoisseurs of the Ford succession saga recall the lightning dismissal in September 1969 of the previous president and seeming heir, 'Bunkie' Knudsen. At that moment, Iacocca sat on the platform smiling and smoking a large cigar. Knudsen had lasted only nineteen months. Before him, quite a few senior executives had fallen to the power of the man who once succinctly explained his strength: 'My name is on the building.'

There was Harry Bennett, for example. Hired in 1916 by Henry Ford, the founding patriarch, he was by the 1940s controlling the company with ruthless determination. Henry II took nominal control in September 1945, [and] he immediately sacked Bennett. In the tense confrontation with John Bugas, the young Henry's ally, Bennett pulled out a revolver. 'My ·38 was just inside my jacket. I was ready if it looked like my life was involved,' said Bugas afterwards.

Henry II brought in a General Motors veteran, Ernest Breech. In 1960 Breech left after Henry reportedly told him: 'I've graduated.' In 1963, Arjay Miller – recruited as one of young Henry's 'whizz kids' – became president. Miller returned from a trip to Latin America in 1968 to learn that he had been replaced by Knudsen.

Financial Times, 19 June 1978

1 Henry Ford's Motor Company

The twentieth century has been the century of mass production. In its early years, the introduction of the assembly line was greeted with acclaim that approached adulation. The man responsible was seen as a miracle-maker. And that man was Henry Ford. He became the hero of the mass-production saga. Wilde's dictum that 'under the right conditions technology will serve men' was taken for granted, for the right conditions were at hand; the age of plenty was around the corner. However, mass production also involved the 'mass worker' and the technological euphoria of those years mellowed in the face of unemployment and the 'speed-up' practised on the line. The miracle-worker became the villain. Chaplin's *Modern Times* depicted the little man crushed by the assembly line. Huxley's pessimistic *Brave New World* imagined a future where men were stunted by coercion and confused by a new religion – Fordism. A technocratic, disenchanted world. Ford became plagued by a similar vision. So much so that he started to buy up parts of 'old America', opening folk museums, closing roads to the motor car.

Henry Ford was born the son of a farmer in Dearborn, Michigan, in 1863. He made his first automobile in 1893 and formed the Ford Motor Company in 1903 when he was forty. He dominated the affairs of the Company for the next forty years. Throughout his life he retained the prejudices and ideas of the small farmer. He was an anachronism. The multi-billion dollar small-town farmer who produced motor cars.

On 18 June 1903 Henry Ford and eleven other men met to form the Ford Motor Company. In its first year, 1708 Ford passenger cars were produced. Ten years later, annual production figures reached the 200,000 mark. In 1915 half a million cars were produced and in 1919 the figures reached one million cars a year – only to soar again to over two million in 1923. Ford had made it. He had broken into the mass market for automobiles. And he was rich. In 1903 very little capital was needed to start a motor company and Ford and his eleven associates had started with $28,000. In its first ten years the Company earned fifty-five million dollars. The following three years brought in over a hundred million dollars. By August 1916 the Company's assets stood at $300,000,000. Ford was a rich man. A rich man who wanted to control his own. As his sympathetic biographers have put it:

> In due course, Henry Ford bought out his associates until he was the Company . . . He had no patience with the idea that the Dodge brothers should compel him to pay out money in dividends which he wished to reinvest in the business . . . He had no desire to see 'outsiders' grow wealthy on the earnings of *his* factory . . . He was a dictator and with his immediate family held complete sway (Nevins and Hill, 1962, p. 428).

He was The Man. And he was to remain The Man until his death. Throughout his life he maintained a single-minded, autocratic hold over his company, entirely convinced of his right to run it as he thought fit. Every car plant was a hard place to work in. The philosophy of Henry Ford was to add a special bite to the organization of work on the shop floor of a Ford plant.

Ford was made by the flywheel magneto moving assembly line which was introduced into his plant at Highland Park in 1913. 'It is', wrote two contemporary enthusiasts, 'the most interesting metalworking establishment in the world' (Arnold and Faurete, 1915, p. 1). Ford describes some of its features:

> Every piece of work in the shop moves; it may move on hooks on overhead chains going to assembly in the exact order in which the parts are required; it may travel on a moving platform, or it may go by gravity, but the point is that there is no lifting or trucking of anything other than materials (Ford, 1922, p. 85).

It was all very scientific.

> The Ford engineers make a point of 'man-high' work placing, having learned that any stooping position greatly reduces the workman's efficiency. The differing heights of the chassis-assembling high-lines are believed to be decidedly advantageous (Arnold and Faurete, 1915, p. 138).

Like most of the other things that Henry Ford did, the introduction of the moving assembly line was surrounded by a good deal of publicity. He was the first to make great use of public relations. As Galbraith would have it – he was the first fraud (Galbraith, 1963). He was hailed as a great mechanic, a great engineer, yet:

> if we actually analyse this new so-called technology, we shall find that it is not a 'technology' at all. It is not an arrangement of physical forces. It is a principle of social order. This was true of Ford's work. He made not one mechanical invention or discovery; everything mechanical he used was old and well known.

Only his concept of human organization for work was new (Drucker, 1950, p. 19).

And his concept of human organization was simple:

The idea is that the man ... must have every second necessary but not a single unnecessary second (Ford, 1922, p. 85).

The implementation of this organizational principle had a considerable effect upon the men who worked in Henry Ford's car plants. Detroit at the turn of the century 'had an international reputation as a city of abundant and docile labour' (Nevins, 1954, p. 516). This state of affairs was perpetuated by the concerted anti-union, open-shop policy of the Employers' Association of Detroit. This policy became difficult to maintain with the expansion of the Ford Motor Company and the automobile industry generally. The owners of the car plants wanted more and more workers. 'Since every vacancy meant so many fewer pieces finished at the close of the day the one thought of the bosses was "get the men"' (Nevins, 1954 p. 517). Labour turnover rates were extremely high. In 1913 Ford required between 13,000 and 14,000 workers to run his plants at any one time, and in that year over 50,000 workers quit. The motor industry at that time was a hire-and-fire industry. There were no seniority rights and everyone was employed from day to day. The plants were run by the iron hand and arbitrary justice of the foreman.

> ... it is not at all surprising to me with our modern conditions that it is difficult to find a boy who wants to continue in employment. Our modern shops are built on such an economical plan that we get one individual doing one thing until he becomes most efficient at that one thing. It is impossible to take a child and set him one task and not expect him to chafe at that task ... Among the thousands or more boys who come to me in a year I find few that hold their positions more than three months. Generally they say they get tired of that one thing. They want to get into a shop where they get some other kind of job, one perhaps as tiresome in the end, but it represents a change temporarily.
>
> Judge Hulbert, Detroit, 1912.

Detroit was a frontier city – squalor, immigrant workers, shanty towns, corruption and violence. In 1911, for example, 22,000 manual workers arrived to work in the expanding industry – many of them European immigrants. Safety standards were appalling and fatal accidents a commonplace. An ideal breeding ground for unionism and radicalism. The Industrial Workers of the World, 'The Wobblies', were making some headway in Detroit – as they were nationally. In 1912 the secretary of the Employers' Association remarked that:

There is at this time more restlessness, more aggression amongst the workmen in Detroit and elsewhere than there has been for several years past ... There is a lot of inflammable matter scattered about the plants and it is up to you ... whether or not a spark ignites it, or it is cleared away before damage results (quoted in Nevins, 1954, p. 518).

Something had to be done.

The Ford Motor Company has never paid piece rates. Ford thought that they 'would have meant endless bother'. He preferred to control his workers by methods other than a simple economic bonus for work completed. Also he suspected that such incentive schemes produced 'botched parts' (Nevins, 1954, p. 525). This opposition to piece rates, coupled with a concern to be directly involved in the control of the work produced on the lines, has been a dominant feature of the Ford Motor Company in America and abroad. In 1914 it led to the implementation of the wages deal that became known as the Five Dollar Day. Publicized as an attempt by Ford to share profits with his workers, it involved an increase in the wage rate from $2.30 a day to $5.00 a day. However the package deal was not a straight wage increase. It was based upon a large-scale rationalization of work through a detailed job evaluation scheme, an accompanying restructuring of wage categories and a series of disqualifying clauses. It produced a rapid decline in absenteeism, lateness and labour turnover, coupled with a vast increase in output and a cut in the average cost of each car produced on the line. The scheme to share profits created a profit boom.

Not everyone who worked on Ford's assembly line qualified for the Five Dollar Day. It didn't apply to workers in their first six months with the Company or men under the age of twenty-one. Nor to women, who were initially omitted from the deal altogether. When asked about this, Ford confessed to an oversight, claiming in defence: 'We expect the young ladies to get married.' Mature men, who had served their period of probation, were eligible for the new rate. They finally qualified only if their personal habits at home and at work were considered satisfactory. Cleanliness and prudence were key attributes, the use of alcohol and tobacco was frowned upon, as was 'any malicious practice derogatory to good physical manhood and moral character' (quoted in Nevins, 1954, p. 556). Gambling was out, as was the practice of taking in boarders, especially male boarders.

The period from 1900 to 1918 in the USA has been termed the 'Progressive Era'. It was a period in which academics and 'industrial experts' first stepped forward to offer help to American businessmen. Rockefeller, who was experiencing the same problems as Ford with his workers, turned to Harvard University and Mackenzie King to help him out. Ford was sought out by John R. Lee. Lee was a reformer who wanted to produce a model industrial relations factory. He 'found Ford and Couzens [Ford's Business Manager] in a responsive mood, for both had been pondering the subject'. Ford took Lee on and put him at the head of the 'Sociological Department' which was to be responsible for the administration of the new pay deal. Lee was a propagandist for the Five Dollar Day. In one of his speeches he outlined an incident which influenced the form of 'The So-Called Profit Sharing System in the Ford Plant'.

I recall a drop-hammer operation that had gone along for a number of years at an even output, when somehow, the standard dropped off. The hammer was in good condition, the man who had operated the machine for years was on the job, but the finished output failed to appear in the old proportions that we were looking for and had the right to expect.

A superficial analysis of things brought no light, but a little talk with the operator revealed a condition of things entirely outside of business, that was responsible for our depleted production. Sickness, indebtedness, and fear and worry over things that related entirely to the home, had crept in and had put a satisfactory human unit entirely out of harmony with the things that were necessary for production. This is the type of incident that played an important part in the conclusions that we reached (Lee, 1916, p. 299).

The Five Dollar Day was introduced. Shorter hours and twice the wages for those who qualified. Thirty investigators were employed by the Sociological Department. The foremen and the assembly line ensured that the men earned their money. It fell upon the investigators' shoulders to ensure that the new riches were spent right and that they went only to the deserving. As Lee put it:

It was clearly foreseen that $5 a day in the hands of some men would work a tremendous handicap along the paths of rectitude and right living and would make of them a menace to society in general and so it was established at the start that no man was to receive the money who could not use it advisedly and conservatively (Lee, 1916, p. 303).

The lifestyle of most of the immigrant families that had settled in Detroit in search of work at Highland Park was frowned upon by Ford and his Sociological Department. For them to become aware of this –

'to see the folly of their ways' – was the prerequisite for admission to the Five Dollar Day.

It can be argued that this welfare programme had some merit; that in helping many immigrant workers to speak English, the Sociological Department assisted them in dealing with some of the worst manifestations of a racketeering frontier city, and so on. But in saying this, it is important not to ignore the strong ideological overtones in which the programme was cast. While Ford spent money developing churches in Detroit for his workers, the teaching of the English language was combined with the inculcation of 'American' values, values which Ford approved of and considered necessary for a stable industrious workforce. As part of their English lessons, for example, workers were treated to a pantomime sketch which involved a couple in peasant dress being stirred into a pot by 'Uncle Sam' to re-emerge, new-clad, as 'all-American'. Paternalism underpinned the whole programme and it often degenerated into petty and heavy-handed interference in the private lives of vulnerable people. In Nevins's words:

> Doubtless the spectacle of an earnest inquirer writing down an array of facts on his blue form aroused conflicting emotions in many breasts. The investigators . . . were asked to throw 'a deep personal interest' into every visit. Sometimes it was tinged with suspicion; the mere word of an employee that he was married was not taken as sufficient, and the agents were instructed to use some ingenuity in getting this information *positively*. Branch managers were instructed, for example, to be vigilant and to make sure 'beyond a shadow of a doubt that the money is paid to those deserving, and to no others' (Nevins, 1954, p. 555).

Those families who did not meet the specification of the Sociological Department were put on probation. After two years of the scheme 90 per cent of the employees were deemed fit to qualify for the Five Dollar Day but qualification had no necessary permanence. If an investigator found at any time that the money was, to quote Lee, 'more of a menace than a benefit to him', that the man had 'developed weaknesses', his bonuses would be lost for a period of six months. If, at the end of that time 'he had not found the folly of his ways, he is eliminated as an employee of the Ford Motor Company' (Lee, 1916, p. 307).

The paternalism of the Sociological Department's programme was deeply influenced by Henry Ford's assumptions about both 'the common man' and 'the good life'. Ford neither smoked nor drank. He believed in the value of the open air and long walks. Hard work and cleanliness. It had all been good for him so it was good for everybody.

'Nobody smokes in the Ford industries.' Ford didn't believe in charity. 'Philanthropy', he said, 'must be productive.' He was a great believer in 'self-help'. If he helped people to help themselves, it helped him. He also believed that people should emulate him and pull themselves out of the common rut. But there couldn't be 20,000 Henry Fords in Detroit. Ford's success depended upon the failure of others. This was the contradiction of 'self-help' – a contradiction that underpinned Ford's contempt for the common man.

When the Five Dollar Day was introduced maximum publicity was given to the new rate and to the fact that the Ford Motor Company would be hiring an additional four or five thousand men. On the first Monday workers arrived at the gates of the Highland Park plant from all over Michigan. Men with Ford badges felt favoured for once as they were allowed through the gates. Some of the newcomers were selected. 'Hey you ...' The rest were told that 'men who formed crowds wouldn't be considered'. In the middle of winter they stood there at the gates, waiting. 'No more hirings today.' Perhaps tomorrow. 'No hirings today.' Hiring continued sporadically for the week. Every day more and more men arrived. It was getting colder. 'What's happening?' On the second Monday it was snowing heavily. At 7.30 a.m. there were ten thousand men outside the gates. Hoping for a job. 'No hiring today.' Ford had got all the men he wanted by the Saturday. Ten thousand men looking for work in the cold. Nevins (1954, p. 544) describes how 'when the fire hose was hauled out and waved threateningly (this was before the days of tear gas) the crowd simply yelled in derision ... A little planning might have prevented this explosive disorder.' So it might. But the hoses were turned on. It was a sign of the times that a man who could plan the organization of a moving assembly line could not plan for men, many of whom were destitute, standing in the cold for over a week. And getting soaked into the bargain. The implementation of the pay deal gives some insight into the way 'the common working man' was viewed by Ford. It reveals the roots of the violence and repression engendered in the Ford plants in the twenties and thirties. Ford had a vision of a new world. He was greatly influenced by the words of Edison, his friend and mentor, 'we've got to start to make this world over'. But his reforming zeal was tempered by a vision of an ideal world in which the lower orders still had their place – at the bottom.

In his autobiography, Ford remarked that 'it is evident that a majority of the people in the world are not mentally – even if they are physically – capable of making a good living' (Ford, 1922, p. 77). In his view the majority of working men were well fitted to a life of drudgery. They knew of no better, nor were they capable of it. While he expressed concern over their domestic habits Ford gives no hint that he worried about the effects of monotonous work upon their lives. The machines were the masters at Highland Park and the men had to keep pace with them. And under the Five Dollar Day:

the pace [was] inexorable, the pressure for ever-better production insistent. 'The top men of all Ford departments', writes a keen observer, 'know that they are expected to make labour-cost reductions, that tomorrow must always better today' (Nevins, 1954, p. 549).

Although the wage rate had been doubled and the length of day shortened, labour per car increased by only a third, and the average cost of a car decreased. Working for eight hours rather than nine, a workforce of similar size produced 17 per cent more engines, and 70 per cent more radiators. Sixty-five men had previously produced 800 gasoline tanks in eight hours – after the Five Dollar Day, five men less produced 1200 tanks. While the Ford employment office had to replace up to 60,000 men in 1913, in 1914 only 2000 men left their jobs on the line. Absenteeism declined from 10 per cent to less than one half a per cent.

Ford had had a very definite problem of labour turnover at Highland Park. He was also faced by threat of unionism and even insurrection. It was in his interest to reform, to ensure his riches and his future. There was more to it than that though. Ford wasn't a complete hypocrite. He was for a time taken up by the ideas of Lee and Marquis, Lee's successor. The idea of putting 'soul' into the Corporation. To some extent he did care about what was happening to his workers and the world. He was rich enough to care certainly, but a lot of other rich men didn't bother. However it also paid to care. In a conversation with Marquis, Ford argued that:

a man who can pay a living wage and refuses to do so is simply storing up trouble for himself and others. By underpaying men we are bringing on a generation of children undernourished and underdeveloped morally as well as physically; we are breeding a generation of working men weak in body and in mind, and for that reason bound to prove inefficient when they come to take their places in industry. Industry will, therefore, pay the bill in the end. In my opinion it is better to pay as we go along and save the interest on the bill, to say nothing of being human in industrial relations (quoted in Marquis, 1923, p. 151).

'The idea is', Marquis continued 'that every man wants to be a sober, capable, industrious citizen, and that such a man is the best investment the Company can make.' A happy conjuncture of good business and humanism. Whether planned or not, one thing is certain, the Five Dollar Day was profitable. Ford was to see it as 'one of the finest cost-cutting moves we ever made'. A statement from the Sociological Department in the *Ford Times* in 1916 made it clear that 'looked at from a cold-blooded point of view of business investment [the Five Dollar Day] was the very best investment [the Ford Motor Company] has ever made' (Baritz, 1965, p. 33). Whatever the ins and outs of *why* Ford introduced the Five Dollar Day, it is clear that:

Ford was a high-wage employer for only a few years. He was not sufficiently convinced of the high-wage philosophy to avoid becoming one of the most unsatisfactory employers in the town (Galbraith, 1963, p. 140).

The paternalism of the Sociological Department was soon to give way to the brutality of the Service Department.

Ford was convinced that his Model T was right. Right for him, right for Americans. It was black, cheap and functional. But it wasn't selling. Ford refused to change his ideas. He changed the price. An even cheaper Model T. At the cost of speed-up. Galbraith points out that Sorensen – for forty years Ford's senior production manager and known to the workers as 'Cast Iron Charlie' – and his associates were the 'masters of speed-up'. In the face of this the Reverend Samuel Marquis resigned from the Sociological Department.

I resigned from the Ford Motor Company in 1921. The old group of executives, who at times set justice and humanity above profits and production, were gone. With them so it seemed to me, had gone an era of cooperation and goodwill in the company. There came to the front men whose theory was that men are more profitable to an industry when driven than led, that fear is a greater incentive to work than loyalty (Marquis, 1923, p. 8).

There comes a time when benevolence conflicts with good business. The 1920s and 1930s were such times for the American motor industry and the Ford Motor Company. In that period the car industry became reduced to the Big Three: General Motors, Chrysler and the Ford Motor Company. These giants were in competition for the share of the market and after the early 1920s, in a period of general economic instability, Ford was losing out to General Motors. Chevrolets were dominating the market. In 1927 Henry Ford ran his plant flat out until May when the last Model T, the Tin Lizzie, rolled off the assembly line. The last of 15,007,003 Model Ts. With enough cars stockpiled to

The philosophy of Henry Ford[1]

On work

Too much good fellowship may indeed be a bad thing, for it may lead to one man trying to cover up the faults of another. That is bad for both men. When we are at work we ought to be at work. When we are at play we ought to be at play. There is no use trying to mix the two. The sole object ought to be to get the work done and to get paid for it. When the work is done, then the play can come, but not before.

And workmen

We do not have piece work. Some of the men are paid by the day and some are paid by the hour, but in practically every case there is a required standard output below which a man is not expected to fall. Were it otherwise, neither the workman nor ourselves would know whether or not wages were being earned. There must be a fixed day's work before a real wage can be paid. Watchmen are paid for presence. Workmen are paid for work.

And charity

Charity is no substitute for reform. Poverty is not cured by charity, it is only relieved. To cure it the cause of the trouble must be located and then removed. Nothing does more to abolish poverty than work. Every man who works is helping to drive poverty away.

On mechanics

We have found ways to cut down corrosion and to limit deterioration by electrolysis, ways to prevent rust. The new chromium-plating process which we are using on airplane parts, for example, makes this metal practically indestructible in so far as the influence of weather conditions on it is concerned. Rust-proof metals are being developed, we are finding ways to preserve wood, means of strengthening and preserving steel.

The point is, if there is enough thinking done along this line, there is no reason why we could not do the same with the human body. There is no law against it. The great problem is to get people in the mental attitude where they are willing to try to do it, willing to use the facts after we get them. There is a certain amount of mental inertia to be overcome in the promotion of any new thing. A few individuals may be quickly educated, but it takes time for society to move, to consent to the adoption of the new way.

1. Many of these quotations are taken from Rae (1969).

And morality

Rightness in mechanics, rightness in morals are basically the same thing and cannot rest apart.

And living

Just as a clean factory, clean tools, accurate gauges, and precise methods of manufacture produce a smooth-working, efficient machine, so clear thinking, clean living, square dealing make of an industrial or domestic life a successful one, smooth-running and helpful to every one concerned. It has always been surprising to me that so few people realize this great fact.

On alcohol

The coming of prohibition has put more of the workman's money into savings banks and into his wife's pocketbook. He has more leisure to spend with his family. The family life is healthier. Workmen go out of doors, go on picnics, have time to see their children and play with them. They have time to see more, do more – and, incidentally, they buy more. This stimulates business and increases prosperity, and in the general economic circle the money passes through industry again and back into the workman's pocket. It is a truism that what benefits one is bound to benefit all, and labour is coming to see the truth of this more every day.

And tobacco

Anything that interferes with our ability to think clearly, lead healthy, normal lives, and do our work well will ultimately be discarded, either as an economic handicap or from a desire for better personal health.

Tobacco is a narcotic which is exacting a heavy toll from our present generation. No one smokes in the Ford industries. Tobacco is not a good thing for industry nor for the individual.

If you study the history of almost any criminal, you will find that he is an inveterate cigarette smoker. Boys, through cigarettes, train with bad company. They go with other smokers to the post rooms and saloons. The cigarette drags them down.

On Christianity, America and the Jews

For the present, then, the question is wholly in the Jews' hands. If they are as wise as they claim to be, they will labour to make Jews American, instead of labouring to make America Jewish. The genius of the United States of America is Christian in the broadest sense, and its destiny is to remain Christian. This carries no sectarian meaning with it, but relates to a basic principle which differs from other principles in that it provides for liberty with morality, and pledges society to a code of relations based on fundamental Christian conceptions of human rights and duties.

meet future demand Ford shut down the plant and laid off 60,000
workers. In that year the city of Detroit paid out one million dollars
more in relief payments than it had in 1926. Ford was building a new
plant with new machines on the River Rouge. There, he was going to
produce the Model A which was going to turn the tide for the
Company. The Rouge would employ a lot less men than Highland
Park. In Ford's mind the six-months' lay-off would have done his
workers a lot of good: 'everybody gets extravagant' – it had 'let them
know that things are not going along too even always'. It would
prepare them for the new regime, a regime which:

by even the most friendly evidence was a machine age nightmare. Recalling the
early twenties, William C. Klann, one of the ablest of the older Ford executives,
said a trifle repetitiously: 'We were driving them of course. We were driving
them in those days ... Ford was one of the worst shops for driving the men'
(Galbraith, 1963, p. 141).

The laudatory acclaim which had once greeted Ford's achievements
in the liberal press gave way to coolness and eventual hostility. By
1928 the *New York Times* was calling Ford 'an industrial fascist –
the Mussolini of Detroit' (quoted in Sward, 1948, p. 369). Accounts of
the assembly line read rather differently from those written a decade
earlier. Leonard visited Ford's in the 1920s and wrote:

the men do not observe the visitors. In most factories they will look around,
perhaps hoping to see a pretty girl in the party. But not at Ford's. The line
moves inexorably onward. The men have exactly time to perform their minute
operation before the work passes out of reach (Leonard, 1932, p. 231).

Increased competition within the automobile industry and a depression
economy made themselves felt in the plant. Work was speeded up and
the wage rate was cut. In 1929 the employment manager of the Ford
Motor Company remarked that 'men between thirty and fifty years of
age are the best for automobile work ... after fifty most of them can't
stand the pace'.[2]

Things became worse. In 1931 only half a million Ford cars were
produced – a million less than 1929,[3] the year of the Wall Street Crash.
Unemployment dominated Detroit. In 1932 a hunger march of the
unemployed was planned, and three thousand unemployed workers
marched towards the tall chimneys of the River Rouge plant. Four of

2. *Wall Street Journal*, 4 July 1929.
3. For output figures see Nevins and Hill (1962), Appendix 1.

them didn't return. The machine guns of the Dearborn Police and the Ford Motor Company's Service Department killed them and wounded over a score of the others. The head of the Service Department, Harry Bennett, was hit by a stone and taken to the Henry Ford Hospital.

To Ford, the idea of working men questioning his prerogatives as an owner was outrageous. He would have none of it. He refused to be involved in Roosevelt's New Deal and the provision that the National Reconstruction Agency made for employee representation.

We will never recognize the United Auto Workers or any other union. Labour union organizations are the worst things that ever struck the earth, because they take away a man's independence.[4]

A lot of workers, however, were eager to lose such independence as they had in the River Rouge plant. The plant was dominated by the autocratic regime of Bennett's Service men. Bennett was an ex-navy boxer. His task was to maintain discipline amongst the workforce, protect Ford's property and prevent unionization. He trained the three and a half thousand private policemen employed by Ford; men referred to implicitly by Frank Murphy, the mayor of Detroit, when he said, 'Henry Ford employs some of the worst gangsters in our city'. Ford's Service Department policed the gates of his plants, infiltrated emergent groups of union activists, posed as workers to spy on the men on the line and helped operate the rackets and gambling in Detroit.

Under this tyranny the Ford worker had no security, no rights. So much so that any information about the state of things within the plant could only be freely obtained from ex-Ford workers. A contemporary writer noted:

Do not attempt to extract it from a Ford worker. He will suspect you of being a spy. Ask the unemployed or the men who have jobs with some strong company such as the Standard Oil. Gas station attendants are accessible and usually as talkative as barbers. Many of them are ex-Ford men. Mention his name to one of them and if you had any impression that the Ford plant was a paradise for the working man, that impression will disappear in a welter of picturesque epithets which your informant has probably been practising for years (Leonard, 1932, p. 230).

Fifteen years later Keith Sward wrote:

Any number of idiosyncrasies bore witness to the stiffening effect of regimentation within the Rouge. Chatting or fraternizing with workmates

4. Quoted in *We Work at Ford*, UAW Detroit, (1962), p. 3.

during the lunch hour was taboo in the old days which lasted twenty years or more. It was then the rule during the noonday spell to see a Ford employee squat on the floor, glum and uncommunicative, munching his food in almost complete isolation. The locked-in manner of the Ford worker supposedly at ease was remarked by Ravmond J. Daniell who observed in the *New York Times* on 31 October 1937, 'The visitor [at the Rouge] is struck by the restraint among the workers; even in moments of idleness, men stand apart from one another.'

Ford men, before long, became noted for their ingenuity in circumventing the ironclad law against talking at their work. They developed an art of covert speech known as the 'Ford whisper'. Masters of this language, like inmates in a penal institution, could communicate in undertones without taking their eyes from their work. If Ford or Sorensen were about to tour the plant, even the plant foremen knew how to spread the word by resorting to the 'grapevine'.

Ford's tool and die men used to be governed by the same taboo, though their work by its very nature compelled them to move about. Long ago, these craftsmen invented their own brand of hidden talk. Their technique was to exchange small talk while gesticulating in mock earnestness at parts of a lathe, or while feigning interest in a blueprint. One highly intelligent artisan in this department invented a type of 'Ford speech' all his own. He learned to talk like a ventriloquist. After spending ten years in Ford's service, this man became the laughing stock of his wife and friends, for the habit of talking out of the side of his mouth without moving his lips finally became ungovernable; he began to talk that way unconsciously, at home or in the most casual conversation with someone outside after working hours.

'Fordization of the face' was once the rule among all Ford men at work, inasmuch as humming, whistling or even smiling on the job were, in the judgment of Ford Service, evidence of soldiering or insubordination. John Gallo, a Rouge employee, was discharged in November 1940 – caught in the act of 'smiling', after having committed an earlier breach of 'laughing with the other fellows', and slowing down the line 'maybe half a minute' (from Keith Sward, 1948, pp. 312–13).

Several of the workers who experienced the Bennett regime at the River Rouge have written of their experiences in autobiographies. John Fitzpatrick, an Irishman and early UAW activist described how:

> Once you got to the gate the tension began, because in there, no matter how good a man you were ... a Service man would come up to you, tap you on the shoulder, and tell you to pack your tool box and go off to Miller Road – this meant the Employment Office.

Those who were lucky enough to have a job found themselves cursing their luck. Fitzpatrick himself became overwhelmed by the fear that dominated the River Rouge plant, telling himself that 'two weeks will be enough here'. Talking wasn't allowed but it went further than that:

> There was no association with other men. Any association with other workers in the department, line, or on the bench where you were working was frowned upon. There was a feeling in the mind of everyone that he was an individual with no connection during working hours with any other man (quoted in Nevins and Hill, 1962, pp. 47–8).

Spies were everywhere. No one was safe:

> The spies and stool pigeons report every action, every remark, every expression. The men are constantly shifted about so they never learn who they can trust. When a new man comes into a section he is looked at with suspicion and observed carefully. They try little stratagems to test him. One of them will risk his job and ask him a question. If a look of genuine terror comes over his face, he is all right. He's a Ford worker like the rest. But if he answers and tries to draw his questioner away from his work, he is a stool pigeon.
>
> The scope and efficiency of the spy system is incredible. A boy on an errand who has stopped to buy a bar of chocolate will find that he has been spotted. The man who wipes the oil off his machine half a minute before the closing bell meets the same fate. The man who expresses himself carelessly in a private conversation finds that his words have been card-indexed in the office. The man who joins one of the pathetically weak unions which exist feebly in Detroit finds himself transferred to the dreaded foundry.[5] When a man has been called away from his work for a medical examination or some other good reason, he is given a slip of paper stating the exact time he started. This is a passport to get him by the spotters in the factory yard. The chances are that it will be examined carefully before he reaches his destination. When he does arrive, a clerk in the doctor's office calculates the time the trip consumed and checks it against a table of distances.
>
> No one who works for Ford is safe from the spies – from the superintendents down to the poor creature who must clean a certain number of toilets an hour (Leonard, 1932, p. 235).

The Ford organization was determined to prevent unionization and any interference with the way its plants were run. It became obsessed by the idea of Red agitators. Anyone who did anything remotely out of line was sacked and so labelled. Walter Reuther, future President of the UAW, was sacked from the River Rouge plant. It made him, and others, all the more determined to have the union recognized by Ford.

---

5. 'The foundry became known as the madhouse. Open hearth workers who had been expected to dismantle 130 used cars a day for scrap lifted their quotas to 190, while the superintendents urged them to go on to 225 . . . Only workers near the water fountains had time to drink' (Nevins and Hill, 1962, p. 152).

During the 1930s a concerted effort was made by automobile workers and UAW activists to unionize the car plants. The spy network was expanded enormously to counteract their development. Between 1933 and 1936, for example, General Motors spent one million dollars on espionage, employing fourteen detective agencies and two hundred spies at a time. The Pinkerton Detective Agency found anti-unionism its most lucrative activity. Ford relied upon his Service Department which along with Chester le Mare and the Detroit underworld kept a close check upon union activity in the Ford plants and in Detroit generally. 'The Service Department bred a state of mind in and about Detroit that could be duplicated only in those localities which have written the darker pages of American industrial history' (Leonard, 1932, p. 18). The Company and the city – one of the largest metropolitan areas in the United States – were controlled by Ford. The Employers' Association of Detroit was his to command.

We find that the Service men . . . were actively engaged in identifying union members and combating union activities, that the activities of the Service men had the sanction of Klump, assistant head of the department, that the respondent made no effort to prevent such activities, and that the respondent, through its officials, pursued a consistent course of anti-union action, which paralleled closely the activity of the Service men . . . We are convinced that at least one of the purposes for which the Service men were employed was to effectuate the prevention of organization at the plant.

Decisions and Orders of the National Labour Relations Board, vol. xxiii (Washington, DC, US Government Printing Office, 1941), p. 560

In these ways union activity in Detroit had been restricted to the smaller component factories. The immense power of Ford's Service Department had prevented any of the workers at the River Rouge plants from joining the union. In 1936, however, the UAW brought the union challenge into the heart of the city when it organized a sit-down strike at Midland Steel, the supplier of steel body frames to Chrysler and Ford. The strike was settled and described by the UAW as 'the most significant union victory in the history of the automobile industry in Detroit'. The sit-down tactic was equally effective at the Flint works of General Motors. And in May 1937 a six-week strike at eighteen of the Company's plants brought union recognition and negotiating rights for the UAW.

After their success at General Motors, the UAW leadership decided to begin a definite campaign to organize the workers in the River Rouge plant. On 24 May they opened a union headquarters in Detroit and obtained permission from the Dearborn City Hall to distribute handbills at the gates of the plant on 26 May. They had been forewarned to expect violence, so women members agreed to do the actual distributing of the handbills. It didn't work. They and the men were given a severe beating by Bennett's Service men. Reuther and Frankensteen, the two leaders, took the worst punishment. Frankensteen led the way up a long flight of stairs to the overpass. The Ford men approached – 'You're on Ford property – get the hell out of here.' Ford Service men – 'Which one is Reuther?' 'Is that Frankensteen?' Frankensteen was struck from behind and given 'the worst licking I've ever taken'.[6] Reuther described his attack to the National Industrial Relations Board's hearing:

> Seven times they raised me off the concrete and threw me down on it. They pinned my arms and shot short jabs to my face. I was punched and dragged by my feet to the stairway. I grabbed the railing and they wrenched me loose. I was thrown down the first flight of iron steps. Then they kicked me down the other flight of steps until I found myself on the ground where I was beaten and kicked.

Cameramen who photographed the incident were chased in a car at sixty miles per hour. They escaped to the comparative safety of a local police station.

The attempt to organize Ford's was set back. There were further defeats at Kansas and Dallas where similar beatings were handed out. Ford seemed to have been successful in opposing both the UAW and the National Labour policy established under the New Deal. In the era of business reform, when the ideology of 'responsible business activity' matured, Henry Ford was an anachronism. He still owned and controlled the Ford Motor Company. In Detroit and Dearborn he did what he liked. He hadn't learned to adapt to the subtler forms of control of the New Deal. His firm remained the vast family firm in the world of executive-run monopolies. He had stuck it out the longest but he was going to have to change, and adapt to the fact that the unionization of the car plants was a prospect as inexorable as the rise of Federal tax. The crunch for Ford came in 1941. Men in the Rouge plant had been joining the union.

On 1 April 1941 came a spontaneous explosion. John Fitzpatrick, furthering union activity, was talking with workers in the afternoon shift when he learned

6. 'Strikes of the Week', *Time*, 7 June 1937.

Ford's Partner[7]

If Bennett had asked for concessions he would have got them, for UAW was prepared to modify its demands to avoid a strike. Instead, his object in seeing Murray was, in the words of an executive of a competing company, 'to make him a present of the whole goddamn industry'.

Not that Ford is the whole automobile industry; but Ford's action is considered as giving the CIO a stranglehold on automotive production and no union which has secured the check-off from a big employer has ever been undermined. Under the Ford–UAW contract, the company's paymaster will be sending a cheque for $130,000 each month to the union's treasurer. Without a 'by your leave' it's going to be deducted from each Ford employee's pay. No one familiar with labour organizations will suggest that the money will be used for any other purpose than to campaign for identical arrangements with all the rest of the industry.

Thus, as the company, in the words of Edsel Ford, 'decided to go the whole way' with the union after thirty-eight years of unmitigated opposition to unionism, its first positive benefit becomes apparent. Ford is off the CIO's target range, and its competitors are going to be incessantly sniped at until they make the same kind of a deal.

The second economic gain for the company is that it comes off the black-list of its most important customer, which could, if it chose, give Ford a great deal more business. That customer, is of course, the government, which under the New Deal has done everything it could under the law to buy from Ford competitors. Intermittent bitter controversies over defence contracts for the company . . . have highlighted the New Deal's attitude. From now on, employing only dues-paying union men, the Ford Motor Company can expect preferential treatment, whenever possible, from Washington. And if the preference flags, the powerful CIO lobby can be counted on to do its share of prodding, since every worker Ford employs means another $1 a month in CIO coffers. And, besides government business, there is the prospect of selling more cars to unionists in their own consumer role.

A third benefit which Ford apparently expects is of a negative variety – a freedom from the labour troubles which beset companies, like all the other auto manufacturers, not operating under an agreement which makes union membership compulsory. In positive terms, it is 'union protection', a kind of plant policing by the union for the company.

Where union membership is not a condition of employment, a labour organization must ever be active if it is to anchor the loyalty of employees and keep them convinced that it is to their interest to pay their dues. To achieve this, it constantly seeks 'grievances', and where they cannot be found it often manufactures them.

---

7. An extract from an article in *Business Week*, 29 June 1941.

that 1200 or 1500 men had gathered at the superintendent's office in the rolling mill . . . he was told that the union chairman in the mill and seven others had been discharged, and that workers had at once shut down at least three buildings. 'Maybe this is it,' Fitzpatrick thought . . . UAW Headquarters in Detroit had been deluged with phone calls: 'A-building stopped work'; 'Rubber plant closed by the Company'; 'Axle plant men walked out'. The whole Rouge except for a few units like the foundry . . . was paralysed.

When Reuther, Widman, and others reached the Rouge and saw 50,000 men gathered in a mass refusal to work, they knew that the movement could not and should not be halted. At 12.35 a.m. word was sent to leaders in the plant: 'You are officially on strike.' The rank and file were told to march through the Rouge on Road 4 to Miller Road, and then to the local headquarters on Michigan Avenue, cheering and singing 'Solidarity'. They did just that. 'It was a thrilling moment,' Fitzpatrick has recalled, 'a wonderful experience, to walk out along with all those men determined on one thing, through Gate Four, with Service men standing there looking at us and not daring to say a word. No supervisor, no officer of the Ford Motor Company, neither Harry Bennett nor any Service men, dared say us nay' (Nevins and Hill, 1962, p. 161).

Faced with this situation, Sorenson insisted that the strike had been provoked by union terrorism. Henry Ford wanted to arm the non-strikers. Bennett was eager to use his Service Department in a pitched battle. The moderation of Henry's son Edsel held the day however. Already there had been bloody encounters on the picket-lines. On 11 April Ford agreed to settle. He agreed to a ballot of the membership. Of the 78,000 votes cast only 34 opted for no union. The UAW received 51,868 votes, and its officers prepared to negotiate the first contract with Ford. It was for Ford 'perhaps the greatest disappointment he had in all his business experience' (Sorenson, quoted in Nevins and Hill, 1962, p. 164). The talks began and all but broke down. But in the end Henry Ford signed. The agreement was extremely favourable to the UAW. Cynics have remarked that the terms were good enough to buy the Ford Motor Company out of union trouble for many years.

Henry Ford by that time was eighty. He was too old to change fundamental ideas. He was still shrewd enough to approve of the workers' UAW dues being deducted at source by the Company. He liked the idea of being the 'union's banker'. Moreover Edsel and his son, Henry, had realized that they were entering the era of the soft-sell; the years of fear, confrontation and of government black-listing were no good for business. After all the UAW wasn't so bad. Why not accept it and use it? Ford, like Alfred P. Sloan Jr (senior executive with General Motors in the 1930s) had opposed trade unionism out of fear of:

persistent union attempts to invade basic management prerogatives. Our right to determine production schedules, set work standards, and to discipline workers were all suddenly called into question. Add to this the recurrent tendency of the union to inject itself into pruning policy and it is easy to understand why it seemed, to some corporate officials, as though the union might one day virtually be in control of our operations.

The sights of the unions were set much lower however. They wanted organizing rights and the right to negotiate. General Motors soon came to realize this:

In the end we were fairly successful in combating these invasions of management rights ... We have moved to ... discuss workers' grievances with union representatives, and to submit for arbitration the few grievances that remain unsettled. But on the whole, we have retained all the basic powers to manage.

So too at Ford. These were the arrangements which set the scene for the post-war expansion in the USA and Europe.

Viewed as a business entity, the renovated Ford Motor Company has three great outstanding characteristics, one of which stands in a somewhat contradictory relationship to the others. It is imposing for its size . . . it has been remarkable for the velocity of its growth . . . Finally, it has retained to a striking degree, in spite of its size and expansion, a special individuality, so that the name of Ford means to the average American something unique.

Nevins and Hill, *Ford: Decline and Rebirth 1933–1962*, p. 436.

Ford's strike proneness was exaggerated in popular repute by its concentration in a few big stoppages and in the development of an 'endemic conflict' situation in certain key plants in the late 1950s. Nevertheless, in view of the company's size, its importation into a British industrial relations environment of elements of managerial policy and attitudes which even in the USA could not always be maintained in the face of union resistance led to a substantial contribution to the car firms' total strike incidence. Its acceptance of collective bargaining only under government and TUC pressure committed it to a singularly clumsy bargaining and conciliation arrangement in the first place, and to a system of workplace representation which was exceptionally divorced from union control and guidance. Its insistence that workloads and efforts were not negotiable particularly invited conflict.

Turner, Clack and Roberts, *Labour Relations in the Motor Industry*, p. 346.

2 From Detroit to Dagenham

In 1944 the workers at Dagenham staged a sit-down strike, forcing the Ford Motor Company to recognize their right to join a union. By that time the Company had been producing cars in Britain for over thirty years. In 1911 it had bought an abandoned car plant at Trafford Park in Manchester and soon became the largest producer of automobiles on this side of the Atlantic. By 1930 it shared 75 per cent of the British market with Morris and Austin. In the following year the assembly line at Dagenham produced its first car, as the Ford Motor Company moved away from the North of England and became established on the Thames.

The basis for the multinational expansion that was to take place in Europe after the war was laid down in the 1930s. The building of Dagenham was accompanied by a scheme (the abortive '1928 Plan') under which the Ford Motor Company of England Ltd obtained the controlling interest in Ford's other European concerns. Dagenham was to be the centre of manufacture, sales and servicing for the whole of Europe.[1] The plan was governed by the calculation that

British manufacture would be cheaper than American, for concentration of European work at Dagenham would permit the adoption of mass-production methods, while labour would cost less and no transatlantic freights would be paid (Nevins and Hill, 1962, p. 79).

Detroit, however, was to keep a firm grip on the European development. A grip that was to tighten with every increase in capital investment. The scheme was solid enough to provide Ford with regular profits throughout the Depression period when production at the Rouge was severely cut back.

Throughout this period the men on the assembly line were unorganized and outside the union. Ford in England was as deliberately anti-union as in America and the chairman of the Company Sir Percival Perry (later Baron Perry of Stock Hansard)

1. This arrangement only lasted intact until 1934 when the German and French companies demanded, and were granted, their independence from Britain.

received the cooperation of the paternalistic William Morris (later Lord Nuffield) in the task of preventing unionization. Arthur Excell has written of how:

Lord Nuffield said he would never have the union in his factory ... The Pressed Steel was very active, but that hadn't yet come under Nuffield. The AUEW was in there on the skilled side. But it wasn't until 1934 that the other men started to get organized. There was nothing at all at Radiators or Morris Cowley. Nuffield kept warning us against the union, but he encouraged us to join the League of Industry, which we all did ... The League of Industry was completely under Nuffield. We had representatives – but Nuffield chose them. The boss elected them, each one, and they were good friends of the boss all the way through ... It was easier to organize outside the factory than inside because you weren't so likely to get the sack (Excell, 1981, p. 11).

At Ford, there was the Service Department. Without guns perhaps, but still ever watchful, as Harry Kay points out:

Those of us who worked in the Dagenham plant ... recall the fear of talking out of turn and the suspensions and even worse if one spoke out. The Gestapo-like Service men, and the cat-walk high above the factory where the superintendent usually patrolled, for all the world like a prison warder, shouting down to any unfortunate who happened to have a word with a fellow worker ... Many former employees will remember the raids by the Service men on the trim and upholstery departments to see whether a worker had committed the heinous crime of having his packet of sandwiches near his job. The company insisted that they be kept in a locker which was above the heat treatment, making the sandwiches uneatable at lunchtime.[2]

British car workers had traditionally been organized in craft unions like the Vehicle Builders (NUVB) and the Engineers (AUEW). Although these unions could recruit assembly-line operatives the opposition to dilutees prevented this. The only union to gain a foothold on the assembly lines, in fact, was Tom Mann's Workers' Union which had a few members in the Midlands. The amalgamation of the Workers' Union with the Transport and General Workers' (TGWU) in 1928 led to some systematic recruitment of assembly-line workers in the 1930s, and this encroachment made the craft unions take some notice of the men on the assembly lines. Mostly, however, these men were on their own.

In the most up-to-date of the twentieth-century industries [the car workers] re-enacted the battle for organization that had been fought many times over by earlier generations. Management rarely granted official recognition until its hand was forced by some degree of existing organization in the plant. To

2. Letter in *Ilford Pictorial*, 20 June 1973.

achieve this at a time when to become a trade unionist – much more to become a shop steward and recruit others as trade unionists – was not uncommonly to invite the sack, involved persistent picket-line and other pressure upon the numerous non-members and sometimes even concealment of membership until enough strength had gathered. Every successful penetration was a breach in the stand of the more recalcitrant managements upon whom the pressure of concessions elsewhere could be brought to bear; and as they gained ground, place by place, the motor workers learned the value, and the habit of shop-floor action under shop-floor leadership (Butt, 1960, p. 11).

Shop-floor skirmishes produced some degree of shop-floor organization. This remained strongest amongst the skilled workers, though even here union members were in the minority. A cut in the rate of six pence an hour produced a strike by toolroom workers at Dagenham in 1933. The strike stopped the plant.

The confusion was so great owing to mass picketing with flying squads, mounted police, firemen with hoses, barricades, buses, cars jamming the entrance that Company Chairman Sir Percival Perry had to close the factory.[3]

Perry talked to the strike committee and the cut was reduced to three pence an hour.

In spite of actions like this one, little union organization had been obtained in the car industry by 1939. In 1936 G. D. H. Cole described the industry as the most weakly organized section of British trade unionism (Cole, 1936). It has been estimated that at the outbreak of war 'seldom more than a fifth and often only a fiftieth of mass-production operatives were union members' (Turner, Clack and Roberts, 1967, p. 193). Yet by 1960 it had become one of the most highly organized sections of British industry with most plants (Vauxhall's at Luton and Dunstable being the main exception) entirely unionized.

As in the USA, unionization in the British motor industry was achieved with the backing of the State, and here the war made all the difference. The demand for munitions, the Essential Works Order and the Appeals Tribunal all made it more and more difficult for the employers to dismiss workers. The war put an end to the sacking of union activists and, at Ford's, the men sat down. In the face of this, pressure from the government and the TUC, and the 1941 about-face in Detroit, Perry allowed the unions into Dagenham. He still wanted to keep the unions at arm's length, however, so he negotiated with the TUC, and obtained an agreement that made no reference to shop

3. *What's Wrong at Ford* (published in 1963 by the Joint Ford Shop Stewards' Committee), p. 3.

stewards or procedures for dealing with disputes in the plant. No union was granted recruiting rights – no one was to be encouraged. This led to an open house and a future National Joint Negotiating Committee (NJNC) on which over twenty unions would be represented. The Ford Motor Company would recognize unions, but it would deal only with the national officers of those unions. it wanted no bargaining on the shop floor. Like Ford in America it wanted to preserve its right to manage, to control the work rate.

In the post-war years Europe presented a vast market with immense growth potential and the motor industry expanded rapidly. By 1959, for example, Ford had constructed large assembly plants as far afield as Antwerp, Alexandria, Cork and Copenhagen. The Company's main concern outside Detroit, however, was still Dagenham. Paying lip-service to the Attlee Government's export drive Henry Ford II proceeded to plan the rapid expansion of the complex. In the twelve years that followed the war the Ford Motor Company installed over 100 million pounds' worth of capital equipment at Dagenham. In 1946 about 400,000 vehicles were produced there, a little less than the Company's pre-war output. By 1950 over a million cars were rolling off the Dagenham assembly lines in a year, a number which had increased to 1,400,000 in 1955. Between 1948 and 1959 the output of the British car industry increased by 180 per cent. An increase achieved with only 18 per cent more workers. Speed-up had arrived.

This expansion increased Detroit's control over Dagenham. The retirement of Perry allowed the last vestiges of the overlordship implicit in the '1928 Plan' to be removed without rancour. From then on dividends were to go straight to Dearborn. And Ford found a man in London who would suit their needs: Sir Patrick Hennessy – in Nevins's words 'a self-made man of energy and resourcefulness' who had 'pushed his way up the ladder rung by rung'. Born poor in County Cork, he joined Ford in the early 1930s, worked with Beaverbrook during the war and 'by wide reading, travel and friendships' he had by 1945 'made himself a cultivated urbane gentleman' (Nevins and Hill, 1962, p. 397). This was the man entrusted with the superintendence of the Ford.Motor Company's investment in the Dagenham plants.

Hennessy was nobody's fool and in a period of strong government control over industry kept in close contact with the Treasury. As he put it, 'I make a point of doing more for the government than others in the industry.' He developed a sound understanding with the ministries of the Labour government. His main problem was with the workers – on the shop floor. For the post-war period produced a struggle over 'the effort bargain' within the car plants. A struggle over who does what, at what pace, for what price, and with whom. These were the issues of the 1950s that came to a peak in the 1960s. The issues at stake were management's 'right' to organize the plants as it thought fit and the workers' 'right' to a fair wage, to be without harassment, without speed-up, without lay-off, without the sack. In fighting these issues car workers found, to an ever greater extent, that their strength lay in their own ability to organize. As with the UAW in America, Ford and the other motor employers in Britain found that it wasn't difficult to achieve an amicable relationship with the national union leadership. But in the long post-war boom – broken only by the setbacks of 1951 and 1956 – the shop steward, the elected sectional leader of the men who worked on the line, emerged as the cornerstone of the men's strategy in the battle over the control of the shop.

As a contemporary writer put it:

post-war experience has thus not only confirmed the pre-war lesson of the need for local initiative; it has established the role of the shop-floor leader in their industry at least, *as the only feasible arrangement* (Butt, 1960, p. 11).

In the piece-work plants of Austin, Morris and Rootes, in the Midlands the workers were in a stronger position. Taking advantage of labour shortage they were able to bargain, through their steward, on a day-to-day basis with management. And the basis of the bargain was the rate. Any proposed change in production schedules – in the speed of the line, the type of model on the line and so on – led to negotiations over the rate for the job. The rate was their protection.[4] But at Ford's there was no protection from the rate because the rate was fixed. Ford had conceded the negotiation of the rate with national union officials. But that was all. There was to be no bargaining in the plants. Either with shop stewards or district officers of the union. The plants were the Company's preserve. The 'right' to manage unilaterally had been bequeathed by Henry Ford to his executives. There could be no negotiation on the line. Professor Turner and two of his colleagues at Cambridge University made a detailed study of the British motor industry in which they drew attention to the fact that Ford was 'the only company which formally maintains an insistence that work loads are beyond the reach of negotiation'. They continued:

4. Piecemeal negotiations however produced widespread differentials both within and between the car plants. Differentials that were based entirely upon bargaining strengths. These gave rise to ideas of 'parity' in the 1960s which culminated in the Parity Campaign at Ford.

Formally the function of shop stewards in Ford was thus limited to a participation (for most of them, indirect) in the firm's Joint Works Committees, which are essentially a procedure for dealing with individual and small-group grievances in each department. And that Ford itself regarded shop stewards as possessing a much more limited role than did the federated firms is shown by the more restricted facilities it has so far provided for them. In effect the steward organization at Ford was thus involved in an attempt to establish standards for the rest of labour informally on a 'custom and practice' basis and in the face of the disapproval of top management – even if it met with frequent concession from lower level supervision (Turner, Clack and Roberts, 1967, p. 215).[5]

The battle for job control in the car plants was fought with greatest ferocity in those owned by the Ford Motor Company, in the 1950s at Dagenham and later in the 1960s in its new plants at Halewood in Liverpool.

Two major, interrelated tendencies worked themselves out at Dagenham during the 1950s. They culminated in the sacking of seventeen workers and the Court of Inquiry of 1963. During a period of boom and ever-increasing output, the Ford Motor Company solidified formal procedures and understandings with the national leadership of the trade unions. On 23 August 1955 a procedure agreement was signed by the Company and the representatives of twenty-two unions. This agreement formalized the Ford policy of centralized negotiations, away from the plants. It was supported by the Company's increasing association with the other car employers and the government. With this centralizing tendency went the widening of the gap between the union bureaucracies and the union organization on the shop floor. This was made all the wider by the fact that Dagenham was a multi-union estate. Stewards there, in one union, would be representing men on a section who were members of other unions which made it difficult for the union officials to discipline members and stewards. As Les Kealey, the TGWU national officer on the Ford NJNC, told the 1963 Inquiry:

In many cases there may well be 70 per cent of my members with a shop steward of another union of only 10 per cent. You can't do much to that shop steward if he calls the 70 per cent out; he is not one of your union and no other union really wants to know anything because not many of their people are involved. This is a complicated issue. I am told by the shop stewards that it

5. The 'federated firms' is a reference to those car employers who are members of the Engineering Employers' Federation. Ford has never been a member. In 1972 only BLMC remained.

works. I have never really been in favour of it (quoted in The Jack Report, 1963, p. 51).

This led to a situation at Dagenham where the shop stewards' committee existed as 'a powerful and efficient organization' which owed 'no allegiance or responsibility to any of the individual unions represented on the Ford NJNC'. It was

a private union within a union, enjoying immediate and continuous touch with the men in the shop, answerable to no supervisor and in no way officially or constitutionally linked with the union hierarchy (The Cameron Report, 1957, p. 26).

In 1946 after a strike by the 11,000 workers on the Dagenham estate, the Company recognized the existence of shop stewards in the plants. For the next twenty years it was to be involved in a conflict over what such stewards could and couldn't do. The 1955 Procedure Agreement formally recognized stewards and indicated their duties and their place in negotiations. The Company's main concern throughout the decade was to deal with the union through the full-time officials – preferably national officers. It was prepared to recognize unions but not the existence of a legitimate conflict over the running of the plant. This contradiction was bound up in the first two clauses of the 1955 Agreement:

(a) The Company recognizes the right of its employees to belong to any of the unions.
(b) The unions recognize that the Company has the right to manage its establishments.

The struggles in the plant were played out around a conflict between these two clauses. A conflict that came clearly into the open when the Ford Motor Company took over the Briggs body plant on 30 March 1953.

Briggs Motor Bodies Ltd was situated on the Dagenham estate and it consisted of two integrated plants – the Main plant and the River plant – which produced the bodies of vans and cars which were taken to the Ford assembly plant and made into finished vehicles. A strong shop-floor organization had existed at Briggs since 1941. A wartime court of inquiry into a dispute over a sacked shop steward led to the implementation of a system of plant bargaining within which the national officers had little or no place. Briggs paid on the piece. Piece rates and the 1941 Agreement ensured that in the boom years the men on the assembly line would have some control over the decisions that affected them in the plant. A situation quite different from the shop floor at Ford. Yet Ford had to amalgamate with Briggs before one of its competitors did. The Company had to secure its supply of bodies. The merger was inevitable. So too was severe conflict on the shop floor. The Ford Motor Company didn't intend to allow variation in the rules that applied in its plants. Briggs was to be brought under the Ford rules. The 1955 Procedure Agreement was the first stage in a process which was completed by the Standardization Agreement of 1958. In signing the agreement the NJNC accepted an entirely one-way standardization. Nothing of Briggs was taken into the Ford structure.

The four years that followed the Ford takeover produced over 600 'incidents' in the Main and River plants. All these stoppages were unofficial and all those after August 1955 in breach of the newly-signed Procedure Agreement. The Company through sackings, warnings and formal notices 'reiterated its intention to obtain discipline in its plants' (The Cameron Report, 1957, p. 13). Its other policies didn't help. Speed-up was one thing. Redundancy was another. Working faster one day, out of work the next. In July 1956 the Company announced that the strike at BMC made it necessary for 2400 workers at the body plant to be made redundant. This provoked a strike 'though no discharges were necessary in the event' (The Cameron Report, 1957, p. 13). In November the Company announced that the oil shortage produced by the battle of Suez meant that 1700 would have to be sacked – in the following January. In response to this the shop committee of the jigs and fixtures department decided that, in the event of a sacking, a meeting would be called immediately. Johnny McLoughlin was the chairman of that committee, and summoned such a meeting in the January by ringing a handbell, after two stewards had been suspended.

Mr McLoughlin's version is that he acted under the influence of the general atmosphere of 'wind-up' pervading the River plant engineering shops after the recent discharge of the older craftsmen and the labourers, and also under a sense of urgency based on his observation that at Briggs 'once you are out of the gate you've had it'. In this mood he had been 'really gripped' by the scene of the suspension of his fellow shop stewards in the manager's office – a quite unexpected blow – and he returned to the shop to consult members of his shop committee about it. Their advice to him as chairman was to 'implement the resolution' ... He accordingly took the bell and rang it ... He had already started ringing when the foreman who, according to Mr McLoughlin, was 'absolutely raging', spoke to him in incensed terms. Mr McLoughlin considered that two courses were open to him, either to square up to the foreman or to pacify him, the best way of pacifying him, according to Mr McLoughlin, being to ignore him. He therefore said 'Leave it alone, Ted; give yourself a rest', and addressed the meeting urging it to 'get on to the national officials ... and get things cracking' in aid of the suspended stewards. The foreman swiftly returned to the charge, now 'quivering like a jelly', according to Mr McLoughlin, in company with Mr Smith, the general foreman, and Mr McLoughlin was suspended and thereafter has remained 'outside the gate' (The Cameron Report, 1957, pp. 14–15).

The whole engineering division came out on strike and the plant was stopped. After a week the men returned to work pending official discussions. These broke down and a ballot split 1118 to 429 in favour of continuing the strike. The strike never took place. There was a court of inquiry instead, it found that Johnny McLoughlin had been justifiably dismissed. He stayed outside the gates. 'Once you are out of the gates you have had it.' In coming to his conclusions Lord Cameron was influenced by McLoughlin's 'demeanour'. He thought him 'glib, quick-witted and evasive', with nothing of the appearance of 'a man ... worried about his job or the results which his action had produced'. He was, in fact, a man who 'showed a considerable capacity for ... agitation and propaganda'. More importantly, though, Cameron was concerned by the 'Communist influence' within the stewards' committee in the body plant and worried that the reinstatement of McLoughlin 'could be interpreted as a gesture of appeasement of the extreme elements in the shop stewards' organization' (The Cameron Report, 1957, p. 19). The report emphasized that the continued existence of an uncontrolled shop stewards' committee was in nobody's interests. It also made reference to the 'attitude of mind' of the Ford executives which was dominated by 'a desire to impose rather than agree by negotiation'. This attitude didn't change. Rather it was encouraged and enforced by the commission's report. It reinforced their determination to control the work process and bring the stewards to heel.

In the following year the Standardization Agreement was signed and to press home the point that Briggs was now a part of Ford's the Company moved 2500 men from the body plant into the new PTA (Paint, Trim and Assembly) plant. If this action was intended to cure the Briggs malaise it clearly failed. By 1960 the Joint Shop Stewards' Committee at Dagenham was selling 50,000 copies of its broadsheet *Voice of Ford Workers* in a week. It had an annual income of £30,000. It was the most powerful unofficial body in the country. It fed on shop-floor struggles over the control of work, and the new PTA, where the pressure of the line was greatest, was at the centre of these conflicts. The Ford Motor Company was facing an intransigent opposition to its 'right to manage'. Managerial decisions were being vetoed in the shop. It was difficult to take. It pushed the Company into alliances. The build-up to a confrontation.

Its insistence on managing its own plants in its own way kept the Ford Motor Company out of the Federation of Engineering Employers to which the British car firms were affiliated. But while it objected to interference from outside, the Company still wanted to maintain contact with the other car employers. In 1950 a senior member of the Ford personnel staff suggested that personnel managers in the motor car industry should meet informally, but regularly, to exchange information on wage levels, and other employment practices. Such meetings took place throughout the 1950s and eventually became formalized into the Motor Industry Industrial Relations Panel. The formalization was in part a response to increasing government concern with the strike record of the industry.

Table 1 **Post-war industrial disputes in the car firms[6]**

Annual average of three-year period	Number of separate strikes	Workers involved	Working days lost
1947–49	10	9000	25,000
1950–52	14	25,000	131,000
1953–55	14	42,000	137,000
1956–58	31	82,000	322,000
1959–61	75	116,000	307,000

(From Turner, Clack and Roberts, 1967, p. 23.)

The trend in strikes was upward. Increasingly the strikes were unofficial, broke procedure and were to do with managerial prerogatives. The tendency was to continue into the 1960s. In 1960 the Ministry of Labour called a meeting of the unions and employers. They

agreed on a number of points on which action should be taken in our respective fields to assist individual companies, workpeople and trade unions in their day-to-day relations.

Procedural behaviour was central. Things had to be done 'constitutionally'. It was felt that the institutional arrangements for dealing

6. This table is based upon the official DEP classification of 'a strike' – i.e. that it involves at least ten workers and lasts for at least a day, unless it leads to the loss of 100 or more working days.

with disputes were entirely adequate providing they were 'operated in the right spirit'. This was the 'firm line' declaration. A joint decision by the employers, the Tory government and the unions that tough action was needed to deal with the trouble in the plants.

In 1960 the Ford Motor Company at Dearborn spent £128 million in buying up the 45 per cent of the British Company's shares held by 'the public'. It was a significant step. It marked the beginning of another period of vast capital investment in Britain and Europe. A period that would produce Ford Europe – a giant transcontinental company. It also marked the twilight of Hennessy's time with Ford and the establishment of an even tighter grip on Dagenham by Detroit. Dagenham management were soon aware of the consequences. The management structure was 'shaken up'. Men moved sideways. And out. Not a few were scared stiff. It affected the shop floor more diffusively but no less markedly. Posters impressing the need for better workmanship appeared in the plants. The motor car is a mass-produced luxury product, and a lot of the luxury is in the finish; in the paint and the interior of the car ... the trim. The drive for better quality centred on the trim. There, the men on the line had to cope with a jittery management, a quality campaign and speed-up. Ernie Stanton, an NUVB steward at the time, describes the situation in 1962:

By 1962 the speed-up had resulted in creating a large labour pool and increased rate of absenteeism. The labour pool was used in two ways: first to fill in for absentees, and second, to bring pressure for further speed-up. When the Company wanted to speed up a line, the chargehand would approach workers individually and tell them that the department superintendent had been looking into their particular jobs. If a small operation was taken away and a bigger one put in its place it might be better for all concerned. If the member protested that he already had too much, he would be approached in the same way two or three times more. Then the foreman would pay him a visit. This time he would be told that he only had to try the new job. If the member accepted his new target on this basis he soon found that if he didn't succeed he would be hauled up before the line desk, confronted by the chargehand, foreman and superintendent, and told that he was 'disrupting the whole line' and that if he didn't make the extra effort they would have to sack him or put him in the labour pool (which meant a different job every day). The Company refused to discuss the speed-up with shop stewards or with district officials (Stanton, 1967, p. 13).

Speed-up. The full meaning of multinational production began to make itself apparent in the PTA at that time. The Company owned another assembly plant in Cologne manned mainly by Spanish and Turkish workers, whose immigrant status made them extremely vulnerable. The sack could mean deportation. Supervisors were frequently taken to the Cologne plant to compare the ways in which the job was run in the two plants. The 'Cologne Yardstick' was increasingly applied to the Dagenham PTA plant in the 1960s, producing a relentless conflict. In 1960 the men in that plant took part in strikes that accounted for 100,000 man-hours. In 1961 the figure had jumped to 184,000 and in the year after to 400,000. In 1963, following the defeat of the stewards' committee, only 3400 man-hours were 'lost' through strike action.

Faced by an intransigent shop-floor organization the Ford Motor Company decided to operate the 'firm line' advocated in the 1960 Ministry of Labour talks. It prepared the ground in the NJNC. In 1958 the Company had signed a detailed agreement with the unions. Most of this agreement referred to rates of pay, bonuses and the like. Clause 15, however, was entitled 'The Achievement of Efficiency in Operations' and it read:

The Trade Unions and the Company agree on the need:
1. To achieve efficient production by all reasonable means;
2. For the introduction of labour-saving machines and methods;
3. For the Company to transfer employees from one job or department to another as may be desirable having in mind continuity of employment and flow of production.

It is not part of the duty of any shop steward whose constitution and duties are defined in the Procedure Agreement to deal with such matters in the shop, but he may refer them for consideration by the Works Committee.[7]

The national officials were as irritated by the shop stewards' committee's activities as the Ford Motor Company. Les Kealey, the TGWU representative on the NJNC, felt that 'unfortunately a number of stewards of certain unions at Dagenham have got into the habit of trying to solve their own problems' (quoted in The Jack Report, 1963, p. 51). William (later Lord) Carron of the AUEW was more explicit with his criticisms. In 1957 he said of the situation in Briggs: ·

For a long time now subversive elements have been at work at Briggs. Last year alone, there were 200 stoppages in the plant. In my view those subversive types were responsible for most, if not all of them.[8]

7. *Agreement and Conditions of Employment* (The Blue Book), p. 32.
8. *Sunday Dispatch*, 24 February 1957; quoted in Weller (1964, p. 23).

In 1962 he wrote an article entitled 'Where is the enemy?' in the *Ford Bulletin*, the house journal of the Ford Motor Company. 'The enemy' it seemed were workers on the shop floor.

The old need for unbridled militancy rapidly diminished with the reduction of our immediate major social and industrial problems. One still finds pockets of militancy which are inspired by motives that cannot be accepted as being based purely upon trade union principles. These motives spring from attempts to change that system of government we have in the United Kingdom and would attempt to replace this system with one that has been rejected in parliamentary and local government elections by an overwhelming majority of opinion. Disruptive tactics with political ambition as a source of inspiration will not contribute to the further wellbeing of our citizenship or, for that matter, our membership, which depends entirely in these modern years upon the produce of our factories and workplaces (quoted in Weller, 1964, p. 23).

The national officials were not happy about the independence of the stewards' committee. Its funds and its strength within the workplace presented an implicit challenge to the official union hierarchies. It served to undermine the position of the full-time officers on the NJNC. All members of that committee were agreed that there was a problem and on 12 October 1962 they issued a statement.

The trade unions recognize the right of the Company to exercise such measures as are expressed within the Agreement against employees who fail to comply with the conditions of their employment by taking unconstitutional action.[9]

The Cameron Commission had already noted that 'good will' existed between the Company and the national officers of the union. The relationships on the NJNC were said to be 'cordial'. They had had their quarrels over who was to blame for particular stoppages in the plants but these had never approached a breach. In 1962 the national officials seemed prepared to give the Company a free hand in doling out the 'firm line'. For months the shop floor had been infused with rumour of the crunch. The Company was going to have a go. Five days after the joint declaration, the crunch arrived. Bill Francis, a steward in the PTA plant was sacked. The PTA plant struck in his support. The stewards' committee described the events that led up to the sacking in a pamphlet *What's Wrong at Ford's*:

The incidents began on the Classic Trim section where our members were assembling the complete doorglass, channels, regulators and quarter-vents at the rate of 35 a shift.

9. *Agreements and Conditions of Employment* (The Blue Book), p. 15.

The last time the work load increased from 32 to 35 the members were told that if they did the 35 no further increases would be asked for. Then the Company sought to increase the number of doors by four per man per shift.

It was proposed to do this by cutting the gang on the operation from nine men to eight without cutting the line speed. The gang agreed under protest to try this and a man was taken off on Monday, 15 October.

As eight men could not do the work previously done by nine they were pulled out of position down the line. This hindered other operations and they were helped get back by additional labour on the job. This continued throughout Tuesday.

On Wednesday morning the Company claimed that three of the eight men were 'leading resistance' to increased production. They were taken off the line and replaced with three other members.

At this stage the doorglass gang stopped work in protest against the three members being 'sorted out'. The three men were replaced and the job continued. After a further hour the convenor and stewards were sent for and told that the three men were being changed. This resulted in a protest.

The production manager, Mr Boxall, left the office temporarily and, in his absence, Francis reached agreement with the superintendent about the replacement of the three men. Boxall quashed the agreement immediately on his return.

Again the three men were taken off the job and replaced; this led to a stoppage, though resumption of work was obtained with the three men taken out but left in the vicinity.

After an hour's delay on the Company side the management started discussions by stating that the eight men on the job were drifting down the line out of position and if this continued the line would be shut down.

The stewards then asked that the original three men be returned to the line since experience had proved in the past hour that, although they had been replaced, the gang could not hold the line. This was refused.

The convenor then asked that before the Company started shutting down the line – which would result in locking members out – procedure should be carried out. He asked for an immediate joint works committee. The personnel manager indicated that this was not likely to be granted.

On this reply the Company was asked to take no further action until district officials had been called into discussion. This also was refused.

Francis, in company with three other stewards of other unions, as was the normal practice, then reported back during the lunch hour to the members on the trim line who, after receiving the report, decided that if the three men were victimized or if the Company locked out any members, the whole area would give full support.

That afternoon the line ran normally and fifteen minutes before the end of the shift Bros Halpin (plant convenor) and Francis were sent for by the plant manager, Mr Cartiledge, and told that Francis was dismissed on the spot for holding a lunchtime meeting.

The Company was faced with a solid strike on the issue of victimization. The mass meetings totally supported an all-out strike until Francis was reinstated. Bill Francis was one of the most popular stewards in the plant with a lot of support from the lads on the shop floor. The crunch had been expected and now it had arrived it was going to be seen through.

The issue, however, became blurred. A situation that had appeared uncomplicated and clear cut became twisted in committee rooms. The trade union side of the NJNC met and O'Hagen and Kealey telephoned Leslie Blakeman at Ford's Labour Relations Department. Afterwards, O'Hagen and Kealey insisted that Blakeman had guaranteed that if the men returned to work there would be no victimization and the issue of Francis's dismissal could be negotiated. Production would be 'stepped up' over a week by which time all operatives would be employed. While there may be 'ordinary redundancy' this would be dealt with through the normal channels. Blakeman was to deny saying any of this. Whatever the case, the NJNC voted for a resumption of work on the basis of the Kealey–O'Hagen assurance, as did the Dagenham shop stewards' committee. The assurance bore only the slightest resemblance to what took place in the following weeks.

Production was stepped up slowly. The first men let back into the plant had received letters informing them that before starting work they would have to sign an assurance of good behaviour. Batches of men started on each day of the week. Each with a letter.

> The Company Service men patrolled the gates and only allowed entry to people who had signed. The letter was scrutinized and the member was directed to the department he was to work in. Many members were sent to strange shops where they had no idea what had been the customary speeds, local agreements, etc.
>
> Before starting work the member was interviewed by the foreman and told how much work he would have to do and 'to watch his step, for there were thousands outside the gates'. In many cases the amount of work expected was a third more than before the dispute (*What's Wrong at Ford's*, p. 11).

After a week there were still 600 men outside the gates. The Company, in selecting who was to return and when, had drawn up a list of names 'in as fair a way as possible'.

> ... they had sought the views of the appropriate members of supervision in the areas where they had experienced the greatest amount of disruption, asking them to provide lists of unsatisfactory employees.

Many of the 600 were reprieved by a cut in the purchase tax on motor cars. This left seventy. The names on the list were eventually whittled down to seventeen.

Their employment had been terminated because the management – in a matter in which they have to be the ultimate judges – had concluded over a period that these were not men with good will towards the Company (The Jack Report, 1963, pp. 21–2).

The seventeen were 'outside the plant' while the others worked on speeded lines and the national officials on the NJNC argued and machinated. It went on for months. Outside the gate. Unemployed soon to be unemployable. The protracted disagreements in the NJNC led to a Court of Inquiry, sitting in public in London on 4 and 5 March 1963, five months after Bill Francis was sacked.

The chairman of the Court was D. T. Jack, a former professor of Economics at the University of Durham. Jack had long since been active in affairs of state. He had advocated that the Treasury should exist as the final arbiter in all wage disputes and had helped in the initiation of the Cohen Council which first proposed the 'wage pause' in the 1950s. He had previously been chairman of a Court of Inquiry into a dispute at BOAC which had recognized that 'the curbing of disruptive elements presents a problem for the trade unions' and advised that 'the disruptive behaviour of the Joint Shop Stewards' Committee is a matter to which the unions concerned should give their most careful attention'.

Few activists at Dagenham held out much hope of salvation from the Court. A group of these wrote in the new rank and file magazine *Solidarity*:

The Court consists of ex-professor D. T. Jack, aided by two assessors from the Ford Motor Company (noted for their militancy). The TUC assessors are two trade union officials (not noted for militancy, other than verbal). Both 'sides' are therefore well and truly 'represented'. The only people left out appear to be the men themselves. It would not be out of place to say: 'What about the workers?'

They went on to conclude that:

It is on the cards that a deal will be made. In return for a promise by the unions to 'put their house in order' by taking action against the shop stewards' committee, the Court might recommend that the Company take back the seventeen men, but as ordinary workers, well split up throughout the plant, or even dispersed in plants elsewhere. The damage will then well and truly be done.[10]

10. *Solidarity*, vol. 2, no. 9, pp. 1–2.

The damage was indeed well and truly done. Not one of the dismissed men was called to give evidence. The Court upheld the Company's right to employ, and therefore sack, whoever it liked and issued warnings about the dangers of shop-floor organizations existing outside the official control of the unions. And the seventeen were to stay outside the gates for ever. The stewards' committee had been

---

63. In conclusion, the Company stated that although the case of the seventeen men should not be allowed to distract attention from their long drawn-out trouble which had cost the Company, and the country, so much, it raised a very important issue of principle, basic to management – namely, the legal right of employers to terminate, subject to contract, the employment of those who in their judgement have served them ill. This was a right which, the Company claimed, was as vital to employers as it was to employees. Just as employees were fully entitled, either individually or collectively, to terminate their employment, so were employers. In the Company's view, to say that it was not the prerogative of management to decide whom it will employ was the way to industrial anarchy. They pointed out that in this country the trade unions have always refused to share any of the risks or responsibilities of management, and while that remained the position, they considered that management, which was responsible for the efficiency of their industry, must retain the ultimate prerogative of deciding, subject to individual or collective agreements, whom they would employ. In the Company's view, this was a question of principle vital to all employers.

From The Jack Report, 1963, p. 24.

---

defeated. Johnnie Cross, a member of the AUEW and a shop steward in the PTA plant, was one of the seventeen. In 1964 he reflected that:

The root causes of the defeat, however, go back much further than the dispute itself. Ford workers used to have a very good link with all other car firms in England ... Once a year there were meetings including shop stewards and committee men from the whole industry. This had the makings of a national shop stewards' movement.

But inevitably the trade union bureaucrats, in the form of the Grand Knight of St. Gregory, Sir William Carron and that Grand Old Left Winger, Frank Cousins ... cracked their whips.

These so-called trade union leaders said they would expel any of their members who attended any of these meetings, even though they were held at weekends. Why it mattered what they ordered I can't imagine. They should have been told to get knotted. But not on your life. The leading Party members among the leadership of the stewards' movement ducked down their little holes and stopped there.

I would say that this was when the trade union movement in the car industry started slipping backwards.[11]

If one thing was needed by car workers in the 1950s it was a national shop stewards' combine committee that could organize trade union activity between the numerous plants in the industry. At a time when car workers were experiencing the same struggles, in various degrees, coordinated activity on a wide front would have seemed to be an obvious strategy. The Communist Party was in a strong position industrially to give such a lead. However it was at the same time vulnerable politically. Its members were banned from holding union office in many unions during this period, and this hangover from the Cold War made the Party reluctant to take a definite stand against the official union hierarchies. It had no committee based on the car industry until after its 1965 congress and it did nothing to encourage the formation of a combine committee by the stewards. As a result the Dagenham stewards' committee was isolated as it approached the 1962 showdown, and (in one of the most glaring conflicts to take place in British industry since the war) received the support of not one sympathy strike from other car workers.

There is also the suspicion that the Dagenham committee was isolated in another even more important respect. The existence of a changing 'Party line' created a feeling within the plant that the stewards' committee no longer *represented* the lads – a critical situation for a mass-based organization. The isolation of the activist from his members means that when the crunch comes he's lost them. And so it proved. Francis's sacking resulted in the immediate stoppage of the PTA plant. Undoubtedly, that strike could have continued. Yet the PTA plant was the only one on the Dagenham estate to stop. Some stewards and a few members left the other plants, but that was all. The stewards' committee was incapable of leading the 22,000 workers into a strike. They lacked the support, and by that time any clear idea of what they could achieve. They settled for a limited strike. And then called it off. They were beaten. And the members of the Dagenham branch of the Party was halved. Cars were being built on the assembly lines of the PTA and the men there knew better than anyone that they'd suffered a defeat.

11. *Solidarity*, vol. 3, no. 10.

> The Company emphasizes that wildcat strikes will not be tolerated in the future. Employees who go on unofficial strike must not assume that they will be able to return to their jobs automatically ... These measures are designed to restore the joint authority of the unions and the Company and to combat the activities of those who have no loyalty to either.
>
> Ford Motor Company notice, issued 20 November 1962, reprinted in *Solidarity* pamphlet no. 26, *What Happened at Fords*.

As we entered the PTA after the sacking of Francis we had to hand in the signed forms which declared our intention to be good boys. When the starting hooter sounded we found that the lines were set at a speed that didn't conform to the labour strength. As the numbers of men increased after the first week, so the speed of the line was increased likewise.

The supervision were having a heyday. They were boasting that they now had the men where they wanted them. Very quickly the tasks became intolerable. The men were forced to a running pace, supervisors had to jump to keep up with them.[12]

The speed-up had a particularly violent effect upon the older workers in the plant. At the best of times men in their fifties can't compete as equals on an assembly line with men half their age. Speed-up and the clamp-down on the organization of work resulted in many of these men asking for their cards.

I wasn't a steward, I can only say how I personally found it. The factory became a place of desperation. Men studied the vacant job columns in the newspapers struggling to get out of the plant. Men were more or less afraid to talk to each other on the job. The fear was the sack and the prospect of years out of work along with the victimized lads.

I hated going to work. But I put up with it as I had been on the job for more than ten years and couldn't see any immediate openings for myself elsewhere.

A year later, early in 1964, the company really did the dirty on me and another 200 blokes, most of them from Stock ...

I was told that the only job for me was on the assembly line. I could take it or get out. Lots of others were told the same.

The shop stewards knew what was going on. But they didn't do anything about it. They were as scared of the sack as anybody else. They didn't want to get on an employer's blacklist.

I know what the Company was up to in my case. They hoped to kill me off. The line had been so speeded up that even young men couldn't cope. And I was

12. 'Murder at Fords', *Solidarity*, vol. 4, no. 4.

fifty-two at the time. I decided to sling the job in – but when it was convenient for me.

So I went on the line. It was terrible. I had a job where I was chasing conveyor belts up and down all the time without a moment for a breather. I used to work myself silly. When I got home I was whacked out.

To be honest, the work was too much for any one man. The foreman kept having to come and help me out. The only reason he did it was because he also knew that the job needed two men.

After I had my holidays and I had stuck the job for a few months, I asked for my cards. When I left two foremen admitted that the job really needed two blokes on it.

I also knew why he didn't go into the office and ask for another man. He was as scared of the sack as anyone else. Yet he's still a Company man ...

When I left, I had no job to go to ... I just wanted to get out of the place. If necessary, I told my wife, I would go on the labour or the NAB. Fortunately I got fixed up all right.

I've known a lot of other long-service workers who've left the PTA as well. When that happens, something is really wrong with a factory.[13]

The shop steward organization at Dagenham had been virtually destroyed. And the men were suffering for it. With this victory under its belt the Ford Motor Company turned a belligerent eye to the North of England. To Liverpool and its new plants at Halewood.

13. 'After the Ford Defeat', *Solidarity*, vol. 4, no. 2.

Ford US made a £128 million bid for the outstanding shares in the British company in November 1960. The deal was completed early in the following year.

The decade that followed saw a massive expansion of the Company's facilities outside the Dagenham estate, which up to that time had manufactured all the Company's products. The first to go were trucks – assembly began at Langley, Buckinghamshire in March 1961. Two years later car model production was split when the three Halewood plants were completed in the Merseyside development region. At the end of August 1964 a £5 million administrative headquarters was completed at Warley in Essex for 2000 staff and a month later Ford Tractor Operations were transferred from Dagenham to Basildon, Essex. In 1965 a new plant at Swansea extended the Company's machining and sub-assembly capacity.

From: *Graduates in Ford*: Ford Motor Company (recruitment pamphlet, 1971).

I have heard some people say that Liverpool men could never put up a fight, but I have always laughed at this idea. The best fighters that I met with in any part of the world were the Liverpool men; but one had to be exceedingly careful in handling them. They must not be told lies – their confidence must be retained, and they will follow their leaders to death.

J Havelock Wilson, President, National Sailors' and Firemen's Union, 1925.

3 Henry Ford Comes to Liverpool

The Ford Motor Company's Halewood estate is situated in the extreme south of Liverpool. Out past Garston and the airport. You probably need at least two buses to get out there. The Crosville or the 80/82c are your best bets. If you catch a 'special' you'll go right to the gates. Otherwise you've a ten-minute walk from Speke. If you're really lucky you have a car or can get a lift with one of your mates. Liverpool is strewn with pick-up points where workers wait, on corners, for their lifts.

The estate is made up of three major plants – a transmission plant, a metal stamping and body plant (MSB) and a paint, trim and assembly plant (PTA). The main capital of these plants was laid down between 1958 and 1963. A considerable amount of new capital was invested in Merseyside and other development districts during this period, attracted by government incentives and the state of the labour market. Subsidiary factories in the Merseyside area paid wage rates lower than those in the parent factories in the South. The reasons which influenced the Ford Motor Company's move to Halewood were the same as those that led it to establish a plant at Genk in the underdeveloped Linsburg region of Belgium. Unemployment means low wages and a vulnerable labour force. At Genk the Company openly used the threat of moving elsewhere in order to obtain an agreement with the unions which offered the workers a lower rate and worse conditions of employment than applied in any of its other European plants. In Britain expansion away from traditional areas of manufacture created the possibility for the motor employers to organize the production of motor cars free from the job control that had built up in the old factories. Ford's moves to Liverpool and Swansea were paralleled by Vauxhall's move to Ellesmere Port on Merseyside and the opening of a Rootes (Chrysler) plant at Linwood. When Ford came to Liverpool 'restrictive practices', the activities of shop stewards and managerial prerogatives dominated the minds of management and supervision.

The managers and foremen who went to the new plant were

recruited from Dagenham. Most of the labour was 'green' and recruited locally. Many of the management team had been involved in conflicts with steward organization at Dagenham and were determined to prevent a similar situation developing at Halewood. The first personnel manager of the PTA plant remembers that 'we went there with the idea of having a good plant; one with good labour relations. We wanted to get a trouble-free plant, to get away from Dagenham and Dagenham ways. It didn't turn out like that though.' Ford's came to Halewood determined to establish 'the joint authority of the unions and the Company'. It had burned its fingers by allowing over twenty unions into its plants. Multi-unionism meant that the full-time officers found it difficult to establish discipline over their membership and their stewards. It had learned the costs of an uncontrolled shop stewards' committee, as well as the advantages of close relationships with the official unions. The opening of its new plants in Liverpool was preceded by an agreement signed with the AUEW and the GMWU – both dominated by a right-wing 'anti-shop steward' leadership – which gave them exclusive negotiating rights for the semi-skilled and upon, by the national officers of these unions, was 1/3d (6p or 20 per cent) per hour less than the Dagenham rate. The national leadership of the TGWU objected to the exclusion of their union from the agreement, and a threat of 'blacked' cars on the Liverpool docks was sufficient to give them recruiting rights in the new factory. The rate, however, remained unchanged by this move, and parity with Dagenham was only gained by a series of unofficial overtime bans in 1963.

The focus of the Company's industrial relations policy during this period seems to have been the regulation of the activities of shop stewards on the shop floor. An extract from a directive to all supervisors from the personnel manager of the PTA plant read:

It is essential to control and record the time that employees leave their place of work on business other than personal break ...

In particular, the amount of time given to shop stewards for carrying out authorized activities must be meticulously controlled from the outset. It should always be borne in mind that a shop steward holds his position by virtue of being a Company employee and his first responsibility is to carry out the duties for which the Company pays him.

Before granting permission for the steward to leave the job, the foreman should satisfy himself that the reasons given are valid and that it is necessary for the steward to see someone other than himself with the matter in hand. Unless he does this he will soon lose his authority over the steward and the section.

To move from his job within the department verbal permission from the line foreman is sufficient but to leave the department the steward should obtain a shop steward's leave permit (Form E.8287) . . .

Only strict control from the outset will prevent the abuses current in other Company locations.

It seems reasonably clear that Ford management went to Halewood determined to control shop steward activity in the plant and to conduct negotiations wherever possible through official channels. It is also clear that the policy failed and that it produced, as in Dagenham, a considerable degree of conflict on the shop floor. In 1964 some 67,000 man-hours were lost through strikes in the PTA and MSB plants.

By 1964 a strong shop steward committee had been established in each of the three plants on the Halewood estate, and the Company had been forced to amend its policy of restriction. The level of strike activity in the following two years was considerably lower than the 1964 peak (each year recording around 10,000 man-hours lost in the PTA and MSB plants) and when I first went to the plant in 1967, there had been only one significant stoppage of work in the previous six months. The plant's new personnel manager saw the emergence of a new 'constructive relationship'. The senior stewards for their part felt that the management was being increasingly cooperative. The stewards had been granted greater facilities and by 1968 the convenor had an office and a telephone. The Company was extending the soft-sell. My presence in the plant was seen as an indication of this new approach by management. The convenor remarked cryptically that I was their 'reward for being good boys'.

This new approach was developed at a time when Ford was planning the construction of Ford Europe. To provide a base for new capital expansion the Company opened, with the unions, the detailed negotiation of a new national grading structure and plant-based productivity agreement. An agreement which hung on the cooperation of the men and their shop stewards. It was signed and implemented in the autumn of 1967 and was followed by a period of intense bitterness. During 1968 some 140,000 man-hours were lost in the PTA alone. And in the February of 1969 the Company's production in Britain was brought to a complete standstill by the first national stoppage that the Company had experienced. The Penalty Clause strike. The main pressure for this strike came from the PTA plant at Halewood. It brought to the foreground once again the issue of 'unconstitutional action', the rights of management, stewards and union officials. The reform of the unions' negotiating team followed in the wake of the strike in which the stewards from the Halewood PTA were an active force. With the backing of the other Halewood plants and the axle plant at Swansea these stewards went on to lead the 'Campaign for Parity' that came out of this. These plants provided the core support for the national stoppage that lasted for over nine weeks in 1971, and again in 1978. In the early 1980s the 'productivity' levels in the Halewood plant were repeatedly referred to as a cause for concern. Frequently during these years television interviewers have asked 'Why is Halewood so militant?'

The particular circumstances faced by shop stewards in their place of work varies a great deal, and this is an important source of variation in the militancy of shop steward organizations. To say this is not to ignore tradition, or the particular culture of the local working class. In fact the main aim of this chapter is to present an account of how the past experiences of the Liverpool working class affected relationships with the PTA plant at Halewood. People who know Liverpool know that 'scousers' are different. A conglomeration of Celts around a busy seaport has produced more 'characters' per square yard than anywhere else in the country. However, there are some docile labour forces on Merseyside. Not all the factories there were in ferment during the sixties and seventies and only a small proportion of them developed a strong shop steward organization. The fact that the PTA workers at Halewood were scousers mattered. The fact that they worked in an assembly plant of the Ford Motor Company probably mattered more. What also mattered was that the production workers in the PTA were almost all members of the TGWU. This was the first time that the TGWU had obtained a virtual closed shop in a large factory in the motor industry and this, in an industry dominated by multi-union plants, had some quite important implications for the way in which the stewards' committee developed at Halewood, and ultimately for the union organization within the whole Ford Motor Company.

At Dagenham the AUEW had always had a large membership in the plants and its members had dominated the leadership of the shop stewards' committees. Unlike the TGWU the branch structure of the AUEW is not usually based upon the plant but upon the geographical area. A typical branch will draw its membership from a number of establishments. This can mean that the shop stewards within a particular factory do not hold office within their local AUEW branch. More complications arise if, as at Dagenham, the workers in a particular plant belong to a number of different unions. This mixture, as we have seen, led to a particular form of shop-floor unionism at Dagenham, with shop stewards relatively immune from the disciplining powers of the full-time officials. It also meant, though, that they existed without the protection of the official union organization. The power of the stewards' organization at Dagenham was largely a power established *in isolation* from the official hierarchies of the unions and in 1962 this power was broken by the sack. This experience, and the absence of a chronic multiplicity of unions within the plants, led to a different type of unofficial unionism being developed at Halewood.

The TGWU has increasingly tended to base its branch structure upon factories. At the beginning of Halewood one TGWU branch spanned the three plants on the estate.[1] The membership was always concentrated in the PTA plant however, and the officers of the branch were invariably drawn from this plant. Members of the TGWU were also the dominant voices in the shop stewards' committee of the PTA. Almost all the production workers were in the TGWU and, apart from the occasional election of a member of the GMWU, all the stewards carried TGWU credentials. In 1967 there were forty-five members of the shop stewards' committee, and thirty-six of these were TGWU members, the remainder being members of craft unions representing the various maintenance workers in the plant. Each year the committee elected from its number a convenor, two deputy convenors and four other stewards to serve with them on the plant's Joint Works Committee (JWC). The convenor remained permanently on the day shift and was concerned exclusively with negotiations. He was compensated for his loss of shift allowance by payments from the shop steward committee's fund. This was financed by raffles and sweepstakes and latterly by regular levies on the membership. The convenor together with the works committee members formed a group of experienced stewards who gave advice to other stewards and were directly involved in all serious disputes that developed in the plant. At no time has the PTA committee elected anyone other than a TGWU member to the position of convenor or deputy convenor. Occasionally a member of the AUEW or the Electrical and Plumbing Trades Union (EPTU) served on the Works Committee but this wasn't common. The union organization within the PTA plant was dominated at all levels by members of the TGWU. These men were

---

1. Later on two branches were established. The old one based on the PTA and MSB plants and the new one on the transmission plant.

particularly active[2] and produced in five years a strong shop-floor organization and a branch that was on the assessment of the regional secretary, 'the most alive in the region'.

This coexistence of the branch and shop-floor organization made it easier for the one to develop in sympathy with the other. It meant that issues which cropped up at the workplace could be discussed by the stewards and taken in the form of resolutions to the branch meeting. They needn't have done this though. The Donovan Commission found that only a third of the shop stewards they contacted maintained that workplace policy was ever decided at the branch. In fact only 4 per cent of AUEW stewards often took plant business to the branch.[3] Partly as a consequence of the 1962 defeat at Dagenham the stewards in the PTA at Halewood were determined to exert an influence within the union and to achieve this they tried to develop a consistent policy at the plant and in the branch.

In 1967 the stewards' committee and the membership were dominated by young married men with children. In spite of the age of the stewards, the committee had a larger proportion of men who had been there for some time than the overall membership. A third of the stewards had been in the plant since it opened in 1962 while none of the forty-three members I interviewed had been there that long. Nine of the stewards were under thirty; three of these had been in the plant for over five years and were members of the JWC. This mixture of youth and experience was an important feature of the stewards' committee of the PTA. The stewards were young men. They wore sharp clothes; suits with box jackets. They thought of themselves as smart, modern men; and this they were. They walked with a slight swagger, entirely alert and to the point of things. They walked, talked and looked as they were. They knew what their bit of the world was about and they were prepared to take on anybody who challenged it.

This came across in many ways. For example, in the March of 1970 four stewards from the Halewood PTA plant arranged to meet the stewards of the Swansea axle plant. The meeting was arranged to take place in the Skewen Rugby Union club, just outside Swansea. I arrived

2. Between 1964 and 1967 I had studied three other branches of the TGWU on Merseyside. On a series of indices – attendance of meetings, number of meetings, activity at and around meetings, discussions with the membership and so on – the stewards at the PTA proved to be significantly more active than the stewards in the other plants.

3. See the *Royal Commission on Trade Unions and Employers' Associations*: *Research Paper* 10, 'Shop Stewards and Workshop Relations', p. 37.

before them and had a drink with a few of the Swansea stewards. These men lived in Swansea or travelled to work from the surrounding valleys. Their heritage was the pits. The pits that were being closed but which lived on in their collectivism. They carried the marks of the pit in blue on their hands and faces. Union men. The solid, traditional heart of the British Labour movement. Home-knitted, zipper cardigans – the occasional floral tie. One of the stewards leaned across the table and told one of his mates, who had just arrived, to keep his eye on the door because 'the Halewood boys will be coming through there any minute now'. They arrived late and the contrast was complete. Not only in their dress but in their very being. That night they stretched hands across and recognized working-class solidarity, they acknowledged their common heritage. Yet a development within the working class was apparent. These men respected tradition but seemed to be less bound by it. In their activities they were bringing a new, perhaps cosmopolitan, dimension to working-class culture and politics in this country. Between them they had attended thousands of meetings: they travelled regularly by Inter-City to London or Birmingham and in a few years they had been involved in more negotiations than most stewards experience in a lifetime. They were born and brought up in the city that produced the Beatles and in the 1960s they had lived in the furnace of shop-floor confrontation. It was these men who worked out a policy for the PTA stewards' committee in the early days of 1963.

In 1963 few of them had had any real experience of active trade unionism. They had been union members. A number of them had held a steward's card but few of them had been dedicated activists. This wasn't entirely coincidental, but rather a consequence of a recruiting policy that fitted a managerial strategy for the development of the Halewood estate. Bill Brodrick was one of the exceptions. He had worked on the dock in a number of capacities and been a strong supporter of the TGWU. His father also worked on the dock but was in the 'blue union'.[4] 'That caused no end of rows in our family that, him being in the blue union. We would argue and sometimes wouldn't talk to each other for days.' In his youth he'd been a bit of a tearaway and had been on the strike committee at the Garston bottle works. His last job had been one of some responsibility on the dock and this explained his acceptance by the Ford Motor Company. Billy was one

---

4. The National Amalgamated Stevedores' and Dockers' Union, which was formed in 1924 as a 'breakaway' from the TGWU.

of the few men with a lot of trade union experience behind him, and once the TGWU became established at Halewood he became convenor of the PTA. He didn't get it all his own way though. One of the best organized plants on Merseyside, the Dunlop factory at Speke, was just down the road from the Ford estate. A number of men were recruited from Dunlop's and although they'd never 'organized a factory' they knew what an organized plant looked like. They kept contact with the Dunlop stewards and often met Stan Pemberton, the convenor, in the best room of the Legs of Man on a Sunday dinner hour. Arguments about Dunlop's and the 'Dunlop way' were central to the early discussions within the shop stewards' committee. As one steward remembers: 'it used to get to a point when Billy would say "I'm fed up of hearing about Dunlop's. I'm fed up of having Dunlop's shoved down my throat. Fuck the Dunlop way, we'll do it our own way." But we didn't you know. We did it the Dunlop way.'

What then was the Dunlop way? Essentially what it involved was a maximum involvement in the democratic machinery of the union but with no illusions. The stewards at Dunlop's had obtained a considerable degree of influence within the TGWU by nominating representatives for the various elected committee seats in the union structure and by following almost parliamentary policies of lobbying and canvassing.[5]

They *used* the union at Dunlop's. If they were in a position where they needed support they had people on all the committees who would argue for them. They did all this and they could still give the two fingers to the full-time official if they felt like it. They got rid of an officer there once. He's joined the bosses now.

The PTA plant followed this pattern. By weight of numbers they were guaranteed seats on a number of local committees. They took up these seats, made sure that they weren't all taken by one man but distributed amongst the stewards, and entered the hurly burly of local

5. The Transport and General Workers' Union is structured geographically – into Regions and Districts – and also by industry into a federation of Trade Groups. The full-time officers are based at the National, Regional and District offices and are loosely linked to particular trade groups. This hierarchy of appointed full-time officials is paralleled by a series of committees manned by elected lay members. Thus at National level, lay members sit on the Executive, the Finance and General Purposes Committee etc. At the Regional and District level there are also lay committees as well as Trade Group committees. Seats are allocated on a number of different bases but a large branch which seeks representation within the union can be certain of a voice at District and Regional level and have a reasonable chance of obtaining an Executive seat.

union politics. By 1967 they were a force to be reckoned with in the region and in 1968 they obtained a seat on the National Executive. In doing this they were consciously following a strategy which drew lessons from the eclipse of the shop stewards' committee at Dagenham. In so doing they formulated and developed an unofficial–official unionism at Halewood.

In substance this strategy was not all that different from that followed by the Dagenham stewards. The fact that the PTA was a one-union plant, and that that union was the TGWU, gave the pursuit of the strategy more chance of success at Halewood in the 1960s. Where the PTA stewards differed most markedly from those at Dagenham was in the way they understood their role as *leaders*. They had gained some things from the defeat at Dagenham. They knew better than ever before that they couldn't trust the national officers of the union. They couldn't trust them, but on occasions they needed them. They had to try to use them. More importantly they learned something else that they already knew. Their strength lay with the membership. *Nothing* could alter that. The failure of the Dagenham stewards was summed up in their failure to get the support of the lads on the floor when it mattered – at the crunch. The Communist Party was held responsible for this. The PTA stewards came to the conscious decision that the steward committees in the plants were going to be the decision-making bodies at Halewood, that they were going to be responsible to the lads and not to King Street; they were convinced that the Party had sown the seeds of the 1962 defeat. And they were adamant in their resolve to keep political parties out of the steward committees at Halewood. (As it turned out this resolve was put to its greatest test by persistent calls from Moral Rearmament.) The Halewood committee was about to develop in much closer contact with the 'official' union than had the Dagenham committee, yet to have much fewer illusions about the full-time officers. They learned to know where their own strength lay. It was on the shop floor. They'd use the union but they wouldn't be taken for suckers. 'They had the plant out in 1962 and they went back – with fuck-all except Kealey's word. That's nor on tha'.'

At Halewood the relationship between the new TGWU stewards and the district officer of the union had an important moulding influence. The plants came under the Garston District Office and an officer called Sammy Glasstone. Sammy died in 1971 but during his lifetime he had entered into the folklore of the PTA stewards' committee and the Merseyside labour movement.

The Transport and General Workers' Union has a larger number of full-time officers than any union in Britain, and it also has a particularly favourable officer–member ratio. In 1961 it was estimated that the TGWU had one full-time officer for every 2200 members. By comparison the AUEW had an officer–member ratio of 1:6300. In 1968 the Donovan Commission estimated that the local full-time officer in the TGWU, directly in touch with the membership, had 120 stewards and 8900 members to look after. His counterpart in the AUEW had 477 stewards and 19,500 members. The TGWU officers had contacted 80 per cent of their stewards in the past four weeks while the typical AUEW district officer had contacted only 28 per cent of his stewards. It could be argued that this proliferation of full-time officials in the TGWU makes for easier control of the membership within that union. There is a lot of truth in this. Talk of bureaucratic control, however, should not serve to obscure the fact that most managers prefer to deal with their shop stewards and are reluctant to bring in the full-time officer. The Ford Motor Company in its reliance upon official centralized negotiations at national level was a clear exception to the rule. Yet Ford's were as reluctant to deal with district officers as they were with shop stewards. It is a mistake to assume that the trade union bureaucracies are simply monolithic structures standing over and apart from the membership. It is not unusual in fact for the local district officer, who may have only recently left the shop floor himself, to be particularly sympathetic toward the wishes of the membership. Such an officer would have built up alliances and understandings with the shop-floor organizations in his particular area and could be used effectively by those organizations in their struggles with management. Furthermore, by turning the occasional 'blind eye' he can protect the stewards from the formal control of the union organization. While it would be difficult to argue that this is the rule, there are enough examples of this phenomenon within the TGWU to make it an important aspect of workplace activity, and shop steward organization.

At Halewood the unionization of the plant took place with the close involvement of Sammy Glasstone. In 1966 Sammy moved to the regional office at Transport House in Islington in Liverpool and the vacancy at the Garston Office was contested by six stewards from the PTA. Bill Brodrick, the convenor, got the job, and with it maintained the close links between the district office and the shop steward committee.

A clear picture emerges of a shop steward committee developing in the wake of the Dagenham defeat, bent upon creating an extra-union base on the shop floor, but equally determined to maintain links and alliances with the official structure of the TGWU. In the early 1960s, when the other general unions were dominated by an overtly right-wing leadership, the PTA committee at Halewood emerged as a powerful force within the motor industry and the TGWU. An understanding of the ideology of the PTA committee and the events of the late 1960s must be rooted in this initial period of unionization.

The stewards in the PTA met each other regularly. They ate their meals together in the works canteen and drank together after meetings. They were friends. Occasionally they arranged social evenings to which they took their wives.[6] On all these occasions they joked and told stories about people and events, about the city and the factories. More often they told stories about the plant, about the early days when the PTA plant was first unionized by the Transport and General Workers' Union. These stories in particular were always told to newcomers (the same stories were told to me dozens of times during the months when I came to know them) particularly to new shop stewards and activists and almost inevitably at times of crisis. In 1969 during the Penalty Clause strike there was continuous talk of the 'early days' in the plant.

These stories provide us with illustrations of the period of unionization. The fact that they were told so often indicates the significance of this period. In their telling, the stories take on a further significance. In handling the present, people call upon the past for guidance. The lessons of the past are learned and handed on as stories. The past structures the present, creating partial explanations of the world which are worked out in action. And told again. It is through stories about events in the past that people make sense of events in the present. The stories of the 'early days' told by the PTA stewards served as a pragmatic guide to their actions in the plant throughout the 1960s. For those early days, the days when the plant was unionized, provided the stewards with an important understanding of power relationships in our society, of the nature of the management and union bureaucracies. Specific conceptions of the Ford Motor Company and the trade union hierarchies were made concrete during this period and

---

6. A number of the stewards, but one in particular, attached tremendous importance to these evenings. They saw it important that 'the wives should meet each other and know that they all have the same problems'. These 'problems' related to the strain of family life created by union activity which is discussed in Chapter 8.

these exerted a strong influence upon the way the shop steward committee at Halewood developed.

The early period of the plant was seen to be one in which the workers were severely exploited. Many of the managers who were in the plant at the time had moved on by 1967 – 'the bastards made their names off our backs'. Many line managers had been removed, leaving the personnel department in a position of ascendancy. Their change in managerial attitude was seen as a direct result of organization and struggle. Without such organization and further struggle 'we'll be back to the days of the ball and chain'. The work then was seen to be hard. As one steward put it:

> It's hard enough now but in those days it was terrible. That was before I was a steward. I was working on the headlinings and I never thought I'd survive. I used to come home from work and fall straight asleep. My legs and arms used to be burning. And I knew hard work. I'd been on the buildings but this place was a bastard then. I didn't have any relations with my wife for months. Now that's not right is it? No work should be that hard!

Accounts such as these are interspersed with specific incidents when men were injured or taken ill while working.

> They wouldn't stop that fucking line. You could be dying and they wouldn't stop it. If someone was hurt the first thing the supervisor thought about was filling the job. He'd start doing the work before he made sure the bloke was all right. I tell you you could have been dying and they wouldn't have bothered.

Occasionally men did die. One, a man of about forty, lay by the side of the line as his mates worked.

> We were in the locker room before the shift had started and he collapsed with a pain in his chest. He went an awful colour but then he reckoned he was all right. We went down the stairs on to the shop floor, walked across to the line and he collapsed again. Y'know – flat on the floor. His face was an awful grey colour. We all rushed round him like and the buzzer went. The line started. The foreman came across shouting 'get to work ... get on the line'. And there we were sticking things on the cars and he was lying there. He must have been lying there ten minutes ... dead. In front of us.

Men and Machines. A conflict of values in a car plant. The stewards tell another story which plays on this conflict. Ronnie Walsh was working on the middle deck in the paint shop.

> I was working on one side of the car and the boot lid dropped. It just grazed the head of the fella working opposite me. I can see it now. He stopped working, had a look round to see if anyone was watching – I was pretending not

to look at him – and then he held his head. He'd had enough like. You could see him thinking 'I'm getting out of this for a bit'. He staggered, and I could see him looking around. You know what it was like in there. Paint everywhere. He wasn't going to fall in the paint ... so he staggered about ten yards and fell down with a moan on some pallets. It was bloody funny. One of the lads saw him there and stopped the line. The supervisor came chasing across. 'Start the line ... start the line. ...' He started the line and we had to work. We were working one short as well. It took them ages to get him out of there. They couldn't get the stretcher in. It must have been half an hour before they got him. Him lying there y'know with his one eye occasionally opening for a quick look round: 'What's happening?' It's funny. But he could have been really ill. For all the supervisor knew he could have been dead. 'Start the line. Keep the cars coming.' That's what they're concerned about.[7]

The speed of the line and speed-up figure in many of the stories about work in the early 1960s. In particular, frequent mention is made of the fact that the line speed would be altered *during* the shift without consultation or alteration in the allocation of work.

You'd be working. Get into a bit of a system and just about keeping the job under control and then you'd find that you'd lost control, like. You'd be working that bit harder again. The bastards had altered the line speed. They'd swear blind they hadn't but they had. We put a stop to that though. Little Bob's got the key now.[8]

On top of this the money was not as high as many had expected and this mixture of overwork and underpay was seen to be supported by a coalition of management and union officials, and put into practice by cockney foremen. This London–Liverpool dimension of the conflict is one which flavoured many of the stories and has had quite important consequences for the development of the committee. In the words of one of the senior stewards:

They thought they could treat use like dirt, them [the Dagenham supervisors]. We were just dirty scousers who'd crawled in off the docks out of the cold. We'd never even seen a car plant before and those sods had been inside one since they were knee-high. We took a hammering. Those fucking stewards at Dagenham have a lot to answer for over that. They were robbing us blind up here. They were getting away with murder. Doing things they wouldn't

7. An American psychologist, R. A. Sokolov, has argued that assembly-line workers have contradictory feelings about industrial accidents. While not actually wanting to get hurt, the accident does have its advantages. As distinct from his position on the line 'he hears his full name used several times ... from a number on an assembly line (he becomes) a person, a man with a name, and ... a disease.' See Sokolov (1967).

8. The key that locks the line at one speed. See Chapter 6.

have dreamed of in Dagenham. And they said nothing. They didn't come up here once. A new plant – you'd have thought they'd have done something but they did nothing. It's funny whenever I see them nowadays I'm always asking myself 'Why didn't you get the sack in 1962? Where were you when they were screwing us in this plant?'

The Dagenham stewards did in fact make some attempt to develop links with Halewood at the time when the Halewood workers were paid on the low rate. These attempts were obstructed by the full-time officials of the AUEW and GMWU. After many weeks they eventually managed to talk to the Liverpool Trades Council through a delegation from Walthamstow Trades Council. The absence of a national shop stewards' committee was felt severely at this time. No contact was established between the steward committees at Dagenham and those on the Halewood estate. This absence of assistance during their critical period of development was to have a great influence upon the way in which the Halewood stewards related to the shop-floor leadership at Dagenham in the late 1960s.

However, Merseyside has a developed labour movement with a lot of struggles behind it. It has developed many 'characters'. Wild men who became legends in their own lifetime. Aristocrats of the people. One of these men came to work for Ford in the MSB plant. Eddie Roberts tells the story of Johnny Jones who had been his shop steward in Dunlop's.

> Johnny Jones was a funny character. An egotist, a very arrogant sort of man, not very well liked. I liked him but I took him for what he was . . . At Dunlop's John was very effective. The lads would go to him with a case and he'd get them what they wanted. That's what you want from a shop steward. Politically he was a cynic. He probably didn't vote: if he could have voted for himself he would have. He used to call himself the 'original bighead'. 'Never lost a case y'know' – and he hadn't. And we had a good shop there. We priced ourselves out of a job there. It was costing them more to make the shoes than they were selling them for.

They were declared redundant. They were offered alternative work but it was 1962 and jobs weren't scarce. They didn't care much for Dunlop's so they said 'sod that', took their redundancy payment and arranged a celebratory evening in a pub. A number of them thought that they'd have a go at Ford's which was just opening. Johnny Jones arranged for a recruitment officer for Ford's to be set up in Dunlop's and two-thirds of the shop put their names down and were accepted. Johnny was turned down. Like a number of other active trade unionists he didn't get through the security net. The local TGWU officials made some vague rumblings about 'blacklisting' and Johnny was taken on under duress 'but he'll have to watch himself'.

Meanwhile in the plant the Dunlop lads had started work:

They hadn't seen anything like this bloody place before. They'd been used to individual piece rates with a shop steward at their beck and call, winning everything in sight for them. Some of the lads started antagonizing the foremen. 'Fucking hell, wait till Johnny Jones sees this'; 'wait till Johnny Jones gets here mate he'll sort you out'; 'wait till Johnny Jones gets *here*'. It was like this bloody folk image y'know. This bloody Robin Hood character going to come here and stick arrows in all the bosses and all sorts. Well Johnny Jones sweeps into the place, fourteen feet tall, wearing this mantle of the shop steward that he'd had for years in Dunlop's.

He antagonized everyone in the personnel department on his first morning by refusing to sign for a procedure agreement that he hadn't been given. He had a short run-in with Paul Roots, the personnel manager, and then got on to the shop floor, having 'signed with great reluctance'. He was led toward the press shop:

It was the start of the big freeze-up in 1962. It was a bitter winter. It was freezing. There was only three walls, or three and a half anyway, up in the press shop with a great tarpaulin sheet over it. Up to the knees in ice it was. Fellas there with snotty noses turning to ice, garbed up in duffle coats, mufflers and all sorts. Well Johnny said, 'Gor blimey: we're not having this.' Eighteen of them were sent over to the press shop so Johnny gets over to the first bloke he sees who looks like he's in charge and says 'Eighteen duffle coats and be quick about it. Eighteen duffle coats or we're not starting work.' Well, Ford's had this fearsome reputation at the time. They were sacking lads left, right and centre. This bloke says to him: 'You can't go round telling me what to do': 'I'm bleeding well telling you,' says Johnny, 'who are *you* anyway – the foreman? – well take me to the *general* foreman.'

John carried on in this vein. He kept a notebook with verbatim notes on who said what about what. He knew the lads who were running the union and he didn't like them. He crossed the branch chairman who 'was a phoney'. For a man of his experience he played his cards very badly wrong. He went around with his chin hanging out and he got taken. Roots called him to the personnel office. The Company was operating with a probationary period that allowed instant dismissal and Mr Jones was told to get his cards.

A bighead to the last was Johnny though. 'No thank you,' he said, 'You can keep them, I've got work to do now, tarra.' He goes on to the section and goes to Milburn [the Branch Chairman]. 'Here Milburn, you phoney, call a meeting quick.' Milburn wouldn't – half of the men weren't in the union anyway – and the next minute Johnny's getting escorted off the premises with a security man on each arm shouting, 'I'll be back. You haven't heard the last of me.' We hadn't either, he came to branch meetings for about a year after that. In fact he nominated Bob Hendo for Chairman. I was sick. I was sick at heart, y'know. John Jones gone y'know. I had visions of being at Ford's with John Jones as steward on my section. Carrying on as we were before, winning everything in sight. I thought 'Bloody hell, this is some place this. This Ford's'.

Johnny Jones left Ford's early on. While he was the only Merseyside 'character' to be shown the door, many less voluble men were given their cards by the Ford Motor Company.

There were blokes getting sacked hand over fist. Y'know blokes who stood up for themselves. There were no incidents because nobody knew. You didn't know a bloke was getting sacked; 'ten hours' notice' they could just say to a bloke 'get your coat on, off you go'. You might hear about it weeks afterwards or somebody might come up to you in a pub and say, 'Our kid was at Ford's. He got the sack and the union didn't do a blind thing about it.' He might even have been on your section. You didn't even know him. You'd never even *seen* him, y'know. He'd started there and he'd had a run-in with the foreman and said 'Look the line's going too fast' or 'I'm not doing tha'' and they'd put 'unsuitable' – finished. I don't know how many there were. We probably exaggerate it. But it was enough to have effect on people who knew how easy it was to get the sack.

The period then was one of struggle. A struggle to get organized in order to deal with a very hard employer and the first part of this struggle had to be with the unions. During the first months of production the Ford management recognized a number of shop stewards – Johnny Jones's 'phonies'. These were not elected and were members of the AUEW and GMWU. Many of these stewards were defeated or replaced, and the local officer of the TGWU had an important role to play in this process. As one of the stewards put it:

When I came here I was in the T&G but I wasn't bothered either way. They were all a bunch of bent bastards as far as I was concerned. I'd been a bit active when I was in Dunlop's – helped to collect the dues and that. They had some great stewards at Dunlop's. People like Stan Pemberton and Johnny Jones ... real heroes they were. So when I got here, put on a section, I asked around for the steward. I eventually found out who he was but when I went up to him he told me that we couldn't talk about the union in the company's time. The management would object he said. So I thought, sod you. He asked me what union I was in and I said 'not yours you bastard'. It was really bad, no organization at all. The foremen were like slave drivers. That's when I went down the Garston Office [of the TGWU] and met Sammy. He gave me a handful of cards and I started distributing them on the section.

The union district secretary was in his forties at the time. He had been a convenor at the Royal Ordnance Factory at a time when Leslie Blakeman was personnel manager. He had been in the job for ten years and had never had anything as big as the Ford Motor Company on his plate before. He saw the opening of the estate to be 'a bit of a challenge I suppose. A big new factory. A chance to get a lot of new members into the organization and establish a strong branch.' The stewards, however, were much more forthcoming in their tales of Sammy Glasstone. One of them put it like this:

The thing about Sammy see is that he's shop steward at heart. His heart is on the shop floor. Even now if you meet him in Transport House and ask him for advice on a case you can *see* his mind working. 'You shouldn't do this, mind,' he says, 'but if I were in your position . . .'

And another:

Sammy Glasstone organized this plant. While all the other bastards were sat on their fat asses Sammy was at the plant. He was there every evening. You could ring him up and ask him to give a meeting and he'd be there. I could never do that. He'd just stand up and talk. Call them fools and bastards if they wouldn't join.

Sammy didn't have a car. He would catch a bus from outside the Garston Office to the Speke roundabout and walk from there to the plant. In the winter he often got drenched.

He'd arrive with water oozing out of him, dripping off the end of his nose and everything. He'd go squelching into meetings laying down the law: 'We're not having this, you're not fucking us about. We're the biggest union in the country; we'll stop the docks.'

Sammy's early activities on the site included walking around the partially completed factory with a ruler in his hand, posing as a building contractor. He would spend his days tapping the ruler into his palm and muttering to every new Ford employee that he met sweeping up, 'Are you in the union yet? There's only one union worth bothering with, mind – the T&G.'

He became part of the furniture in the PTA, more like a steward than a district officer. The management barred him from the works canteen. They insisted on taking him for lunch in the managers' canteen. He didn't want to go: 'Honestly, I'd sooner sit with the lads. I want a plate of chips.' But they insisted. They knew about him plotting and scheming in the corner of the canteen surrounded by a small meeting. The time came in fact for the stewards themselves to ask

Sammy to stay away and not come to the plant so often. Management was becoming used to him. He was called in on almost every case. As a result he was losing his effectiveness and also retarding the development of the stewards' organization. The big guns are often more effective in the background.

If you've got a good district official you should try to make use of him as a threat to management: 'If you do that we'll bring him in and if he comes in you're not just dealing with us you're dealing with the entire T&G organization.' So we asked Sammy to start staying away a bit and he agreed. He said 'Right, you don't have me in so often, you're becoming too dependent on me.'

Sammy, then, was the bureaucrat who wasn't bent. The shop steward at District Office. Through his energies and those of several extremely gifted young men, and with some bending of conventional union behaviour, the TGWU was established as the dominant union in the PTA plant. New stewards were elected but were given no facilities in the plant.

The ball and chain we used to call it. You couldn't come off the job let alone off the section. Everywhere you went you'd have foremen following you around. If you moved off the section for some reason you could hear the jungle drums beating.

Facilities were fought for, gained only to be lost again.

They blew hot and cold for a long time but we wore them down in the end. I think it was Eddie's sacking that marked the turning point. That was their last fling. They've tried to live with us since then.

The sacking of Eddie was an extremely significant event and the story of how the stewards' organization was able to defeat Ford management was told to me on innumerable occasions. The incident took place at a time when the stewards' organization had established itself within the PTA plant.

We were organized then. We weren't a joke any more. We were able to challenge their decisions. We were able to sort the bullies out. You see, people like Paul Roots weren't opposed to the development of a union, as long as the company got a 'fair day's work'. But the production people were bastards. Y'know, cases of men being allocated eighty minutes' work in an hour. Once we got organized and could get past the initial stumbling block of middle management we were finding that we were winning case after case with higher management. In fact we had an inquiry. Somebody came up from Central Department. We thought he was Father Christmas. He agreed with the steward on every case. 'We'll put this right, we'll put that right.'

In implementing the clamp-down at Halewood the production management were breaking even the flimsy agreements reached in the NJNC on shop steward activity. In the first stage of the development of the stewards' committee a level of organization was reached which enabled the workers to take advantage of regularized codes of behaviour that had been agreed by the unions and the Company. To obtain these rights they had to fight plant management and in doing so, by making shop-floor events public, they were able to use senior, national management as allies. It didn't stop there though, because the stewards and the members wanted more than their formal rights. This marked the next phase in the development of the union in the plant.

After we'd won all the 'legitimate' cases we began to challenge the whole bloody system. Not altogether consciously mind you, but we started saying things like 'you can have too much efficiency'. We wouldn't work overtime unless we had twenty-four hours' notice. Things like that. They didn't like that because it meant that they didn't have absolute control of the labour anymore. They had to consult not instruct. And that wasn't their style. They'd have to enter into negotiations about what they were going to do. Before, if you like, we were winning cases because higher management said what we wanted was fair. Then we started saying *to them*, 'All right so its "fair" but we're not fucking having it anyway.' Y'know what does 'fair' mean?

There were lots of things going on. Meetings springing up at all times all over the place. We were organizing weak sections. There was lots of evidence of collective activity. We were putting leaflets out on the floor regularly and they didn't like that. Y'know, saying 'Good morning' to him when we came in in the morning and then writing down what we really thought of them – 'a bunch of conniving bastards'.

The growing militancy in the PTA plant at Halewood took place at a time when conflict was becoming increasingly bitter in the car industry generally. The 'firm line' applied at Dagenham had produced only limited results elsewhere. Strike incidence leaped in 1965 much to the annoyance of the new Labour government. Ministers angrily condemned unofficial strike action and the Prime Minister called a meeting of union officials and employers at Downing Street. The meeting was apparently presented by the Minister of Labour with a virtual ultimatum: either the industry 'puts its own house in order' or the government would feel obliged to take action itself.

As it was, the already existing 'fact-finding commission' was converted into Jack Scamp's Motor Industry Joint Labour Council and the members left determined to sort something out. Ford's moved Boxhall the 'Dagenham hatchet man' to the Halewood PTA and the newly constructed management team decided to have a go. Eddie Roberts was sacked.

Eddie was one of the younger stewards. In 1966 he was twenty-five. He had come to Ford's from the nearby Dunlop factory at the time of the start-up. He had been to grammar school but had to leave without trying his O levels. 'I wish I'd had a chance to have a go at some O levels. Especially Spanish. I used to like Spanish.' He was very bright and very sharp. He was a leading figure in the PTA committee and very popular with the lads. At the time of the sacking incident he was deputy convenor. In 1968 he became the plant convenor.

The sacking of Eddie arose out of a manning dispute on the two-tone section in the paint shop. It was a period of slack demand with low schedules and management had begun to tighten up on the manning in a number of sections. On the Friday day shift Frank, the steward on the two-tone section, had been informed that eight men were to be pulled off the section. 'We were in a bit of a tricky position. They were making a move. It was obvious. They'd already reduced the manning on the trim. The headlining section was calling Mick [the convenor] "Judas". It was all a bit tricky.'

Eddie was working nights. He had the same lift to work as Ronnie Walsh, Frank's opposite number. They discussed the problem and agreed that Ronnie should stay over to meet Frank on the day shift. The two-tone sections on both shifts were strongly opposed to the manning reductions. On the Tuesday night the men were told to 'work or else'. As senior steward on the night shift Eddie was involved in the negotiations. He takes up the story:

Donelly [the convenor] had come back because there was obviously going to be trouble. One of our complaints was that the reduced manning involved a safety problem. It involved a man having to cross *over* the line with an air line. When I said we weren't having that, Evans, the senior foreman, said that it was easy. He decided to show us how easy it was and he fell over. Flat on his arse he was. I was made up. All the lads were doubled up with laughing. Evans wasn't too happy. 'Either start up or go home.' You know, over his shoulder as he was disappearing into the distance.

During the hiatus provided by the disappearance of Evans, Eddie explained the situation to the men who worked on the adjoining section in the enamel booths. He already knew that he could rely upon the backing of his own section of the paint shop, and found that it wasn't difficult to get a promise of support from the enamel booth workers. Meanwhile back on the two-tone section the general foreman

was daring the men to strike. This they did and were followed out of
the gate by the entire paint shop.

A meeting was held in Transport House on the Wednesday to
discuss the situation. At this meeting the strike was unanimously
supported and the reduction in manning strongly opposed. On the
advice of Sammy Glasstone and the convenor, however, the men
agreed to start work on the Thursday morning in order to allow official
negotiations to take place. As a result of these negotiations some small
manning reductions were accepted. More importantly, management
insisted that Eddie should no longer be a steward. 'They wanted to
sack him. They wanted him off the plant. If he stayed on the premises,
they weren't going to have him as a steward.' Eddie explains:

I wasn't involved in the negotiations but Mick and Sammy told me that they
wanted to sack me and that they were generally out to get me. I wasn't too
surprised. We called a stewards' meeting that evening to decide what to do. A
lot of the lads were all for a strike but it was quite clear that Ford's wouldn't
mind a strike. I was against striking. I remember Les Moore saying that they
were 'just egging us on'. It was obvious. It was just like Dagenham in 1962.
They were working to the Dagenham blueprint. Sack a popular steward, get
them out the gates and keep the gates closed on half the bastards. So we decided
not to strike, to do it the *proper way*, to put it in procedure. I went on the sick
and Sammy went in to tell them that I wanted leave of absence.

In this dispute the PTA shop stewards' committee gained an important victory. And with it it broke out of the shadow of Dagenham. It
met a management assault and turned it back with guile rather than
brawn.

The national officials were called in and Kealey of the TGWU and
Baker of the GMWU came to Liverpool. 'It was so blatant, it was
hanging out. Kealey said that he was prepared to go all the way on it.'
Eddie stayed on the sick until his case had been settled. Under
pressure from the national officers the Company agreed to the
reinstatement of Eddie as a steward. But he had to accept a verbal
warning. He had to be disciplined. Eddie, however, was still on the
sick, and he stayed on the sick for several more days. After a number
of letters and telephone calls he agreed to attend a meeting in the plant
to be formally disciplined. The victory became a rout.

It went on for days. 'Mr Roberts, will you *please* come to work to be
disciplined.' 'I'm sorry but I'm not well.' Anyway, I eventually get there and go
into the Plant Manager's office with Billy and Mick. It was like a Broadway act.
I grinned and looked out the window while I got my formal warning.

This then was an important victory. It was a victory for the steward committee, a confirmation of their strategies, and it was also a victory for scouse wit. They were to lose many battles but never their humour; their acute sense of the absurd. The stories of victories that were relished most were those which were deeply imbued with humour.

Mick Donelly figured in most of the stories that involved jokes. His past, like his age, was something of a mystery but as near as I could tell he was about forty-five and had been a seaman and bus driver before coming to Ford's. He'd been a road steward on the buses and became immediately involved in the shop steward organization at Halewood. He had a marvellous, battered face which he could keep completely unmoved as he told stories and played ingenious tricks on people. In the early chaotic days of the plant this was an enormous asset for a militant steward, and Mick *was* a militant. He worked in the paint shop and his job was to sand down the blemishes and bumps on the painted shell. He never did it. He'd pretend to but he never did it – 'they tell you they've got an inspection department ...' Mick, then, was a joker and like most jokers he had a serious side of which he wasn't too certain. While his tricks became the hallmark of the emergent PTA committee, and though they scored many victories through them, you never quite knew where you were with Mick. This was to become a severe problem when he became plant convenor.

Most often Mick played tricks on foremen. He enjoyed confusing them. One of the stewards tells of one of Mick's most famous escapades.

The supervisors were real bastards, see. So what Mick started to do was to play with them. We'd get to a telephone point and he'd ring the foreman. We'd be able to see him like. Mick would ring and say he was somebody fantastic – he'd think of some fantastic names – Dongittering or something from the Service Department. 'We're just testing your phone' he'd say. 'When I tap the receiver I'd like you to count up to ten.' Well, he'd start counting and Mick would say 'Could you speak up please' and he'd start to shout a bit. It would go on until the supervisor was purple in the face. He was for ever doing things like that, Mick.

He played tricks on workers as well. Often they had no purpose, they were just a joke, but occasionally they were used to good effect.

We had a nark on our section once. Everything we did the supervisor knew about it before we did. I thought I knew who it was so I told Mick about it. He'd just been made convenor. 'You leave it to me,' he said, 'where is the little bastard?' Anyway he came down on the section and told this lad that he was the Training Officer on the lookout for likely supervisors. 'I've heard good reports of you,' he said, 'Tell me, what do you think of the way things are run on this section?' Well this lad went on about how the supervisor was much too lax and how the other blokes didn't take the job seriously enough, and how the shop steward had too much power. Mick was there see, egging him on. I don't know how he kept a straight face but he said to this lad: 'Listen, you're the sort of chap we're looking for. You've supervisor material. So don't just sit quietly by and let these things carry on. Next time something like this happens I want you to stand up against it.'

Occasionally though his jokes were just plain disruptive like the one he played on Eddie. This one is worth telling because it reveals clearly what the stewards made of the full-time officers of the union. John, a close friend of Eddie and a senior steward, tells the story:

It happened right at the beginning I suppose. None of us had been here that long. Eddie had taken a bundle of cards into the Garston Office, and had left them with a note asking for them to be stamped and returned to him. Mick went into the office and saw this note. I think he thought Eddie was being a bit big-headed or something – I can't always tell what Mick thinks – but anyway he wrote Eddie a letter on T&G notepaper signing himself something weird as usual and as District Officer of the union. Mr Esmereldar. that was it, that's what he signed himself. I don't know how he thought that one up. Anyway this note gives Eddie a bit of a ticking off. 'How dare he leave a pile of cards' and all this bollocks. Eddie was taken in. While he was reading it Mick was going on 'The bastard. I know him, little short fat bastard with glasses.' There are so many of them up there we didn't know most of them from Adam. So Eddie wrote back to this Mr What's-his-name telling him that the union officers were supposed to serve the members and that while stewards were slogging their guts out the likes of him were sat on their fat asses. Anyway Mick intercepted the letter somehow – I think in fact he said he'd deliver it for him. Then he wrote back to Eddie: 'You talk about recruiting members. I'll have you know young man that in the days when I was a lay member of this union I unionized the entire candle-wick dipping industry of the Midlands. I recruited eighteen candle-wick dippers to the cause.' Just like the bastards write, you know. Mick could take people off pretty good. Well when Eddie read this he went bloody stone mad. He was in the canteen. 'Look at this' he shouted. He was banging his fist on the table. 'I'm not having this. I'll get the bastard for this.'

I think Mick took it a bit too far in fact. But nobody could tell Eddie then, he was raving. He wrote a long letter to the Regional Secretary, Harry Wall. He didn't know what the hell to make of it. Sammy explained that it was just us lot fooling around.

Eddie was anything but a fool. It wasn't stupidity that allowed him to be taken in by the candle-wick dipping story. Rather it was a developed understanding of what 'the bureaucrats' were like. It was just possible that a Mr Esmereldar was a District Officer. It was possible that some 'arrogant bastard' who knew nothing about a car factory could be in a position of power in Transport House. This story, like the others, demonstrates quite vividly an important element within the ideology of the shop steward committee of the PTA at Halewood. The ideology was based upon the fact that the Ford Motor Company and the union bureaucrats had between them severely exploited the workers on the shop floor. The understanding of this exploitation was essentially simple and rooted in the factory situation: in order to prevent exploitation you develop an organization at the shop-floor level. The further away from the shop floor you moved the greater was the possibility of becoming bent. The committee had no clearly developed conception of politics. In 1964 it had contributed to the Labour Party's election fund but by 1966 it had regretted it. Essentially the stewards were suspicious of politics and politicians. In 1967 the committee was avowedly anti-political. Politics were seen to get in the way of the job. Instead of politics it had humour. The ideology of the PTA committee was essentially factory based. It was opposed to the bosses and the bureaucrats, it was wary of the political sects. What it represented at the time was a highly developed awareness of the nature of conflicts within the factory situation – on the shop floor – and comedy played a crucial part in this awareness.

But we should be wary of drawing a crude distinction between a political and a non-political understanding of the world. Although the Halewood stewards were suspicious of both politics and politicians they cannot be termed *apolitical*. Politics is basically about power. About who does what to whom. Viewed in this way it is obvious that these men had quite a developed political understanding. The boundary of this politics, however, was the factory floor. It knew about the bosses and the bureaucrats. About exploitation and being screwed. And this knowledge manifested itself in periods of sustained militancy. But it was a politics that was not easily transferable to other areas of class exploitation and power.

While the ideology of the committee was essentially rooted within the factory it cannot be seen as a simple, 'direct' reflection of experience within the PTA. Although it may often *appear* to be not the case, people *do* learn from the past, and the experience of the working class in Merseyside provided a basic core to the understanding which the stewards developed of work and trade unionism within the plant. More specifically, however, they had learned from the mistakes of the shop stewards at Dagenham. The Dagenham committee was destroyed in 1962 by a coalition of management and the union bureaucracy.

While the committee had developed a strong unofficial base within the plants this base had proved vulnerable. In understanding this vulnerability the Halewood stewards argued that the politics of the Communist Party had prevented the stewards from developing a flexibility in their relations with both management and the union bureaucracies. As such the nature of 'unofficial unionism' which they developed at Halewood was quite different from the Dagenham model. In particular it demonstrated a conscious ambivalence toward the bureaucrats. The bureaucrats may be bent but they could be used. The victory with Eddie's sacking was seen to demonstrate, above all else, a victory for this approach.

The business of manufacture

Industry is organized to make profit. Most people accept this as a fact, and recognize that the more profit their company makes the better chance it has of providing a good standard of living and security for its employees and their families. This is not only because everybody's future earnings depend on the Company continuing to make a profit, but because a good profit encourages more investment – a good safeguard for the future.

A look at profits in our own business shows that they are closely linked to how much use we make of plant and equipment. This is because it takes a lot of expensive space and plant to make our products and the more we make with the same resources the more profit we get. In fact, unless we are building at a good rate we are not even paying our way – on a two shift system without overtime our plants are standing idle for a third of the day.

From *Two Heads are Better than One*: Ford Motor Company Department of Labour Relations (pamphlet for employees, 1967)

The people

Plant is only one of the factors, however. In Britain today, people are, by and large, enjoying a good standard of living and compared with many countries wages are high (although, of course, not as high as most people would like). Human resources, however, are scarce and expensive and therefore it makes sense to see that they are fully used and not misused. Just as it does not make sense to build more plants before we fully use the ones we have, neither does it make sense to keep on hiring men when some of those we have cannot make a full contribution because of bad organization or working habits. There are two ways, therefore, in which a company can increase its efficiency:

1. By better use of plant.
2. By better use of people.

One way to achieve these aims is to work plant and equipment more hours either by adding hours on to existing shifts, i.e. overtime or by working different shifts, or by a combination of both. Not everybody understands the reasons behind this.

From *Two Heads are Better than One*: Ford Motor Company Department of Labour Relations (pamphlet for employees, 1967)

4 Eldorado

Ford began operating in Liverpool toward the end of 1962. 'This place was a bit of an Eldorado at the time,' said one of the stewards. 'Everybody wanted to come here. They were coming here from all over Lancashire. Y'know expecting the pavements in the press shop to be lined with gold.' Entry into Eldorado, however, was limited. Merseyside and Lancashire was a depressed area. Traditional industries were in decline. Unemployment figures were high and wages were low. Everybody wanted to go to Ford's but not everybody was allowed in. Ford's had the pick of the labour market, and the Company followed a recruitment policy which was consistent with its aim of obtaining a trouble-free plant on Merseyside. It aimed to recruit from 'the cream of the labour market' and although the rate of pay it offered was lower than at Dagenham and significantly lower than the rates operating in the Midlands, the state of the labour market on Merseyside made it high enough to serve the Company's purpose. Family men with commitments came first. Stable men who were tied down with debt and responsibility were given priority. Men under twenty were formally barred and there was little welcome in Halewood for men off the dock or the buildings. Seamen weren't very high up the list either. Neither were the unemployed. Two of the personnel officers on the plant at the time have recounted their experiences of recruitment. They explain that they were on the lookout for adaptable men from whom years of 'service' could be expected. Eighty-nine per cent of the earliest recruits were aged between twenty and forty. Only 14 per cent of these early Halewood workers came to the factory off the dole and 'it could reasonably be supposed' that the recruiting officers 'regarded the unemployed with some element of suspicion' (Goodman and Samuel, 1966, p. 358).

The Ford Motor Company was after 'green labour'. Something over 60 per cent of its first recruits were entirely new to factory work. They never knew what hit them. A steward recollects that 'they were a really green bunch of lads. Not a typical Merseyside labour force at all. Y'know, they weren't objecting or complaining. They were trying to

do the job. I'm not decrying those lads. They came here from all over –
Wigan, Widnes, everywhere. They tried to do the job but the job just
couldn't be done. Not the way Ford's wanted it.' The recruitment
policy ran into difficulties because the recruited labour wasn't staying
at Halewood The stable men were moving on. They weren't used to
factories, let alone the Ford assembly line, and the pay wasn't that
good. By 1965 enough of them had left for the age requirement to be
dropped to eighteen. Turnover rates were high and continued to be so
throughout the 1960s. The story that management and workers told
most often recounts how men arrive at the plant for their first shift, see
the job and ask for their cards. In 1966 the PTA plant lost 1140 manual
employees out of a total labour force of 3200. The number declined to
about 800 in 1967 but in 1968 it was 1160 and in 1969 it was 1800. As a
result of men voting with their feet the Company recruitment policy
foundered. All they were left with was a watchful eye for the militant
and the intelligent. As one personnel officer put it: 'Anyone who puts
an intelligent man on the sort of job that we've got here is asking for
trouble. We've had it as well. Whoever recruited intelligent blokes like
Roberts and Flaherty want their arses kicking. Intelligent blokes are
bound to get militant if you stick them on the trim line.' Apart from
this they'd take all comers. One of this personnel man's colleagues
argued that 'there's only one way to recruit men in this industry. You
don't want to bother with aptitude tests and interviews. If you want 200
men just send down the labour for 400. Get them to come to the gates
for 9.00 and let them in at 10.00. That's how to recruit men in this
industry.'

Over 80 per cent of the manual jobs in an assembly plant contribute
to the productive monotony of the assembly line. In 1967 the men who
performed these jobs were called operatives, classified as semi-skilled
and paid an average of 8/9d (44p) per hour. For a forty-hour week, on
days, they earned £17 10s. They worked a night shift fortnightly about,
and were paid time and a third for doing so. All the men in the sample
of members were assembly-line workers. They, like men in the PTA
generally, came to Ford's with a diverse work experience. They had
found their previous employment across a wide range of semi-skilled
and unskilled jobs in the area. Many of them had 'moved around a bit',
always looking for somewhere better. Seventeen of the stewards and
eighteen of the members had had three or more jobs in the ten years
that preceded their employment at the car plant. They had been lorry
drivers, hod carriers, seamen, dockers, telephone engineers and
butchers. In the main they were young – all had been under forty when

recruited – and were married with young children. They came in search of Eldorado and in 1967 at least they were still helping to make motor cars in the PTA plant at Halewood.

Often it is quite inappropriate to talk of 'car workers' in the same way as one would talk of 'miners', for many of them do not consider themselves to be 'car workers' in that sense. They see themselves more as workers who *happen* to be working in a car plant. They've done other jobs in the past and they expect to do others in the future. They don't want to grow old on the line. They work in a car plant because of the money: 'Money and a five day week' was the stock response to the question 'Why Ford's?' Occasionally the size of the plant was mentioned, together with the general idea that work in a car plant would be a bit different, a bit interesting and afforded the chance to get on. In the main, though, it was the money – thirty-two of the stewards and forty of the members mentioned this as one of their main reasons for coming to the plant. They came to Ford's because they needed to make a living and there were limited opportunities for doing that on Merseyside. For many people Ford's move to Halewood seemed like the big chance. As one man explained:

> You see I'm a labourer, just a labourer. When all is said and done all I can do is labour. That's all I can sell, isn't it? What's 'ideal' for me? You know what you are and you've got to make the most of it. It's a good job here really. The conditions here are good compared with the buildings. You appreciate that. When I married the wife first we lived with her people in this fucking great house. It was freezing in the mornings. I used to look forward to coming to work, to go to the toilet and have a warm wash. I used to look forward to coming to work. This is a hard company. There's no doubt about that. But you appreciate things like that.

When I asked people how Ford compared with an 'ideal firm', it became clear that for many workers the Ford Motor Company was, in 1967, the nearest things to an 'ideal firm' that they had come across on Merseyside. A worker on the trim line made this explicit when he said 'If I tell you that this is the most ideal firm I've worked for, you can picture the others. Compared with the alternatives this *is* ideal.' Many of the stewards would have agreed with this, nevertheless they were highly critical of the Company and the wage rates paid to Ford workers. While the majority of the workers I interviewed based their evaluation of the firm upon their own immediate experience of the labour market on Merseyside, the stewards consistently tended to take a wider view. Frequently they based their evaluation of wage rates upon what they felt the company could *afford* to pay, supporting their arguments by reference to profits and the rates paid by other motor manufacturers in the Midlands. This wider awareness, combined with their experiences of low rates and a rampant management during the start-up period at Halewood, crystallized in a sophisticated understanding of how wage rates were established and changed.

The stewards considered that all the good things offered to workers at the Ford Motor Company had had to be fought for. They were seen as the fruits of trade union organization and struggle rather than grace and favour of an ideal employer. Many of the stewards made some reference to the early days of the plant and made it clear that certain lessons had to be learned from this experience. Eric put it like this:

> What we've got we've fought for; and fought hard at that. When I came here first we were worked really hard and if you had a complaint you couldn't get a steward. Now a man can get a steward pretty quickly. It took a lot of hard work. The rate was bad and the job was bad...People have got short memories though, and new ones come. They see the job now and they think 'this isn't so bad'. They forget that it wasn't always like this. We *earned* it like it is and if we don't watch out with this Company we'll be back where we started.

Involvement in the shop stewards' committee and identification with its aims clearly affected the thinking of the shop stewards at Halewood. In particular it affected their understanding of trade unionism and the function of management within the factory, and this in its turn affected their relationship with their members and fellow workmates. While the past can be seen to have structured the present in the way that it provided the steward with a 'pragmatic charter' for his everyday activities in the plant, such charters are invariably questioned and need defending in a complex society. Part of the process of being a steward at Halewood involved argument with the members over the *correct* interpretation of the present. There is no easy, straightforward way of dealing with the fact that shop-floor union activism differentiates the steward from the mass of the membership. The nature of the differentiation will vary from situation to situation. What is clear, however, is that at Halewood in the 1960s involvement in the early struggles in the plant, together with day-to-day contact with events throughout the plant, created within the shop steward committee a more radical critique of the Ford Motor Company than existed generally within the factory. This was revealed most clearly in the way the stewards and their members understand the Ford management.

*

The motor industry is a highly competitive industry. Large companies with excess capacity in their plants compete with each other across a wide range of models. Computerization, technological sophistication, increased productivity, regular changes of models and increasing competition have been acute features of the British motor industry since World War Two. A visit to the office of a production manager in a car plant vividly highlights the consequences of these changes. The walls are covered with charts – output, labour costs, projections – everywhere you look. They dominate the consciousness of the manager and his aides. They point them out to you as one would a particular piece of countryside. At one point during my stay in the plant I went into the trim assembly department with a personnel officer in the hope of obtaining the release of some workers off the job for a talk. We had to meet the production manager. 'Could we possibly have about ten operatives for a short while?' – 'Fuck off' – 'But be reasonable. I'd only want them for about half an hour' – 'Half an hour, ten men, that's five hours, do you know how many cars that is . . . How much that will cost me? Get me a note for five hours from the works manager and you can have them. Otherwise fuck off.' Time is money and money is everything in a car plant. The cars take shape along an assembly line. Over the length of the line some 16,000 components are screwed, stuck or spot-welded together. Each of·these components has to be delivered to the assembly plant, stored and allocated to the various assembling points along the line. Spatial and budgeting constraints prevent large stores being kept. Time and space are money. Unexpected interference with supplies will cause havoc in no time. Model changes don't help much either, for this means a complete retooling of the plant and a·redefinition and·redistribution of work tasks. Also it means 'teething problems'.

If a car plant is about money a plant manager's job is about pressure. In him complicated administrative and technical tasks coexist with market pressures, deadline dates and the like. It's not surprising that Turner should suggest that these managers often welcome, if not provoke, strikes which can get them off the hook of a missed output target (see Turner, Clack and Roberts, 1967). There is frequent evidence in a car plant of the pressure that production management works under. At Halewood, for example, the three plants formed an integrated technological unit. This integration was not reflected in accountancy practices. The manager of the trim assembly department bought painted body shells from the manager of the paint shop who had previously bought the shell from the manager of the body plant.

Wrangles and stand up rows were not uncommon along the frontiers of the departments. 'Take the fucking things back. I'm not having crap like that. Look at that fucking finish. I'm not having that.' The lads watched, waited for their foreman to get a bollocking and kept their eye on their steward.

The production managers are the hard heads. For them money is success, the difference between failure and success lying in the extra car or two that they can squeeze out of the lads. They're not daft. They know this. They are the hard heads, the supporters of the 'firm line'. Often they come into conflict with 'Personnel'. The history of the Halewood estate in fact is one in which power ebbs and flows between these two managerial power groups. The 'firm line' doesn't always work. While the personnel manager's job is less easily appraised in terms of money, he too is out to make his name. While I was at the PTA I bumped into a man I'd met in the Regional Headquarters of the Electricity Generating Board. He was a personnel officer in the MSB plant. He'd come there 'for the experience because there's no place like a car plant for negotiating experience. You get as much experience in this place in a year as you'd get in a lifetime in the Electricity Board.' A successful negotiation is a feather in the cap and a failure can be put down to experience.

All plant managers have something in common. Unless they're on the scrap-heap they're looking upward. In the car industry to look up is to look out. To be on the move from plant to plant. A success here, a killing there, and you're near the top of the tree. The Company's management training scheme is on the lookout for extroverts and individualists – polite parlance for 'big heads'. They take them on, build them up and not infrequently cut them down, for with competition and technical change comes organizational change. You may be left and overlooked, but that may be preferable to finding that your job no longer exists. British Leyland is still in the throes of such rationalization. Ford went through it all in the late 1960s. In 1967 brick walls started appearing across offices in the administration block at Halewood. Everything was to be changed. A new administrative structure left several middle managers with a salary but no 'function'. 'They should give you longer than two years' one said. He had tears in his eyes. 'If you've got a family they should give you more than two years. I thought I'd be settled for a bit here. It's not right. It's...' The young, ambitious graduate smiled in reply and said: 'You've got to keep moving. It's no good standing still.' He'd move all right. What else could he do?

> **Sixty per cent of the graduates recruited by the Ford Motor Company in 1966 had left the Company by 1971**
>
> Whilst these figures appear to be high, by comparison with British Industry as a whole we know that we have a lower than average termination rate for graduates within the first years of their employment.
>
> There are various reasons why people leave the Company. Some decide that Industry is not for them and return to the academic life, either to pursue postgraduate studies or to go into lecturing or teaching. Others leave to take jobs of increased responsibility in a smaller company or to move into a consultancy, both of which we would regard as a reflection of the excellent experience they have obtained within the Company.
>
> From *Graduates in Ford*, Ford Motor Company (recruitment pamphlet, 1971)

Pressure and strain is structured into the very heart of a car plant. Structured into a game in which there are no real winners. In this world negotiations were often a battle, occasionally a subtle psychological war. Out of this the stewards came to an understanding of the role of management in the plant and the way to relate to managers as individuals. Neither the stewards nor the workers interviewed thought that the Ford Motor Company rated highly as a 'considerate employer'. Only three of the stewards considered that the Company was even 'average' in this respect, while thirty of the sample of members considered the firm to be no better than average. Even its strongest supporter considered the Company to be a hard employer who was obsessed with production. The stewards, however, were vehement in their criticisms of the way the Company's management treated the workers. An indication of the strength of this feeling is shown by the fact that twenty-eight of the stewards considered that it was the attitude of the management that was most in need of change in the Company. Some of their comments illustrate this:

They treat the labour as machinery here. The Personnel Department just don't exist. In many cases they are just *cruel*. All they're concerned with is production problems. It's production, production all the time with them.

They go on about getting people to cooperate. To spend their lives here and make a go of things and all that bullshit. But they don't even assist in making it bearable.

You're just counted as a number here. Treated like a lot of robots. You could be in desperate trouble and they wouldn't help you.

Several of the stewards made explicit the fact that their criticism of management derived from their experiences as stewards:

> The supervisors here are just not trained in the right attitudes. That's why we're young. We've got to be to take it. We're young and we're militant. Not militant in that we take the blokes outside the gate – but in sticking up for them against the foreman. Standing up for their rights.

> As a shop steward I see the main problem to be the centralization of power on both the management and trade union side. This is bad for the operator as well because both the steward and the operator get frustrated when things get taken above their heads. You need to have much more autonomy for shop-floor unionism.

> I've found that with management it's always the case of passing the buck. They're all *afraid* to make a decision in case they drop a goolie. If anything goes wrong they don't want to know. They don't want to find out what or why they just want a scapegoat. Always find someone to blame.

In their discussion of plant management the stewards continually made reference to the fact that an unpleasant job was often made intolerable by management's self-interested concern for production and their own careers. A concern which rode over any consideration for or obligation towards the workers. Management, as far as the stewards could see, were out for themselves. Tied in with this is the idea that management aren't their own masters anyway, that all the important decisions are taken at Warley, or Detroit, and that plant management simply wants to keep its nose clean and get a good name. These two themes crop up continually, and can be seen as elements within what might be called a working-class *factory consciousness*.

The history of British trade unionism is built on various levels of factory class-consciousness. Trade unionism and workshop organization are, and always have been, a direct response to economic forces. A response to a world where goods are exchanged as commodities on an open market; where workers have nothing to sell but their labour power and where this too is bought and sold on the market. A factory class-consciousness grew out of this; it understands class relationships in terms of their direct manifestation in conflict between the bosses and the workers within the factory. It is rooted in the workplace where struggles are fought over the control of the job and the 'rights' of managers and workers. In as much as it concerns itself with exploitation and power it contains definite political elements. But it is a politics of the factory. Implicitly tied up with the day-to-day battle with the boss. Factory class-consciousness finds its historical antecedent in syndicalism – the idea of workers' control of the factories, adhered to most strongly by skilled workers – which was most developed in Britain in the shop steward movement that occurred during and after World War One. While this was the high-water mark of this tradition, strong elements of it still permeate the British working class. In its least developed form it is revealed in sporadic bloody-mindedness and 'malingering' – the 'fuck 'em' attitude that most managers are familiar with and find distasteful. The underlying structure of this view is not radically different from that which underpinned the consciousness of the stewards at Halewood. Their class consciousness can be seen as a higher development inasmuch as they had worked out a sophisticated understanding of how they were exploited in the factory and how they could best combat management there. Not infrequently this involved them in bloody-mindedness.

Particular features of the PTA plant at Halewood during the 1960s contributed to a heightened development of class awareness in this plant. All of the stewards and each of the forty-three members I interviewed felt that if management were given the chance they would 'put one over on the workers'. This view was either supported by the simple statement, 'They've *done* it', or by the claim that all managers were the same in this respect. One paint-shop worker put it this way:

> Well it's the same everywhere really isn't it? That's what management is for really isn't it?...to get as much off you as they can. To get away with things like. This lot here is probably a bit worse than most, mind. The pressures are greater here.

In the interview I asked the stewards and members whether or not they agreed with a series of statements about management. What became clear was a consistently critical attitude towards management amongst the shop stewards. A clear majority of these men felt that management was paid too much; that although they understood the problems faced by the workers, they were not prepared to do anything about them, that they were mainly concerned with efficiency, and that they wouldn't be prepared to assist the workers even if they had a clear opportunity to do so. These views were expressed firmly and consistently and reflected the development of a clear and sophisticated understanding of the role of management within the factory. In comparison with this, the responses of their membership were markedly uncertain and even confused. To take one example: I asked whether people thought that management would assist the workers if they were given the opportunity to do so. Three quarters of the workers were at least prepared to give them the benefit of the doubt, whereas twenty-four of the stewards were adamant in their judgement that Ford management would *never* do it. To an important extent this difference can be seen as a *consequence* of trade union activity. The stewards had had much closer contact with managers, and justified their scepticism by detailed reference to incidents where they felt that management had had an opportunity to assist the workers at little or no cost to themselves but had failed to make use of it. One said:

They've had golden opportunities here to help the lads and they've done nothing. Just take that Blue Book. That Blue Book is just a licence to rob. Whoever signed that for us ought to be shot. This Company thinks it's so powerful that it can change the clock. On a Bank Holiday the lads have to come in for the night shift – that's for a start like – but then they don't get paid the time and a half for the morning that they're working during the Bank Holiday. No. The Ford Motor Company says that the Bank Holiday starts at seven o'clock in the fucking morning. It's OK for them. We spend half the weekend in bed.

And another:

They've *always* got opportunities but they never help the lads. Even when the opportunity isn't obvious they could make the opportunity if they wanted to. You should see them move and manipulate when they want something for themselves. They forget there's rules then...when production is threatened.

What would be a good example? Well just take an easy one – holidays. We get a problem with this every year. What we try to do before the holidays is to arrange so that the lads on nights work a 'lieu shift' instead of the Friday shift. You want to get off perhaps on the Saturday and you're knackered after a night in this place. This year they said 'all right work a "lieu shift"' – they want to arrange it as much as us, you see, because they know half the lads won't turn in on the Friday anyway – that's the only reason they consider it at all – 'but you'll have to work the Sunday previous'. Well, we said 'what's wrong with Saturday?' – they wanted the lads to work for *single time* on the Sunday you see. And they replied 'you'll work when we say you work'. They had ample opportunity to show some good-will to the lads there. The lads told them to stick it and no one came in on the Saturday, Sunday or Friday.

You get a lot of things, a lot of little things, when everything would be so much easier if they'd bend a bit. But they won't. I don't know what it is. I think they just don't trust the lads. But the lads are OK if you treat them all right.

These two quotations are interesting in the light of arguments over the 'instrumentality' of the new 'affluent' sector of the British working class. Some sociologists have maintained, for example, that this sector of the working class, during the 1960s, became increasingly concerned about money to the neglect of 'traditional' solidarity with their workmates. While these responses appear superficially to be indicative of some form of 'pure' instrumentalism, a concern for money and nothing else, it should be noted that, for the stewards, the question of premium payments was a moral question. One of them said: 'I think it's morally wrong to ask a man to work overtime, nights and weekends, it's even more wrong to ask him to work it without a premium payment and it's a crime if that man accepts. Because it's wrong, morally wrong...' If you are going to sell yourself you should at least attempt to have *some* say in the terms. Others took this further.

Well, let's get this straight. I don't want nothing from this Company. I don't ask for no favours. If they want to be nasty that suits me. You know where you are then. They're just a bunch of crooks and we're going to stop them doing too much thieving. So I don't want any handouts. It's just that I think they're stupid that's all. I don't think they ought to be nice to us, I don't even want them to be nice to us, but you can't help thinking how fucking stupid they are. We have a great time with them. But seriously you get it all the time. The job could be run twice as good, with everybody having a better time and *more* work getting done if it were more flexible. All the supervisors here, see, are shit-scared. They've got a big book in their office and if it isn't in there it can't be done. If it isn't in Mr Ford's book they've never heard of it, it can't happen and they don't want to know. Now as I say that suits me. It's not my job to run the section.

The men who came to Halewood to work for Ford came from diverse employment backgrounds yet brought broadly similar expectations to the plant. In this respect the stewards were in no way different from the sample of members. Their direct involvement in the early struggles with management in the plant produced within the committee a critical understanding of the function of management at Ford, and this understanding was reinforced by their day-to-day contact with management and with each other. The collective involvement of the stewards in building an organization and struggling with management produced a committee with a coherent ideology – a highly developed awareness of the class structure in the factory. It is in its coherence that this ideology differs from the understanding arrived at by stewards in many other plants and by the membership as a whole in the Halewood plant. And their critique of management can be seen to demonstrate this awareness. It was a central pivot within the ideology of the stewards' committee.

Since the war sociologists have taken it into their heads to interview workers and ask them whether or not they consider the factory to be like 'a football team'. Affirmative answers have been taken as an indication of a lack of class consciousness. This, however, misses the fundamental point about capitalist production. It isn't an either/or question of being like a football team *or* being like two opposing camps. Factory production involves *both*. Because production has a social basis the factory can obviously be seen, at some level, as a collectivity with management operating in a coordinating role. The contradiction of factory production, and the source of contradictory elements within class consciousness, is rooted in the fact that the exploitation of workers is achieved through collective, coordinated activities within both the factory and society generally. Frequently the PTA stewards attempted to resolve this contradiction in moral terms.

The stewards' critique of management can be presented in terms of two dimensions. The one structural, which places the action of management within the structure of the large capitalist corporation; the other moral, which involves a criticism of the action management takes in the plant and a moral judgement of the managers as men. The last quotation (on page 111) illustrates the tension between these two aspects of the critique. Management is there to make profit, therefore you expect them to be concerned about efficiency and the like; you don't expect them to be considerate to the lads, in fact, it might make things more complicated if they were. Nevertheless they *should* treat the lads better – if only because the lads would be that bit more cooperative if treated decently.

Car plants are about profit and pressure and so is plant management. A perpetual struggle to reduce costs by increasing the rate of output. Keep the line going continuously! There is an inevitable conflict on the shop floor of a car plant. This is one of the facts of life, something the shop steward has to live with. It can push him along the road to militancy or stifle his spirit – because this is the guts of it; the inevitability of struggle, day in, day out. To see this, accept it and carry on is to expose fundamental questions about the structure of relations within the plant and within society generally. This can lead to an understanding of management as mere pawns in the game, victims of forces that they cannot adequately control or understand. Bill McGuire put it like this:

Well it's a bit difficult to work it out actually. I've thought about it a lot. With some of them it's easy because they're bastards; they're not all like that though. Some of them are quite nice blokes who believe in the Ford Motor Company. They do you know. Some of them believe all the shit that's given them.

I don't see myself being any better than them *as a man*. It's just the situation that they're in. They've just got to make a profit or they get the sack. It's as easy

---

Revised nightshift hours

As you all know, the most recent attempt to improve the conditions of the nightshift workers has been our application to Management that for the period that overtime is not being worked on nights you should only have to work nine nightshifts instead of the ten each fortnight; production time to be made up by one hour of overtime being attached to eight of the shifts worked. This request seemed to be met by local management with a not unreasonable response, and it was clear to your JWC Members that some Managers were openly in favour of what is a perfectly legitimate and logical submission by us. However, at the time of writing, our request has been turned down after having been referred to 'Central Staff'. Again our Managers here at Halewood have demonstrated their ineffectiveness and their inability to truly negotiate with us. The reasons given to us for the rejection have not been accepted by us as valid, and have the usual lame ring of feeble excuses about them. We now await a meeting with higher management in the hope that common sense will prevail, and for once Ford Management can demonstrate that they do have the wisdom to manage and respond to the reasonable wishes of their employees . . . We are sceptical.

From *PTA Voice* 1970

---

as that. They've got to screw the blokes or they get screwed. That's the way it is . . .

But trade unionism cannot resolve this problem, for trade union activity in itself is manifestly incapable of altering the entire *raison d'être* of the capitalist enterprise. The activity of the steward stems from a much less complex concern – from the need to obtain at least some control over the decisions that management make. To obtain at least some slight reform of the system of control that operates within the factory. The structural criticism is given strength by a moral criticism. It may be inevitable that the blokes get screwed but this doesn't make it right. Screwing people is wrong and it must be challenged. Management may be pawns, they may be just doing their job, they may be nice blokes, but by challenging the political rights of workers they make themselves morally culpable. It is by this means that the stewards come to activism. It is this which gives force to the ideology of trade unionism and the idea of trade union principles. Johnny Craig said:

Well it's like this you see Huw, a lot of things that management do I consider to be morally wrong. I fight Ford's because of this. Take dismissals – we'll *always* fight a dismissal. I believe that when a man is about to be sacked – his livelihood taken off him; a man with kids say – then everything ought to be brought into account. I had a number of dismissal cases last week, blokes who'd been late over the last month – they'd already had their final warnings like. Now as far as Ford's go – you know the disciplinary procedure they've got? – well as far as they're concerned when a bloke's had a final warning he's had it if he sets a foot wrong. That was it you see, I was called in and they just assume six dismissals as if there was nothing to be said. I think that's wrong. I think it's wrong to just sack a man no matter what he's done. We've had terrible weather this past month – ice, fog and everything. I said to Obbart – 'You look at the records of some of the best timekeepers in this plant over the past month – look at mine, look at Eddie Roberts's – and they'll be as bad as these lads.' Oh it had been really bad. It took me three hours to get to the plant one morning. It had been murder getting in. Anyway I only got one lad off, the other five got the sack. It makes me sick that not being able to get a lad off. You see what I mean. Those lads shouldn't have been sacked but it didn't matter much to Ford's. It just goes on their turnover rate.

Maybe the Company had to make a profit. Maybe that was the way things were in the world, and management had its own problems but it was, nevertheless, bloody hard for the lads on the line. The working class. The idea that workers and managers belong to different classes and as a result have different loyalties and understandings is central here. Unlike managers, workers have to get up at half past five in the morning, catch buses or wait on the corner for their lift. Getting to work is, for them, often a struggle and the stewards understand these struggles because they experience them themselves.

The plant then can be seen, and was seen by most of the stewards, as an arena of limited class conflict. A shop stewards' committee which had developed out of the conflicts within the PTA plant was held together by a sophisticated factory class-consciousness. A consciousness which told them that management was on the other side and had to be opposed by the lads. This understanding also revealed management as pawns in the profit game, and here was the difficulty. To know that you are involved in an inevitable economic conflict, a perpetual day-to-day struggle with the boss can take you so far. There comes a point when it brutalizes you. Many stewards balked long before this, weighed down by the contradiction that management may be on the other side but they are human 'like us'. These stewards just didn't have the stomach for confrontation after confrontation, slanging match after slanging match. They were too nice, too soft, they lacked, as one of them put it, 'the killer instinct'. At certain times in a car plant, however, a steward who lacks such instincts gets into severe difficulties. A humanitarian act in the office can have adverse consequences for the steward's membership. Management may be pawns, but in a car plant they're paid to be lethal pawns. One of the stewards said: 'If you've got one of them down, he's bleeding and everything, there's just no point in going over to help him up because as soon as he's back on his feet he's going to start hitting you.'

To take an extreme case. One of the middle managers at Halewood had been worn down by his career with the Ford Motor Company and was receiving regular psychiatric treatment. The stewards knew this: 'He was a nerve case, Ted. He used to go off every month to get his shock treatment. He'd be right as rain when he came back, but in a couple of weeks he'd be shaking again.' This man occupied an important position within the negotiating procedure. If the stewards failed to obtain an agreement in their negotiation with him the problem would formally have to be referred to the national committee, which would take time without guarantee of success. Ted Bates (a pseudonym) was at the time a key man in the negotiations set-up at Halewood. Management often uses procedures as stalling devices. At Halewood the stalling devices were quite complex. Fall guys would be set up to block demands for a period of time. Supervisors were regularly used as fall guys, so was Ted Bates. The shop stewards' convenor and the district officer had developed an understanding with Ted Bates's superior – Goodman (another pseudonym). Although not formally in the procedure Goodman wanted to act as a backstop. If all else failed his door would always be open to the convenor. The convenor had as a right something which few middle managers were confident of. He could see Goodman whenever he wanted to. Goodman had specifically asked him to see him if a problem cropped up which seemed likely to stop the plant. Both the convenor and the district officer knew that they had immediate recourse to a senior manager, outside the formal procedure, and they also knew that Goodman used Bates as a fall guy.

It didn't happen once you know it happened very often. It was a regular occurrence. Ted was all right. If it was something within his domain you'd get a decent decision out of him. Regularly though we bloody well knew that he had no power in the situation and that he'd been sent in by Goodman to sort us out. 'I can assure you,' he used to say, 'I can assure you that I have complete management backing on this item and the answer is no.' It was all pretty despicable really in human terms because he had been used so blatantly. We'd say all right we'll go and see Goodman. 'I'm not sure if Mr Goodman will see you.' 'He'll see us Ted, tell him we're coming.' It was really sick because we'd go out of this office along the corridor into Goodman's luxurious suite and we'd get what we wanted. Ted would be there eyes standing out of his head, almost crying.

How did Goodman justify all this to Bates?

I don't know. He'd probably say something like, 'What's the matter, Ted? We're paying you a good salary, aren't we? We're making motors aren't we? Quality's all right isn't it? We've got to placate these bastards. Go on back to your cage.' And off he'd go for his shock treatment. Strapped to the battery again.

Some stewards wouldn't be able to cope with this, they wouldn't have the stomach. But what should a steward do under such circumstances? Humanitarian considerations might lead him to go easy, take Ted's word for it, let the issue pass over or refer it to the NJNC. But where does this leave the lads on the line, the subjects of the dispute? This is the crucial point. Managers negotiate with stewards and union officials about the lives of other people, people not directly involved in the face-to-face negotiation. Men who regularly negotiate with each other get to know each other and develop a certain amount of give and take with each other. They come to some day-to-day accommodation and in this situation both the manager and the union negotiator will be inclined to go easy if their opponent is on the ropes. That such give and take is an important feature of management–union relations throughout industry is undeniable. What is also undeniable, however, is that this institutionalized leniency often breaks down. While the negotiating situation has an important degree of autonomy from the work situation, ultimately the pattern of negotiations will always be coloured by the balance of forces in that situation. Under certain circumstances any humanitarian concern that the steward may feel for his opponent across the table will openly conflict with his duty as the representative of his workmates. It cuts even deeper the other way. A manager in a car plant may let a steward off the hook, but if he does it often enough, on issues important enough, he'll find his journey to the top halted. Car plants are about profit and pressure. They very quickly sort the men out from the boys. You've got to be a very hard man to get to the top in the industry. You've got to be equally hard if you want to be a useful steward and union organizer.

As I have hinted shop stewards occupy an ambiguous position within a factory. The steward is frequently involved in the process of translating experiences – of explaining to one group of people the significance that a particular occurrence has for another group of people. Quite often this ambiguity, derived from regular contact with 'the office', can turn the steward against his workmates and encourage him to take the job as supervisor. Shop stewards are regularly, and have always been, bought off in factories up and down the country. The same ambiguity however, can, when allied with other factors, serve as an important radicalizing agent. This proved to be the case at Halewood. A severe period of struggle during the early years of the plant provided the experience which moulded the ideology of the stewards committee. Struggle over line speeds, lay-offs, victimization and the like fostered the articulation of a highly developed form of factory class-consciousness. This class-consciousness has been termed a *factory* consciousness because as an ideology its cutting edge is essentially limited to the confines of the arena of production. We shall pick up the threads of this argument later. In the meantime we must examine the core of the workers' experience within the car plants which is the root of factory consciousness – the line, the job and worker control of the job.

At Ford we have developed and successfully applied industrial control and automation systems to the process of automotive manufacture. We are using process control computers in the fields of automated component and assembly testing, production monitoring, machine control, vehicle checkout and certification and terminal based date-acquisition systems.

In order to continue development work in this area it has become necessary to expand our existing process control group.

Recruitment Advertisement in the *Sunday Times*

I have not been able to discover that repetitive labour injures a man in any way. I have been told by parlour experts that repetitive labour is soul- as well as body-destroying, but that has not been the result of our investigations. There was one case of a man who all day long did little but step on a treadle release. He thought that the motion was making him one-sided; the medical examination did not show that he had been affected but, of course, he was changed to another job that used a different set of muscles. In a few weeks he asked for his old job again. It would seem reasonable to imagine that going through the same set of motions daily for eight hours would produce an abnormal body, but we have never had a case of it. We shift men whenever they ask to be shifted and we should like regularly to change them – that would be entirely feasible if only the men would have it that way. They do not like changes which they do not themselves suggest. Some of the operations are undoubtedly monotonous – so monotonous that it seems scarcely possible that any man would care to continue long at the same job. Probably the most monotonous task in the whole factory is one in which a man picks up a gear with a steel hook, shakes it in a vat of oil, then turns it into a basket. The motion never varies. The gears come to him always in exactly the same place, he gives each one the same number of shakes, and he drops it into a basket which is always in the same place. No muscular energy is required, no intelligence is required. He does little more than wave his hands gently to and fro – the steel rod is so light. Yet the man on that job has been doing it for eight solid years. He has saved and invested his money until now he has about forty thousand dollars – and he stubbornly resists every attempt to force him into a better job!

Henry Ford I

5 On the Line

Working in a car plant involves coming to terms with the assembly line. 'The line never stops,' you are told. Why not? '... don't ask. It *never* stops.' The assembly plant itself is huge and on two levels, with the paint shop on the one floor and the trim and final assembly departments below. The car shell is painted in the paint shop and passed by lift and conveyor to the first station of the trim assembly department. From this point the body shell is carried up and down the 500-yard length of the plant until it is finally driven off, tested, and stored in the car park.

Few men see the cars being driven off the line. While an assembly worker is always dealing with a moving car it is never moving under its own steam. The line – or 'the track' as some managers who have been 'stateside' refer to it – stands two feet above floor level and moves the cars monotonously, easily along. Walking along the floor of the plant as a stranger you are deafened by the whine of the compressed air spanners, you step gingerly between and upon the knots of connecting air pipes which writhe like snakes in your path, and you stare at the moving cars on either side. This is the world of the operator. In and out of the cars, up and over the line, check the line speed and the model mix. Your mind restlessly alert, because there's no guarantee that the next car will be the same as the last, that a Thames van won't suddenly appear. But still a blank – you keep trying to blot out what's happening. 'When I'm here my mind's a blank. I *make* it go blank.' They all say that. They all tell the story about the man who left Ford to work in a sweet-factory where he had to divide up the reds from the blues, but left because he couldn't take the decision-making. Or the country lad who couldn't believe that he had to work on *every* car: 'Oh no. I've done my car. That one down there. A green one it was.' If you stand on the cat-walk at the end of the plant you can look down over the whole assembly floor. Few people do, for to stand there and look at the endless, perpetual, tedium of it all is to be threatened by the overwhelming insanity of it. The sheer audacious madness of a system based upon men like those wishing their lives away. I was never able, even remotely, to come to terms with the line. Mind you, I never worked on it. But that's another story.

In 1970 I talked with a Ford worker in Swansea. His son had recently bought a Capri – the Company's latest model. 'I wouldn't touch them,' he said and pointed repeatedly towards his own car, a Morris Oxford, 'that's my "Ford" there. I wouldn't touch the bloody things: not with what I see going on in that plant.' This denial of any identity with the Ford product is, and always has been, a general phenomenon amongst workers in the motor industry. Continually Ford workers tell you 'never buy a Ford'. Neither is this peculiar to Ford. In the early days of the motor industry in the United States, General Motors workers are reputed to have bought Fords instead of Chevrolets because they 'knew how Chevrolets were built and would not advise anybody to buy one' (see Fine, 1969, p. 38).

Living in a society ruled by the tyranny of the market place men frequently find themselves attracted yet at the same time repelled by features of that society. Nothing better demonstrates this state amongst Ford workers than their relationship with the motor car. Most workers would like a car and Ford workers are not exceptions. They want a car because it allows you to leave for work that much later, to go away for day trips with the wife and kids. In short it gives you some freedom. There is also something attractive about the automobile itself, the intricacies of its internal combustion engine, and its glamour. Many of the men I talked to in fact mentioned that they were first attracted to the car plant in some sense by the very fact that cars were produced there and that they might 'find out' about how cars are made. They found out as they put hub-caps on, stretched rubber around windscreens or struggled with the dashboard wiring. In our society the motor car has an attraction which makes people endure all sorts of deprivation in order to possess one. Some men talk of little other than cars and the roads are thick with them. The position of the car worker, though, is doubly complicated, for the deprivations he endures in order to possess a car are actually defined in the very production of the desired object.

One way of coping with these tensions may be to deny any identity with the *particular* product, with the particular car that has been the source of your agony on the line. Few Ford workers were proud of the fact that they produced Ford motor cars. The Ford Motor Company, however, doesn't allow *their* workers to rest easily with this non-identification. Frequent quality boosting campaigns are designed

Partners in Progress

A Sales Scheme for Ford Employees

A personal message from
Mr S. Gillen
Managing Director
Ford Motor Company Ltd

As an employee of Ford Motor Company Limited it is quite likely that your own particular job is not directly concerned with sales.

However, we are all very much dependent upon sales of our products, and the idea behind 'Partners in Progress' is to offer you an opportunity of playing an important part in actively selling the products you help to make and being handsomely rewarded for your effort.

All of us have friends or acquaintances who may be thinking of buying or exchanging their car or van and you can win attractive and valuable prizes simply by talking and recommending your Company's products.

　　With best wishes and good luck
　　　Stanley Gillen

'Partners in Progress' is open to all Ford employees (excluding Car and Truck Group staff at Warley).

This is an opportunity to assist in the sales of cars/5/7 cwt. vans and help maintain and increase our level of sales.

You can help Ford Motor Company and yourself by telling friends and acquaintances about the products you help to make: at the same time both you and your friends can take part in a wonderful prize winning competition.

How you can win is clearly outlined in booklets containing full entry details, and these will be distributed by your Employees Vehicle Sales Rep. during the week ending 16th September.

Broadly, all you have to do is hand a card to a potential customer and when he buys a new Ford car or 5/7 cwt. van, you will both qualify for entry into a series of draws for attractive prizes.

by the Company and its house journal The *Ford Bulletin* regularly carries articles that are specifically designed to increase identification with the product amongst its employees. It also allows its workers to purchase Ford motor cars at a reduced price. The Company sells some 5000 cars each year to its own employees.

One worker on the trim production line spent some time telling me never to buy a Ford because 'its madness in here. If you saw some of the things that happen you'd never entertain buying one.' Some time later I saw him behind the wheel of an Escort. Yes he knew he'd told me not to buy a Ford and in truth he didn't feel that he ought to buy one, but it was cheaper to buy from the Company. He could have trouble with it, he hoped not, but were not all cars the same *really*? 'I know we all go on a lot about not buying Fords but I think that's because its Fords that we are to do with. We know what goes wrong with them because we know we don't care how we do the jobs. This Escort now, I know that me and my mates probably put the trim inside it. It's a funny feeling riding along in something you really hated when it was a shell on the line. That's why we go on about it. Because *we* made them not because they're any worse than a BMC car or anything.'

A Ford employee may find the cost of a Ford car reduced by almost 20 per cent. The *real* cost of the car though is the hours that men spend working on the line. The measure of the freedom obtained on a day trip to Southport is the time that freedom is denied while working in the Ford plant at Halewood. How do men make sense of this; how do they come to understand their jobs; above all else how do they come to terms with the line?

One of the ways that I thought I could explore the way these men came to understand their work was through the notion of an 'ideal job'. This, however, ran into difficulties, as many stewards in particular reacted to this as they had done to the idea of an 'ideal firm'. Bert was very explicit. 'What are you on about now? You work for money. That's what it's all about. I've told you before. I'd shovel shit for money.' Bert was the wet deck steward. He'd go out with you for a night, buy lots of beer, give you fags, beat you at darts and tell you stories about his family. When you met him next day he'd say, 'Here he comes, the man with no hands. You want to watch out for him. Don't go out with him for a night unless you've a spare fiver and a pocket full of ciggies.' He only worked for money – he'd 'shovel shit for it', he said – yet he'd refuse overtime and spent hours at the weekend organizing football matches of the PTA teams. His finally resigned as a steward because he was 'fed up with representing a bunch of selfish bastards'.

Now although few of the stewards were like Bert Owen, if one were to attempt to typify the 'lifestyle' of the stewards this peculiar mixture of a brash, uncompromisingly hard exterior with an almost naive sentimentality and warmth would be an important element within it. I discussed this at length with several of the stewards, not least because they often laughed at my own 'romanticism' and 'sentimentalism'. To paraphrase the comments of one of them: ˙

> Yes: we're all sentimentalists to some extent. We laugh at each other, criticize each other by calling one another a sentimentalist but I think we're all a bit that way inclined. Believe in the 'brotherhood of man', a better society and shit like that. But you've got keep it in check or you've had it. You've got to keep your feet on the ground. If you go around the world with rosy ideas about things, about the members, they'll pretty soon come unstuck because the members can be bastards . . .
>
> A steward will come up to me and say 'I'm not representing that shower of shit any more', or he'll say 'You call this a shop steward committee . . . half of them aren't worth a candle'. I say this see 'You can't pick your team. You've got to make do with what you've got.' It's all very well having your high ideals but we've got to deal with that company in that plant and we can't pick and choose and um and ah.

This particular principle had become incorporated into the ideology of the shop stewards' committee, and in its emphasis upon the need to tackle day-to-day problems it can be seen as a 'direct' reflection of working-class experience. People, living their lives, develop a pretty accurate idea of their own life chances, of the odds they face and the hopes that they can realistically entertain. One of the more obvious criticisms of much that passes for social science is that it drastically underestimates people's intelligence. Working-class people are faced with a limited number of employment prospects all of which are pretty dreary. If you're young, with family responsibilities and want to move out of the house you know to be a slum you attempt to get as much money as you can by selling to the highest bidder. In a hard world you become a hard man. This doesn't mean that you are not aware of alternative things, better ways of living, but merely that these are unlikely to be open to you. If you work at Ford's, on the line, you let your mind go blank and look forward to pay day and the weekend. As one man put it: ˙

> I just adapt to it. I suppose you could adapt to anything really. It depends upon your circumstances. I'm married and I've taken out a mortgage. This affects your attitude to your work. I just close my eyes and stick it out. I think about

the kids and the next premium being paid. That's about all there is with this job. It gets frustrating but that's it. What can you do?

I had previously talked to him about the notion of an 'ideal job'. As I have said this involved problems but he did say this:

> Oh. You're talking about in my dreams, like. The sort of thing I'd *really* like to do if I had the chance. Oh yes . . . I'd like to work on a newspaper. I'd like to meet people. To do something like you're doing yourself. Find out the facts about people's problems. You know about social problems. I've a reasonable knowledge of English. I used to write in the school magazine. I've always had it in the back of my mind. My school teachers said I should do it. I often think about it. There's no possibility now, like.

Another man made the relationship between the real and the ideal more explicitly:

> Your choice of job is governed too much by money. You've got to be a realist. You've got to be a realist. What I'd like to do though would be a sports teacher – teach physical education to lads. That's my ideal job, it's important, it would give me a better outlook on life.
>
> You don't achieve anything here. A robot could do it. The line here is made for morons. It doesn't need any thought. They tell you that. 'We don't pay you for thinking' they say. Everyone comes to realize that they're not doing a worthwhile job. They're just on the line. For the money. Nobody likes to think that they're a failure. Its bad when you *know* that you're just a little cog. You just look at your pay packet – you look at what it does for your wife and kids. That's the only answer.

Most of the Ford workers that I talked to expressed sentiments broadly similar to those quoted above. There was a tendency for men working on sub-assembly operations, which involved them in preparing a batch of components for the line operator and enabled them to 'make their own time', to find the work less frustrating than the men who were actually on the line. The differences weren't all that great, all the men I talked to felt that their job was either 'completely dull and monotonous' or 'dull most of the time'. Similarly most of them had some idea of the sort of job that they would like to do if they had or had had the opportunity. The two quotations are unrepresentative in one sense however. While all the 'ideal jobs' mentioned were chosen for their intrinsic qualities, a majority of the sample of members opted for jobs which took them 'outside the system' where they were 'their own boss'. They talked of being back in the services or at sea or driving a lorry again. In this connection it is interesting that in addition to songs about leaving Liverpool, going home again to Wales and fighting the English in Dublin, a favourite pub song in Liverpool is 'Let the Rest of the World Go By':

With someone like you
a pal good and true
I'd like to leave it all behind
and go and find
a place that's known to God alone
just the spot to call our own.

We will find perfect peace
where joy will never cease
and there beneath the starry sky
we'll build our own little nest
somewhere out in the west
and let the rest of the world go by.

The stewards were much less inclined to talk in terms of being their own boss and as a rule had a much clearer idea of the type of job they would really like to do. They wanted a worthwhile job, preferably one which allowed them to help other people.[1] None of them, or the sample of members for that matter, wanted to be business men while several of them felt that a union organizer's job *could* be ideal. Gerry was one of these. He was the branch secretary, young and very intelligent. He was the hard-nosed one who wheeled and dealed in local union politics. He is now a district officer of the union.

Most officers are bent. We know that but they could do so much for the blokes on the shop floor if they weren't. There's hundreds of places in Liverpool for example with no union organization. Now I think we've done a pretty reasonable job at organizing this factory. We've gained a lot of experience – which we could put to good use organizing other places. It could be really important to do that I think.

Other choices were less obviously related to their present situation: Billy was a woolly-back from St Helens. He'd been in the pits for donkeys' years and had come to Ford's to escape the dole. He was a round, wild, defiant man. He worked on the 'backs and cushions' and didn't like it much. He would have really liked to be able to work in a hospital.

1. All the stewards answered a fixed choice question on the two most important and the least important aspect of an 'ideal job'. Using a score of 2 for the most important, 1 for the second most important, we find the 'security' scored 27, 'worthwhileness' 24, 'wages' 22, 'helping others' 21, 'working with people' 8. Thirty-three of the stewards considered 'status' to be the least important attribute of such a job.

I'd like to do hospital work. I'd like to have studied and to have used my brain. I wish I'd had the opportunity ... no I suppose I did have the opportunity if I'd had the guts. Anyway I'd like to have been able to be a doctor. I wouldn't want a bossy job or a factory job. I'd want to be able to help people and be respected for it. That's what I've always wanted to do. That's what I'm like really. 'If I've got it they can have it' sort of thing.

Stan was a timid man who'd taken the steward's job against his better judgement. He'd worked on the railways, been unemployed and spent his time searching for a quiet life.

I don't think that I could pin it down to one particular job but I'd just like to be able to go into work of a morning without being scared of what you're going to face. A clerical job I suppose. It's something you dream about.

Frank was a tearaway. Expansive and carefree yet deeply earnest. He was a very good organizer but couldn't settle to it. Frank was all chained in. Often he didn't know what he wanted.

I'm very interested in helping the working class The underdog. I don't like to see people gaining from people who aren't as fortunate. The ordinary worker is bewildered by all the nonsense that gets thrown at him. You know I'd really like to *do something*.

Bill was a moderate. He believed in reason and discussions. He came from a family deeply involved in politics and the Labour Party. Most of the other stewards felt that he could lose them when it came to philosophy. A thoughtful, sincere, steady man who was to become the convenor of the PTA.

I'd like to be a teacher, I think. Something like that anyway. I think I've been through the mill. I'd really like to work with young people. I think that something like you are doing must give you a lot of satisfaction. You're fortunate because you can see your work. It's something tangible which you can get to grips with ... come back to ... think about ... You must feel that you are doing something. With us you do something and its gone. Part of your life on the back of a car.

In the absence of an 'ideal job' these men came to terms with working in a car plant; with working on or around the line. They arrived and were put straight on to a job. The Ford Motor Company doesn't have, or need, much of a training programme for its new operatives. The automobile industry is the domain of the new 'semi-skilled' worker. Less than one worker in a hundred in a car plant can call himself skilled in any real sense. As early as 1925, in fact, Henry Ford had estimated that 79 per cent of his workers could be made proficient in eight days and as many as 43 per cent of them required only one day's training. In the PTA plant at Halewood it would be difficult to claim, without doing severe damage to the meaning of words, that the production workers were trained at all.

Oh they've got a *great* training programme here. A great training programme. I can't remember how long it is ... two days I think. I'm not sure though. I didn't get any training at all when I came here, but I think they get two days now.

What does this training involve? Do men still go straight on to the line?

Oh yes, they go straight on the line all right. You know the sort of thing – 'This is Fred, he'll show you what to do.' 'Hello,' says Fred 'you stick this in here and that in there – I'm not paid for this y'know.' You either do it or you don't. If you don't you're 'unsuitable' and you get your cards.

As a consequence of this the introduction to the line was often a harrowing experience. A mate of mine went to work on the assembly line in the Vauxhall plant at Ellesmere Port, over the water from Liverpool. He was six feet two, a bit dozey and not too agile. He was put on the night shift, fitting electric wiring through the dashboard of the Viva. He lasted two shifts. While his mates were trying to do the job that bit faster so that they could work back up the line and create a few minutes break in every hour, he found himself working just that bit slower. He was ending up several stations down the line. Getting in the way of his mates; falling over; getting cursed. Tall, dozey men don't belong on an assembly line.

Most people survive their period of probation and become fully fledged assembly-line operatives. The men I talked with all found the experience painful and had established means of coping with it. They 'blanked out their minds', perfected 'mental blackouts' or thought about crossword puzzles. Complete social isolation may be a 'solution' but many of the assemblers felt this to be unbearable. They make great efforts to communicate with their mates but there was the problem of the noise. 'You can talk but you can't have a conversation in this place.' They develop a system of handsigns, they gain minutes by working back up the line, all 'to have a laugh and a joke. That's about all that keeps you going.' If they're lucky they can get a change of job, and if they're very lucky they can get off the line.

A twenty-three-year-old fork-lift driver put it like this:

When you're doing the same job, day in, day out, you'd rather do almost anything for a change. I'm used to it though. Sometimes you look around and ask when are you going to be anything other than a clock number. Now take you, you can pick, you know you'll do something worthwhile. With me it's just a case of asking 'is it ever going to change?'

And a twenty-one-year-old worker from the final assembly department:

There's nothing interesting in the job. It's just boring. Whenever there's a vacancy I ask for a move just for a change. I moved from the Anglia to the Cortina engine dress because I was really fed up. It's not much of a change but it's a bit different for a few shifts at least. I'd prefer to be on sub-assembly really. You can make your own time there.

And another thirty year old:

I place the car off the hoist, I've been doing that for three years now. With the line you've got to adapt yourself to the speed. Some rush and get a break. I used to try and do that but the job used to get out of hand. I just amble along now. Thirty seems a lot when you're working here. Some jobs you're on you can't talk or you'll lose concentration. When I came here first I couldn't talk at all. Now I can manage a few words with the man opposite me.

To be off the line is to experience an immense sense of relief. Those who have escaped or dodged the line dread the thought of being caught up in it again.

It's a relief when you get off the moving line. It's such a tremendous relief. I can't put it into words. When you're on the line it's on top of you all the time. You may feel ill, not one hundred per cent but that line will be one hundred per cent. Being on sub-assembly is like getting off the roundabout. Y'know . . . day in, day out . . . never stopping. I still have nightmares about it. I couldn't go back on that line. Not for anything.

They feel no moral involvement with the firm or any identification with the job. No one that I talked to thought that he'd feel too bad about leaving Ford's for a 'similar job in the area'; seven of the sample in fact thought that they'd be quite pleased. To quote a man on the cross-feed:

I bring books and crossword puzzles to work. This gives me something to think about when I'm doing the job. You walk out of here in a dream.

I *will* leave soon. It's getting me down. It's so monotonous, tedious, boring. I was just going to make a convenience of Ford's for a few months but I'm still here. Not for much longer though. Yes: I'm leaving soon. I'm not happy here. I'm definitely not going to stay for much longer.

And another on the trim:

It's the most boring job in the world. It's the same thing over and over again. There's no change in it, it wears you out. It makes you awful tired. It slows your thinking right down. There's no need to think. It's just a formality. You just carry on. You just endure if for the money. That's what we're paid for – to endure the boredom of it.

If I had the chance to move I'd leave right away. It's the conditions here. Ford class you more as machines than men. They're on top of you all the time. They expect you to work every minute of the day. The atmosphere you get in here is so completely false. Everyone is downcast and fed up. You can't even talk about football. You end up doing stupid things. Childish things – playing tricks on each other.

The only regrets they'd have would be the mates they'd leave behind. This comes across most poignantly with the stewards, twenty-eight of whom felt to some extent that if they left they would let down their fellow stewards and the union organization in the plant. Eric Temple put it like this:

I wouldn't miss this firm at all. It's the worst firm I've heard of for scandalizing people. When I started I never thought I'd last three weeks. I'd only miss the lads. I've got some good mates here in the union. We're all together. If Mick's in lumber, we're all in lumber. It's a good feeling. The organization here union-wise is pretty decent. It gives you peace of mind to be able to speak your mind. That's what I'd miss if I left here. Being in the union with the lads. I'd feel that I'd let everyone down if I just left.

The stewards felt the same about the work as the members. They were, after all, workers and were forcibly reminded of this fact by members of management. They were also stewards and although many of them pointed out that it was impossible to make a clear-cut distinction between their job as an operator and their responsibilities as a shop steward – 'It's all part of the same thing isn't it. You'd have to be schizophrenic otherwise' – they all saw the experience they gained as a steward to be intrinsically satisfying, in direct contrast to their job on the line.

I can't imagine anything more boring than assembly-line work – can you? The steward's job is something different. Every man is a human being and he's different. All cars are alike but every man has something different about him. So every case is a different case. You're learning something all the time.

They could use their brains as stewards, they could do something that had a beginning and an end, and they could assess themselves. They may handle a case well or badly, and they cared about that; but they cared nothing about the cars on the line. The steward's job had something they could get their teeth into. Above all else it allowed them to help their mates. All these things made it something worthwhile, something that, no matter what else, was at least *worth doing*.

If I get a clear-cut decision for a bloke with a genuine grievance I get a lot of satisfaction. I certainly get *no* satisfaction from the job. Wind me up at 8 a.m. and that's that. I'm just here waiting for the buzzer.

This reference to the idea of helping someone, 'your fellow man', cropped up continually and was a central force of the ideology of the shop stewards and is taken up again in Chapter 9. It can be seen as that aspect of a factory class-consciousness which specifically relates the steward to his work. The ideas of 'helping people' and 'doing something worthwhile' were seen by the stewards to be important aspects of an 'ideal job' (see page 125). The steward's job offered elements of that ideal because:

It's obvious isn't it. You're doing something worthwhile. You're making use of the little brain that you have to help your fellow man. To solve somebody's problems. If I weren't a shop steward I don't think I'd work at Ford's. I take all the worries home but I get a kick out of it. I know that we're respected for working for the men.

I don't want to give the impression that I'm afraid of work but as a shop steward you achieve something. If you're an operator you're faced with the same thing today as yesterday and it will be the same tomorrow. When you've got a case it's always different. If you solve it you've achieved something. You've done something worthwhile. You've put someone's mind at rest.

This guarded reference to workshyness is important and gives some indication of the vulnerabilities of shop stewards. They are always open to the charge by management that they are 'shirkers'. Many of them guard themselves against such a charge:

I've got an attitude on this ... I like to be able to say that I can do my job. That I can work as well and as fast as the next man. I can eliminate them being able to pick on me then ...

It is impossible for a steward to do a full operator's job and to represent his members adequately. Many stewards try though. By 1967 a lot of the stewards in the PTA had obtained 'facilities' from management to attend to the grievances of men on their section. The extent of these 'facilities' varied over time and from section to section. On some sections the steward worked on the line and was expected by the supervision to do the same amount of work as the men who worked alongside him. On most of the sections though the steward was allocated a sub-assembly job and was allowed time to deal with grievances. Some of the senior stewards did little or no work as operators.[2] While the establishment of shop steward 'facilities' as 'rights' was seen to be of great importance by the stewards, and although none of the members I talked to felt this to be in any way improper, many of the stewards felt some sense of guilt when they made use of these rights. One steward put it like this:

> We've just got to have facilities if we're going to do the job. If the membership are going to be protected you've just *got* to be able to call a steward *immediately*. And that means that the steward mustn't be expected to do a full operator's job. I believe in that. I believe in trade unionism and I'd fight for the right of a man to have his shop steward when he wants him. But when I get called off the job, and leave the rest of the lads there sweating, working their balls off, I feel guilty. It's funny but I don't like leaving. I feel as if I ought to apologize to them.

One of the senior stewards in fact refused to take advantage of the facilities available to him for this very reason. He worked on the high-line, he had done all of the jobs on his section and in 1967 he was putting the petrol tank inside the body shell. He worked on the line – he had refused sub-assembly jobs – and he dealt with the grievances as he worked. He wanted 'fuck all off them that the lads don't have'.

The position of shop stewards can be seen as the focus of a number of ambiguities and contradictions which are rooted in the nature of production and position of the trade union in the factory. The shop steward lives out these ambiguities and contradictions and in so doing he attempts to make sense of them. The shop stewards at the Halewood plant had collectively established a more coherent understanding of these problems than most, but this understanding did not extend to a developed form of political consciousness, rather it represented a very direct, common-sense reflection of workers' experience in the car plant. Frequently problems were handled through humour, self deprecation and personal trauma. What they had also developed was a rudimentary code of ethics for shop stewards – a form of morality if you like – and it will be useful at the moment to explore some of the features of this code.

A moral commitment to the firm was almost totally absent in the members of the sample and the shop stewards. One man described the situation acutely when he said:

2. This variation between sections relates to the job control established by workers in the past (see Chapter 6).

It's strange this place. It's got no really good points. It's just convenient. It's got no interest. You couldn't take the job home. There's nothing to take. You just forget it. I don't want promotion at all, I've not got that approach to the job. I'm like a lot of people here. They're all working here but they're just really hanging around, waiting for something to turn up ... It's different for them in the office. They're *part* of Ford's. We're not, we're just working here, we're numbers.

Most of the men felt like that, 'waiting for something to turn up'. None of them wanted to be working for Ford when he was forty, yet they all became slightly hesitant when asked what job they'd be doing in ten years' time. Few of them (six) definitely felt that they'd have moved from Halewood and if they didn't they thought they'd be on the same job – if it was there, 'you never knew with Ford' – or on sub-assembly. One man asked me at this point in the interview what I thought I'd do when I'd finished my studies. I replied that I didn't know, that I had no idea. He looked at me for about thirty seconds and then said 'it must be great that ... not knowing'.

We have already seen that the steward through his involvement in the union organization in the plant felt a greater commitment to continuing at Halewood. Although five of the stewards felt that they would have left in ten years' time, three of these said that they would only move if they were offered a job as full-time union officer. The remainder felt that they'd be in the same job and most of them stated that if they were still elected by the membership they'd be pleased to continue as a shop steward. An important aspect of the stewards' 'moral code', as well as significant difference between them and the sample of members, is revealed in their conception of 'the next ten years'. The stewards were stickers. 'It's all very well saying that you don't want to be in Ford's when you're forty,' said one of them, 'but you may have no choice. It's our job to make this a place where you can work when you're forty.'[3] To stick and to organize was obviously in your own interests but it was also important for other workers:

I don't like going through life just doing a job. You get a bad job and all right you can move on, but some other poor bastard will be doing it after you've gone. If you're doing a job I think you've got a duty to the man who follows you in that job to make it a bit better. Anybody can just leave.

3. This in fact because one of the important slogans of the committee. In 1969 a forty-year-old assembly-line worker had a heart attack and was eventually threatened with dismissal by the company. The stewards fought the case strenuously and produced a leaflet for the membership headed 'On the Scrap-Heap at Forty'.

The idea of 'sticking it out', of 'having a job to do and doing it', was an important aspect of the stewards' 'moral code'. The resignation of a steward always became the focus of discussion, and stewards who talked of resigning were chided as 'quitters'. On one occasion when a steward had threatened to resign if he lost a particular case, the district officer, Bill Brodrick (the ex-convenor), remarked in conversation with Mick the convenor:

We can't have this though. It's no good a bloke threatening to spew it if he loses. Let's face it, we're going to lose more than we win. If everyone started to do that what sort of organization would we have? You've just got to be prepared to take it if you're going to be a steward.

The stewards, then, believed in the need for organization and felt that individual stewards should be guided by the 'needs' of that organization. A number of the stewards, for example, felt that they should always be in a position to take on a struggle and that they should never be too dependent upon the company. Many of them talked of keeping their hire purchase debt low and one or two explicitly argued against house purchase.

You see what happens to supervisors. They get made up, earn a lot more money and then the company start encouraging them to buy a house, to get a car on the company's scheme. I *know* this for a fact. Then when they're up to their neck in debt they put the screws on them, and they've got no chance. A shop steward should never be in that position . . . where he can't afford to go on strike pay. I'd never buy a house while I was a shop steward. I don't think any steward should.

While fifteen of the forty-three members were buying their own houses, in 1967 only five of the stewards were doing so. Twenty-six of the stewards in fact lived in rented terraced houses.

To be effective the steward, and the stewards' committee, had to be able to rely upon the support of the membership. Every steward was aware that this support could quite easily be undermined and as such many of them felt that they had to be seen to be clean, that they had to be indisputably honest, fair, scrupulous men. This had a number of consequences, for in a corrupt society people expect corruption. The steward had always to guard himself against the charge that he was using the privileges of office for his own ends.

Overtime is a bastard. I hate to say this but that's what gives me the most trouble on my section – the overtime rota. You'll always get some clever fucker who'll say 'I bet you're doing all right out of it' so I never work overtime at all. I've always got my last year's pay note with me so that I can say 'I'll bet you that

I earned less money than any man on this section last year'. No one's taken me on yet and it's just as well because I'd always win. A lot of stewards are like myself. I don't think a steward should work overtime, or at least he shouldn't work unless everyone on his section is working.

This view was almost universally held by the stewards in the 1960s. The extent to which it was held, and the extent to which their trade union activities came to dominate their lives, is revealed in the way this 'personal morality' was extended to their families. In 1967 several of the stewards felt that a steward's wife should not work as this could cause antagonism, which could be particularly severe and damaging during a strike.

During a strike a man whose Judy is working is obviously better off than the man with a wife and three kids about the house. So you're bound to get some backbiting – 'Oh it's all right for him, his missis is keeping him in ale and ciggies.' A steward just can't afford to be mixed up in that sort of thing, especially a senior steward who may have to recommend to the men that they stay out.

The shop stewards, therefore, knew that there was a need for a shop-floor organization and were acutely aware that such an organization was fraught with difficulties. The steward had to be prepared for defeat, for graft without glory. More than that, he had to recognize that the organization was dependent upon the support of the membership and that this support couldn't be guaranteed. To get the support he had to show that he wasn't bent, that he wasn't out for himself or benefiting in any way from being a steward. This obviously had implications for the way in which the stewards related to promotion. The promotion of the steward to the foreman's job is one of the oldest tricks in the book, and many of the stewards would get worked up about anyone who turned coat. Almost all of them in fact felt that a shop steward should not seek out or accept promotion to the position of supervisor. Those supervisors who had once been stewards were pointed out to me like lepers. 'Did you see that bloke in a white coat we just passed? He used to be a steward ... the bastard. The lads gave him hell for a bit though.' The stewards weren't interested in promotion, in becoming 'dedicated Ford men'. For them to take the white coat at Halewood would be to join the other side – 'I couldn't do that. Leave the lads? Not in this firm anyway. They're a crowd of gangsters here.' They felt a 'sense of obligation' to the people who had elected them and to the union organization. To become a foreman would be to let everyone down. As one of them put it:

If I did the foreman's job I'd never be at ease – because of the union. I'd be bothered by that. And the idea that I'd used the union as a stepping-stone.

This personal morality is bolstered by the needs of the shop steward organization:

We've done a big job here in building up the union, and the most important thing we've had to do is build up the blokes' confidence in the union. To get their trust. The lads on my section trust me because they know that I'm honest with them and that I'm not out for myself. A lot of the lads, see, think of the steward as someone who's out for himself – who wants to be a supervisor, and we've had enough traitors here to give them reason to think that. Well if you're going to have a good section you've just got to convince them that they can trust you. As I say, the lads on my section *do* trust me because they know I stick my neck out for them.

Neither the members nor the stewards thought 'good promotion prospects' to be a particularly important feature of an 'ideal firm'. Furthermore they felt that the chances of promotion at Halewood were rather poor (see Chapter 4). The stewards considered their chances of promotion to be even less good than did the members. No steward considered that he had an even average chance of promotion. Many of them qualified this by making it clear that it was impossible for them to assess their 'chances' as they were completely uninterested in the supervisor's job.

You might as well stab me in the back. I'd sooner be dead. Have you seen them walking about here. They're like zombies. I don't think they're allowed to go for a piss by themselves in the fucking night. Ford *owns* them. They'll *never* own me. If I've finished my work and I want a sit down I have a sit down and I read the *Mirror*. I don't care *who* walks in here. He can fuck off. Them though, they're on pins all the time. They've been brainwashed. If they had any brains to wash. They lose their own identity. They're Ford's and they live it.

Not a few of them intimated that they'd 'had their offers'.

I've been offered the foreman job several times. I've no intention whatsoever of accepting it. I've no intention of being a party to the decisions that those people are a party to. The foreman *must* accept the boss's decision. I don't have to. That's the only way I could be. I couldn't do that job without selling my self respect.

Generally speaking the Ford workers had little interest in promotion. No one I talked to considered it at all likely that he would be promoted in the near future and only three members felt it remotely possible that they would be a supervisor if they stayed at Halewood for another ten years. A number of members (twelve) and stewards (seven) thought that one of the problems with the Company was the fact that men couldn't 'get on' or feel that they were getting somewhere because it was important for men to have a chance to 'use their brains' and 'be more than bloody robots' or 'numbers'. However, the supervisor's job was not seen as a solution to this, and the lack of promotional prospects caused very few sleepless nights for the lads on the line. On the other hand only a few of them shared with the stewards an ideological antagonism toward the supervisory function – a feeling that they wouldn't want to give orders to the lads, to be an outcast, on the other side and one of 'them'. By far the most general feeling was that the supervisor's job in the PTA was completely and utterly unattractive. As some of the members put it:

> The foreman's job is the worst job in the factory. Everybody's at them. I just wouldn't have that job no matter how much it was paid. I just couldn't take it. They're the lance-corporals.

> The supervisors here are treated like dirt. The way they are shouted at in front of the men is terrible. The manager shouted at our foreman the other week: 'You stupid fucking bastard you'll be sacked if you carry on like this.' He said that in front of us. Their job isn't as secure as ours. All they get out of it is a white coat. They can walk around the paint shop all day in a white coat and you're married to the firm.

> I've never applied to be a foreman. Anyway I don't think you should have to apply. They should ask you. You belittle yourself by asking for a job like that. I'd like the money though, but they suffer worse than we do.

> The only advantage in being a foreman is the cash. The worse thing would be Ford's attitude. They are a shadow on your life. It's too complicated to explain – you'd have to work here. Work on the line and watch them. It's much worse than the army.

> I've never applied to be a supervisor. When I came here I thought I'd like to do that. But watching them walk around has changed my mind. They're just like robots. They get told off all the time. I couldn't take that.

Many of the members, then, considered the supervisor's job to be even worse than their own. The only attractions of the job were the money, the security and, disparagingly, the white coat. In return for those advantages, supervisors were seen to suffer the abuses of management and the isolation of being between the firm and the lads. The responses of the stewards were even more clear-cut and damaging. The stewards' day-to-day activities in the plant foster deeper insights into the functioning of the firm than those achieved by many of the members. Unlike the rank and file member, the shop steward is allowed some access into the 'back stage' of the company's operations and this is most marked in its consequence for the supervisor. Most of the shop stewards in the PTA dealt with their supervisor on a day-to-day basis, and were frequently involved in negotiations at a higher level. Each shop steward had, by 1967, immediate right of access to the convenor who was in continual day-to-day contact with plant management. Many of the stewards were, therefore, in a position where they could effectively 'upstage' their supervisor, and this comes out clearly in their responses to the questions on supervision. While many of the members had witnessed the public humiliation of their supervisor, most of the stewards had been involved in disputes during which the supervisor had failed to obtain the support of higher management. To the steward the supervisor was a 'hand rag' – an irrelevance – 'I wouldn't be a foreman for a big clock'. Again to quote a few of them:

The supervisor gets kicked about from pillar to post. We see more of it than the workers do. You know they're just used by management . They're told what to do ... management put them up as a front and then when we push a bit management won't support them.

You see it every day really. They're hand rags. The foremen here are just selling their self respect for the money. They can have no self respect with that job. The shit they've got to take. Many of them know it too. All they can say is 'Look at you ragamuffins. You've got clean consciences, but what about your wife and kids.' I'd do a lot for my wife and kids but I couldn't do that job.

What amazes me most is how they can take it. I suppose they've got to ... they've sold themselves to the firm. My supervisor is just an ordinary bloke and I begin to feel sorry for him. You're in with management and you know before you go in there that you're bound to win, that he's just being used again, and that's the way it goes. You know – the manager apologizing to me 'it won't happen again' and calling him all the names you can think of. But he *takes* it. That's what gets me. He's just afraid to do anything for himself. He must know what's going on ... he must know. That's his job I suppose ... to pretend that he doesn't know ... to stall us for a bit until we can get into the office. What a fucking job. It is though, isn't it? Fancy doing that for a living.

The shop steward's position within a car plant is such that he can see the supervisor very clearly as buffer between the men and the plant management. Having seen this he can play on it. Negotiations in a factory involve large elements of bluff and a shop steward with a well organized section in a car plant has, during periods of boom, more to bluff with than his foreman. Most of the 'victories' that a steward achieved were at the expense of the supervisor and – unless the supervisor happens to be 'a bastard' – were hollow ones as a result. But this raises questions of job control and unionization which need to be looked at in detail.

Since the general pattern of union–management relations, and in many cases the day-to-day differences, are settled by top management without the inclusion of first-line supervisors, it seems that it is entirely erroneous to view the foreman as the 'key man' in this relation. He is rather a person who enters secondarily as the implementor of policies which have already been decided, and his success of failure depends on his ability to act on them, instead of in his own positive actions. Any deviation from union–management decision will bring forth censure from one or both sides, but in no case can the supervisor himself enter into the formulation of the rules under which he works. This activity is vested in the union officials and higher management. The supervisor gets criticism from both management and union, but he is pushed aside when decisions are to be made.

Donald E. Wray, 'Marginal Men of Industry: The Foreman'

We have three thousand foremen in this Company and so if each one of them makes only one mistake a year that's ten a day. That's why we are placing so much stress upon foreman training and education. It's all right having all the brains at the top, but its on the shop floor that it counts. That's why we need to have intelligent, skilled foremen.

An executive of the Ford Motor Company

6 Controlling the Line

Most workers endure supervision while they are at work. Many of them resent it and have built up defences against the supervisor. Coal mining perhaps provides the most well-known examples of the sort of controls that workers have developed at work. Writing in the 1920s Carter Goodrich describes a court case which arose out of the Minimum Wages Act. An overman was asked whether a particular miner did his job properly: 'I never saw him work,' he replied. 'But isn't it your duty to visit each working place twice a day?' asked the magistrate. 'Yes,' replied the overman, but 'they always stop work when they see an overman coming, and sit down till he's gone ... they won't let anybody watch them' (Goodrich, 1920, p. 137). Particular features of mining, not least the danger involved in the work, have contributed to the proliferation of quite extensive job control by the miners. While such controls are not highly developed in every work situation there is every reason to expect that, in a society where most people have only their labour to sell, a conflict over control will be a feature of work situations. Although the syndicalist call of 1911 – 'the mines for the miners' – has died away, the idea of worker control still exists within the British working class. On the shop floor of many factories the division between the supervisor and the men can be characterized as a 'frontier of control' – management's rights on the one side and those of the workers on the other. It is in this way, in disputes over control at work, that the class struggle has been fought out by the British working class during this century. At the lowest, and most fundamental level, it has involved a conflict over how much work the men do and how much they get paid for it. At its most developed level it has produced an ideological conflict over who runs the factory and why, to a questioning of the essential nature and purpose of production within a capitalist society.

The unionization period at Halewood was marked by very severe conflicts along the frontier of control. It involved the workers in a major struggle for a degree of job control within the factory, and this struggle was based upon the relationship between the worker and his

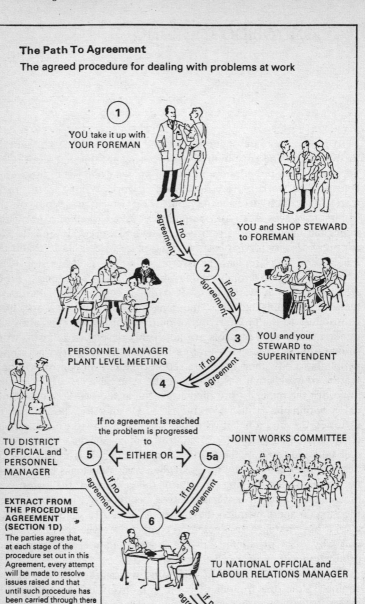

The Path To Agreement

The agreed procedure for dealing with problems at work

(1) YOU take it up with YOUR FOREMAN

YOU and SHOP STEWARD to FOREMAN

if no agreement

(2)

if no agreement

PERSONNEL MANAGER PLANT LEVEL MEETING

(3) YOU and your STEWARD to SUPERINTENDENT

if no agreement

(4)

TU DISTRICT OFFICIAL and PERSONNEL MANAGER

If no agreement is reached the problem is progressed to

(5) ⇐ EITHER OR ⇒ **(5a)**

JOINT WORKS COMMITTEE

if no agreement   *if no agreement*

(6)

EXTRACT FROM THE PROCEDURE AGREEMENT (SECTION 1D)

The parties agree that, at each stage of the procedure set out in this Agreement, every attempt will be made to resolve issues raised and that until such procedure has been carried through there shall be no stoppage of work or other unconstitutional action.

TU NATIONAL OFFICIAL and LABOUR RELATIONS MANAGER

if no agreement

(7) NATIONAL JOINT NEGOTIATING COMMITTEE

supervisor. Victories in these struggles were far from hollow ones, for in their defeat of the supervisor the workers and their stewards laid down the essential basis for a say in the way their lives were to be regulated while they were in the plant. These struggles were of crucial importance for the development of the shop stewards' committee and in examining them it will be useful to begin by drawing upon the experiences of the small-parts section of the paint shop.

Eddie Roberts was the shop steward for the section, George was his stand-in and Kenny was their close friend. All three of them had been on the section from the early days. Kenny was a militant.

I don't know what I am, or what I want to do. I hate Ford's. I'd give up a wage increase to have Henry Ford on this section and give him a good kick up the arse. I'd thought of going to Australia. Of opening a shop. Can you be a socialist and own a shop?

Kenny hated Ford's and loved a fight. He hated having to get up early in the morning. He hated being told what to do. He hated having to work his balls off for nothing. He arrived on the section from the wet deck. Bert (the wet deck steward) couldn't handle him. 'I spotted him so I thought I'd unload him on to Roberts ... It worked out good.' Kenny was amazed by the small-parts section.

I came there and I was put on the front of the line. There was all these hooks and they *all* had to be filled with bits and pieces. I tell you Huwie it was murder. I'd get home and I'd go straight to bed. I couldn't stand it. So I decided that I'd had enough. I started to fill every other hook – to leave big gaps. The foreman went mad. Berserk he went. He started jumping on and off the line, running down the shop filling up the hooks. I ask you. He was shit-scared. 'You *must* fill them all' he kept screaming. Well the lads caught on and they started leaving empty hooks. He was going crazy. Then we got hold of Eddie to complain that the foreman was working. We did that every day.

The situation is a lot better now. In fact we've got one of the easiest sections in the plant. It can be done see. You can control it if you have a go.

The paint shop is the earliest process that the car shell passes through in the PTA. Stoppages of work there will stop production and lay off the rest of the workers in the PTA within a matter of hours.[1] The paint shop workers were aware of this and during periods of market boom when they were working high schedules they pressed their advantage. Certain sections were able to establish and maintain control over line

1. This power is not without its responsibilities. A fiercely fought issue within the shop stewards' committee was over 'sectional' as opposed to 'plant' interests.

speeds and the allocation of work. In the small-parts section the advantages of their position in the production process had been exploited to the full by a high level of solidarity and cohesion amongst the men on the section and an audacious, gifted leadership. As a result of this, and the decline in through-put of the section which accompanied the new fascia panels, the manning of the section in 1968 was almost twice as high as management considered reasonable. Eddie explains:

We've just had to destroy the foremen. When we were here first the foremen really threw their weight around and it took a bit of time to sort things out. Kenny was up at the end of the line. He did a great job. Since then they've tended to send weak foremen down to us. They leave us alone and we leave them alone. One or two of them have tried to get on top but they're easy to beat. There are lots of things you can do to make it bad for them. The lads would do half the job, and play around with them. I'd set him up for cases and destroy him in the office. Every time I was in the office I'd say something about him. That's what we *had* to do. We *had* to destroy the foremen.

We've got it pretty easy now. The blokes are told what has to be done at the beginning of the shift and they work out the speeds, and the times when they're going to take their breaks for tea and cards. Occasionally the foreman will come on to the section during the shift and tell me or George that they want some more parts done quickly – so will the lads do it, as a favour? He goes on about how appreciative he is and that, and the lads do it for him. They just take longer breaks.

I don't know what it is. Some sections like this one are good sections with all good jobs. It's because you've had blokes like myself and Kenny and George who've come to stay I suppose. We've decided not to be beaten down by Ford's or to leave. On other sections the jobs are really bad. I can't understand it. I've been down to talk to the lads on one of those sections, to try to persuade them to do something. They just say they'll be leaving soon. At the other extreme you get the daft buggers in the boiler house who've been here since the start-up and still haven't done anything. For all we say though, there's no easy job in this plant. We're going to have to give way on manning on this section soon. We've just been fortunate with the change in the fascia panels. Most jobs in this plant, even the easy ones, are pretty bad really. There's no joy in putting things on hooks.

In the small-parts section of the paint shop the method of work, along with the strategic position of the section in the plant, assisted the organized attempts of the workers to obtain strong areas of job control. The fact that they were able to maintain these controls during a period of declining work schedules was largely due to the influence that Eddie – the steward and deputy convenor – was able to exert over the supervisor and plant manager. It has already been suggested that bluff plays an important part in negotiations between shop stewards and representatives of management. Periods of months can go by without either side calling the other's bluff. In some factories the bluff is never called. In a period of expanding output it would not be worth it for management to challenge the areas of job control in the small-parts section because this carried the risk of a stoppage. In the long-term, however, the bluff would be called and Eddie knew this; he also knew that when that happened they would have to settle for a reduction in manning.

The extent and durability of job controls are subject to the market. Fluctuations in the sales of cars, in the rate of capital investment, soon reveal themselves in the social relations on the shop floor. It is in this sense that unionism and workplace organization can be seen as a direct consequence of economic forces. Workers who restrict their output, who 'malinger' at work, frequently justify themselves by their need to regulate the supply of labour. 'If we all worked flat out it would be dead simple what would happen. Half of us would be outside on the stones with our cards in our hands.' The Labour government's notion of 'shake out' in the 1960s was but a euphemism for the fact that by maximizing the return on capital working men are put out of a job. The idea of maximizing returns and cutting labour costs is instilled into the minds of modern managers, particularly those who have attended courses in business economics in our universities. Yet a similar understanding is denied to workers because they are in a position to see beyond it. Maximizing returns makes sense only if you're not going to be maximized into the dole queue. Workers who understand this are called 'bloody-minded' because they have come to understand something important about how the economic system operates.

We are left with arguments about 'fairness'. 'A fair day's work for a fair day's pay.' But what is fair? Fair for whom? What sort of fairness commits some men to a life on the line while others write books about them. It's not a fair world and there is no way of deciding what is a fair day's work from these men. The very act of asking them to work there *at all* is manifestly unfair. People who sit in offices, ride in lifts and Company cars have no right to demand that the lads on the line work harder, because to ask the same thing from themselves would be unthinkable.

It's got nothing to do with fairness. What it has to do with is economics and power. In these terms it is important to examine the strengths and vulnerabilities of the job controls established by the

Halewood workers, and in doing so I shall now concentrate upon the experiences of the workers in the trim and final assembly departments. The situations in these departments differed in a number of important respects from the paint shop. In these departments the assembly line exerted an even greater pressure upon the nature of work and work relationships. In these departments the operator, the steward and the foreman were under a greater, and more continuous, pressure than that experienced by their counterparts in the paint shop. Here thousands of components are assembled around the painted body shell, which moves upon a line that never stops. To miss a job means the threat of chaos because someone further down the line has a job which depends upon your job. In the small-parts section an empty hook was an important act of defiance which laid the ground for a movement toward job control, but it did not involve the *sabotage* of the job. On the assembly line a missed job could mean precisely this. Although this means that the individual operator has a greater amount of power at his disposal, in the early days of the plant this power was essentially superficial and illusory. Unless you were sure of the support of your steward and workmates, to miss a job on the line at this time meant that you took on the whole world.

One of the most firmly held policies of the Ford Motor Company has been its opposition both to piece rates and to negotiations over job manning and individual workloads. The Company has held consistently to its right to manage its factories as it thinks fit – to employ whom it likes and to use those in its employ as it likes. In 1969 I had a conversation with a senior Labour Relations executive of the Company, who made clear to me his objections to 'mutuality agreements' with the trade unions over such things as the timing of jobs and the allocation of work. Such an agreement would make the management and the trade unions jointly responsible for ascertaining the time for a particular job, the organization of work, speed of the line and so on.

No. We cannot accept mutuality at this time. Where the trade union movement fails to see these areas of common interest we are inhibited from going down the mutuality road. The first duty we have to our employees is the business. We're not going to be a loss maker. People can look at Ford's, look at its assets and think that the company is safe. Ford's can go to the wall like any other company. If we're not competitive, we make losses and we go to the wall. It's in their interests – share-holders, customers and workers – for us to stay competitive.

Clearly, therefore, any move toward 'mutuality' or the establishment of extensive job control by the workers through their union is seen to involve a direct threat to the competitive position and profitability of the company. It was not felt that this insistence upon the manager's right to manage and pursue efficiency should of necessity give rise to conflict. To quote from the same conversation:

No: I may be naive over this but I can't see that at all. Management don't set difficult work standards. All we want is maximum use of the plant; we can do this in a number of ways – overtime, shift working. All we want then is the plant to produce *the number of cars that we know it can produce* – we're simply asking for *good continuous effort*. And it's here that we need a good working relationship between the foreman and the shop steward in order to achieve these standards. On the track, for example, there may be a work allocation on the basis of three two-doors followed by one four-door followed by three two-door and then a mistake occurs and three four-doors come down together. Now it's in these sort of situations that a good working relationship with the steward is vital. If the relationship is good they can work out whether to put men in on the line or to let the bodies go down the line and gradually move them back again. In these sort of cases cooperation becomes so important.

The unions have taken the wrong turning over this. They seem to think that increased efficiency means that we are asking the men to sweat blood. We're not doing this at all. We aim to set standards that can reasonably be met.

In spite of this, however, it would be true to say that there was no common agreement in the Halewood plants over what constituted 'good continuous effort' or a 'reasonable' workload. The management's insistence that it was its right to make the vital decision on these issues, in itself produced mistrust. The question of job timings and job control was the source of very severe conflict in the Halewood assembly plant throughout the 1960s.

On the assembly line each worker is termed an operator, he works at a particular station and work is allocated to him at that station. He is surrounded by stacks of components and maybe a man is sub-assembling these for him. His job is to attach his components to the body shells as they come to him. Obviously the faster the line runs, the less time he has on any particular body shell, and consequently the smaller the range of tasks that he is able to do. If the line is running, for example, at thirty cars an hour, he is allocated two minutes' work on each car that passes him. The allocation of the two minutes' work is done on the basis of the times recorded for each operation by the Works-study Department of the Ford Motor Company. Most of the assembly-line workers I talked to were suspicious of the timings. It wasn't so much that they thought that the times were rigged but more that they thought the whole idea of timing jobs to be a questionable one – both ethically and scientifically. As two of them put it:

> They say that their timings are based upon what an 'average man' can do at an 'average time of the day'. That's a load of nonsense that. At the beginning of the shift its all right but later on it gets harder. And what if a man feels a bit under the weather? On night shift see, I'm bloody hopeless. I just can't get going on nights. Yet you've always got the same times: Ford's times. It's this numbering again. They think that if they number us and number the job everything is fine.

> *They* decide on *their* measured day how fast *we* will work. They seem to forget that we're not machines y'know. The standards they work to are excessive anyway. They expect you to work the 480 minutes of the eight hours you're on the clock. They've agreed to have a built-in allowance of *six minutes* for going to the toilet, blowing your nose and that. It takes you six minutes to get your trousers down.

The 'science' of the stopwatch was conceived in America at the beginning of the century. Much of it emerged from the factories of men like Ford, but the chief publicist of 'scientific management' was Frederick 'Speedy' Taylor. Like Ford he was an eccentric. As a boy he insisted when he played with his friends that their games conform to detailed, rigid rules. The longer he lived the less he slept, for he had perfected a device that woke him if he dozed in his chair. His mission was to make labour scientific; to calculate the most efficient means of working, through detailed timings of physical movements, and by related incentive payment schemes. His schemes met with considerable opposition and eventually in 1912 a Congressional Committee was set up to investigate his methods (see page 147).

Men still claim scientific status for work-study methods. Usually, however, such claims come from those who are not on the receiving end of the stopwatch. (The extent to which the 'professional classes' support increased rationalization and productivity on the shop floor yet deny the applicability of such criteria to their own work is one of the more interesting phenomena of modern society.) Unbiased opinion rarely disagrees with Professor Baldamus's contention that the whole work-study operation hinges upon 'intuitive guesses as to what is in fact a normal, reasonable, fair, average or right degree of effort for any particular task'. Even writers closer in their identification with the aims of management are reluctant to make sweeping claims for science and objectivity in work study. One of the books written for students of management on methods of payment makes it clear that 'the allocation

CHAIRMAN: Then, how does scientific management propose to take care of men who are not 'first-class' men in any particular line of work?

TAYLOR: I give it up.

CHAIRMAN: Scientific management has no place for such men?

TAYLOR: Scientific management has no place for a bird that can sing and won't sing.

CHAIRMAN: I am not speaking about birds at all.

TAYLOR: No man who can work and won't work has any place under scientific management.

CHAIRMAN: It is not a question of a man who can work and won't work; it is a question of a man who is not a 'first-class' man in any one particular line, according to your own definition.

TAYLOR: I do not know of any such line of work. For each man some line can be found in which he is first class. There is work for each type of man, just as for instance, work for the dray horse and work for the trotting horse, and each of these types is 'first-class' in his particular kind of work. There is no one kind of work, however, that suits all types of men.

CHAIRMAN: We are not in this particular investigation dealing with horses nor singing birds . . . what I wanted to get at is whether or not your scientific management had any place whatever for a man who was not able to meet your own definition of what constitutes a 'first-class' workman.

TAYLOR: Exactly, there is no place for a man who can work and won't work.

CHAIRMAN: It is not a question of a man who can work and won't work; it is a question of a man who doesn't meet your definition of 'first-class' workmen. What place have you for such men?

TAYLOR: I believe the only man who does not come under 'first-class' as I have defined it, is the man who can work and won't work. I have tried to make it clear that for each type of workman some types of work can be found at which he is 'first-class', with the exception of those men who are perfectly well able to do the job but won't do it.

of points encourages one of the major fallacies about job evaluation',[2] that it is 'a scientific or at the very least an objective technique which introduces definitive criteria into the emotive and subjective matter of determining levels of remuneration'. It goes on to conclude that 'the measurement is spurious', and overwhelmingly laden with subjective evaluation 'as any examination of the way factors and their weightings are determined will reveal' (North and Buckingham, 1969, p. 197).

The works-study engineer, the man with the clock, bore the brunt of much of the antagonism engendered by job timings in the PTA plant. The *Solidarity* pamphlet, *What Happened at Ford*, produced a cartoon which amply demonstrates this (see page 149). This cartoon was later used by *Big Flame*, an emergent rank and file organization on Merseyside, and was popular with the lads.

The works-study engineer, the man with the clock, bore the brunt of them were young men. Their dads were workers and they'd been to grammar school, got a few O levels and jacked it in. They didn't believe in the Ford Motor Company either. It was just their job.

Some of them were attending evening classes, for a qualification in works management, or personnel management. A bit of work study and a bit of industrial sociology and psychology. They didn't like it much. 'It's all a load of baloney tha'. As far as I can see it's all about manipulation. And the lecturer's only there for the cash. I don't blame him, like, but it's a bit difficult to take it seriously. I'm going to pack it in and go to India.' The few that I spoke to were sympathetic towards the workers, one of them in particular being even more dubious about the science of job timings than the lads themselves. Tony coped with it all through jokes and a heavy irony – by laughing and calling himself 'the worker's friend'.

Apart from the timings themselves, the main problems faced by the operatives on the assembly-line related to *speed-up*. The history of the assembly line is a history of conflict over speed-up – the process whereby the pace of work demanded of the operator is systematically increased. This can be obtained in a number of ways, the most simple involving a gradual increase in the speed of the line *during* a shift. In other words a man may start a shift with a work allocation of two minutes to coincide with a line speed of thirty cars an hour and then find that he is working on a line that is moving at thirty-five cars an hour. He gets suspicious after a bit because he finds that he can't make

2. A detailed job evaluation scheme was introduced by the Ford Motor Company in 1967 which gave rise to severe conflict on the shop floor (see Chapter 7).

'Did the dead man have any enemies?'

time on the job. He can't get those few stations up the line which allow him a break and half a ciggie now and then. We have already seen that this practice was common in the pre-union era of the American motor industry and also at Dagenham. The long-service stewards and workers at Halewood insist that plant management made frequent use of this type of speed-up in the early days of the plant. Production managers out to make a name for themselves can only do it through figures – through their production and their costs. They abuse their supervision to this end. To serve the god of production is also to serve yourself and in this climate a few dodges are all part of the game. These dodges could be controlled though. They provoked a number of unofficial walkouts on the trim lines. 'The lads said "Sod you. We're not doing it, we're just not doing it." It worked as good as anything else y'know. We just said "no" and if they pushed it we went home.' No procedure could sort out issues like these. This was naked aggression being met with violent defiance. Management was trying to force the lads to do the unthinkable and they weren't having it. An agreement had to be reached and management conceded to the stewards the right to hold the key that locked the assembly line. Little Bob Costello had the key on the A shift, and the line speeds were changed with great ceremony, watched and cheered by the workers on the line. This wasn't enough for some sections. Some stewards had been able to obtain an additional safeguard. The first man on these sections was given an extra time allowance for counting the cars that entered the section. If the number of cars in any hour exceeded the stipulated line speed he was able to stop the line.

Some control then was obtained by a straightforward refusal to obey – by rebellion. Instances such as this one were commonplace in the plant before negotiated agreements had been made over the control of the work. Individual acts of sabotage were also common at this time. Men pulled the safety wire and stopped the line. These acts were part of a general movement toward job control and in substance differed only slightly from the formally articulated acts of defiance just mentioned. In an organized plant, however, sabotage takes on a different significance.

In the late 1960s the management at Halewood was forced to lower the minimum age of recruitment to eighteen, letting in a flood of lads who couldn't believe their eyes. What a place this was. These lads wanted the money. They dressed well, lived it up, with girls and music. The PTA plant at Halewood had nothing to offer them but money. They wanted to take their Fridays off and have a good time. They didn't want to put petrol tanks in motors. A gang of these lads worked together on the high-line. They started by peeling the foreman's orange, carefully, removing the fruit and filling the skin with Bostic The new remoulded orange was returned to the supervisor's bag. And they watched him trying to peel it. Bostic is a marvellous substance. It sticks and it burns. Bostic bombs were manufactured and hurled into the steel dumper rubbish containers. Explosions . . . flames twenty feet high. Someone could have been killed. On the trim lines they started pulling the safety wire. On one shift after the 1970 strike the line was stopped on thirty-six occasions. Foremen were restarting the line without checking.

In one respect incidents like these involve a fundamental challenging of the whole thing because these lads just didn't want to produce motors. This denial is so fundamental that it has nothing whatsoever to do with trade unionism. In the summer of 1969, for example, the convenor met the works manager who asked him if there was any dispute outstanding that they could sort out. There wasn't, but the weather was beautiful – hot and sunny. The lads kept coming in late from their dinner breaks. 'If they can play football they can work. They're just a lazy bunch of bastards.' It got hotter and hotter, it was too hot to work. 'But they played football . . .' They weren't going to work – take the roof off. Senior plant management went into the paint shop to check the complaint. One of them was streaming with sweat. 'What did the lads want?' They wanted iced lime juice. This unfortunately couldn't be supplied but would orange be all right? Yes, orange would do fine. They drank it and went home.

Trade unionism is about work and sometimes the lads just don't want to work. All talk of procedures and negotiations tends to break down here. The lime juice incident illustrates this well. It could be coped with, it was good fun but it had little to do with conventional union–management relations. There comes a point, however, where certain sorts of individual action come into direct conflict with the very nature of trade union collectivism. The steward organization was developed to protect the members against management and, as such, an important part of its function was to obtain a degree of internal discipline within the workforce. Bostic bombs could kill someone. The lads *had* to stop. They had to be sorted out and the convenor had to do it. Once more that was all. Just one more Bostic bomb and they'd be outside the gate.

All right Eddie. We'll take it from you Eddie. We'll not take it from him [the supervisor] though. We'll not take it from him. Treating us like little kids. We're not at school y'know.

They're not bad lads. It's just working in this fucking place.

Controlling the membership is part of the steward's job. The nature of the relationship between the union and the employer can mean that the steward rather than the manager disciplines individual workers for not working properly. This is one side of the picture. In an organized shop individual acts of defiance or 'laziness' can threaten the unity and organization achieved by the mass in collective action. But although individual acts of sabotage *can* be antipathetic to unionism, not all sabotage need be.

In the paint shop the car, after an early coat of paint, passes through the wet deck where a team of men armed with electric sanders – 'whirlies' – sand the body while it is being heavily sprayed with water. From the wet deck the car shell goes right through the painting system and emerges finished some three hours later. In 1967 Bert Owen was the steward for the wet deck. The lads on the deck played in a football team, went away on coach trips, drank together in the pub. They had their own nicknames for each other. A lad called John Dillon worked there. So they all took *Magic Roundabout* names: Dougal, Florence,

Zebedee. 'Did you see it yesterday?' 'It's clever mind – how they do it.' There was also Mumbles, Big Ears and Uncle Fester. And Bert. They sang songs. Played about.

If there was a problem on the wet deck, a manning problem, speed-up, if the foreman had stepped out of line, they always had a comeback. They could sand the paint off the style lines – the fine edges of the body that give it its distinctive shape. And nobody could know. The water streaming down, the whirlies flailing about, the lads on either side of the car, some of them moving off to change their soaking clothes. The foreman could stand over them and he couldn't spot it happening. Three hours later the finished body shell would emerge with bare metal along the style lines. They *knew* it was happening.

'The bastards . . . now look here, Bert, this has gone far enough. I've taken as much as I'm going to from them fuckers. You tell them to stop.' Stop what? Bert was always prepared to urge them to improve their work but really it was the equipment, or the paint, or the metal. 'All right, Bert, they can have what they want.' They'd sing then. After a victory. They'd stand there with their whirlies – singing. In the wet. 'Walk on through the wind, walk on through the storm, and you'll n – e – ver walk a – lone . . .' For the rest of the shift.

Few sections had this degree of cohesion or such assistance from the means of production. Things were quite different on the trim lines where the car assembly workers at Halewood met speed-up in its most developed form. While little Bob's key foiled the more flagrant excesses of management, other, more sophisticated, means of increasing the work content were more difficult to combat. These derive from the fact that fluctuations in the market demand for cars result in the speed of the line, and the mixture of models (and therefore jobs) coming on to the line, varying from week to week and even from day to day. As a consequence of this both the allocation of jobs and the number of men employed on a particular section has to be altered and renegotiated with each change of speed or model mix. In this situation speed-up can be obtained by an increased rationalization of work allocation at the higher speeds, i.e. a less than proportionate increase takes place in the number of men employed on a section and this manning ratio is maintained when lower speeds are returned to. For example, a hundred men might work on a section with a line speed of thirty cars an hour; with an increase in the speed of the line to forty cars an hour (by 33 per cent) the manning might be increased to 125 (or only 25 per cent) and then when the speed is dropped again to thirty the manning might be cut to ninety-five. Again the stewards maintain that such practice was commonplace in the early days of the plant.

The establishment of controls over speed-up achieved through variations in the manning ratios was obviously difficult to obtain given the company's principle of refusing to negotiate the allocation of work – a principle formally recognized in the agreement signed by the company and the trade unions. In spite of this, however, several sections had established unwritten agreements as to the manning ratios that would operate at the various speeds. By 1968 most of the sections in the trim and final assembly departments had established a code of custom and practice which governed the allocation of work and it is important to look at some of the ways in which these controls were established.

By 1968 the shop stewards' committee was in a position to establish a level of consistency in the job control exercised by each of its stewards on their section. Its ability to secure this consistency derived from the actual controls over job regulation that had been built up unevenly throughout the plant. Within the trim department areas of strongly developed job control coexisted with sections where such control was quite rudimentary. These strong areas of control were invariably associated with the fact that sometime in the past, the steward, or another operative on the section, had stuck his neck out and opposed the supervisor. One steward describes what happened on his section:

I've told you that it was pretty bad when we came here first. The supervisors used to treat you like dirt. I've always been able to stick up for myself like, they knew that if they messed me about they'd have some trouble on their hands, so it wasn't too bad for me. You see I don't think any man, any supervisor, should consider himself above another man. I don't think he should ask another man to do what he wouldn't do himself. A lot of the lads who came here first were given a really bad time. I've never been able to sit back and watch another man take a beating. To see a man struggling with a job. So I started telling the supervisor that he was out of line. Then the lads asked me to represent them – to be the steward – and I've done that ever since.

Such opposition frequently produced situations of severe conflict and sometimes this conflict developed into a personal battle between the steward and the supervisor. In order to establish controls over the supervisor's decisions, the stewards resorted to a number of different tactics. One of the most successful stewards on the trim sections obtained his autonomy by restricting his negotiations with the supervisor to a torrent of abuse and a recorded 'failure to agree'. Les explains:

I expect everyone has told you how bad it was down there in the beginning have they? It was murder. We had no representation. We were just supposed to do exactly as we were told. Well I started shouting my mouth off and the lads asked me to be the steward. That started it. I was working on the line. A member would have a dispute with the foreman and ask for me, but the foreman wouldn't get me a relief. I'd have to wait he said. So we stopped the job. Yes it was really bad then. You had no say in anything – in who did what or how much work or nothing.

Anyway we stopped the job a few times and things got a bit better but not much. They still thought that we hadn't to be listened to. So I thought sod this, we won't listen to you. I used to swear blind at them all the time – I still do a bit, it's the only way sometimes – swear blind and 'fail to agree'. Then we'd go up the office and I'd abuse him again. Call him a stupid bastard in front of management. It was the only way on my section. I had forty 'failure to agree's going at one time.

The bitterness in this situation exploded when one of the supervisors attempted to plant a component in Les's haversack which was subsequently searched by a security guard. Les, however, had been forewarned. Another steward tells the story:

Yes that did happen. Les used to curse the supervisors all the time on the trim. He used to cuss them up in heaps. He used to call them everything. I can't remember what his favourite one was now but he had some beauties. They're not supposed to lose their tempers see, the supervision, and they're definitely not supposed to hit a man. So there wasn't much they could do except put it in procedure. And they were a bit afraid of that, because Les was no fool and they knew that he could make them look stupid. Les had a tough job down there on the trim at that time and he did a hell of a lot of good work. A lot of the stewards didn't like the way he carried on, but he was the only steward on the trim on his shift who got anywhere. 'Failure to agree' we used to call him.

Anyway, he drove the supervision to distraction. They just couldn't handle him. So one of them put a flasher unit in Les's rucksack, and tells the security guard on the gate to look out for him. You couldn't miss Les. He used to wear this lumber jacket with a big sheepskin collar. Fortunately one of the lads on the section spotted this and told Les – 'Look out for your bag mate.' So anyway Les goes through the gates and the security bloke grabs him. Les throws up his arms – he's brought a few witnesses like – and shouts 'It's a frame-up'.

It was a pretty nasty situation. Paul Roots came up from Warley and didn't believe any of it. He knew Les like, and Les was for the sack. Anyway little Jimmy stuck to his story. They questioned him for hours, tried to catch him out and all sorts. It was like the SS. But little Jimmy didn't change his story once, and I think Roots suddenly saw that he was speaking the truth. He gave the foreman a bit of a grilling. It lasted all night long. In the end he broke down . . . in tears he was. He said he couldn't stand hearing Les cursing one of the older supervisors.

After that of course Les couldn't go wrong. He was the man they tried to frame.[3]

While this incident is obviously an extreme example, it should not be readily dismissed as an entirely misleading and atypical one. Many of the stewards experienced periods of perpetual confrontation with their supervisors. During the autumn of 1967, for example, the issue of job control became important within the material handling sections of the plant. These sections had previously been relatively unorganized, but had by this time produced two active shop stewards. The material handling department receives and stores components, and then distributes them to the stations on the lines. The workers in these departments were part storeman, part clerk and part fork-lift driver. They were split up all over the plant, and organization was difficult. Jack Jones was another of the young stewards on the A shift. He was smart and a bit cheeky. Like so many others he'd come to Ford's for the cash and with some idea that he might 'get on a bit'. He had been a long-distance lorry driver and then a storeman at English Electric. Ford's made him into a unionist. 'It was so obvious when I came here. It was obvious that you had to have an organization. Everyone was getting screwed. This place without an organization would be last.' Bill Brodrick who was a mate of his encouraged him to take on the steward's job. Jack became a steward in 1964. He had a lot of trouble organizing the section. His job made him isolated. It was impossible for him to be on the spot with a grievance. He had to be told of the problem and relieved from his job. Frequently he had up and downers with the foreman and the superintendent. In 1967 one of these culminated in Jack being sued for libel. In building up an organization on the section the steward enforces unwritten agreements from his supervisor. When the supervisor is placed under pressure by his superiors he often breaks these secret understandings. Jack committed his feelings to print. He filled in a procedure report calling the supervisor a 'perpetual liar' and a 'deceitful bastard'. The supervisor went to law, but he wasn't allowed to push it too far. Higher management persuaded him that the case was better dropped and Jack Jones escaped his chance to testify in the dock.

The right of the shop steward to have freedom of access to his members on a section, and his right to negotiate with the supervisor over

3. Les was a very complicated individual who eventually had his steward's credentials removed. He asked to be moved off the trim and eventually became a foreman. See Chapter 9.

allocation of work and the like were therefore established in the main by way of periods of severe conflict between the stewards and supervision. These rights were minimal requirements for a degree of job control by the men on the assembly line, and they had to be fought for. Once they were obtained the steward and the shop stewards' committee were able to build upon them.

This conflict over 'rights' is a fundamental one and permeates union–management relationships. It is not restricted to the shop floor. During a meeting of the Ford NJNC in 1970, the Company's director of labour relations, Bob Ramsey, clashed with the committee's secretary. Reg Birch, of the AUEW. The basis of the clash appeared trivial. They were arguing about the men who worked in the Ford plants; Ramsey claimed that they were Ford workers who happened to be members of the AUEW, the TGWU or whatever, Birch that they were first and foremost union members who happened to be working for the Ford Motor Company. There is no doubt that Birch and Ramsey were touching the nerve end of quite fundamental differences in principle. This clash of principles reveals itself on the shop floor in the conflict along the frontier of control. It is these principles that are at stake when the foreman starts to allocate work and the steward retorts 'Hang on a minute. *You* tell us what's to be done and *we'll* decide who does it.' It is a direct clash over management's right to manage. A clash of power and ideology.

The position of the steward in the car plant is rooted in this clash. In the early years at Halewood the day-to-day life of the plant was virtually one endless battle over control. The establishment of a steward in a particular section was clearly related to the attempt by the workers to establish job control in that section. If the steward wasn't up to the job he was replaced, or he stood down leaving the section without a steward for a while. Where a steward stuck with the job, he and the men on his section were involved in a perpetual battle with foremen and management. Even in 1967 the stewards felt that the overwhelming majority of the problems that they had to deal with on their section were related either to speed-up or 'the blue-eye system', the favouritism practised by foremen in allocating work and overtime or in moving men from one section to another.

The problem of overtime is an important one. Initially it can be seen as a point of tension between the steward and his members. The stewards didn't like overtime. As I was writing down one steward's comments he remarked 'that looks bad tha', going down there like tha' – "overtime". But it is my biggest headache.' Another steward made the situation quite clear:

> What causes me the most trouble? It's a sore point with me but it must be overtime. The distribution of overtime, insufficient notice, etc. I detest overtime but it's my job to represent the lads and if I wouldn't sort it out they'd soon get someone who could. Overtime and the movement of labour cause most disputes on my section.

This tension between the steward and his members over overtime is part of a general ideological struggle and is taken up later. At the moment it is important to recognize issues of overtime allocation as part of the conflict over control which the workers are involved in on the shop floor. Assembly-line workers work for money and they want overtime because it gives them more money to pay off hire-purchase debts, mortgages and the like. The foreman allocates overtime. He says who works when. This is part of his prerogative. His right to manage. The individual operator can exercise no control over the supervisor's decisions – apart, that is, from buying him pints in the local. On the assembly line one man is as good as the next man. The operator can stake no claims on the basis of ability or expertise. He is in the supervisor's pocket. If he doesn't behave, or if the supervisor just doesn't happen to 'like' him, he can lose his overtime for a week or forever. In a skilled work situation things are slightly different. At the Rolls Royce factory in Bristol, for example, men can control their right to overtime on certain jobs by virtue of the fact that they control the tools, or the knowledge, vital to the completion of the job. The foreman *has* to ask *them*. The assembly-line foreman can ask *anyone*. The emergent shop stewards' committee was a response to this situation. On many sections, the allocation of overtime was taken out of the hands of the supervisor and replaced by an overtime rota, administered by the steward.

Men became stewards in their battles with supervisors over injustices, over the workers' rights as opposed to management's indiscriminate right to manage. Frequently their response was crude. The vulnerability of their situation defied subtlety.

> We just said 'No. We're not doing it.' It was as good as anything else at the time.

> They'd say: 'You've got a complaint?'

> We'd say: 'No, we're all right. We've not got any complaints.'

They'd say: 'But what about the line speed, the work allocation. I thought you were complaining about that.'

We'd say: 'No, it's all right now. We're happy as it is. We're only complaining if you try to change it.'

They'd say: 'Oh, but we are going to change it. The speed must be changed.'

We'd say: 'Well we're not doing it. Y'er not on.'

Richie Rowlands had a classic. He'd say 'all right off we fucking pop'. It used to drive them to distraction. We used to say to some of them 'All right, put it in procedure' and y'know the stupid buggers would.

As part of the logic of management's 'right to manage', the supervisor can expect his instructions to be obeyed. In case the operator objects to the order a procedure exists whereby he can object personally and then through his steward. Where no agreement can be obtained it is assumed that the man will obey the order until a decision has been reached at a higher level in the procedure. The procedure, therefore, assumes that the supervisor has authority. It exists to safeguard the worker from a wrong decision. It makes no sense for the *supervisor* to put a complaint in procedure for such an act negates management's authority and the very nature of the procedure. In a climate where the 'right to manage' was being perpetually challenged by the 'rights' of the workers it is not surprising, and certainly revealing, that many supervisors became confused about what was theirs 'by right'.

As the organization developed the stewards presented more subtle challenges to management and supervision. In order to deal with disputes over work allocation most of the stewards (thirty-four) had had some training in the techniques of work study. Twelve of them had in fact decided to become work-study experts and had attended an advanced course on the subject that had been organized by the WEA. By virtue of the expertise gained on such courses, and also by their length of service in the plant, a number of the stewards had developed a far greater understanding of these techniques than had their supervisors. This had a number of consequences. For example, it meant that if an operator complained that he was being asked to do too much work, the steward was able to base a case upon the efficacy of the job timings which often served to drive a wedge between the supervisor and the works-study department. In these arguments the steward usually had to rely upon intuition, but one steward who had been bought a stopwatch by the men on his section was able to make more accurate checks upon the timings. It was through negotiations of this sort being carried out by individual stewards on their sections that the shop stewards' committee was able to establish an agreement for the whole PTA plant which prevented management re-timing any job without the prior agreement of the steward involved. Controls that were established within certain sections could therefore be extended through the committee to other sections which previously had not achieved such controls. Certain sections, however, still demonstrated greater worker control over job allocation than others, and the expertise and experience of the steward was one of the factors which explained this uneven development. Given the timings of the jobs that had to be manned on a particular section, there were any number of ways in which these jobs could be allocated to the men who worked on the section. As with most things there is an easy way and a hard way, and on several sections of the trim and final assembly departments the steward was more likely to know the easy way than the supervisor. A combination of this expertise and support from the men on their sections resulted in the steward's allocating work on at least six of the eighteen sections of the trim and final assembly departments in 1967. Given the speed of the line and the model mix, these sections functioned almost autonomously, with all the coordinating tasks being performed by the shop steward.

One of the stewards described the situation in this way:

I'm always in early. This means that I can check with the supervisor on line speeds and the model mix. Then I walk up and down the section to show the lads that I'm in. I talk to all the lads to make sure that everything is all right. I explain to them the manning changes if there are any. I discuss things with them to make sure that they are right in the picture.

You see I've been working on this section now for six years and I know the jobs much better than the supervisor can. The other thing of course is that the lads trust me more than him. So it's easier all round.

These controls over the job gained the operative a degree of autonomy from both supervision and higher management. Through their steward they were able to regulate the distribution of overtime, achieve a degree of job rotation within the section, and occasionally sub-assembly workers, in particular, were able to obtain 'slack' work schedules. But there were quite precise limits to the way in which workers can run the section. An example of these limits was revealed on the wet deck. The lads didn't like working in the plant. They looked forward to the weekends. The Friday shift was the worst. Particularly on nights, because it messed up your Saturday as well. So the *Magic Roundabout* lads decided to have a rota. Eight of them contributed to a pool. Every eighth week one of them took the Friday shift off, and got paid a shift's money from the pool. It became too regular, too open and was noticed by management. Friday absenteeism is a problem in a car plant. Perpetual absenteeism, like lateness, is a sacking offence. So management intervened with threats and the pool was abandoned. Not a few managers found examples of working-class collectivism such as this one emotionally attractive. A member of the Central Industrial Relations staff at Warley, for example, explained the militancy of the Halewood plant in terms of Liverpool's working-class tradition:

They say that there are a different type of people in the North. They're not as materialistic as the people in the South. They've not got their own houses or their own cars. They're much more easy going altogether. They don't take life so seriously. Apparently if they go in for a claim that is just not on, they prefer to be told to 'fuck off out of it'. That's how labour relations are conducted up there. Now in Dagenham they'll come in with a claim that you know and they know is hopeless and you'll argue round and round it all day. In Halewood you'd just say 'fuck off' and that would be the end of it. They're much more easygoing there; the men are much more independent of their wives; they drink more; go and watch the football ... I suppose they'll change. When they get into debt with buying a house they'll have to go to work I suppose.

Do you think that that would be a good thing?

Ah, now that's a *philosophical* question not a *business* question. It's like those questions on class we were discussing earlier; they make life very complicated if you think too much about them. I can see that it wouldn't be a good thing. I can see that there's something attractive about that way of life; but it's not much good for business. And business is what counts I suppose.

And business *is* what counts. However things *should* be, that certainly is how things are. The need for capital to produce a surplus, a profit, is an inexorable need. It is this which structures the world of the shop steward in an assembly plant. The stewards may be able to prise away some of management's controlling rights but they can hang on to these for only as long as the needs of business dictate. Essentially the controls obtained over the job by shop floor union activities involved little more than a different form of accommodation to the more general controls imposed by management. Johnny saw this very clearly:

As I've said, I don't like Ford's. I don't like what they do, what they stand for, or what they've done in the past – in this country and America. I can see the time when the bomb goes up, you know. I can see myself leading the lads off my section and just destroying this place. I can see that happening. But you've got to cope with this plant as it is now, you've got to come in every day and represent the lads. That means you've got to set up some relationship with the supervision and with management. Sometimes I think 'what the hell are you doing? you're just doing management's job.' But I think its better for the lads if I do it. It *is* better for the lads if I allocate the jobs and the overtime because if I do it it will at least be done fairly.

While the controls established within the sections may not have involved a very radical challenge to management's organization of the plant, they were radical enough to reveal conflict between a worker rationality and a management rationality, and it was at times when this conflict became manifest that the vulnerability of worker control over work was cruelly exposed. While the stewards were able to exert a degree of influence over the way in which jobs were timed, and a strong degree of control over work allocation, they had not established any control over the market, and its expression in the variations in the speed of the assembly line.

A district secretary of the GMWU, an ex-convenor of the MSB plant at Halewood, explained how the absence of piece rates increased the vulnerability of the steward's position when alterations took place in line speeds.

They're killing themselves up there in that plant. A steward on that estate is on a hiding to nothing. They just won't be able to last. It's different with piece rates. A steward's job is a lot easier then. He can negotiate the rate and then let the lad make his time. If management wants to change anything the steward can start talking about the rate. Now up there the rate is fixed so the steward's got nothing to bargain with. He spends all his time arguing about workloads. They set a line speed and they get things sorted out and then they change the speed and he's back where he started. It's heart-breaking and back-breaking. They're killing themselves up there in that plant.

With severe variations in the speed of the line, even the most well organized sections had difficulty in maintaining and re-establishing 'traditional' areas of job control. One of the senior stewards concurred with the union officer. 'We're mad,' he said, 'we're crazy I think, sometimes I don't know why we do it. We're running flat out all the time and just to stay in the same place.'

The effect of the market upon the controls established by workers in the factory deserves further treatment, and in discussing the problems of job security in a car plant it will be possible to examine this and the vulnerabilities of the shop steward's position a little further.

Mr Ford declared that . . . there was much dissatisfaction in the United States as well as around the world with the British Company's situation.

Unless there was stability over a long period, such as three or four years, Ford of America, which this year has £328 million to invest overseas, could not consider making any new commitments in Britain. Things needed to be cleared up and trade union relations improved.

The motor chief, who as a boy aged eleven in May 1929 watched his father dig the first sod of Thames marshland to start the building at the Dagenham complex declared, before going off to his German plants, that there must be peace with the labour force on some lasting basis before any announcements of new capital facilities could be made.

The Times, 16 March 1971

Ford looks to Spain

The Ford Motor Company was given permission in Madrid at the weekend to set up a factory in Spain – a week after the latest visit here of Mr Henry Ford, president of Ford Motors.

The Government announced a general authorization for foreign car manufacturers to establish plants in Spain after a Cabinet meeting.

The news agency, Europa Press, said that the Ford Company is planning to build a factory near Valencia with a capacity of 300,000 cars per year, and that 90 per cent of the Fords made in Spain would be exported.

The report of the new Ford plant may be bad news for British car workers. Europa Press said that a new factory in Spain would not necessarily mean closing any of the Company's plants elsewhere, but it would certainly limit further expansion of existing plants in Europe.

Ford has long been interested in manufacturing in Spain, where labour costs are low and the Government bans most strikes.

Commenting on the decision to open the doors to foreign car manufacturers, the Minister of Industry, Senor Jose Maria López de Letona, was quoted today as saying: 'Ford is the manufacturer who has probably shown the greatest interest.'

Guardian, 27 November 1972

7 Insecurity and Struggle

In spite of publicity to the contrary, and talk of easy times on the dole, the life of a working man without work is often desperate. What most working men want of a job is that it offers them some security. Married men with children value a regular wage above all else in their work. Such men dominated the labour force at Halewood, and they consistently mentioned security to me as the most important aspect of a job.

The significance attached to job security becomes all the more important when placed alongside the fact that the production of motor cars has been characterized, almost above all else, by instability. The interdependence of the car plants, the proliferation of small, independent suppliers and market fluctuations have synthesized in the lay-off and short-time working. All of the Halewood workers I talked to had experienced a period of lay-off in the time that they had been employed in the PTA, and eight of the stewards and fifteen of the members mentioned instability of wages as a major drawback to working in a car plant. The Ford Motor Company in its move to Halewood attempted to handle fluctuations in the demand for cars through regulating the hours worked by a stable labour force, rather than by seasonal recruitment and lay-off. As a personnel officer put it: 'this has been a hire and fire industry for too long. What we have tried to do in this plant is to keep a stable labour force. Not to kick them out at the drop of a hat, but to try to give continuous production. That's the way to build up a loyalty to the Company.' Ford's operation of this policy made overtime for the workers on the line almost obligatory during periods of peak demand. The shop steward organization grudgingly accepted this, provided that 'proper notice' was given. However, the policy was no safeguard against the market. Market recession brought with it short-time working.

In the summer of 1965 for example, the Company introduced a period of short-time working in which the hourly paid employees in all its British plants were put on a four-day week. The joint steward committee of the three Halewood plants met to consider the situation and produced a three-page leaflet on short-time working which was distributed throughout the trade union movement. In this they explicitly attack the meaninglessness of 'continuity of employment' at Ford's – a concept which had been one of the keystones of management's negotiating position within the Halewood plants. To quote from the leaflet at length:

The trade unions agree to commit their members to a policy of a high amount of overtime during the peak spring and summer periods when schedules are running high, as opposed to the hiring of extra labour who would be fired when a schedules drop. They also agree to 'mobility of labour', whereby men are constantly redeployed to maintain efficiency of plant operations, often with great inconvenience to the men concerned. Both these measures are patiently endured, and much cooperation is given. The reward for this is labelled 'continuity of employment', virtually a guaranteed five-day week, and yet the Ford Motor Company, the only company to have secured such agreements, is the first of the motor car manufacturers to cast its employees on to short-time working and imperil their livelihood with redundancy tactics.

The trade unions are also angry at the complete lack of prior consultation and ultimate refusal of negotiation. This, despite the case that can be made by ourselves for the non-necessity for the Ford Motor Company to resort to the drastic measure of introducing short-time working. Had the desire been great enough, here was a splendid opportunity for the Ford Motor Company to make a magnanimous gesture to its workpeople and at the same time reap tremendous benefits for its Halewood plant. This plant, so stricken of late with quality problems of the highest magnitude, from a multiplicity of sources, also in the throes of a mighty expansion programme, could have set its house in order and benefited immensely by merely cutting back its production schedules, at an estimated negligible cost to this wealthy company of some £300,000. This measure could have presented the Company with valuable time and an excess of labour which could have been utilized to successfully clear the back-log of defective vehicles in the selling line area, which at the time of writing, number a daily growing congestion of approximately 1300 cars. The workers in this plant are aware that schedules not intended for production until the October/November period, have already rolled off the production lines, the reason being that for some fifteen weeks prior to the annual summer shutdown, this plant had obviously greatly overproduced. During this period men were actually disciplined for failing to comply with excessive fifteen hours per week overtime demands, in addition to Saturday, which in the main were readily adhered to. Now we are callously confronted with 'short time'. After impressing upon us for months the importance of building 'quality' into the job, which responsibility we have readily accepted as it is our 'bread and butter' at stake, the Company now choose to ignore our suggestions to improve the situation. We are now facetiously informed that it is not Ford's intention to attempt to build Rolls Royces, thus indicating that once again it is the sole prerogative of the Ford Motor Company, to the exclusion of the trade unions, to determine the future of Halewood and its workers.

The committee then was severely critical of management's failure to enter into consultation with them before arranging the short-time working. In this, and in their treatment of quality and overproduction, the stewards raise the questions of market forces and managerial prerogatives. This strikes at the heart of power and politics within a car plant; and the history of the Halewood stewards' committee, and of motor car production generally, is played upon themes such as these. Again and again they occur. During the last six months of 1967 the production was halted in the PTA plant on two occasions and the workers were laid off and sent home. One of these lay-offs occurred in the middle of the night, the other at a more civilized hour. This one occurred at 2.30 on a Wednesday afternoon and lasted until the following Monday. During the previous weeks the number of cars in the storage parks around the estate had been increasing gradually. The plant was overproducing. The cars that were being produced weren't being sold and so on the Wednesday production was brought to a halt and five thousand men were laid off.

On that day I was in one of the material handling sections talking to the steward and a few of his members. After the dinner break several of the men reported a rumour that the plant was to shut down. The steward asked me if I had heard anything about a potential lay-off. I told him that I had been in the Personnel Department that morning and had talked with the convenor during the dinner break but had heard no mention of a lay-off. By two o'clock the rumour was confirmed by the section supervisor and by half past two production was halted and the plant was empty and silent.

The men in the material handling section were angry about being laid off. They considered it to be wrong and unjustifiable that they should lose half their wages for the week.

It's always us. We *make* the fucking cars, we chase around here all day like fucking morons and as soon as anything goes wrong it's us who get the shit. They'll be all right up there in the office. They'll get their wages. It's always the same, we take the knocks for their stupidities. We've got kids and mortgages as well. They don't seem to consider that.

They didn't consider the lay-off to be unavoidable or a logical consequence of large-scale production. Rather that it was the fault of management. The management had made faulty predictions and had planned badly, but it was *they* (the workers) who suffered.

Furthermore it was felt that once management had created the situation by way of their own errors, or inconsideration, they then proceeded to manipulate the situation to their own advantage.

All you've got to do is to watch the car park. You watch the car park and you'll get a pretty good idea of what will be going on inside this plant. When the park starts filling up a bit they start to push a bit. Little things like, but you haven't got to be a genius to work out what's happening. Whenever we have a strike here we have it when it suits Ford's. Never when it suits us.

The market, then, affects relationships in the plant. Economic fluctuations reveal themselves in the balance of power on the sections. Given this, the actual decision to shut the plant becomes one of a number of strategies in the power game, and the game isn't over once the decision has been made. The men's biggest complaint was that they weren't given more than half an hour's notice of the lay-off.

They take a terrible attitude to the men on the shop floor here. I don't know how they behave as they do. They tell you nothing. Look, we've been laid off this afternoon and we haven't even been told that officially. They tell you nothing. All your pay can be stopped and they tell you nothing. That's typical of this firm.

Members of the Personnel Department explained the shortness of the notice by the fact that the decision didn't become inevitable until after the dinner break, and that right up to that time it was hoped that a lay-off could be avoided. Even if there is some truth in this explanation – even if the Halewood management were hoping for a reprieve from Warley – it doesn't adequately explain why the possibility of the lay-off was kept as such a closely guarded secret. The reason given for this secrecy by the stewards and several of the members I talked to, was simply that management was afraid of the consequences.

They see it like this see: they're going to shut the plant down at 2.30 and by that time they'll have produced so many cars. Then they'll know how many cars they'll have to get rid of, they'll be able to work their numbers out. So what they're afraid of is what the blokes will do once they know that the plant is stopping. Nobody trusts anybody in this place. What they're afraid of is the lads saying 'sod you' and either going home or doing bad jobs. It happens you know. When there's trouble like this you often get lads going down the lines with pennies or knives, scraping the paint off the cars.

In a situation ridden with latent conflicts, the decision to lay men off can be likened to a declaration of war, and it is not only the workers who attempt to exact reprisals against the other side in this situation. Often a depressed demand for cars encourages a supervisor to settle some old scores with his steward or with men on his section who have given him trouble. On the material handling section, for example, a skeleton crew was to remain in the plant during the shut down. The decision on the manning of the crew was left in the hands of the supervisor who announced that he intended to 'draw up a list'. The shop steward and several of the men on the section opposed this violently. One of them remarked that 'that bastard wants to fill the place with his "blue eyes" '. A group of the men wanted to crowd into the supervisor's office and 'have it out with him'. Jeff the steward persuaded them against this, arguing that it would be playing straight into his hands. Instead he went to see the supervisor and after a long furious argument it was agreed that the names of the skeleton crew would be picked out of a hat. Jeff said:

That's what we've got to put up with here see. Big Joe wants to run this section his way all the time. He'd have us saluting if he could. We've managed to get it through to him that we're not having it, that we want some say in what goes on here, by standing up to him. But it only takes something like this for him to think he can start waving the whip again.

The men objected strongly to being laid off; they had children, hire-purchase debts and mortgage repayments to make, and to lay them off with half an hour's notice wasn't right. The lay-off can be seen to produce a heightening of the critical attitudes that these men held toward the company. Turner (Turner, Clack and Roberts, 1967, p. 331), in fact, attributes the industry's strike record and the militant demands of its workers to the fact that men who possess a low moral commitment to their employer and who tend to be more like 'economic men' than other workers experience a very considerable instability of earnings. This example clearly reveals how the lay-off is structured into the world of the assembler, how the elements of instability, monotony and conflict over the wage–work bargain all cohere to produce situations of heightening conflict.

There seems to be some evidence that members of management in the motor industry are aware of the significance of insecurity of earnings. To quote Bob Ramsey, the Ford Motor Company's director of labour relations:

Men have been too easily bounced out of this industry in the past. We have been much too inclined to lay people off. We don't lay people off now unless it's absolutely necessary. You've got to draw the line at some point. But we don't do it if we can help it. We feel that the track shouldn't be stopped by either side. If we keep laying people off they are quite right to say 'why should I worry about production?' We want to get away from all that.

It seems likely that statements such as these, if carried into practice, would have a considerable effect upon work relationships. Nevertheless, it is important to remember that is is not so much the lay-off *in itself* that has given rise to conflict in car plants, but the coherence of other elements in the work situation around the insecurity of employment. Furthermore it should also be remembered, as Ramsey indicates, that the market sets very definite limits upon the extent to which any motor car company in Britain can guarantee security of employment to its workers. Given the instability of motor car production and the severe dependency of the assembly plants upon the supply of components, it seems likely that even where fall-back rates have been negotiated, the assembly-line worker will continue to experience insecurity of earnings.

This leads to a second, more general point. Apart from administering the selection of skeleton crews on sections where such crews are required the shop steward is virtually helpless in the face of a lay-off. Job insecurity brings home very clearly the fact that while a degree of job control may be established by workers through the shop stewards' committee, to work in a factory means to work, to a very large extent, on management's terms. While a shop steward may well find himself in a situation where he has to challenge management's authority on the shop floor, he is more often in situations where he is forced to play the game management's way. Another senior executive of the company saw it like this:

It's difficult to say what type of steward does best for his members. A militant may well force a few concessions, but we'll always be waiting to get them back or to make life a bit difficult for him. While a quiet, more reasonable bloke may be less dramatic he'll probably get more for his members because if he's in any trouble we'll help him out. We make concessions to him that we wouldn't make to the other bloke.

In the face of a powerful, prestigious adversary, the soft-sell is often the best form of attack and self-defence. This is particularly the case if you're meeting him on his home ground. It takes a lot of courage, conviction and confidence to stick out a confrontation with a manager in a posh office, desk, carpet, good suit. And you in your overalls. It's even more difficult if he flatters you and appears reasonable. Many stewards rarely get over this. For most of the time they play negotiations management's way. They learn the limits of the game and in the routine of their lives in the plant tend not to step outside them: 'You can't fight a battle every day.'

But sometimes they've got to. And this is what makes nonsense of most public debate on industrial relations. Too often it is assumed that if only the shop steward and his members had the 'right attitude', strikes and industrial conflict generally would be tremendously reduced. The only attitude that would ensure this is one of subservience and stupidity. For what the pundits fail to recognize, or choose to ignore, is that we live in a world dominated by capital and a capitalist rationality. In this world decisions are understood as 'investments', what makes a thing good or bad is the 'return' on it. Not it in itself. Everything becomes a commodity valued not for what it can do so much as the price it can be exchanged for. People too become commodities, for the commodity world has men's labour at its centre. Spun round by capital and transformed into charts on office walls. 'Labour costs' – that sums it up. Production based upon the sale of labour power. By men, putting themselves at the disposal of other men for over half their lives. In order to live they preserve capital and their bondage. It is not perversity that makes assembly-line workers claim that they are treated like numbers. In the production of motor cars they *are* numbers. Numbers to be manipulated by people who are trained and paid to do just that. To cut costs, increase output. And lay men off. As a commodity, so is their power to labour treated. This is not to say that managers are necessarily inhumane people. Many managers, and employers, deeply regret the need to lay men off, to make them redundant. But they recognize that it is a need, a necessity dictated by market forces, for this necessity applies to them as well.

There are real lines of conflict within a car plant. A conflict that will be more obvious at one time than another. But it can never be assumed away, for it runs deeper than the 'cooperativeness' or otherwise of the assembly-line workers and their union representatives. It is underpinned by the very existence of wage labour and the market. While a shop steward may well attempt to play the game management's way, in many circumstances this attempt will be fraught with severe tensions. These tensions, together with the vulnerability created for the steward by his position of mediator, can be explored by reference to two incidents. These incidents like the lay-off that we have just discussed are important in themselves. They have a wider importance in that they can reveal some of the general problems faced by the shop steward organization within the British motor industry and more generally still they can tell us a great deal about life and the human condition within our society. The first of these incidents took place in the July of 1968 and the second a year later.

On Thursday, 4 July 1968, 370 workers on the B shift of the PTA plant walked off their jobs. They elected a strike committee which contained no shop stewards and went on strike for two days. In the face of a threat of the sack, most of the men returned to work on the Monday leaving a core of around forty isolated at the Pier Head. The strike was provoked by a notice from the Ministry of Employment which informed the men that payment of dole for a period in which they had been laid-off was to be held up pending an inquiry. The importance of the lay-off as an issue in the plants is revealed again here. This particular strike involved much more than this, however, for it focused many of the conflicts and tensions that were prevalent in the plant during 1968. To understand these it is necessary to begin in the September of 1967.

Between 1969 and 1972 the British Leyland Motor Company and Rootes–Chrysler were involved in a long series of negotiations aimed at 'buying out' piece work and replacing it with measured day work. The Ford Motor Company had never paid on the piece anyway, but in 1967 it had completely restructured its payment system through a detailed job-evaluation exercise.[1] In September 1967 the NJNC signed an agreement which accepted the principle of measured day work and the introduction of a five-fold classification of jobs. Previously, jobs had been grouped under the headings of 'skilled', 'semi-skilled', 'unskilled', and 'women', with almost all the production workers falling within the broad band of 'semi-skilled' work. This was replaced by a complicated system of job grading. The system was based upon twenty-eight characteristics of jobs – which included such things as 'responsibility', 'level of fatigue', 'working conditions' and the like – each of which was given a particular weighting. The operation of job classification was performed under the guidance of Urwick–Orr, a firm of management consultants. Under this system five job grades were recognized and identified as A, B, C, D and E. The scale of payments for women being 87 per cent of the men's rate. In practice, grades E and D coincided with the old 'craft' category, there being no such grades for women. The agreement was linked to a wage increase which because of other changes cannot be simply computed. Most workers in the PTA at Halewood, however, stood to gain around a shilling (five new pence) an hour.

---

1. It is of some interest to note that many of the Ford managers involved in the implementation of the New Wages Structure at Ford's moved on to do the same thing for the Company's competitors. It would seem that we have witnessed an interesting variant of the 'politically motivated group of militants' theory of industrial conflict.

Money and the rate of pay had been a niggling problem within the PTA plant for the past two or three years. They had begun as the Cinderella plant, with a lower basic rate than the ones at Dagenham. Although they had been able to remove this disparity through organized activity they had not been able to wangle the advantageous 'plus rates' over the odds, for 'good behaviour' and the like, that had grown up with Dagenham. The rates paid by the car firms in the Midlands provided a further thorn for their flesh. These rates had been established through local bargaining over the prices of jobs in piece-rate plants during periods of full employment. They were quoted in near disbelief by the Halewood workers. 'Could they really be that high?' To state them was almost to ask for their confirmation. The failure of the union officials on the NJNC to obtain a satisfactory answer to their pay claim in 1966 did not ease the situation. The shop stewards published a 'wage claim' leaflet at this time which clearly indicates the discontent felt by workers in all the Ford plants. This leaflet (see over) drew attention to rises in the cost of living, increased productivity, the Company's profits and the rates in the Midlands. In it can be seen the embryo of the Parity Campaign and the sophisticated Ford wage claim of 1971. The Ford workers weren't that confident or that well organized in 1966 though. To have asked for 'parity' then would have been to ask for the moon. What they wanted was a rise and the 1967 package offered them just that. It offered the workers at Halewood the first substantial wage increase that they had received since they came to work for Ford. It meant that an assembly-line worker with four years of service would move up from nine to ten bob an hour.

The Company was not being philanthropic. As with the Five Dollar Day, there were sound business reasons for making such an offer at that time. Firstly, there was the problem of *merit money*. This involved the locally negotiated payment of money above the national rate. During the post-war period, strongly organized sectional groups on the Dagenham complex had been able to force local management into making quite extensive merit payments. By 1967 it had become an important issue within the Halewood plants. Already the payment of 3d an hour to the toolmakers had resulted in a stoppage of work in the PTA. 'It was a question of principle more than anything else. They told us that they weren't going to be pressured into making merit payments – that's fair enough – but then they go and give the toolmakers 3d.' The Company had never liked the merit system and it didn't relish the idea of its extending to Halewood. The system hinted

Wage Claim

On Monday, 16 August, the national officials met the Company directors to discuss the claim for a substantial increase in wage rates for *all grades of workers*. The results of these discussions have now been published on the clocks, and once again the generosity of the Company is *conspicuous only by its absence*, our employers saying that they *could not consider any increase until the end of the year*.

Most of us are aware that in order to secure an increase in rates, two main arguments must be established. 1. It must be justified and 2. Ability to pay. Whether these two points are made, the few brief facts as set out below will enable you to judge for yourself. The last increase, made early in 1965, represented an approximate improvement of 4 per cent, while the cost of living had risen, since the last rise in 1963, by 5.7 per cent in December 1964, the basis of these figures being the *official retail price index*, which was 109·2 in 1964 as compared with 103·3 in 1963, so it can be readily seen that in spite of the last increase our standard of living was that much lower and our wage value has deteriorated considerably since – so much for the justice of our claim. Now let us have a quick look at ability to pay. The number of vehicles produced and sold was 674,815 in 1964 as against 658,673 in 1963, an increase of over *sixteen thousand* vehicles, this being achieved by a much lower hourly paid labour force – indeed we had redundancy in 1964, followed by heavy and increasing terminations since. Profits in 1963 zoomed up to 25 per cent of capital employed, which means simply that our poverty-stricken employers made a mean average profit of £387.12.0d. per worker, presuming of course, that 'every employee' includes our directors, who are struggling to make both ends meet on an average income of £32,000 per annum. As a matter of interest, just work out how many years you will have to work to reach that sum in a lifetime – who was it said' – you Jack, I'm alright'? The Company have always maintained that the wages paid to their employees compare favourably with other firms engaged in the industry. Just how favourably, we will see, by a few comparisons.

Coventry: Hourly average rates: Standards 12/9d; Jaguars 12/9d; Humbers 13/0d.

Liverpool: Average hourly rate: Standards 10/6d and Massey Fergusons (tractors) a high of 15/9d is reached, and even in Scotland, allegedly noted for an attitude on thrift, BMC as long ago as December were paying 9/7d. American-owned Vauxhall pay 9/4d to Grade 1, 8/9d to Grade 2, 8/7d to Grade 3, all with a merit plus up to sixpence per hour.

Our officials have rightly emphasized to the Company the unprecedented feeling of discontent and frustration existing in all plants, a situation that has led to large-scale terminations of all grades of workers, and including many with long service.

Our union officials have taken up the cudgels on our behalf, and we should now demonstrate our dissatisfaction with the Company and our support for our officials by *positive action*. The ball is now at your feet, and the goal, a substantial increase, can be reached. Consider this and make your views known to those who represent you.

at a challenge to the hallowed prerogatives of Ford management to manage their plants as they thought fit – to make the 'right' payment for the 'right' work. One of the attractions of a new payment system was that merit money could be done away with and be replaced by a *controlled* basis for paying higher rates to particular groups of workers. It wasn't the payment of an extra 3d an hour to toolmakers in itself that the Company objected to, rather it was the mechanism by which such payments were made. Merit money allowed other 'less deserving' groups of workers to demand similar treatment. Measured day work offered an escape from this cycle.

Perhaps more important than this was the fact that in 1967 the Ford Motor Company's operations in the United Kingdom and Western Europe were entering a new era. Ford Europe was just around the corner and with it the planned, integrated production of Ford vehicles on this side of the Atlantic. Large increases in the rate of capital expansion were planned for the British plants and the Company was looking for a lucrative return on this investment. It wanted an increase in productivity and a guarantee of continuous production in the plants. These two aims often conflict and this turned out to be the case for Ford. The 1967 package, however, was an attempt to achieve both these things – to 'rationalize' production and industrial relations at one and the same time.

The Company needed to introduce measured day work and the Ford workers needed a pay increase. Agreement over the package proved difficult, however, because the men were being asked to sell their traditional job practices. Each plant was expected to produce a productivity agreement and the workers in the plants were required to agree to the new system before the Company would accept the signatures of the national officers on the NJNC. Under the package some categories of workers, and those in some workplaces stood to gain, or lose, more than others. Minor crafts like plumbers would lose out as would the production workers in the older plants on the Dagenham estate, while the production workers at Halewood would gain the greatest benefit from the package. The Company exploited these divisions within their labour force to the utmost.

The negotiations lasted over a year. Throughout this time the management was sensitive to any criticism that they were grading men. It was the jobs, they insisted, and not men that were to be scientifically categorized. The shop stewards at Halewood were not convinced. 'They say that all the time, that they're not grading the men, but you've got to pass their test before you can move from a grade B to a grade C job. I can't see much difference myself. If that's grading jobs I'd like to see what they *could* do if they decided to grade men!' The stewards were in a cleft stick. They knew that the new agreement was bound to lead to trouble but they also knew that the lads expected a pay increase. Also the management was playing on their antipathy towards Dagenham. After several meetings the stewards' committee finally agreed to recommend acceptance of the package. Throughout this period Mick Donnelly, the convenor, was pointing out that 'they've never had a money strike at Dagenham. All the strikes they've had, they've not had one that got the lads an increase.' In the last of a series of branch meetings discussing the agreement he recommended the four hundred workers present to 'accept the agreement, get the money into the lads' pockets and sort the problems out as they come our way'. There was more division amongst the membership than anyone realized. The four hundred at the meeting split evenly over the acceptance of the stewards' recommendation, which was carried by the casting vote of Bob Henderson the chairman. 'On reflection I don't know if I did the right thing but at the time I was duty bound to back the stewards' recommendation.'

The PTA, with the other Halewood plants, had committed itself to the new measured-day work agreement. The stewards knew that it was going to cause problems in the plant. But they had given very little away in their productivity agreement and they thought they could handle the struggle they would face when the agreement came into force. As yet there was no agreement anyway. Some plants, and the smaller unions were holding out. Faced by this intransigence the Company advised the national officers of the large unions, and the stewards in the Halewood plants, that they should put their house in order. Pressure was brought to bear upon the dissidents and the agreement was signed.

At Halewood the local management and the shop stewards cooperated to a considerable extent in the construction of the job profiles. Interestingly enough the plant management was kept as much in the dark over the weightings carried by each job characteristic as were the stewards. A member of the senior administrative staff at Warley explained that 'it was very necessary to ensure that no one in the plants knew of the weightings, otherwise the whole purpose of the new structure would have been lost. Local management would have been tempted to give a few more points to those jobs that they knew were going to give them trouble.' The implementation of the agreement soon brought that trouble to the door of the stewards and the plant management of the PTA at Halewood.

A grading grievance procedure had been set up as part of the agreement. Under this the Company intended to deal with disputes over job gradings as they occurred on the shop floor. The Company insisted that 'group claims' (i.e. a grievance that covered more than one type of job) could not be accepted. 'Grievances' had to be associated with a particular job. They mustn't involve many men at a time. They mustn't be big claims. The six months which followed the agreement produced over a hundred grading grievances in the PTA at Halewood. Only three of these resulted in an upgrading of the job. It became apparent that whereas the grievance procedure could deal adequately with 'mistakes' – such as the incorrect labelling of jobs – it was being faced with conflicts that were too fundamental for it to arbitrate. Continually the rationality of job evaluation was conflicting with the common-sense rationality of workers in the work situation. The nature of this conflict was revealed by the first grievance that was submitted by the PTA. The stewards considered this to be their strongest case and it was presented first for obvious tactical reasons. It was 'knocked back' by the grievance machinery and the PTA stewards knew then they were in for a fight.

The grievance came from the small-parts section of the paint shop. Prior to the new system of grades, all workers in the paint shop were classified as semi-skilled and paid the same rate. The new agreement created differentials within the shop and in particular it placed the small-part sprayers on a grade below the sprayers on the other sections. In its attempt to impose a new system of wage differentials the new agreement can be seen as an attempt to restructure certain aspects of work relationships in line with a new (secret) system of values. In the paint shop there was a clear conflict between these values and those subscribed to by the workers. The rationality of managerial efficiency conflicted with one which was based to some extent upon a collective experience of work. The slogan 'equal pay for equal work' cropped up in most arguments over this issue. The men were convinced that they were right. The grievance was placed in the procedure on three separate occasions and each time it was confirmed in its original grade 'by the computer at Warley'. Small-part paint spraying was to be Grade B work, and small-part sprayers Grade B workers. After a series of overtime bans and walk-offs, the small-parts section went on strike for two days in April and the rest of the plant was laid off.

By this time the stewards were likening the plant to a 'volcano waiting to erupt', and the approach to eruption was marked by two events. Firstly the fork-lift truck drivers had their claim for upgrading upheld and secondly the women machinists after two strikes – both of which caused lay-offs – had their work schedules slackened and their wage rates increased. These two events had a dramatic effect upon the workers on the line. The fork-lift drivers' job was seen to be one of the better ones in the plant. Compared with working on the line it was a 'cushy number'. Before the agreement it was a semi-skilled job, like all the jobs on the line, now it was a grade above assembly-line work. One assembler put his complaint this way:

> There are no good jobs in this place but theirs is one of the best ones. I don't see why they should get paid more than us. Why? – I just can't see it. We *make* the cars, and we work a damn sight *harder* than they do. Yet they're on a higher grade than us ... it don't make sense to me.

Two things were happening to the assembly-line worker. He saw himself being paid a rate just above that paid for sweeping up, and he was being laid off. He didn't understand why the new payment system was discriminating against him. He didn't like it and he liked being laid off less. The strikes by the women increased the frustration of these workers. It was like a whip to their backs. Here were they being laid off because the women were 'having a go'. Why for Christ sake didn't they have a go as well? At least that would be something positive, if only blindly defiant. 'The women', they claimed, 'are the only men in this plant.'

A further, extremely important, feature of the situation was the crisis that the 1967 Agreement had created for the stewards' committee. The committee hadn't anticipated the problems that they had come up against and which they were having to face every day. It hadn't anticipated them and it had no plan to deal with them. The committee was abdicating its position of leadership and the plant was becoming fragmented.

The strikes by the women had a cathartic effect upon the assembly-line workers who claimed that 'those tarts have taught us a lesson. We ought to go down there and shout a fucking big "thank you".' Of no less importance was the effect that the strikes had upon the women and the shop stewards. Mick, the convenor, had too many problems. He had been one of the main advocates of the deal within the stewards' committee. While he had not been convinced of the philosophy behind the deal, he did see the implication of job grading to be an important breakthrough for the production worker against the craft worker. Mick believed in the evils of capitalism, but he also believed in science, reform and progress. In the November of 1967 I spent a long drinking evening with him and Frank Banton in the Garston Hotel. Throughout the evening he argued that the grading agreement was an attack on the skilled worker who had for too long benefited at the expense of the semi- and unskilled. This it was. But it was an attack on only *some* skilled workers. It was also an attack upon some of the practices of the production worker. The failure of the grievance procedure to sort out disagreements put Mick in an impasse. It also created a lot of work for him. As he walked around the plant he would be stopped frequently and regularly by stewards. 'Hey flat face when are you going to . . .' The stewards understood that he was busy. He had a hell of a job – 'More than one man can stand. He's back in the plant most evenings. He hardly ever gets home.' But he was becoming a bit blase. 'If I took everything up that they asked me to I'd be in and out the office like a fucking yo-yo.' In a way he was right of course but by 1968 he wasn't in a position to tell the good from the bad – the issue to fight on and the issue to play down. The grading grievances had thrown him off course and he was no longer sure where he was going.

One of the problems that had been left to solve itself was in the sewing room. This was not one of the strong points of the steward organization and the supervision there were very much in the ascendance. The women had been complaining for weeks about working 'tight schedules'. They were being asked to work too hard. In Mick's absence at a National Conference Eddie and Gerry had made some headway with the dispute. They were a lot younger than Mick. They were concerned about the women and their problem. The women liked them and they became a pair of folk heroes in the sewing room. Trouble flared up when Mick returned. His sense of humour at last got the better of him. 'Shut up you cod face' he said to one of the older women and that was that. This wasn't a folk hero. He was the devil incarnate. They took off. Another lay-off was in sight.

By this time the plant was in such confusion that Mick's only policy was to prevent lay-offs – keep the plant running, play down sectionalism and hope for the best. After some negotiations with management, an agreement was reached over the schedules and the women were summoned by telegram to a plant gate meeting at seven in the morning. Keep the plant running at all costs. But the women weren't having any. They all turned up in their going-out clothes. They'd go back to work all right, but not today. They were off to town, they'd come back tomorrow.

The grading strike came soon afterwards. The sewing machinists claimed that they should be Grade C and a demand for reassessment had been placed in the procedure. After months of waiting they had got no reply. In frustration the Dagenham women went on strike with the Halewood women in support.[2] The strike ran for over a week and after a meeting and a cup of tea with the Labour Minister of Employment the Dagenham women voted to return to work. Jack Scamp was going to investigate. But where did this leave the Halewood women? Again they received telegrams. This time they were to meet at 11 a.m. on the Sunday in the Adelphi Hotel. A return to work was certain but the women felt that they were being used. All through the strike they had felt that. Now it was Mick again with his telegrams and the Adelphi Hotel. I stood at the back. A bit different from Transport House. Thick, plush carpets and seats. I hadn't been in the Adelphi before, neither had most of the women. I'd seen Harold Wilson wave from the balcony in 1964, but I'd never been inside. Now it was full of factory women. They had a laugh in their best clothes. Solid middle-aged women with round faces and brown coats with small fur-trimmed collars. Slight girls with short cropped hair, short green leather coats, lace-up shoes and small square handbags. Not your Chelsea girls. These were girls with more than a touch of hardness about them. A hardness that comes from early mornings in the cold, late nights and terraced back-to-backs. A hardness that comes from being working class in Liverpool.

They went back to work but they didn't like it, and they liked Mick less and less. 'How do you get rid of convenor?' asked one. A year ago it would have been a violation of a question. In the summer of 1968 it was becoming more and more of a concrete possibility that had to be dealt with. Gerry and Eddie were perplexed. Gerry was the secretary and money man but he didn't know who was paying for the Adelphi and the telegrams. 'It must be Ford's I suppose,' he said, looking at his shoes. By July, then, things were confused in the PTA plant.

Before looking at the July walkout it should be made clear that the introduction of the grading system which had triggered off the chaos was not a managerial foible but a direct consequence of capitalist production. A vital economic necessity created by the state of

2. For an account of the development of the strike at Dagenham see Friedmann and Meredeen, 1980.

> Job evaluation must by its nature contain subjective elements or as the ILO manual, *Wages*, well put it, points rating 'uses system but not science in the grading of jobs'.
>
> The discrimination against the machinists was symptomatic of the Company's more general discrimination against women. Of 38,000 male production workers, 9000 were on Grade C – roughly one in four. The 850 female production workers included only two in Grade C – one in 400. Even with technical and clerical work included there were only 12 women in C. There were no women at all in the two top grades D and E.
>
> Report of the Court of Inquiry under Sir Jack Scamp into a dispute concerning sewing machinists employed by the Ford Motor Company (Cmnd 3749, August 1968, p. 16).

competition in the motor industry in the 1960s. A necessary feature of the new agreement was that it cut across traditional and accepted patterns of differentiation within the labour force. Conflict was an almost inevitable consequence of this process. In 1968 some 14,000 man-hours were lost through strikes in the PTA at Halewood. Most of these stoppages were connected in some way with the new grading system. By 1969, if not before, higher management had come to recognize this. Ramsey made this clear:

The system in the Midlands is a jungle. There is no supervision; the rate is the supervisor. It's just sheer moral blackmail. We grasped the nettle in 1967 and introduced a new wages structure. We knew what to expect. Men who originally were paid the same found themselves in different grades. It was an immense job and it caused great bitterness – you were in Halewood at the time so you couldn't help but notice it. But it had to be done. It was one of the inevitable consequences of change.

On 4 July 1968 then, as part of this inevitable consequence of change, some 370 men walked off their jobs in the trim and final assembly departments of the plant. Not all of the men in these departments participated in the strike. Those who worked on sections with a strong shop steward and established areas of job control were persuaded by their steward to stay in the plant. One of these stewards describes the situation:

It was just after the dinner break. One of the lads on the section said 'the trim lads are walking out'. Well all the lads stopped work then. They didn't know what was happening and they wanted to find out. They wanted to be in on it like. It was something exciting I suppose, and they were all steamed up about how the women had been on strike. Anyway we had a bit of a meeting and I had a talk with them. I told them it was stupid to walk out without knowing what was going on. Without knowing what it was all about like. They agreed and I said that I'd try to find out what was happening so that we could talk properly about it.

On the trim sections the situation was rather different. At that time, a number of resignations by shop stewards had resulted in a situation where there was no established steward within the department. In the trim there were no sectional meetings or discussions. The men simply walked out. Again a steward describes what happened:

It was all over the notice from the Labour about the dole. A number of the lads on my section were really pissed off about it. We all were in fact. The section next to us stopped work and a lot of lads started walking past. Some of them were running and shouting. The lads on my section said 'fuck it' and joined in. They were really fed up like. Ready for anything half of 'em. I couldn't see any sense in what they were doing. I couldn't see what they were trying to achieve. I couldn't stop them though. They were past talking. They just wanted to get outside the gate. I thought, 'If that's what you want you go ahead and do it.'

Another remarked:

I've seen nothing like it in my life. We had no warning or nothing. They just went outside the gate. Hundreds of them just walking off the job; just like that.

This then was a wildcat strike. The lads were out the gate, over the road and on the hill. Bob Henderson was shouted down and a strike vote carried unanimously. The shop stewards' committee had lost control. An unofficial strike committee was elected and a meeting was called at the plant gates that evening to picket the night shift. The picket was unsuccessful and within two days the strike was over. A letter sent by the Company to each of the strikers threatening them with dismissal resulted in all but forty of them returning to the plant for work on the Monday. A meeting at the Pier Head, arranged for that day, was attended by only three of the strike committee and was addressed by Mick and Bill Brodrick. The formal leaders had regained control, as they were bound to, and it was left for them to negotiate the reinstatement of the intransigent forty with the Halewood plant management.

Strikes are complicated phenomena. Moments when the commonplace of everyday life take on a depth and richness that pushes back the grey. Elements of the mundane become highlighted; they are

Five views of a dispute

The branch chairman (the constitutionalist)
We've got to accept it [i.e. the lay-off]. As long as we have unofficial stoppages – and we'll always have them – we're going to be laid off. It's no good moaning about it. It hits some sections more than others but that's the way it is. That's the way things are.

The district officer (the organizer)
I don't know what the bone of contention is. What is their grievance? When you get them back in the plant you want to get a vote of confidence in the stewards or we'll be losing members. I believe the NUVB have taken some off us already.

The convenor (the cynic)
They're going to stop out for six weeks for two quid dole. Marvellous isn't it?

The deputy convenor (the strategist)
There's no section in that plant with a grievance that the others haven't got. It's a plant issue and we've got to make it a plant issue.

The striker
I don't know what we're out for but I'm staying out for six weeks.

captured symbolically and return a critical glare on the daily routine. For strikes like this one interrupt the routine. And in the moment of the walkout its continuance was questioned. The symbolism of women, militancy, grades, humanity, dole, equality and much more besides, were jumbled together with an antagonism and a defiant 'no – fuck off'. They'd had enough and they didn't want to know any more. They wanted to do *something*. Anything so long as it allowed them to make some claims to manhood. It had all become just too much and they'd gone over the edge. Even in their anger they knew this.

They had returned to work on 1 July after a three day lay-off while the women were on strike. They would receive only two days' pay for that week. The dispute disqualification clause of the 1964 Insurance Act meant that many of them had been refused unemployment benefit payable in lieu of the two days lost through the sprayers' dispute in April, and the notice confirmed that this payment of benefit to Grade

B workers would be delayed until a test case had been considered. This notice captured the conflicts that the men had experienced in the plant over the past months, and the issues they raised at the evening meeting across the road from the main gate were particularly revealing. They were harshly critical of management and the Company, and their abuse echoed that of the men in the material handling section at the time of the lay-off. They objected to being numbers, to being graded and to being laid off. 'What's it to do with the Labour what grade I am?' asked one of them, 'I'm a worker. What's it to do with them if I'm B or fucking Z. Its Ford's this. Ford's and their fucking new wages structure.' A short crimson man, rounded into a navy donkey jacket was shouting to no one in particular. 'They lay us off when it suits them. They don't ask us. Its always when it suits *them*. If it suited them they'd keep us working on the brush until Christmas.' Men were standing around talking to their mates, talking to themselves or just shouting at the world. Someone tried to organize a picket-line as the A shift lads were already going into the plant. Somebody called someone a bastard. The A shift stewards came to the gate. Mostly it was confused. A man near me told me that the problem was profits. Someone else took up the theme, 'Yes, that's it. It's dead simple really. They want to get as much as they can out of us and pay us as little as they can. And we've got to stop them. That's what it's all about. We've got to stop the bastards.'

I was with Eddie and Jack Jones, another A shift steward who wanted to find out what was going on. 'For fuck's sake Eddie what's happening? Where the fucking hell are we going? We're going to have to get something sorted out. This is fucking crazy. We're going downhill fast. Really fast.' The strike committee stood on the wall by the embankment. Tom, a forty-five-year-old branch regular, was acting as chairman. They were trying to formulate a policy. The new wages structure had to be done away with for a start. They'd had enough of grades; they wanted to be semi-skilled again. They wanted no more lay-offs. The Company should pay a guaranteed forty-hour week. And what else? 'Equality with the Midlands.' They wanted to be paid the same rates that assembly workers were paid in the car plants in the Midlands.

They were also highly critical of the stewards. The elected strike committee insisted that they had been elected to do exactly what their fellow workers wanted. One of them addressed the meeting and claimed:

We're up here to do what you tell us to do. We're not here to tell you what to do. We're not going to boss you about. All we're going to do is to make

---

223 Strike at Assembly Plant – Halewood

Letter from the Company was considered relative to a strike of approximately 370 employees, mainly production personnel, which commenced in 4 July 1968. It was reported that the men had now resumed work.

Noted

Minutes of the Meeting of the Ford NJNC (TU side) held on Monday, 8 July 1968 in Transport House, SW 1 at 2.30 p.m.

---

suggestions. If you don't like them you can turn them down and suggest something else instead. If you don't want us you can vote us off. All we are is your voice. This is going to be a democratic strike.

For these men, the shop steward and the trade union represented their main source of control over a hostile work situation. By accepting the new agreement, the method of job evaluation and the grievance procedure, the stewards increasingly came to be seen as responsible not to their members but 'the computer at Warley'. The new wages structure was effectively isolating the shop steward from the men on his section. The structure also served to fragment the shop-floor organization of the stewards' committee. As claims were put into the procedure, sections came into competition with each other and a coordinated policy across the plant became increasingly difficult. Even a guarded acceptance of a managerial rationality had created considerable problems for the stewards' committee and the individual steward. The men became isolated from the decisions that were affecting them and on all but the best organized sections this led to a loss of confidence in the stewards and the stewards' committee.

This strike raises most poignantly the condition of these men. They spent their days on the line blocking out the world. They wanted to be things other than they were. Something they didn't know, which they might hate but 'it must be better than this'. They tried to keep their minds blank but the world wouldn't let them. They *needed* a strong steward organization. Without it they were without hope. They had been deserted, kicked when they were down, set adrift by their anger. And what they wanted, what they asked for was a form of peace. A guaranteed week, a rise, and things as they were. But the world isn't like that.

The strike was crucial for the stewards' committee because it marked a further fragmentation of the labour force and decline in the standing of its leadership within the plant. They thought that the strike itself had been a nonsense. A craziness. Going on strike for dole money. Where was the strategy in that? For years after it was referred to as 'the daft one'. For them an unorganized mass of workers was 'like a snake without a head'. The failure of the strike and in particular the moral abdication of the strike committee's leadership at the end was seen to support this view. As one steward put it:

> It's all right shooting your mouth off, but with this Company the chips are likely to be down pretty quickly and unless you know what's what then you've had it. You've got to know where you're going and you've got to know that the lads will follow you.

The strike flew in the face of all the principles of leadership and strategy that the stewards had built up over the previous five years. It was answering the madness of the lay-off with a corresponding madness and there was no sense in that. Nevertheless their disapproval of the tactic did not prevent many stewards from drawing some definite conclusion about the state of their organization within the factory. The strike was very much a sign of the times. By this time the stewards had come to realize that their involvement in the new grading system had seriously undermined the position of the shop stewards' committee in the plant. This particular incident demonstrates well this dimension of the shop stewards' vulnerability. Frequently, the steward is placed in a position where he can only obtain concessions for his members by accepting management's terms of reference, and often as a consequence of this he finds himself at odds with the men on his section. Although the strike may have been 'a daft one' it did bring home to many of the stewards that they were in danger of losing their troops. As a consequence of this the shop stewards' committee of the PTA reconvened the joint stewards' committee of the three plants on the Halewood Estate. The joint stewards' committee had been set up in 1963 with the opening of the plant and had performed an important coordinating role during the early struggles at Halewood. As production got under way the management structures of the PTA and MSB plants separated and a convenor was recognized in each of the plants. This, together with the establishment of committees within the three plants contributed to the demise of the joint committee. To a large extent the PTA committee had decided to go it alone. The transmission plant was much more of a key plant than either the PTA or the body plant. A stoppage of the transmission plant could stop the whole of the Ford Motor Company Ltd, UK. The wind didn't blow so cold on the lads in that plant and their stewards' organization reflected these easier conditions. The PTA and MSB committees did cooperate but the effectiveness of this was undermined by the personalities of the two convenors. Chalk and cheese you could call them. One a lifelong member of the AUEW. A dedicated unionist. A whimsical, fastidious man. Careful to the point of being fussy with a lean, long face that seemed permanently furrowed by concern. No one could have been less like Mick – old 'flat face' they called him, 'Nelson's Cabin Boy', the joker who'd seen the world. You could love him and hate him in a breath. An incorrigible trickster whose unionism was of the guts. Crude and to the point. They got together again at last and the joint stewards' committee met for the first time in three years and it met twice in a week.

The plant was in a turmoil. Bill Brodrick had been worried that a lot of the lads were going to tear up their TGWU cards and take out NUVB membership. At the first meeting of the committee the stewards of the trim lines made a strong plea for a new concerted policy on the grading agreement. Ronnie Davies and his mate, Bob Costello, both made speeches. Ronnie agreed that with some of the demands the lads were making they might just as well ask for the Birkenhead Brass Band, but something had to be done. The lads on the line had had a gut full. A lot of stewards wanted to terminate the agreement and go back to square one. That was impossible, out of the question because the agreement had been signed by the unions and was a commitment. Bill Brodrick was insistent on this.

If they couldn't go back they were going to go forward. But they had to go forward in unity. What was needed was a policy that would unite the men again; section with section and plant with plant. A policy that would let the lads forget about being Grade B, and that policy had to be a move for a pay increase across the board. The paradox of a world infested by money is that money is the only sure basis for collective action. The infestation is complete. The broadsheet *The Voice of Halewood* was resurrected and a two-page issue (see page 186) severely attacked the agreement, the grievance machinery and the government's Prices and Incomes Policy. It gave notice that the stewards had instructed the national officers of their unions to reopen wage negotiations with the Company. The 1969 strike and the restructuring of the NJNC were the dual outcome of these negotiations. More of that later (see Chapter 10).

This series of incidents reveals a lot about the steward's position within the factory. Earlier, this was typified as one which translated

Voice of Halewood

On Monday 8th July a meeting took place in Transport House, Islington, of the joint shop stewards of the Halewood Estate. It was called to discuss and form common policy on the steadily worsening situation arising from 'Wage Structure' grievances.

The chaotic situation existing of late, due to sectional or part-sectional grievances, is playing havoc with the trade union organization within the plants. It is dividing workers into fragmented groups and presenting Ford management a disunited and consequently weak front. Only by reconstituting a strong joint shop stewards' committee embracing the three plants can the divide-and-rule tactics of the Ford Management be combated . . .

Many sections and stewards are currently advancing the idea that all production workers should be Grade C, and that all the craft workers should also be in one grade. In other words a return to the old wage structure of skilled, semi-skilled and unskilled work.

Many of the stewards agree that this should be so. Part of the argument advanced in its support was the vulnerability of most production workers who are continually laid off without compensation. It was proposed that a strike be called in support of this claim. The committee gave his proposal detailed consideration. It was however felt that a better issue with which to unite the workers of the plant against the Ford management would be a claim for a substantial wage increase, coupled with a demand for a guaranteed week. This can be justified by the increase in living costs such as rents and the effects of devaluation. We also feel that the freeze on wages imposed by the 1967 Agreement has been penetrated by the action of the sewing machinists. It was decided that the joint shop stewards' committee, the committee representing all workers at Halewood, should support this campaign, and recommend a complete withdrawal of labour if these two objectives were not speedily achieved by our officials.

This pamphlet is the start of the campaign. Copies of the resolution demanding a pay increase and guaranteed week have been sent to officials of all unions. A series of sectional meetings will take place to report progress back to the shop floor. It is also intended to communicate with workers in all of the Company's locations and seek their support.

Never has it been so vital that Ford workers stick together and jointly present their demands. The company for which we work is becoming increasingly more organized. We are now merely a part of the Ford Europe combine. German personnel have made the well-known competitiveness of the Ford management even more intense. Much of the export targets of £225 million can only be achieved at the expense of the workers. We must be as eager for higher wages and improved working conditions as Ford's are for profits. The Company will not yield to us willingly. We will have to fight for it. We must be organized and we must be united.

That is our intention. It must be yours.

experiences – from one class to the agents of another. Unless he's careful he can find himself in the netherland. A hell where he's everyone's enemy including his own. In negotiations with management the steward must be particularly sensitive to the feelings of his membership. Without such sensitivity the steward, among other things, faces the danger of losing a credible negotiating stance. Although negotiations may be conducted around bluff, bluff can be called, and at that time the steward must be sure of his support. The steward – whether or not he is a militant – can, as a result of the action of his members, find himself revealed to be without clothes. At Halewood a well organized, militant shop stewards' committee found that its acceptance of the rationality implicit in a new wages structure, had placed its very existence in jeopardy. After years of struggle, planning and organization they'd been 'up-staged' by the membership. The nature of the militant's vulnerability, the very guts of his existence is captured by Sartre who writes:

> He is a leader when they are on the move; when they scatter he is nothing . . . He cannot realize his personal ambition, if he has any, except by inspiring in the masses a confidence renewed from day to day: and he will inspire confidence in them only if he agrees to lead them where they are going. In a word, in order to be himself he must be *all of them* (Sartre, 1969, p. 194).

The leader has an important *autonomy* from the masses, an autonomy based on the necessity for planning and preparation. Things that the masses have no time to do. But if the leadership becomes *isolated* from the masses, its autonomy degenerates into empty talk. A difficult position made all the more so by the nature of trade unions and their peculiar relationship with capitalism. As bargainers over the *price* of labour they are forced into an implicit acceptance of their position within the factory. In 1967 a bargain struck around such an acceptance caused a crisis for the stewards' committee. True, an overt challenge of management's 'rights' developed out of this, but the extent of the challenge – the degree to which the rights of capital could be challenged – was, and is, severely constrained. This challenge built up to the national strike of 1969 and the parity campaigns of the early seventies. But even then, the unevenness of the contest between capital and labour in the factory was apparent. So too were the dilemmas created for workers and trade union activists. These dilemmas became acute in the seventies and eighties.

The activist is not only active in such institutionally prescribed roles as meeting attendance and such formal organizational roles as the processing of grievances, but also in the playing of political roles within the union.

A. S. Tannenbaum (an American sociologist)

I left my car and went amongst them hoping for a rational discussion. They were a 'yarling mob' – crude, vulgar and unfit to lead the decent men I know in the pits. How in heaven's name men like this can possibly be elected as leaders of good Yorkshire miners, I cannot understand.

Lord Robens (a British businessman)

8 The Roots of Activism

The public school idea of the 'ringleader' takes a long time to die. It still infects the writings of many commentators on industry and it informed a great deal of the thinking behind industrial relations legislation. Yet recourse to the idea of a 'ringleader', a 'trouble-maker', distracts attention away from an examination of the *position* of the shop floor leader within the factory and in particular the nature of his *relationship* with his members. To understand the shop steward is to understand this relationship. The quotation from Sartre at the end of the last chapter gets to the heart of this. The steward acts and lives through his members. They are in him and he in them. The relationship is not the same in all factories or at all times. It is the living product of circumstance.

The unionism of skilled men for example is quite different from the unionism of the car assembler. The men who printed this book control their place of work through their skill. The skill controls the job and is solidified in the union. Their 'branch' is termed a 'chapel' and the leading figure in the chapel is the 'father', who is a highly skilled man. Nor are his skills solely physical ones. The union as the collective controller of these skills creates within the union leader other skills. In his negotiations with the employer he is able to call upon as great a variety of subtle arguments as his members have control of the job. Printers can refuse to print parts of a newspaper if they find it offensive. To suggest that an assembly-line operator might want, let alone try, to affect the colour or the shape of the automobiles he works on brings home the differences between their worlds. The skilled worker already has a freedom. A freedom which finds its expression in the dignity which printers and other skilled men derive from the superiority of their work. A freedom which, however inadequate, has characterized the unionism of skilled workers for a century and which found its political expression in syndicalism. Assembly-line workers are not dignified. There is no dignity to be gained from screwing on wheels so they don't think about dignity. The leaders of skilled men have many cards to play, both in their hands and up their sleeves. By contrast the steward on the assembly line deals only in the physical presence of his members on the line. They may be able to affect quality slightly, here and there, but basically they either do the job or they don't. Unlike the father of the chapel, the convenor of an assembly plant has few stopping points this side of a strike. One of the most significant consequences of mass production for the working class has been the increasing use made by workers of the mass strike, the sit-down strike and the picket-line.

The steward in the car plant operates within the continuous world of the assembly line. The content of the work creates no relationship between him and them. They don't want his advice on how to attach the petrol tank to the car body; all they want from him is the regulation of the quantity of work that's demanded of them. The Halewood estate is dominated by a large mushroom-shaped cooling tower. On one of my first visits to the plant I pointed it out to one of the senior stewards and asked him what it was. 'I don't know,' he replied, 'it never gives us any trouble so we leave it alone.' I didn't know if he was joking or not. You walk around a toolroom with a skilled craftsman and you know the difference.

The steward on the trim line will represent between 70 and 140 operatives depending on the speed of the line. Fluctuating line speeds, absenteeism and labour turnover all work against the development of a stable relationship between the steward and his members. On top of this the men he represents see themselves as small cogs, numbers; they hate their jobs and their life in the factory. One of the trim-line stewards put it like this:

> The point about this place is that the work destroys you. It destroys you physically and mentally. The biggest problem for people is getting to accept it, to accept being here day in and day out. So you've got low morale from every point of view. You're inflicted with a place of work and you've got to adapt because it won't adapt to you. So morale is terribly low. But you can build on this you see. You can't get much lower than hell and so you can increase morale through the union. Pull together sort of thing rather than dog eat dog. That's how I've found it on the trim. We're all in hell and you can get a bond out of that. We're all in it together like. That's where the union comes in.

This, after all, is what trade unionism is basically about. It is rooted historically in a working-class collectivism; not necessarily a class-conscious brotherhood, but certainly an awareness of a clear identity of interest between yourself and the next man. In an assembly plant this mutual identity is fostered by the fact that the next man could be you, for on the line you are nothing – interchangeable numbers.

What sort of collectivism do men create in this situation? What is the character of the trade unionism of assembly-line workers? In trying to answer these questions it is obviously necessary to consider the nature of the relationship between the activists and the lay membership – the masses. How do these activists emerge, as leaders from the mass, in a work situation where the machine age has done most to reduce all men to a common denominator?

The same steward describes his election:

> Three years ago this place was in a very bad way. Ford's controlled everything. We had no steward on the line at the time. The lad who had taken it on broke down. The frustrations and the pressures were too much for him. I knew Eddie, I'd met him at some of the meetings and he told me to have a go. So I stood. Somebody had to do it. I didn't want to be a shop steward. That's the last thing I wanted when I came to this place first. I wanted to get on a bit. But I could see all the injustices being done every day so I thought I had to have a go. It wasn't right that they were having to take all the shit that Ford's were throwing.

Frank Banton also became active in the early days of the PTA plant:

> When I came here first we had no representative. The odd steward was recognized as a spokesman but all the negotiations were done through the convenor. I knew that the lads were being brainwashed and kidded. The T&G was trying to organize the place and they were asking for volunteers – to work behind the scenes as it were. I volunteered and took up a job as a collecting steward. Eventually they persuaded me to take on the shop steward's job. I was pretty well known by that time and I was elected. I wanted to do it to look after the interests of my fellow workmen on the shop floor and to fight against these bastards here.

These two accounts summarize a wealth of experience. They contain the crucial elements of the emergent shop floor organization – conflict, sponsorship and a commitment to a humanistic collectivism, a strong desire to 'Help your fellow man'. The structure of the shop stewards' committee in the PTA was created during a period of severe, continuous conflict, by a few activists who couldn't stand back and watch 'injustices being done every day'. This is not an uncommon pattern, but rather one which characterizes the entire history of the motor industry. Plants are unionized by men who stick their necks out and survive because of their mates' support. Eighteen of the thirty-six stewards that I talked to were elected in 1963 or 1964, and each of these mentioned conflict with supervision or management as an important contributing factor in his election. These men had come to Halewood to get some more money, perhaps even to get on a bit. They quickly realized that they didn't particularly want to 'get on' in the Ford world and that as workers the Ford Motor Company was a force they had to reckon with. The lads were unorganized – 'it was like Fred Carno's Army, you wouldn't believe half, if I told you' – and they were taking a beating. People like Jimmy Black who had been a steward at Dunlop's, and Bob Costello with a life on the building sites behind him, expected to get involved. It had always been Bob's ambition to take out a steward's card, but men like him were exceptional. The vast majority of stewards had no intention of becoming active when they walked through the gates at the start of their first day of work for the Ford Motor Company. The Ford Motor Company made them active.

The influence that the structure of work relationships exerted upon the pattern of shop floor union activity at Halewood cannot be overstated. The stewards at Halewood were the men who said 'Yer nor on'. The conflict along the frontier of control was the backcloth upon which the history of the shop stewards' committee was woven. It forms an essential background to the issues discussed in this chapter. Having said this, however, it is still necessary to ask why it was that *particular* men became active within the car plant. Why didn't the men who became stewards remain on the sidelines? The short answer to this question is that the situation in the PTA plant created a need for them. But why *these* men?

Merseyside has a strongly developed trade union tradition which is lived out in the day-to-day lives of men and women – in factories, but also in pubs, shops and in the home. All the stewards were sons of manual workers, and well over half of them (twenty-one) thought their fathers to be 'strong supporters of trade unionism'. The heritage is handed down from father to son, to be remembered and fought for again. This doesn't mean that 'tradition' is handed down in a simple way, for class consciousness isn't the same as scouse pie, something which you eat regularly and acquire a taste for. Class-conscious workers don't magically produce class-conscious sons. The process is complex and troublesome. Sons rebel against their dads and what their dads stand for. But what is guaranteed in this process, is that the sons are aware of ideas which explain society in terms of opposed classes and these ideas can be turned to and called upon to interpret future situations.

My old fella was a trade unionist. Branch secretary, shop steward and all tha'. He always used to be on about the bosses ... the capitalists, the General Strike an' tha'. I didn't pay much attention to him. Him and the union caused a lot of trouble in our house. I wanted to be out in the street, dancing or having a few bevvies. The old lady used to side with me.

But when I came to this place ... Jesus ... what a place. It's funny I've remembered all the things my da' said. About the movement an' tha'. I've become as big a unionist as him now. Sometimes I wish I'd listened to him a bit more. He's dead now like and I'd liked to have talked to him ... I'd like to tell him tha' *I* know now.

The stewards were 'union minded' from the start. They accepted trade unionism unquestioningly. They didn't have to be asked for their dues. They asked for the steward when they arrived. Many of them had been active in the union in their other jobs. They hadn't been wild-eyed militants, the Ford Motor Company made sure of that, but they had done their bit. All but two of them were paid-up union members when they first walked through the gates of the PTA. Nineteen of them had had some experience of being a steward or a branch officer before they came to work for Ford's. By way of contrast, although only seven of the members in the sample were not union members when they came to Ford's only one of the remainder had previously held any sort of union office

What sort of blokes were the stewards? We already know that they were quite young – significantly younger than the national average for stewards. It could also be said that they had little respect for authority. In 1968 the stewards and their wives went to a dance organized by the Regional TGWU in the Bootle Town Hall. Frank Cousins, the General Secretary, was there to present awards to long-serving unionists. It was a good night and it was Frank Banton's round. Cousins was speaking as Frank got his feet to get the order. Pat was far away. Listening to Cousins. 'What do you want. Never mind listening to that stupid bastard what do you want to drink?' In the main then they weren't shy, retiring types. While they weren't all magnetic personalities, they all had something about them. In truth it would be difficult to serve as a steward in a car plant unless you possessed more than a hint of bravado – a bit of go. When I asked them how they would feel if the union had to pack up at Halewood, the emphasis of their answers was different from those given by the group of members. Everyone I talked to, stewards and members alike, would have been mortified if the union folded up at Halewood. Everyone felt that Ford's would have a field day and that the situation would be impossible. One man thought that 'it would be back to the salt mines here with this company's attitudes. It's only the union that stands between us and the rule of the whip in this place.' While many of the members (thirty) thought that they'd leave if there was no union, the stewards knew that they'd have no option – they'd be sacked immediately. After the initial shock many of the stewards attacked the whole, artificial basis of the question. It was impossible to imagine. It just couldn't happen. It couldn't happen because blokes like them wouldn't let it happen. If it was knocked down they'd build it up again – them, or somebody like them. 'Gorblimey, can you imagine this place without the union. That's a daft question tha'. You'll always have the union here. What could knock it back? All right, so they sack all the stewards, but you'd only get more stewards in their place. The only way that you'd get rid of the union is if you get rid of the men. After all, that's what "the union" is isn't it – the men.'

Others were less forceful, but nevertheless to the point:

I'd emigrate – I wouldn't stop here without a union. The iron fist would be back – y'know, 'stand by your beds'. The whips would be back . . . it couldn't happen though.

I'd make some attempt to form something again. Knowing Ford's as it is at the moment, the worker would be in a hell of a position. Without the trade union at Ford's there wouldn't be a factory. No one would stay here. The place would be in a terrible state. It couldn't happen though y'know. It would just *have* to start all over again. It's inevitable.

I'd feel sad from the sentimental point of view. We've put a lot of work into the union here and it means a lot to me. Then there'd be the practical problems. I would simply turn round and try and organize something. A workers' council . . . anything. Because without some sort of leadership it would be chaos here.

I couldn't see it happening. You couldn't leave it and accept it. If it came to that here I'd smash the plant up . . . have a revolution. If it came to that we'd all be lined up to have a go. We'd tear this place to pieces.

The stewards were the ones who would 'have a go'. Obviously psychological factors are important here.[1] The steward's job involves argument, perhaps above all else. Some people just can't cope with this. The men who came forward as stewards were, in the main, men

---

1. It is perhaps worth mentioning that the stewards and members were asked to reply to a series of statements which were intended to assess the extent to which both were inclined to *do* things rather than fret or forget about them. The stewards, not surprisingly, were significantly more inclined to respond in a positive way toward statements that favoured activism than were the members. This shouldn't be used to bolster the idea that there are different *types* of workers. People change. Events can change a man's relationship to the world and to 'activity'. The fact that a man wasn't active at Ford's doesn't mean that he will not become active. There is in fact some evidence to suggest that ex-Ford employees did become active trade unionists when they moved to other plants in the 1960s.

whose personality fitted them to stand up and oppose the powerful. While it is important to recognize this, it would be dangerous to leave it there – to explain activism in terms of different types of people. Much more than this is involved. There are many car workers with bravado who don't end up as stewards but are dismissed by their mates as 'bigmouths'. Some men take on the job, though ill-suited to it because they feel they ought to because 'somebody's got to do it'. Not infrequently these men find that doing the job revealed hidden qualities which they didn't expect to possess. Activism is, above all else, a social *process*, and talk of different personality types directs attention away from this. Men who become stewards have to recognize the potential in themselves and to have it recognized by others. This is why 'the steward and the union activist' cannot be formally distinguished and cut off from 'the masses'. The relationship between the two is – to use the precious and much-abused word for once – a dialectical one. Psychologism ignores the dialectic of social life. It also ignores *ideology*. Dominant personalities can dominate for good or ill. The use to which they put their abilities is not determined by those abilities. Activity is directed by values and systems of belief. An adequate account of shop-floor activism and leadership needs to go beyond the personalities of the people involved and consider the ideology of the activists and of the organization within which they are active.

Eric Pemberton worked in the garage at Halewood. He moved to Liverpool in 1963 having worked in the assembly plant at Dagenham for the previous two years.

I was in Dagenham in 1962 at the big crunch. The atmosphere down there was so much different from up here. Down there you could have a laugh and a joke and still get the work done. Up here when you're on the line you're just dreading coming to work. It seems as if it's a different firm altogether up here. It's push, push, push, all the time here.

In discussing how he came to be a steward at Halewood he said that he always seemed to get involved in the union. Often in spite of himself.

I decided to leave it alone when I came here but I couldn't. I went to the branch meetings and I was asked if I'd be a collector. Then the constituency was broken up and I was nominated as the steward for the new one. It's surprising really. People hear you talking about the union and that's it. You're the 'union man'.

I always think about what went on about fifty years ago. Think about what the trade union movement has done for the working class against unscrupulous firms. And there's still people coining in the profits. I suppose I just couldn't keep quiet. So they said 'take the job'.

There's no easy answer to the question 'what makes a union man?' They're often perplexed by the question themselves, but Eric, in drawing attention to both social process and ideology, provides us with a basis on which an answer can be pieced together.

To take social process first. In 1963 the Halewood plant was riven with conflict. A convenor was recognized for the PTA and MSB plants, but there were very few stewards. Several of the men who were stewards were 'phonies' – 'responsible men' approached by management and who had little credibility with their members.

Many of the workers didn't hold a union card. During this early period the important tendencies were present in the PTA which related to and supplemented each other. The earliest activists were attempting to establish the union in their own section and also to expand it to non-union areas in the plant. In these un-unionized areas activists were emerging, in response to the needs of their mates and of the embryonic stewards' committee. The emerging activists stood out in conflicts with the supervisor and attended the first union meetings called on the site and in the branch. They were recognized by their mates and by the 'established' stewards, and were prodded towards taking the steward's card. Many stewards tell the same story. It is worth spending some time listening to them.

Gerry Flaherty was to become the secretary of the branch. In 1963 he hadn't had much direct experience of unionism; but his dad had been a docker.

He was forever on about the union, the Blue and White. I worked on the buildings for five years, on the lump so I wasn't in a union but as soon as I came here I went straight down to Garston Office for a T&G card.

When I came here first there was just one shop steward in each department. I wasn't all that bothered about unions but I found that I was getting pushed around. So I thought I'd have a go at Ford's because Ford's were having a go at me. I started helping the steward out and then I was moved onto an unorganized section. I got a 100 per cent membership on it and was elected as the steward. I suppose it got spread around that I wasn't afraid to have a go.

Billy Rees worked in the trim manufacturing department. He was the only steward who read the *Morning Star* at Halewood. He was a quiet, deferent man who had decided to give the union a rest for a bit. John Castle was his steward. Earnest, if fussy, and 'a good bloke'.

John Castle was the steward for the whole area. He was being badly messed about by management. He was in a really difficult situation. On top of that I was really disgusted by the way we were being treated. Y'know we were being sent home at 1.30 in the middle of the night shift with no warning. I said to myself 'I'll have to get involved here.' But it was out of loyalty to John Castle really. He was on his own and he was getting no backing whatsoever. I had no intention of getting involved when I first came here.

These men came forward to support the organization and spread it across the plant. On several sections the earlier stewards were being deposed. Those men were either completely unsuited to the sort of job the steward had to do at Halewood or they were 'phonies' – 'careerists'. In either case they did not have the support and confidence of their members and were opposed by men who did. Men like Ritchie Rowlands and John Craig.

Ritchie:

I used to criticize the shop steward on our section. He was a nice guy but he was too nice. He just wasn't cut out for it. A lot of injustices were being let slide because he couldn't stand up to the foreman. It wasn't my idea to stand. I was asked by the lads to oppose him. They gathered from the talks in the tea breaks that I knew a bit about it. Y'see it was all one way in here at that time. It was the big boot all the time. I know that we came here to work but this place was amazing. The men still had a bit of pride. They also had their indignation.

John Craig:

In the early days we had a steward on the section who wasn't doing his job. You had to be prepared to have a go at management in those days and this bloke just wasn't prepared to stick his neck out. There were only two or three of us in the section who were at all active – me and Jimmy Black mainly – we asked the steward to stand down. He agreed I'd do a better job and stood down. If he hadn't I'd have opposed him though.

By 1966 the shop stewards' committee had established itself in the central production departments of the PTA. This didn't mean that the struggle was over. The organization was still not strongly established in all sections across the plant, and established sections could fall back if stewards resigned and management pressed that bit harder. Yet it was vital for the committee, if it was to exercise a coherent leadership, that such across-the-plant stability be established. An enormous part of its power within the TGWU derived from the fact that it organized and represented a mass of TGWU members – over 5000 of them. Sectional breakaways to the NUVB or GMWU, or even a large increase in the number of men 'in arrears', could do immense damage to the organization. Because of this the senior stewards and especially the branch secretary were on the lookout for likely stewards in unorganized sections. All stewards kept in mind the possible need for them to be replaced in the future; they groomed deputies to this end.

Billy Brodrick was the convenor and branch secretary in 1966. One of the problem areas at the time was 'material handling'. The area could justify a steward but no one would take it on on one of the shifts. Billy talked to a number of the blokes but only made headway with Jeff Burke.

> Billy Brodrick worked near me. There were twenty-four men on our section in arrears and so he asked me to be the collector. So I was a collector. They didn't have a steward on our section but the union had been pressing for one and got it. When the notice went up in the branch nobody put in for the job. In the end Bob Henderson (the branch chairman) persuaded me to stand. I knew no one would put in for it but I knew there was a need for a steward. So I thought I'd do it. I had to do it. Someone had to do it. I don't really think I've got the talent for the job. At times you've got to be a bit of a bully and I couldn't seem to turn it on.
>
> I thought I'd be a bit of a stop-gap. When I came up for re-election I went around every man on the section and asked if they'd take it on. No one would so I stood again. You'd be dead here without a steward. Things on the section have improved fantastically since we've had a shop steward. There's the presence of the union.

What the existence of the shop stewards' committee did was to impose upon its members a commitment to the continuance of the organization itself. That's why they were on the look out for likely activists and why the issue of a steward's resignation was such a horrendous one. The resignation issue will be taken up later. It is important here to bring out the fact that when asked about it almost all the stewards remarked, 'If I did resign I'd bloody well make sure that there *was* someone else.' Shop stewards are only human, occasionally men can no longer take the strain of the job and they resign. Although twelve of the stewards felt that in the case of their resignation it would be difficult to find a replacement, the general feeling was that someone *would* take the job on. 'It's a funny game. They come from out of the woods. I can't think of any *one* person but I'm pretty sure somebody would do it.' Other stewards – twenty-four in number – found no difficulty in naming the most likely candidate for the steward's job if they did resign. This continuity of office-holding is important and is borne out by the fact that the stewards elected in the 'established' sections after 1965 almost invariably mentioned an approach by their predecessor as their main reason for taking on the job. John Jaeger's account of his election on the trim in 1965 is revealing:

You're supposed to be here twelve months. In fact I had only been here ten months when I took it on. I was working with the steward when I came here first and we got into a bit of an argument with the supervisor. Anyway I kept my end up and when the steward left the Company he recommended me to take over from him. I wasn't too keen as I'd had experience of the job before. I knew how thankless it could be. But eventually I accepted and here I am. There's a hell of a lot of extra work you know. Especially if you're uneducated. There just didn't seem to be anyone else around who'd do it. I wanted the men on the line to have a representative who would do what he could for them. Rather than any idiot taking it on I'd do it.

Billy Lally had a similar experience:

The shop steward before me was a good bloke. I agreed with him and I used to help him. Then he was taken ill and resigned in the end. I used to deputize for him when he was off sick. I was his card steward [collector], you see, and I was the only one who would do that. Anyway when he resigned another bloke stood for his job. He said it ought to be me, that I was the best man in the section to look after the lads. So I stood. And I won. I just thought I could do a good job. Also of course it's good to have the respect of the lads.

If no immediate replacement could be found, necessity exerted itself before long, as Kenny Johnstone discovered.

We'd had no representation on our section for three to four months. It's impossible tha'. Being without a steward in this place. Nobody else would do it so I said I'd give it a try. I'm not all thar 'ot but I'm better than fuck-all.

If you work on a production line in an assembly plant you've got to have a shop steward. It's a necessity of life. At Halewood the potential stewards revealed themselves in conflicts with the foreman, in their attendance at meetings, in their talk in the canteen. Few of these men pushed themselves forward, their qualities were noted by their mates and by other stewards. They were approached and cajoled into taking the steward's job. They were trade unionists. Their dads were trade unionists and their ideas were sparked into life by incidents in their workplaces. The Ford Motor Company put the finishing touch on it. Around the assembly line their ideas hardened. They would never forget them now. Nor will their sons and daughters.

It will be remembered that the ideology of the shop stewards' committee was described as a form of working-class factory consciousness, the dominant element within this consciousness being the irremovable conflict between 'us', the workers, and 'them', the bosses. The stage for this conflict is the factory floor and the shop stewards' committee is its organizational manifestation. The basis of the shop stewards' committee, therefore, is the collective defence of shop floor workers against the bosses and the unions. It provided the stewards with a coherent understanding of the position of the union within the plant and it also served to support the individual stewards through times of personal crisis or trauma. They were all in it together.

The stewards were held together by the stewards' organization and by a common ideology. Jointly they provided each other with guidelines on how to act in specific situations. They also jointly moulded the way in which they came to understand their collective position within the plant – as the leadership of the shop floor. To take first things first. A central principle which underlies the idea of 'us' is that of the collectivity. The whole basis of trade unionism is collectivism of one form or another – 'united we stand, divided we fall' – and this doesn't end with the collective bargain and the strike. Collectivism permeates the very fabric of relationships within the union and is imprinted upon the position of the shop steward. The steward's election brings out some of the ramifications of this.

Most stewards, once established, carry on as stewards, unopposed in elections. To a public versed in the aura of the ballot box, and Her Majesty's Loyal Opposition etc., such a state of affairs smacks of despotism. The world, however, is more complicated than this. Ronnie Walsh describes an annual ritual:

> Every year when it's coming up to election time I go around every man on my section. I tell him the election is due and I ask him if he wants the steward's job. Up to now they've always said 'no it's all right Ron. You're the man for the job' sort of thing. I do the job because of that. If there was somebody else I'd stand down and let him have a go.

The dominant culture in our society is basically individualistic. It is enshrined in ideas about best men winning and the like. This way of seeing things doesn't fit the shop floor very well. Particularly the floor of an assembly plant. This doesn't mean that individualistic elements aren't readily identifiable in such work situations – given the overwhelming influence of the 'dominant culture' it would be truly amazing if they weren't – but that collectivistic modes of thought most readily fit these situations and are more evident in trade unions than any other institutions. The steward understands his position as the collective mouthpiece of his members. In this situation the emergence of a challenger does not immediately provoke the urge to fight it out, but rather is greeted as a criticism of the way in which the steward has been carrying out the job. For the steward an unopposed election is seen as a vote of confidence. When faced with a challenge he will immediately check with his members. If he finds that his opponent has any degree of support on the section he will be inclined to step down. All this takes place *before* the election. Generally the stewards only fought an election if their opponent was 'a headcase' or a member of another union.

The emphasis of the collectivism is important for in its concern with unity it harks back to the idea of the bond which unionism could provide for men who have been driven to the limits by a capitalist rationality which reduces everything and everyone to numbers (see page 190). Such an emphasis is also clearly evident in the mass meeting. In 1969, for example, at a meeting of some 3000 Halewood workers held during the strike at the Liverpool Stadium, a man got to his feet and demanded a ballot. To a tumultuous applause Bernie Bradley, the convenor of the transmission plant, declared that no man was a man who couldn't put up his hand alongside his fellows; who couldn't speak his mind in front of his mates. The euphoria of this, and other such meetings, can only be understood in contrast to the loneliness of work on the assembly line. As a mass, in unison, numbers become strong, they add up. Through the mass the assembly-line operator becomes a man and not a nonentity. It is through the mass, not through skill, that the assembly-line worker obtains his freedom. However momentarily, the mass meeting created in these men some sense of being alive.

These points are crucial ones which will be returned to frequently in the pages that follow. For the moment they beg a number of questions about the nature of the trade unionism developed at Halewood:

> I've been a trade unionist all my life, like my old fella. When I started to work on the buildings as a lad the older men advised me to join. As I grew older I realized how right these old buggers were. Trade unionism is essential for working men. Management are always driving the worker. Like a slave, they'd drive him till he drops if it wasn't for the union.

This comment is a pretty typical summary of the general way in which the stewards understood the need for trade unionism. Views differed, of course, but for all these men trade unionism is not seen as a peculiarity, a problem or a phenomenon of some abstract interest. While it may be all these things at times, essentially and above all else it is a *necessity*.

In this respect the stewards and their members had almost identical views. The stewards had more experience and there were one or two members who weren't too happy about having to join, but the overwhelming emphasis in their thought was that working men *need* trade unions. In their view, no matter how fair management claimed or even tried to be, there would always be disputes, and a man alone in a dispute with a company is 'on a laying-on to nothing'. This was particularly the case when the company was a large one and even more so if it was the Ford Motor Company. These men thought, to a man, that the Ford Motor Company's management would 'put one over' the workers if given the chance. Without a union the working man would have no *rights*. If you're a number you can easily be counted out. So you need the union to ensure that you have a point of view. In the words of one of the workers in the paint shop:

I've been in the union since 1960 when I was on the docks. You need a union for your own protection. To protect your *rights*. A firm like this would have you working like horses without the union. I believe in the union. Everyone should be in it. It's for their own good. For their protection.

Trade unions exist because working people need them. It is this need that leads straightforward 'ordinary men' like Billy Lally to become shop stewards and to say 'I've always been a believer in trade unionism because unions represent the cause of the working man and I'd fight for that cause ... I'd fucking well die for that cause.'

It is the depth of commitment expressed here which differentiated the activist from the ordinary union member in the PTA plant at Halewood. While there was a general agreement that working men need trade unions for protection, the union meant more than that to most of the stewards. While it was an essential form of protection it also stood for something almost apart from this. It represented the struggles fought by workers over generations, it was a living tradition, based upon collectivistic values of unity and brotherhood. While the core of the stewards' committee and many (just over half) of the members openly and positively exalted these values, there was a tendency for many of the 'non-active' members to appreciate the union more in terms of the 'service' it provides for the workers. To quote two of them.

A young lad on the cross-feed:

I've always been in the T&G. It's better for yourself. If you're in any trouble you've got someone to appeal to. If you've a good steward you're laughing. All men should join. It's their security.

An operator on the trim line:

I've been in the union for nine years. It's a good thing to be in. It's good because you've got a mouthpiece then. You call the steward. You don't have to argue. If you think something is wrong you call the steward.

Everybody should be in the union. It's better for themselves and it also makes the union stronger.

There is no essential contradiction between views like this and the strong ideological support mentioned above. Trade unions are in fact built upon this dualism – between what have been termed the 'ideological' and 'business' dimensions of unionism. The last quotation clearly indicates the complementary relationship that exists between individual ends ('it's good because you've got a mouthpiece then') and collective action ('everybody should join ... it makes the union stronger'). What is absent from these two quotations (and eighteen others like them), is any positive commitment to the values of collectivism. It is here that the members as a group differed from the shop stewards, because it was such a commitment, bound up in an ideology that directs and enforces it, that made it impossible for the men who became stewards to escape the struggle. They couldn't simply sit back and 'call the steward' because they saw themselves bound up in the injustices that were being committed all around them. For them an injury to one was an injury to all. They just had to do something.

The stewards in the PTA plant, then, were committed union activists. They were the ones who attended all the meetings, spent their evenings preparing cases for the next day, going to night school and the occasional week at the union's summer school at Cirencester. The extent of the commitment demanded from a steward at Halewood was the main reason given by the members for their lack of interest in the job. That and the binds the steward gets into with both management and his members alike. While none of the members I talked to was particularly keen to take on the steward's job, very few of them were completely uninterested and opposed to the idea. There were a few smug ones who worked as many hours as God made and Ford allowed, and didn't give a monkey's about who they had to tread over. These, however, were the exception. More general was an ambivalence, an uneasy apathy. About 40 per cent of the group of members thought that they would take on the steward's job if they were pushed. They hadn't bothered in the past because they didn't feel they had the ability – 'I just haven't got it. I'm not the type. You've got to be able to argue but I get lost for words. I worry a lot anyway' – or the time. Ray worked as a fork-lift truck driver:

The reason I've not taken the job on – and I could have once – is because of what you've got to give up. If I did it I'd want to do it properly. I'd go to all the meetings, read up on things like. The lads expect their steward to know what's going on and they have the right to expect that in my opinion. To be honest, I think I could do the job all right, probably a bit better than the bloke who's doing it at the moment, but I think that I think too much of my family to take it on. Y'know you'd never see your kids hardly.

What will you do if this steward resigns?

Well, he's said he's going to. I don't know. I wouldn't want to take it on but if no one else does ... You know what this place is like. You'd die here without a steward. If no one else will take it on I'd just have to do it.

The road to activism is not an easy one. Others of the members thought that they wouldn't become involved in union activity, no matter what. Jimmy was a good example. He was twenty-eight, married with two kids and he worked on the trim lines. He joined the union because he had to:

It was a condition of the job. I didn't mind though – it's a good thing. They're not as they should be but we must have them. All workers should certainly be in the union. You need the security. You'll always get the bosses and the supervisors who abuse their authority. The union is worth a lot for the working man.

Well, would you take on the steward's job on the section if Gerry resigns?

No. No I wouldn't do that. We've got a good steward now, perhaps he's too good really. But if he left I wouldn't do it. I would never want to be a steward. You've got to be bothered. You've got to care a little bit – go to all the meetings and that. I certainly wouldn't want to worry so much about everybody. You've got to be a special kind of person I think. That's the trouble I suppose. That's the trouble with unions ... People like me.

This tangled mixture of self-criticism and self-doubt is not peculiar to Jimmy, or to the PTA plant for that matter. Similar patterns are revealed in the way the members understand other forms of union activity like the branch meetng. Only six of the members in the sample claimed to attend branch meetings regularly. Mostly they just didn't go. But also they felt that they *should* go. Only eight of the forty-six thought that there was no need for workers to attend the branch meeting. This quotation from a worker in the paint shop is typical:

Obviously people should go if they can. That's where you get to know what's going on in the union. That's where you can have your say in what goes on. But I wouldn't cry anyone down who didn't go. I don't go very often. I'm not a regular attender. I admire people who go all the time they must be really dedicated. I'm just not that dedicated I suppose. You see the meeting is on

Sunday and, unless there's a really vital issue on, there's lots of other things that I want to do on a Sunday. People have other interests. It's just apathy I suppose.

'Apathy' has, of course, become the commonly accepted explanation for just about every social evil. It explains everything and nothing. Certainly most PTA workers don't care enough about the union to attend branch meetings. In that sense they can be called apathetic. But a lot of them care about not caring. Their lack of dedication worries them.

Apathy, like commitment, doesn't fall from the skies. The men who work as operatives, five or six days a week on the assembly line at Halewood ache by Saturday night. They have a grey-blueness around the face. Especially after a week on nights. By the weekend they need a break. If only to sleep. Many men spend more of their leisure time than they care to know with their eyes shut. Working at Halewood is physically tiring, it is also tedious and boring. It's not something you want to remember. Quite the opposite in fact. Craft unionism is held together by the skill, by the sympathetic relationship that the craftsman has with his tools and his work. Car assemblers hate their work and long to forget about it at weekends. Add to all this the fact that Halewood workers are spread all over Liverpool and most of south-west Lancashire and you have a pretty clear idea why branch meetings are sparsely attended.

This is not a new problem. The sporadic involvement of unskilled workers in union activity has been a continual feature of the 'general unions' throughout this century. The car workers present this phenomenon in a heightened form. Within this situation the stewards maintain the working-class tradition of collectivism. As they try to understand it they mould it and reformulate it. Collectivism isn't an arbitrary tradition, something you can take or leave, it is a basic part of working-class life. But how in the midst of 'affluence' and tedium do the stewards make sense of their unionism? The branch meeting is perhaps a convenient place to start. What does it imply for the steward's relationship with his members?

The branch meeting of the 12/62 of the TGWU takes place once a month in the main meeting hall of Transport House, Islington. At 11.00 a.m. on the appropriate Sunday, Brother Bob Henderson, the Branch Chairman attempts to call the meeting to order. That takes some time because people come drifting in for a good fifteen minutes. Some are greeted with laughs – 'on the piss again last night' – others with a hand in the air and some assembly-line face-pulling to indicate a vacant seat. Bob Henderson usually admonishes the latecomers and the meeting gets under way.

The Transport House of today is a modern building overlooking the St John's precinct. As a result of plans made for Liverpool's traffic, the old office was knocked down and the hall with it. It's missed by some ('a hell of a lot of things happened there', 'lots of memories') but in truth it wasn't a particularly attractive place. Wooden floors, pipes around the walls, wonky radiators and rows and rows of stack-away chairs. Frosted windows and grey skies. A slight platform up the front with a table and the branch officers. Bob would be sat there with Gerry at his side, Mick the convenor at his shoulder ready to give his plant report and Eddie in the background taking minutes. Bill Brodrick would be down in the front row with his arms folded. If it's a big meeting Sammy would be there in the far back corner telling anyone who is excited that it's all happened before and will again. Bob Henderson calls the meeting to order again and the minutes are read.

Usually there were about eighty people in attendance out of a total membership of over 5000.[2] If there's anything slightly important to discuss a couple of hundred may turn up. The branch meeting that made the final decision on the 1967 wages structure was attended by 400 members. Bob Henderson, the chairman, sets the tone of the branch. He's the constitutionalist, the father of the branch and the stewards' committee. He works in the quality control department, and has spent a lifetime in the trade union movement. He's a quiet man, he doesn't drink or swear, after the branch he's straight home for his Sunday dinner. He's a nice man and he's universally respected. During one branch meeting in 1970 a new member, a Labour councillor well versed in the art and practice of committee procedure, challenged the independence of the chair. Bob had become involved in the discussion and the Silver Fox (the nickname they flattered him with) demanded that he vacate the chair. This move was shouted down, people stood on their feet in Bob's defence. Bob Henderson acting improperly – never. It was unthinkable. Not Bob Henderson.

Almost all the stewards will be there. Absences will be mentally noted. The meeting is under way. Kenny will be shouting the odds, old Tom will stand up and read a speech from his notes. Usually there's something held over from the last meeting or a particular sectional dispute to sort out. Mick, the convenor, makes his report on who said what to whom. If there's something important he will end his report

2. The membership of the branch increased dramatically in 1969 when some 2000 members of the GMWU disaffected to the TGWU during and after the Penalty Clause strike (see Chapter 10).

with a recommendation to the meeting which is discussed and voted on. The meeting goes on until about one o'clock. File out of the hall along the passage into Islington. The regulars have regrouped and are across the road for a pint or off to The Clock on London Road for a few. Home for dinner at 3.00.

In addition to this meeting the stewards would have been to a stewards' committee meeting the morning before. If something big was in the air they'd have recently had a mass plant meeting in the Liverpool Stadium and a joint stewards' committee. The senior stewards will have gone to London. A conscientious steward will give up several hours a week of his free time to trade union work. And there's the drinking on top of that. One steward reckoned that the first word his baby daughter uttered was 'meeeting'. Others tell how their children ask on a Sunday morning, 'Are we going out in the car today, or have you got a meeting?' One senior steward claimed to have never had a Sunday dinner with his family since he took up with the union.

Most stewards find that their trade unionism brings them into some conflict with their wives. Few of them consider their wives to be directly opposed to trade unionism as a principle, but simply that trade union activity comes into direct conflict with family-based activities:

Your personal life gets interfered with a lot in this job. What with meetings, preparing each evening for the battle the next day and studying works study and the like. It doesn't leave much time for the wife and kids.

The fact that trade union activity is voluntarily undertaken for other people's benefit does cause strain in a society where self-advancement and self-interest are dominant values.[3] 'You've got to have a very understanding wife in this game.' One steward said of his wife:

She's not got much time for trade unions. She believes in what the trade unions have done for the working class, but she disagrees with me being a shop steward. Her attitude is 'Why doesn't someone else do his share?' She doesn't like the time it takes up. It leaves me no time for her and the family. She thinks I'm making the family suffer for my trade union principles.

And another:

'Let somebody else do it for a change,' that's what my wife says. 'Why does it have to be you?' All I can say is 'Somebody has to do it.' I ask myself privately too. But I just can't stand on the side lines.

3. The difficulties and problems faced by the wives of active unionists are too numerous and complex to be dealt with at all adequately here. Carol, Eddie's wife, insists that it's not the women's fault, 'it's the men tha'. They never tell their wives nothing. They don't tell them about the union. About what's involved. They just come in at all hours and expect to be fed.'

Occasionally family disputes flare up into resignations, but these are rare. The possibility of a resignation over 'the wife' was not taken lightly by the stewards. They all tried to keep each others' marriages on an even keel. In 1969 Johnny Craig became very worried about Eddie. Eddie was the convenor then and was speaking to meetings all over Liverpool and a lot of England most nights of the week. Johnny thought that he was doing too much. 'He's got enough to do with the plant without doing all these other meetings. He won't say no. And everybody wants him to speak. It must be putting a strain on Carol. We've told him he's got to cut down the numbers of meetings he does. He does a hell of a lot.'

Mostly the family life of a steward carries on from one spoiled Sunday dinner to the next. Occasionally they all organize a night out together – them and their wives. Frank was a great believer in these meetings: 'they can talk together and see that they've all got the same problems.' They were always good nights.

When you talk to the stewards about the membership most of them will tell you that the average member is just too lazy, too idle, to give up one Sunday morning a month to attend a branch meeting. They think that all members should attend as many meetings as they possibly can so that they know what's going on outside their section, so that they've got a healthy branch, with discussion and no fear of a minority takeover. They see it to be in the members' own interest to attend and speak his mind (as do the members themselves, even the inactive ones). They also have a sneaking sentimentalism. For many of them a good meeting is 'like a slap on the back. A "thank you" for the effort we've put into the fucking thing.' More usually, however, realism prevails.

In their more sober moments most of the stewards will admit that '11.00 a.m. on a Sunday morning' is the sole explanation of low attendances. They don't seriously expect more than a handful of members to turn up to a run-of-the-mill branch meeting. 'It would be all right if everybody came but we'd have to get a bigger fucking hall for a start.' Billy Lally's view is a generally held one:

The members should go. It's more important for them than it is for me. I can always sort something out with the convenor. But they just leave it to me ... 'if it's all right for you it's all right for us' seems to be their attitude. But very little goes on at the branch to interest blokes ... and I can always get the information they want, and on a weekend people want to watch football or take the wife and kids out for a day. If it was held at work then everyone *would* attend. Your leisure time is difficult to give up when you work in a place like this.

Some of the stewards were worried about this situation and thought that a cohesive effort should be made to get the lads to the branch:

> I've got members on my section who are *good* trade unionists who *never* attend the branch. They should get there when big issues crop up, but mainly it's the shop floor that counts. They could do a lot to make the branch more attractive for the members. The branch secretary could do a lot – arrange special talks, political talks, on the £15 minimum week, the Common Market, things like that.

Most of the stewards, however, didn't worry over much. They too recognized that 'it's the shop floor that counts'. They accepted the low branch attendance as a fact of life and developed the union activity more positively in other directions. Strong elements of ritual, therefore, permeate 'the branch' and the branch meeting. This is how Ronnie Walsh saw it:

> We don't really need to go to the branch. In a way there's no need for the branch at all. We all go because the members like to know we're there. There's hardly any need for us to go because we're already in possession of all the facts. We do most of our work before the branch.

The branch exists and because it exists the stewards have to attend the meetings. They meet and they talk and they have a few pints. They plan and they laugh. But there is a bit more to it than this. In Chapter 3 it was pointed out that the shop stewards' committee in the PTA consciously used the branch as part of their armoury against the employers and the union. Jack Jones expounds the significance of this:

> I like to see a good attendance but it *could* be a bad thing in a way – three thousand people is a hell of a lot of people. We moan about attendances but we don't really want them there. Morally they *should* go, but it may well create problems for an organized branch policy. The situation at the moment is that the branch meeting is a place where the stewards go to *represent* their sections. As far as the members are concerned he has the responsibility.

The tension between the need for trade union organization and mass participation in that organization is a vital and irresolvable one. A gap exists between the shop stewards and the rest. A gap created by the very fact of sustained activism and enforced by its organization. Ultimately there is no way out of this. The complexity of modern society coupled with the physical and mental strains of factory work make some form of 'full-time' activism essential. Even at the shop-floor level. In coping with this the steward finds himself torn between the forces of representation and bureaucratization. Between the need to represent the immediate wishes of their members and to provide a long-term strategy that will protect the interests of those members. The membership, enveloped in the here and now of factory production, find little time or inclination to study and work out detailed plans, demands and tactics. But such activity must be done by someone. In order to maintain pressure upon the national officers, the stewards and the other active members were concerned that regular, militant demands emerged from the branch in the form of resolutions, sometimes telegrammed to London. 'It keeps them on their toes. They know you've met and you've been talking about them.' Frequently the resolutions are moved by the same men – the men who had worked out the best wording and had written it down the night before. The stewards were aware of the dangers of the concentration of power and advantage that went along with this in the branch, but they saw these to be dangers that had to be met and dealt with. The idea of a representative system of branch government advocated by Jack is one way out of this dilemma for the stewards. But it is no real solution. When I asked Frank Banton if he thought all members should attend the branch meetings he replied:

> I do and I don't. But I must say yes. They should go for their own interests. It would also make my job a hell of a lot easier if the members had all the information that they could get at the branch. That's the problem see. It's apathy. The union is so well organized here they know it will carry on no matter what they do. It's wrong that, very wrong.

One of the problems of slack attendances at the branch is that a minority could dominate branch policy ... the branch could be taken over by 'undesirable elements'. The ideology of the stewards proved some safeguard to such abuse. During a conversation on this subject in The Clock, the Silver Fox once argued that in all organizations – political parties and trade unions – the activists want power. 'They want to be at the top. The Number One. You'll get this wherever you go.' This gave rise to a detailed argument. John Craig, for one, didn't agree. 'Take our committee. Now I would never oppose Eddie for the convenor's job, because Eddie is the man for that job. He's the one who can do the best for the lads. That's what I'm concerned about. What's best for the lads, not power for its own sake.' This ideology is a dominant one and is underpinned by a dependence upon the lads. For while the problem of control falling into the hands of a minority *is* a problem it can be overestimated because, whether the branch officials are 'undesirables' or not, the membership have the final veto. The paradox and deep tragedy of mass production is revealed here. In spite of himself the assembly-line worker is made apathetic by being made a number. He doesn't go to branch meetings and he may not know his steward well. He just screws on wheels. But there is strength in numbers and their strength lies in the strike. So does the negotiating strength of the steward. He has to know that they'll follow him out the gates. Sometimes they won't. They'll dig their heels in and carry on. Sometimes they'll go out on their own accord. For the stewards to act as a viable leadership they've got to know what their members are thinking. They have also to keep their members informed about events outside the confines of their particular work situation. This is the problem of unionism in a car plant. This is why the stewards worry about 'apathy'.

Mass meetings

It will continue to be the policy of the PTA stewards to hold mass shift or full plant meetings whenever the occasion necessitates, and like our campaign last year, we will supplement them by leaflets . . . This is not to say that you should neglect, as too many of you do, your attendances at branch meetings – the place at which your official union policy is formed.

From *PTA Voice*, 1970

The steward works with his members day in, day out, in the plant. This is the basis of their relationship and canteen or gate meetings are used to do what the branch meeting cannot do. These meetings derive from particular issues that have developed, often that same day, in the plant and are invariably attended by an overwhelmingly large percentage of the members. Formal meetings are only isolated events. The steward's main contact with his members is entailed in the everyday life of working on the section. This is the content of the steward's world and it is out of this that he grapples with trade unionism and the problem of leadership.

Where are those who will come to serve the people – not utilize them for their own ambitions?

Kropotkin

The position of the shop steward is not without its dangers . . . (it) could have a disruptive effect upon trade union discipline since by its very nature the steward–member relationship cannot be rigidly controlled.

Les Cannon, late President EPTU

9 Leaders and Followers

I was sick. We came in here after the meeting. I got a pint and sat down at this table and I could have cried. I wanted to cry. All that work. All that work and those stupid bastards threw it all away.

This was one of the kinder things said by the PTA stewards about the membership in the February of 1970. The stewards had gone to The Clock after a meeting at the Liverpool Stadium. A few of them decided to make a night of it. They all went out together, with their wives and got very drunk.

The stewards at Halewood had spent many hours in every week for the past six months organizing and preparing for a strike in support of their wage claim. As a result of a strike in 1969 their wages had been increased by about thirty shillings a week but this still left them well behind the wages paid on piece rates to workers in some of the plants in the Midlands. In 1969 dissatisfaction over this disparity was organized into a concerted campaign for parity of earnings with the best rates paid in the industry. This campaign derived its impetus from Halewood, and by February 1970 everything was set. They knew that they had the Company on the run, that its position would be made vulnerable if it lost its supply of cars. The stewards knew that a strike would bring a large settlement. They were reasonably sure that the lads would vote for a strike. Moss Evans, the TGWU National Officer, had said on television that the Ford workers would strike 'to a man'. But Bob Ramsey was boxing clever. 'We knew that if they offered four pounds we could be in trouble and if they offered a fiver we'd be in the shit.' Ramsay offered an increase of four pounds dead. The offer was rejected at the newly constituted NJNC and referred to mass meetings at the plants. The Halewood workers met on the Sunday. At a meeting attended by men from the three plants the stewards' recommendation was turned down. The front of the hall was dominated by lads from the transmission plant, equipped with placards advocating acceptance of the Company's offer. Amid their chants the meeting voted overwhelmingly against the recommendation of the stewards. I wasn't there myself. I arrived too late. Billy Brodrick was relieved. 'I'm really glad you missed this one. I'm glad you weren't there to see it. I was ashamed. It was a disgrace. It's enough to make you want to jack it in.'

On the Monday the line in the PTA was running as usual. Things weren't 'normal' though. The lads were getting a roasting from the stewards.

I gave them fucking hell. Every week I'd met the bastards and told them what we were doing. They've never been better informed. And they all said that they wanted parity. It was all too easy for them. You don't appreciate anything unless you fight for it and they were offered four quid on a plate for fuck-all.

Ronnie Walsh 'nearly drew blood' on his section. 'I called them a shower of bastards. You didn't have to ask who'd voted against. You could tell by just looking at them. They couldn't look you in the face.'

Eddie was one of the stewards who had been drinking well into Monday morning. He was the convenor and enjoyed immense support in the plant. It was he who made the speech recommending strike action at the Stadium. The recommendation that was turned down. He didn't manage to get up for the start of the shift. 'I wasn't feeling too good so I thought "fuck it, let the bastards stew in it for a bit".' The rumour spread through the plant that he had resigned, both he and Gerry Flaherty.

I felt like it I can tell you. The effort we'd put into that. But its no use throwing the sponge in. You've got to go back. Just go back in there and start again . . . but don't make the same mistakes next time.

He got to the plant and was picked out by everybody's eyes; smug managerial ones, the downcast, fleeting glances of the lads. 'They were coming up to me, "What can we do", "We're sorry", and all that shit. I wasn't in the mood for that. I told them it was a bit late and they should have done something in the Stadium – y'know half of our lads were so sure that it was going through that they didn't go to the fucking meeting – I told them to fuck off, that they couldn't look to me to save their consciences.'

Car production took place sporadically during that shift. Quality was bad. There was a lot of sabotage. Everything was uneasy. It came to a head on the night shift. The Swansea plant was out. At their mass meeting the stewards' recommendation had been accepted and the men were on official strike. That was salt in the wound. For the stewards *and* the lads. The lads were also worried. As Billy McGuire put it:

They wanted the four pounds. They thought they could get an easy four quid for nothin' but Swansea upset tha', because there was a fight after all. In a fight you get casualties and the lads were worried that Swansea was going to get clobbered. That the lads in Swansea were going to get hurt while they pocketed the rise.

Hughie Wallace, the Swansea plant convenor, appeared on television in the evening. He saw it as a question of principle. The Swansea plant may be out on its own, but there was no question in his mind who had behaved correctly. The lads in the other Ford plants had let down their officials and their elected stewards. They had taken a wrong decision.

Work had been sporadic on the Monday day shift. It was chaotic on Monday night. The line started but the lads wouldn't. Groups of men were meeting and arguing all over the plant. Some sections started to work, others never did. Then the chant went up: 'Swansea; da da da; Swansea'. A phalanx of Liverpool Kop-ites heading out of the plant. SWANSEA ... SWANSEA ... It was the same the following day shift. The PTA plant was on stop. Jack Jones describes his experience:

> It was in the middle of a fucking snow storm. I came in and changed into my comfortable shoes. Then I heard that there was a meeting outside the gate so I pissed off to change into my outside shoes again. Then there was no meeting so I changed back. Then the bastards were outside the gate. I was like a fucking yo-yo.

The position of the steward in a car plant can often be like a yo-yo. These February events brought that home to the PTA stewards in an acute way. Their credibility as leaders of the shop floor was again under threat. An examination of how they made sense of this position can tell us a lot about their understanding of rank and file leadership.

The first problem they had was with management. They'd been confident that there was going to be a strike, and the whole tenor of the negotiation with plant management up to the Sunday meeting had been based on the understanding that the plant would be empty on the Monday. The stewards had to save a lot of face. 'Y'know they were all there grinning. Getting ready to gloat. I told them that they could wipe their fucking smiles off their faces. That they could be in trouble in the plant and that we'd be back. It might take a year but the shooting wasn't over yet.' Face saving isn't all that's involved however. The steward occupies a position of fine balance within the car plant. As one steward put it:

> The Ford Motor Company tolerate the union but they don't *recognize* it. The shop steward is out on a limb with this Company. There's no recognition of him in any real way in the Blue Book. You've got to be requested before you can get involved in a dispute. You can't initiate anything. You're always on the defensive. You can know about a problem but you can be unable to do anything

about it. I know that some of us have built up pretty good understandings on our own sections but we don't have these things as a *right*. They're all unofficial and if the Ford Motor Company felt like it they can shout 'stop'.

The balance which the steward tries to keep is very much a balance of power. The steward has facilities because management are afraid of the cost involved in withdrawing them. If the cost appears to drop the steward will find himself under some pressure. Half the stewards in the PTA felt that the plant management there hindered them more than they helped them. The other half said that it would depend. Management would help sometimes – if it suited them; they spend a lot of their time playing politics and a lot of this politics involves manipulation of the 'industrial relations situation'.

They're very inconsistent here. They play politics here. When there was a bit of a split in the branch and we happened to be going the way they wanted we had everything easy. But the opposition were in trouble. Stick from us and stick from them.

Generally, then, management try to manipulate the stewards. When the cards are stacked in their hands they can afford to play a bit harder. A slack market period brings about such pressure.

That's something they're specialists at. They vary. In a busy period they help you out. Sometimes they'll do *anything* to help you. All the rules count for nothing then, but when things are slack they come back. You've got to *negotiate*.

The market is one part of the situation. Another is the amount of support the stewards can expect from their members. Management and supervision are always tinkering with this support.

Basically as a shop steward you're despised by management here. When you first take the job on they obstruct you in every way possible. They try to belittle you in front of the men. Put you on bad jobs . . . You know the sort of thing. If you're going to make it as a shop steward you've got to get over the hurdles they put up for you and get the respect of the men.

For a shop steward to operate as an effective leader he has to have the respect of his members and be sure of the support that they will give him.

The worst problem you're faced with is the lack of interest shown by the men on the shop floor in what you're trying to do. As soon as that happens, if management are aware that the men are not giving the steward their active support they will *always* use it against the steward. They *always* use it.

That's the worse thing tha'. When you go into the office and they say to you 'this isn't your mates, this is you. The lads don't want this.' You've got to know that the lads are behind you. They only let me down once. I went back to them and they didn't want to know. It hurt tha'. Y'know, the thought that management knew the lads better than I did. I never go in now unless I'm certain that I'll get their backing.

That's what hurt the stewards in 1970. They had built up an organization with the support of lads, and the lads had turned around and proved Bob Ramsey right. That's what stung. But they had to get over their hurt pride because they faced a real possibility of management offensive. That's why Eddie Roberts couldn't think of resigning. The organization, and paradoxically the lads – 'the bastards', as they were for a day – were under threat. Swansea and the walkouts averted that threat and allowed the stewards to ease into the saddle, to plan again.

Swansea visit

As we reported to you at one of our meetings on 'The Hill' (outside the main gate of the Halewood estate), four of us visited Swansea a short time ago, the idea being that progressive elements within the Ford combine should have a closer understanding of each others' policies. It was an extremely useful trip, and we were warmly received by the Swansea workers' representatives. It was immediately apparent that the brave stand made by the Swansea plant during the 'Parity Campaign' was no flash in the pan, and the boys down there really mean business when it comes to fighting for higher wages and improved agreements. Their attitudes are identical to our own in the PTA and we look forward to jointly spearheading the struggle for a better deal in the next round of pay talks. We will shortly be inviting our colleagues from South Wales up here for a taste of Merseyside hospitality, and to further discuss the whole question of our wages and conditions, and our future aspirations.

From *PTA Voice* 1970

The Swansea strike and the Halewood stoppage 'in sympathy' was soon ended, but it was only one skirmish in a war of a lifetime. There would be other days and these had to be prepared for. Four of the senior stewards from the PTA plant travelled to Swansea for the weekend, to have a post-mortem and to plan strategy with the Swansea stewards. The meeting was much publicized in Halewood. Eddie remembers that 'the management didn't know what to make of it. An unofficial meeting between the two renegade plants. They kept asking me and I told them that we were "plotting and scheming". Their eyes would go glazed. Y'know, mouths sagging open. They thought we were gangsters or something and they couldn't understand why we didn't keep it a secret.'

The meetings with the Swansea stewards took place in the Skewen Rugby Club. By this time the PTA stewards had decided that the stewards in the other two Halewood plants hadn't done their jobs. That they hadn't been reporting back to their members, or they hadn't been representing the feelings of their members at the joint stewards' meeting. They decided that for the next phase the organization on the Halewood estate would have to revert to plant organizations organizing their own mass meetings. 'You've just got to know what the support is, and we just had to take their word for the situation in their plants. We took a hammering. You can't run on organization like that. You've got to be able to deliver the decision.'

The PTA plant intended to go it alone again for a bit, but in collaboration with Swansea. This was to be the twin spearhead of the revived Campaign for Parity. They formed in Moss Evans's words 'the catalyst'. This strategy was formulated at the Skewen meeting. It was formulated through a withering attack of the traditional Dagenham leadership. The leadership that took over in 1963 after the showdown. At a meeting of the Ford Stewards' Combined Committee, with stewards from all the Ford plants in Britain represented, the Dagenham stewards had held the floor and insisted that the workers in their plants would support a strike call. Few of them did, all the Dagenham plants voting overwhelmingly for an acceptance of the deal. 'McCrae [the convenor of the Dagenham body plant] got up and said with his hand on his heart: "the lads are raring to go". The only place they were raring to go was back to work. He never knew nothin' about what those lads were thinking.' The Halewood and Swansea stewards were not blaming the Dagenham lads however.

It's not the fault of the Dagenham lads. All working-class blokes are the same basically. It's the leadership that's at fault. All those bastards down there have done is sit on their arses telephoning *us* and telling us what we should be doing. They can't have been reporting back to those Dagenham lads. They hardly ever see the lads.

We've got a whole history of working-class militancy behind us in Liverpool and South Wales. We've got the tradition, the equipment . . . everything. And we're cashing in on it too. We're going to take over this show. We're off. We've got to tell them that we're going, and if they want to get on board they're welcome but we're driving from now on.

Obviously we can't think of leaving the combine but we've got to sort this one out. We've got to be hard with them.

The Dagenham convenors were the Armchair Generals. This label sums up the criticism of them and their style of leadership. They'd been at Ford's for years – 'you can see them there in the King of Prussia with their gold badges on' – and stewards for almost as long. The convenors had their own offices, they were regularly on the hot line to Reggie (Reg Birch the AUEW national officer on the Ford NJNC) or handing out advice to the Halewood and Swansea stewards. They were the 'southern professionals', and the scousers and the Welsh had had enough. They'd been misled by 'the clever fellas' for the last time.

These are crucial points. Stewards and convenors can pose as shop floor leaders. They can attend committee meetings, make speeches, sit on official union committees for years on end. It is only if they try to *do* something that their bluff will be called, because to *do* anything they need the lads. The stewards at the PTA plant in Halewood and the axle plant in Swansea wanted to *do* something. They weren't phonies. They were the representatives of the lads – that was the basis of their position. Everything else flowed from this. Hughie Wallace was the convenor of the Swansea plant; a Scot in the midst of the Welsh, smartly dressed, elegant grey hair, twinkling eyes which gave away his jokes and tricks; a skilled man and lifelong member of the AUEW. He was in earnest that weekend:

We've got 1500 shop stewards in the plant. Every one of them could do the stewards' job as well as the stewards. This isn't a game. This is a serious business. It's about those lads' lives. They're intelligent lads, you can't pull the wool over their eyes and they come before everything else. The unity of my plant comes first, before the union, before everything. I'm not allowed the luxury of a personal opinion, I'm bound by our committee and the meeting of the lads. But no committee tells the likes of McCrae and Bedford which way to go. They listen to no one.

How do the stewards understand their position as representatives? How do they deal with the responsibilities of leadership? What do they consider to be their duty as shop stewards?

For a start they think of themselves as *of* the men, and because of this they feel that they have to be *with* the men. A conversation between Eddie (the PTA convenor) and Billy and John (the deputy convenors):

EDDIE: In Dagenham all the JWC [Joint Works Committee] are on days.

BILLY: *Are* they ...?

JOHN: No you're not quite right there Eddie. They could all go on days, but some of them still elect to stay on shifts. There's one or two there with some integrity. It's not right that, all the JWC being on one shift.

EDDIE: It's no wonder their organization is like it is: they can have no contact with the lads. There can be no continuity.

BILLY: Would you go on days John?

JOHN: No, definitely not. It's not that I wouldn't like days. It would be great to be on days; it wouldn't be right. We've got to have a man on days and that's Eddie.

It's only this contact with the membership, this sharing of a common situation, which gives you the *right* to speak for them. It is also a strategic necessity, because only by being *with* them do you know what they are thinking, do you know and understand their moods. If you ask the stewards in the PTA what they consider to the main duties of the shop steward, they won't treat you to a definition of a shop steward's role that you might find in an industrial relations manual. As likely as not they'll say 'to look after the welfare and interests of the members'. This was the reply I got time and again. One man would simply say 'to do my best for the membership I represent'. Another said:

As a steward I'm mainly concerned with helping people who've got problems. People tend to be timid and frightened by the white coat. They're just afraid to stand up for themselves by themselves.

> In a sense, the leading stewards are performing a managerial function of grievance settlement, welfare arrangement and human adjustment, and the shop stewards' acceptance by managements ... has developed partly because of the increasing effectiveness – and certain economy – with which this role is fulfilled.
>
> H. A. Turner, G. Clack and G. Roberts (1967), *Labour Relations in the Motor Industry*

Or, as his mate put it, 'Some people just can't look after themselves.' Obviously the stewards could expand on this. They could point out that they have a duty to collect the dues off their members. Or that they perform a particular function at one stage in the procedure, but that their overwhelming sense of obligation is to their membership. At its simplest they see their job as a steward to be to ensure that the lads on the line don't get messed about. To keep the lads happy – to look after their interests. It's not for nothing that the steward has been termed 'a badly paid personnel manager'. In controlling the job he finds himself acting as a foreman (see Chapter 6). And his duties don't stop there.

If any of the lads on my section have a problem, with their tax, with the law, anything, troubles with their kids or wife, they don't go to the foreman. They come to me and if I can't sort it out I have a word with the convenor. They come to me because they trust me. They know I'll tell them the truth and not give them a load of bull.

Shop stewards in a car plant can be seen as 'watchdogs' but they also act as counsellors. By their own criteria a good steward was someone who had gained the respect of the lads, someone who the lads trusted. Most of them were highly aware of their responsibilities to their members, and not a few of them worried that they weren't up to it ... that they couldn't do right by the blokes. Ronnie Davies had such doubts. At the end of the interview I had with him he said, 'Well you've asked me a lot of questions, you've talked to a lot of stewards, what do you think? Do you think I'm up to the job? Am I a good steward?' It was a humbling experience because Ronnie Davies by any standards was a good man. He joined the union on the docks – 'it was just like putting your coat on' – he had:

no ambition to be promoted. I'm not interested in that, I'm interested in my fellow workmates. I just want to try to do something to improve the conditions of the men. I'm a trade unionist ... It would be a loss to me if I wasn't the shop steward, I know that the men here have confidence in me. I think I'd miss that. It's pride I suppose. You know that they look up to you and respect you. I'm only a number in the Company, but not with these men.

It was this service to the membership and the respect which it occasionally brought, which gives the steward his main satisfaction. The shop steward's job is a pretty thankless one. Ask anyone who knows about factories and they'll tell you that its the worst job in the place. The steward gets stick from all sides, 'its like being on a roundabout'. What keeps them going is the idea that the men need them. One put it like this:

When you're taking part you can see what progress is being made for the worker and you know that you're a part of it. You're doing something for yourself and everybody else. You do it for the goodness of it. Help to get some of the profits for the workers.

The idea of 'goodness', doing something 'good', is a central one:

Helping people out. That's what I get out of doing the steward's job. To get a man what is his by right is to do something good I think.

As is respect:

The best thing about the steward's job for me – in fact the only thing that I get out of it all is the *respect* of the members. There's a satisfaction to be got in helping your fellow workmates and to know that you're doing a good job for them.

While they may say that they're not interested in 'scoring points' or 'getting a dig at Ford's', they like to win a case, especially one which management think they have tied up. Victory then is doubly sweet, they get the men their due and they, as 'uneducated workers', outwit Henry Ford's graduates. These 'little victories' keep them going, especially when the members say thanks.

No one likes trouble but you can't move away from it. I like to see the blokes getting a fair crack of the whip. It's great when you get a good case. You work hard on it and win it. It's a great feeling. Doing something well and doing it for your fellow man I suppose.

The best feeling a steward can get is winning a case. When you've got a man who's been wrongly done to by management that man's in a bad position. If you can *prove* it and have the situation revised you've done something for that man. You've done *something* I think.

The biggest satisfaction I've had is to get a man off who was sacked. They thought that we were on a laying on to nothing – but we beat them. They gave this man his notice of the sack and then they granted us a meeting and we made them withdraw it. It was great. Getting somebody his job back. We get plenty of little victories to keep us going. Very few big ones though. Mostly it's from sorting the foremen out.

In 1966 I had a series of detailed conversations with about forty shop stewards in a steelworks in South Wales. The steelworks was a long established one, and the town very much a Company town. The stewards were long-serving men, and most of them held responsible jobs as leaders of teams of workmen. In this union stronghold the stewards also articulated an ethos of service, but on top of this they tended to draw attention to the education which they derived from being a shop steward. They pointed out how they got to learn more about the economics and technology of steel production. The integrative aspects of trade union activity is clearly evident here. These men clearly identified themselves with their work and their jobs, and their unionism reflected this. If anything the opposite applied in the Halewood assembly plant. No steward mentioned the educative aspects of trade unionism in this sense. Their trade unionism was much blunter. They get satisfaction and some sense of purpose from being an active unionist, from 'doing a job that needs to be done' and 'belonging to an organization you believe to be right'. But all of this was wrapped up in a day-to-day struggle with the foremen, the time-study men, the superintendent, along the frontier of control. Looking after the interests of the men. It is this idea of protecting the shop floor worker against adversity which justified their activity and coloured their trade unionism and their politics. It provokes the question: In what ways can a shop stewards' committee look after the interests of the rank and file worker?

Apart from the time it takes up and the problems that it can lead to in your home life, being a shop steward can be a thankless task – 'You get it from both sides, you're like a piece of elastic.' On the one hand you're up against it with the Company. With management and supervision. A lot of the stewards at Halewood found that they were watched much closer by supervision once they became the steward on the section. Many stewards have to work harder than their members in order to keep up. The crucial problem with the job though is that:

> You must consider other people before yourself and often people don't appreciate it. It gets frustrating then because your enthusiasm can go in time.

Relationships with other shop stewards within the committee bolster the steward's enthusiasm, but management can do a lot to crack it. The steward attempts to represent the best interests of his members, he tries to do what is best for them, but he has to do this through a trade union organization. The stewards' committee has an important degree of autonomy from the full-time officials of the union, but it is, nevertheless, a trade union organization. Its structural relationship with the company is basically the relationship of trade unionism to capitalism. It opposes, but the opposition isn't total, for in its opposition it accepts the existence of capital. In order to serve the interests of the membership, the steward has to negotiate with management. In negotiations, especially with a powerful opponent, some recognition of 'the rights' of the other side is to be expected. Such is the case in management–union relations. Sometimes this breaks down – management denying workers any 'right' in certain areas and union officers defying the 'rights of capital'. One of the senior labour relations executives of the Ford Motor Company remarked:

It's incredible sometimes. They come up here to negotiate and we go through it all, output, costs, profits etc. And we say 'Clearly what you're asking for is out of the question . . .' and they'll come back with 'That's your problem. We want to nationalize you anyway. Don't talk to us about profits.' You can't carry on negotiations on that basis. It would be chaos.

Pat Lowry, the senior Industrial Relations executive at BLMC, made a similar assertion on BBC television's *Late Night Line Up* in May 1972. IR (industrial relations), he claimed, has nothing whatever to do with politics. Its aim is to come to a negotiated settlement within the ambit of existing social and political structures. This undeniably *is* the prevailing ideology of all 'IR' work. It is this ideology which shop stewards and union officials have to deal with and which can lead them, indirectly, into severe problems with their members. For many of the problems experienced by their members are produced by the very social and political structures which 'IR' ideology accepts as inviolate. The right of management to manage is an example of this. It is this 'right' which creates severe dissatisfaction, and not occasionally despair, amongst working men and which is ruled out of court as a legitimate area for negotiations. Thus a steward can lose a case which to the man on the floor is a banker. He loses it not because the arguments he uses are flawed, but because they are underpinned by an ideology that differs fundamentally from the ideology of corporate management. Even if the stewards are persuasive, if they are able to present their arguments forcefully in a way that convinces plant management that they *do* have a case, success isn't guaranteed. Negotiating situations are, above all else, power situations, and where there is power there is politics. Not party politics perhaps, but politics nevertheless.

The biggest problem I find in being a steward is having to relate to management. You can have a 100 per cent case, an easy winner and they will *refuse* to negotiate. Often though they can't. They've been told not to. Now and again you'll break them down. They'll accept the logic of your argument and they'll say 'all right, all right, but it's not up to me. I *can't* give it you. It's as simple as that.' You can argue till you're blue in the face but you can't budge something like that.

It's no easy job explaining to men why you haven't been able to do what they want you to.

The worst thing about this job is having to tell a man that you've lost his case. That things will have to be done this way – the Ford Motor Company way – from now on . . . Also there's very few decisions that keep everybody happy.

Often the loss of a case can produce a severe crisis for a shop steward. Bob Costello lost a sacking case in 1967. It was a 'no hoper', but the sacked lad had been unceremoniously dispatched with his cards without any negotiation taking place. This sickened Bob:

I live or die on this one. If I lose this one I can't go back down to face those lads. All right he was wrong but that's no excuse for them to treat him like shit.

He got over it and faced the lads. He had to. If you've the confidence you can carry it off and turn their anger against the employer. Often, though, stewards aren't altogether clear why they lose the case.

The thing I hate, I hate most of all, is when things crop up and there's nothing that you can do about them. The average operative thinks that you can wave a wand and sort every grievance out. Sometimes you've got to approach the supervisor with a case that you've not an earthly chance of winning. You can't please everybody. They seem to think that you can achieve the impossible. You're only the same as they are really – an uneducated worker.

The nature of the position of the steward within the car plant creates problems for the man who tries to do the steward's job. Often he finds himself in a 'heads you win, tails I lose' situation. The members can't be expected to help either. They can be 'self-interested', 'narrowminded', and 'ridiculous'. They can have 'very silly views', be 'backward looking'. 'The members', said a senior steward, 'can be bastards.'

You are always 'number one' if something goes wrong. You're the middle man. You get kicked from both sides. You can win all the cases then lose one and you're the world's worst. Y'know?

It is out of this situation that the stewards developed their concept of leadership. The nature of their situation produced contradictions for the stewards but they didn't go through all these things entirely blindly. They had some idea where they were going.

The central principle which guided the activities of the shop stewards' committee was the autonomy and sanctity almost of the shop floor situation. The members may be bastards but they were all there was and they *needn't* be bastards. Given the correct leadership they could behave properly. A prerequisite for this correct leadership was continuous contact with the members. The members didn't attend branch meetings, so the decisions taken by the branch were relayed to the shop floor by the stewards. Regular sectional and plant gate meetings were called. Leaflets were produced and handed out on the sections. The members then had to be kept in the picture, but the stewards also had to watch *themselves*. They had to ensure that they weren't corrupted. That they hadn't become 'bent'. I'd only been in the plant a few weeks when a steward said to me ' "Bent" . . . I bet that's a word you've heard a lot since you've been here. We seem to be thinking about it all the time.' We walked on for about fifty yards and he turned to me again, 'Do you think I'm bent?' Arguments about who was 'bent' and who wasn't took place quite frequently. In 1967 all the trade union officials, 'the bureaucrats', were unequivocally 'bent bastards'. The stewards were determined that it wasn't going to happen to them. Johnny Craig explains their concern. John is a short dapper man. A committed trade unionist; above all else he wanted to be a full-time officer of the union. He'd take a drop in money to do that job because 'my heart is in it. I'd be doing something that I really believe in.' 'Mr Respectable' they called John. He didn't raise his voice. He'd look at you earnestly fixing on you with his bright black eyes. 'When he says to management, "Look Mr So and So you're wrong on this one. I'll lay my job on the line on this one," they know there's something wrong.' A quiet thoughtful man:

It's part of a problem we've got I think, Huw. We've built up a good organization here. A really good organization. But we've got to be careful that we don't become too professional. I fight Ford's because I think a lot of what they do is wrong – morally wrong. I think it's wrong to sack a man, and I think we should fight every case we get. It's difficult though. You get a case – bad work record, lateness, absenteeism, cheeking the foreman, the lot – and you think to yourself, 'No chance – a loser'. You probably don't know the lad, so you don't try too hard because it's a loser. We can get too professional if we're not careful.

You see we're meeting plant management every day. You get to know them; get to know their weaknesses, what you can get away with and what drives them mad. So you adapt the way you behave, you present your case – 'professionally' if you like, but you don't go in there and say 'this is a bloody war and if we don't get it we're going to smash you'. We don't say that but I think we ought to now and again. Because it *is* a bloody war.

Here is the root of the stewards' ambivalence – they are at war but must pretend they are not. They cope with this in any number of ways. They refuse to be consistent. Eddie explains:

Well you go in there with a case. A lad they're going to sack. And they say 'You're not defending this one are you?' and I say 'You bet we are. We're going all the way on this one.' They can't understand it, they'll say 'But you had a case like this one last week and you agreed . . .' 'I agreed nothing.'

Y'know if you're in this place you've got cases all the time. And almost all of them you want to win. You want to get the lad off. What they want is to say, 'Well Mr Roberts, this is a case of something or other and we've agreed that this warrants the sack'. I won't have that. I fight each case on its merits. I want to be able to fight any and every case that comes up in this plant.

They fight against being routinized. In fact they struggle all the time. It's like pushing a rock up hill. There's always the chance it will roll back and crush you. You can't properly see where you're going and if you could it's all uphill anyway. But you develop big muscles.

The PTA stewards developed into a strong organization. It had strength but also guile. The stewards didn't think it advisable to oppose management continuously. Brawn had its use, but management could also be played like a fish. On productivity bargaining, for example, the stewards were under no illusions about what management was after. They knew what productivity meant. But they intended to *use* it.

We knew what they were after. They wanted control of the job. We *knew* tha'. We also knew that they weren't going to get it. No matter what was said in the office. No matter how many cups of tea we drank, we *knew* that we had that shop floor sewn up good and that they could do *nothing* to touch it. So we went along to their meetings. Agreed to things that didn't matter, to some high sounding principles, and used it as a platform. All right we said, you want to talk 'participation', well there's one or two things which *we'd* like some participation in.

In dealing with management, therefore, the stewards didn't want to be tied down. Their commitment was to the lads on the shop floor and it was this commitment that gave them their cutting edge in negotiations with management. It also served them in their dealings with the union bureaucracies. 'It's all right for those bastards, they haven't got to work in this fucking place. Making motors all their life.' Like managers 'the bureaucrats' could be used, but in an important respect they were different. The stewards gave no time to the idea of 'changing management'. Management were unequivocally on the other side. The bureaucrats, however, were at least supposed to be for the workers. In a way that makes them more dangerous, and the stewards were aware of the dangers – 'I don't have any illusions about any of 'em.' But for all this the idea of *changing* 'the union' was one which had an appeal and made some sort of sense. From the middle sixties onwards the stewards were continually attempting to reform the TGWU. They lobbied the meetings of the Ford NJNC and demanded the referral of all national decisions to the plants. They demanded that the national officers, like the stewards, should represent the lads instead of feathering their own nests. They also wanted more information, a better service:

Look, this union has got fantastic funds. Millions of half a crowns every week. What do they do with it? They hoard it away somewhere. Cousins keeps it under his bed in an old sock. Y'know? You've got to move a bit with the times. The people we're negotiating with in the factory aren't stupid. Ford pays for the best. They've got figures at their finger tips. Now we've always got a way out of that – y'know tell them to stuff it. But if we knew the score I'm sure we'd be in a better position. It we had the union organization behind us. With our own people from the universities.

But wouldn't that mean even more direction from the top? Wouldn't the *bureaucrats* use these experts. Wouldn't the experts end up telling the lads on the shop floor what to do?

No. Definitely no. We'd tell *them*. We'd say that we've got a problem. We want some information on this one. We'd ring up Transport House and we'd get hold of somebody who'd tell us the score. That's all. You ring up Transport House now and all you get is 'Oh he's too busy ...' If you get hold of anyone they can't tell you fuck-all. They're all a bag of wind.

What I'm saying see is the union *could* do a good job. If there were decent officers, research people ... they could do a lot. We're landed with this shower of shit and all we can do is to try and alter them. Make them do something.

In this respect they were optimists – almost naively so. As one said, 'You've got to try to do something, or you'd hang yourself.' This naivety didn't extend to formal politics however. Like many other people they had some hopes of the Labour Party in 1964, but these soon turned to cynicism. By 1967 they had no faith in politicians and firmly believed that the unions should leave party politics alone. One or two of the stewards had turned their cynicism into a definite political perspective. One was a member of the Communist Party:

We *must* get more involved in politics. With the Prices and Incomes Board we've got to take the government on. We've created this monster that's in control now. We've got to organize to ensure that it stays in power but that it changes its policies to socialist policies.

A thorough-going cynicism was more general:

This Labour government has been an eye-opener for me. *And* the lads on the floor. We've talked about it quite a bit. Most of the lads think you can forget about the Labour Party, y'know. Forget about it because it's never going to do anything for the working class. The general feeling on the floor is then we're on our own. Y'know, we've got to fight our own battles. Do everything ourselves, from now on.

This just about sums it up. The stewards' committee was going it alone. It didn't mind company but it had to be company that could be trusted and had proved itself. It also had to be company which didn't meddle in the affairs of the lads on the floor. Two incidents will illustrate this. An ex-student and member of the *International Socialist* group came to work in the paint shop at Halewood. He attended union meetings and after he'd been in the plant for a year was talking about standing for shop steward. He was strongly advised against standing by the senior stewards.

He isn't a bad lad, he's been here for a bit, but he's going to leave after another year so he reckons. I had a word with him, 'Look,' I said, 'all you want really is to have a go at this Company isn't it.' He said 'yes'. Y'know he hated Ford's, like we all do, and he wanted to take out a steward's card and go beserk. I told him it wasn't on. For a start if you go in there with that attitude, Ford's will destroy you. They know what the game's all about. But there's the members as well. I said 'Y'er nor on. You're not going to use those lads for your vendetta aginst the Company. If you take out a steward's card you *represent* those lads.'

The second incident took place at a meeting in the Swan Hotel on London Road in Liverpool two weeks after the debacle of February 1970. In the early months of that year a new left-wing broadsheet appeared on Merseyside. It took its name, *Big Flame*, from the title of

---

Big Flame newspaper

Lots of you will have seen the new rank and file newspaper named after the play on television about the Liverpool docks. This paper is an independently run fortnightly publication and most of the articles are written by shop stewards or other activists in the Merseyside area. This paper, if it's to improve its size and circulation, needs your support, so order your copy now from your steward.

A readers' meeting is to take place on Sunday 17 May at 7 p.m. in the Swan Hotel, London Road, Liverpool. This meeting is to determine a firm editorial policy, and it is our view that decisions on policy should remain firmly in the hands of rank and file workers on the shop floor. You are therefore urged to attend this meeting to vote and express your particular point of view, and so keep the control of this paper out of the hands of small sectarian and unrepresentative groups.

From *PTA Voice*, 1970

the television play about the Liverpool dockers written by Jim Allen. The people behind the paper were mainly Liverpool University students whose concern was to produce a paper that was for the people and also of the people. They wanted the copy to come from the rank and file. This idea had an appeal to the PTA stewards and five of them attended the first public meeting called by the group. One of them acted as chairman. The meeting was attended by representatives of most of the left-wing groupings, and an argument developed about the political line of the paper. The Halewood stewards consistently argued throughout this discussion that they would not be a party to any grouping that attempted to dictate policy within the plants. People who didn't work in the plants didn't know the problems of the plants. The stewards were responsible to their members, they knew what was involved on the shop floor, they knew how to deal with management, and no outside group could interfere with their activity in the plant. They had problems enough, they said, without the smear of Communist infiltration: what was needed on Merseyside was a newspaper which supplied the lads on the shop floor with information about the struggles of other workers in other factories in the area. What the lads wanted, and what would be a great help to the stewards, was a newspaper which told the story from the point of view of the lads. Eddie Roberts made the point forcibly:

> The capitalist press give you the bosses' point of view and the left-wing papers like the *Newsletter* [now *Newsline*] tell you what ought to be done without knowing what the correct situation is. Nobody tells it as it happens from the point of view of the lads on the shop floor. You talk about Revolution and I agree with you. We do need a Revolution in this country and when we go to the barricades I'll be fighting there, probably harder than a lot of you, but there's not going to be a Revolution for a bit. That's the problem. What we've got to deal with is that plant up there as it is now.

During the exchanges that followed the Halewood stewards were criticized for being 'afraid of being called Communist'. After the meeting Eddie said:

> I don't give a shit what names they call me. It doesn't matter to me if they call me 'a Communist' or 'a Trotskyist' or whatever. It's just that it gets in the way of the job. Y'know, the lads get enough propaganda as it is without having it thrown at them that their convenor is a Communist getting orders from Moscow or something. It doesn't matter to me personally, it just makes the job of the stewards in the plant that much harder.
> Whenever I go to these meetings, I find myself asking, 'What sort of a job

would *he* do on the shop floor? What sort of a steward would *he* make?' A lot of these political fellas wouldn't have a leg to stand on if they had to deal with Ford management.

These incidents clearly illustrate the ideology of the stewards in the PTA plant. The firmness of the position they took in the meeting was in part a reflection of the February 'strike'. This had brought home to them, what they knew only too well – they could go only as fast as the members would let them. The only way they could lead the members was by sticking close to them. At a time when many important words have lost their meaning, ones like 'Communist' and 'intellectual' can all too easily be used as a smear. The charge of 'outside interference' can be a damaging one to a shop steward organization. At such a time the unions can take on a new significance for, surprising though it may be, working people still turn to the union. The notion that 'the men are the union' has been worn down to a cliché, but it still means something. The leaders may be bureaucrats, but they used to work on the shop floor and, in a way, you know where you are with them. They may be bent, but they can still speak the same language. It all may be remote, but still in a sense 'the men *are* the union'. And that's the only way in which car workers can come to *be* anything, for the union is the only institution that they can make any real claims upon. That's why the stewards, for all their criticism of the bureaucrats, are trade unionists, because it's only through the union that they can see any hope at all.

The stewards at Halewood therefore were class conscious trade unionists. They knew that the working class has been exploited by the capitalists for centuries. Not a few of them saw the need for a revolution in some ultimate sense. They were socialists and they wanted a better society, but they were uncertain how to obtain it. What they did know was that the worker on the shop floor needs protection, now. At Ford's it took up most of your strength to provide that protection. The stewards would give up some of their surplus energy to activities away from the plant, but they were not interested in 'pie in the sky'. Ultimately they were interested solely in activities which could dovetail into their activities in the plant and which they could use to develop the ideas of the membership. This doesn't mean that they were opposed to students and left-wing sectarian politics. They were not a little intrigued by students, by their lifestyle and their ideas. They weren't completely prejudiced against them. It was more a question of relevance. Their overwhelming concern was 'the plant' and the practicalities of living in the here and now. Basically, left-wing politics provided them with no answers to these questions. Neither did it provide a vision for the future, an understandable, realizable goal. They'd listen and argue, but when it came right down to it they couldn't see how it helped. That there was a failure *to meet* is certain. In answering the question 'Why?' no small emphasis should be given to the vacuous state of modern socialist theory, to the failure of the 'revolutionary left' to penetrate in any meaningful way into the lives of working men and women. This, together with the strong hold 'syndicalist' consciousness has had on the thinking of radical trade unionists in Britain throughout this century.[1]

The stewards were trade unionists, over half of them would have liked to be a full-time union officer, and their class consciousness was essentially a factory-based one. They were extremely sensitive of their relationship with their members. Does this mean that they led from behind; that they were always following the members and not directing them? This notion of 'leadership' comes from the same stable as that of 'the ringleader'. It is essentially aristocratic and militaristic, part of the world of the jutting chin and the stiff upper lip. It reduces 'leadership' to the qualities of the individual leaders, their moral fibre. Leadership needn't be like that. The shop floor leadership was itself produced through the struggles of workers on the shop floor at Halewood. These struggles, and the unity that carried groups of workers through them, were crystallized in the shop stewards. The shop stewards' committee was a testament to these struggles. It remained fixed in the world after the fires had died down, it embodied the lessons learned in past struggles and ensures that the embers never become cold. It retained a degree of autonomy from the membership, but the very existence of the members ensured that the committee did not become isolated from the practical needs of the working class. Leadership, therefore, is a two-way process. Not only are the policies followed by shop stewards limited by the willingness of the membership to follow them, but it is not given that there should be any willingness at all: what there is can be a result of the activities of the leaders. At the level of the section,

1. In effect this means that in times of crisis the stewards revert to the old style 'proven' leadership of either the Communist Party or the left wing of the Labour Party. The take-over and 'work-in' at UCS only highlight a general tendency within the politics of militant shop floor committees. On Merseyside the Communist Party is the only 'left' group with long-standing membership amongst proven militants. Also a man like Eric Heffer, long-established union activist and Labour MP for Walton, still maintained strong ties within the Liverpool Labour movement. He speaks at all the major rallies and raises questions brought to him by the shop stewards in the House of Commons.

for example, the steward is responsible to the members, who are able through him to negotiate with management. But no steward takes up every case, he doesn't act upon every complaint that his members bring to him. Initially, as we have seen, he will want to know how strongly the whole section feels about the particular complaint. 'You get some lads who complain about everything. They're always in the right, sort of thing. No one else has got a point of view.' Usually the steward won't take up a complaint unless he's sure that it is genuinely felt to be an irritation by the lads. Even then he will be influenced by what he knows to be his chances in the office. The members may complain against a supervisory decision that is legitimate within the terms of an agreement signed by the unions and management. In these situations the stewards may 'kid the members along a bit', pretend to take up issues.

You've got to do it sometimes. Tell them you've done something when you haven't. You've got to do it to prevent them from making fools of themselves. I'd never deceive them for my own gain – but sometimes I've got to for theirs.

In taking up an issue, therefore, the steward will be influenced by the level of opinion of his section, the nature of his relationship with management and also by the shop stewards' committee. The action by any one group of workers in a car plant has a clear consequence for other groups of workers in the plant. As such the stewards' committee and the convenor, its elected head, perform a particularly important role, for through it and him the *particular* problem of an operative on a section becomes related to the general position of the three-thousand-odd workers in the plant. The stewards attached great importance to the committee because it was through this that they could push their heads above the water of the section and get some idea of where they were going. One of the dominant ideas within this committee was that it should provide a 'progressive leadership' typified by 'forward thinking'. On the floor of the car plant men are involved in small struggles day after day. The shop stewards' committee was seen to allow the stewards to *anticipate* problems which could be planned for. It was seen as a vehicle whereby stewards could relay to their sections the experiences of other sections. Simply it was seen as the basis for a united 'plant policy' with which to face management and the union bureaucracies.

What does all this add up to?

The shop stewards' committee, then, can be understood as the leadership of the shop-floor workers in the Halewood plant. In that sense it maintains an important autonomy from the shop floor. The way in which this autonomy was used, i.e. the form of the committee's leadership, was determined by the fact that the shop stewards were active *trade unionists*, and their shop stewards' committee was a trade union *organization*. Activism and organization held together by a class consciousness that derives its politics from a detailed understanding of relationships within the factory. A politics that finds its expression in 'taking the piss' out of the foremen, in a laugh and a joke, and in the strike. A politics that is structured by ambivalence. A dislike and distrust of the employer but a need of employment.

But politics by its very nature is about the whole of society. It is concerned with class relationships not only at their base in the work situation but in their virulent manifestation throughout society. Because of the enormous power established within the apparatus of the state (government; the army and the police; education ...) all important changes to modern society are achieved through a political party. Trade unions are remarkably unsuited to the task of changing society. Their very existence is a testament to the existence of employers and capital. This acceptance of capital and, to some extent, the 'rights of capital' has made it difficult for trade unions to restrain their incorporation into the state through the 1960s and 70s. At their core trade unions are defensive organizations built and supported by workers who need protection in the labour market. Protection against the power of the supervisor, collective defence of 'the rate'. Undoubtedly trade unions involve more than this. They are working-class organizations and the numerous conflicts experienced by workers find their expression within the union. The disjuncture between what has been termed a 'trade union consciousness' and a 'political consciousness' is not a clear one. Politics and a political understanding can be contained implicitly in the way in which workers and activists deal with and come to understand their union and their employers. What is clear though is that while 'politics' is contained within trade unionism, trade unions restrain rather than develop this political awareness. Fundamentally they are economic bargainers. Traditionally the British trade union movement has coped with the contradiction of opposing the employer while at the same time recognizing him through a dichotomy of the 'industrial' and 'political' wings of the Labour movement. A distinction not too different from that employed by Pat Lowry and other IR ideologists (see page 224). Anything to do with changing society has been hived off to the Labour

Party. This tactic held some degree of conviction in the past but it held little credence amongst working people after the 1966 Labour government. In the absence of a party with any meaningful politics the lads at Halewood decided that they were on their own. They were thrown back upon the trade unions and their grassroots organizations within them. The main feature of a trade union is its stability. It is its strength and weakness.

Was, and is, a shop stewards' committee enough? The nature of the situation, the absence of anything else, means that in a way the committee had to be enough. Because it was all they had. Nevertheless it is clearly possible to see how the nature of the committee creates immense problems for both the shop steward organization, the individual steward and, not least, the men on the line. The switching of capital investment, from Halewood to Dagenham or elsewhere in Europe and the world is a threat which raises the issue in starkest form. Bob Costello's anguish as one of his lads was sacked is but another manifestation of the same phenomenon. In a real sense the committee is nothing like enough. This fact compounded the crises faced by the stewards and the lads on the line.

There is more. The *facts* of trade unionism create crises for the stewards. So does the nature of organization itself. Trade unions are large organizations administered by full-time officers. Full-time negotiations in offices away from the shop floor. The bureaucrats. The problems of organization, of specialization, a degree of concentration in decision-making, also exist at the shop floor level. At Halewood the convenor and his deputies acted as full-time negotiators. The seven senior stewards, the JWC members, did very little work as production workers. They were known as 'The Magnificent Seven' by the lads on the line.

The facts of trade unionism and the facts of organization forever play upon the gap that separates the rank and file member from the stewards. The uneasy synthesis of leaders and followers.

In the summer of 1968 (see Chapter 7) the union organization within the PTA plant was in disarray as a result of the implementation of the 1967 New Wages Structure. The plant was riven with sectionalism and not a few stewards felt that the 'whole thing is falling apart'.

It's getting pretty bad in fact. I'm getting lads coming up to me saying 'what sort of an organization have we got here anyway?' Y'know, good lads. Trade unionists, not yer fly fellas.

The state of the *international* competition within the motor industry had produced a crisis on the shop floor of the Halewood plant. The nature of international economic relations had undermined the position of the shop steward organization at Halewood. It was leading to more and more pressure on the sections, and with it increasing criticism of the PTA plant convenor, Mick Donnelly. These pressures allowed personal hostilities that existed within the PTA plant to break surface. It all proved a bit too much for Mick.

Mick had never really wanted the convenor's job. He would have liked to be the joker and the elder statesman of the PTA organization. In 1968 he occupied a seat on the National Executive of the union. He liked this. He liked going to London. Meeting people . . . having a few pints and a laugh. He'd represent the lads there and make a good job of it. He was at his happiest 'reporting back' from these excursions, with accounts to the lads of who promised to do what and talk of ribaldry over a pint. But he was also the plant convenor and had been since 1966 when he took over from Bill Brodrick. Mick was always a strong contender for the job but Eddie Roberts was a more obvious candidate. Eddie was a powerful negotiator and had a strong following amongst the lads. But he had been warned off by Les Kealey, the National Officer of the TGWU – his relationship with management was such that he wouldn't be able to represent the lads, Kealey said. Eddie wasn't too bothered. He wasn't attracted to the convenor's job. He had a wife and two small kiddies. The time came, though, when Eddie *had* to become the convenor of the PTA plant.

The convenor occupies an extremely important position in a large factory. The day-to-day conduct of plant negotiations is left in his hands. He, before everyone else, is responsible for the effective implementation of the policy of the stewards' committee, or the branch within the plant. He remains on the day shift. Unlike the other stewards he maintains regular contact with the plant management. In many plants he has his own office and telephone. He is *The Man* on the trade union side and he can become as remote from the rank and file worker as the full-time officers. The 'Armchair Generals' at Dagenham illustrate this tendency. The puzzled anger of the sewing machinist – 'How *do* you get rid of the convenor' (see page 178 – is all too typical of the feelings of many workers towards their lay representatives.

There are ways, however, of getting rid of a convenor. At Halewood in 1968 the members were voting with their feet, and it was becoming increasingly clear to many stewards that the committee was no longer *leading* the lads into disputes, but lamely following behind picking up the pieces. And this was getting through to Mick. The daily activities of the members act as a check on the convenor and the stewards. So too does the formal need for re-election. Under certain circumstances these controls can make the convenor's position extremely vulnerable. The stewards aren't the only activists.

At Halewood the convenor is elected annually by the shop stewards' committee. To become eligible for the convenor's job a man *must* be elected steward by the lads on his section. Once he becomes convenor he ceases to serve as steward on the section and this job is carried out by a stand-in. In order to remain in office the convenor has to have an amicable relationship with the men who work in the area where 'his job' is. Even more importantly, he must retain the support of his 'stand-in' – the man in the best position to 'up-stage' him in a subsequent election.

Ronnie Walsh was Mick Donnelly's 'stand-in'. He was, and still is, prone to catastrophe. Ronnie worked on the paint mix. One morning the floor would be green. A half-inch deep in solidified paint. 'That valve ... I'll remember that.' Another morning it would be red. 'Oh, *that* valve ...' Unkindly they called him Mr Plod. He wore a white boiler suit with his cigarettes in his breast pocket. Bert Owen would regularly knock Ronnie's cigarettes up in the air, catch them and light himself one. Bert was fly and brash; Ronnie solid, dependable and honest. He was often late for work. In the winter his house would be the centre of any blizzard that hit Liverpool. He'd have to dig his car out. Then he'd reverse it back into the snow he'd shovelled and have to dig it out again. He had big feet that swelled up. He'd spend ages trying to get them into his shoes. He has locked himself in, climbed through windows and found himself locked out, without his shoes and late for work again.

A catastrophe brought him to active unionism. His first job was on the buildings and he joined the TGWU almost as soon as he walked on the site. Everybody joined, so he did. From there he got a job as an auxiliary plant attendant in the Wallasey Power Station. A better, more regular job than the buildings, although it meant shift work and getting across the Birkenhead docks. In those days Ronnie rode a bicycle. One day on a morning shift he was riding to work in plenty of time when he found the tide in, the bridges up – a chasm of space and time. Late for work, a bollocking and a warning that 'if it happens again ...' The next day he was even earlier getting into Birkenhead. He even made a detour to safeguard himself, only to be caught at the other bridge. Pedalling backwards and forwards in the dark, in a sweat, swearing; late again and the sack.

> The injustice of that rankled inside me for years. It's still rankling inside me. At Wallasey I'd been a union member, I'd paid my dues regularly but I never really got involved. I never knew *why* there were unions or what this system was all about. That sacking taught me that. It taught me about injustice at first hand. Then I went to the Garston Bottle Works and the conditions there made me an even more determined unionist.

He helped organize the workers at the Bottle Works into a viable force, became convenor and got a lot of things changed.

> At Wallasey it was one of those jobs that runs itself. There was no real need for shop floor activism there. All the negotiations were done on national level. At Garston it was entirely different. We all banded together there because the conditions were so bad. They were really bad. The union activity was non-existent, so a few of us got things going and got things changed.

For Ronnie, although the union was basically about wages and conditions, a lot more was involved than this. He objects to the fact that 'human aspects are always forced into the background', that management and union bosses don't 'take account of the sort of lives the lads on the shop floor have to live'. In 1967 he was perturbed by the fact that 'everyone seems to talk about "the union" as something divorced from themselves. They *are* the union and they've got to act as if they are.' When he came to Halewood, Mick was the steward on his section. Ronnie supported him and became card steward. When Mick became convenor he asked Ronnie to take over the steward's job.

> I've always been on Mick Donnelly's section. I've always shown an interest and the lads knew that I had the experience. I was already the card steward so when Donnelly was elected convenor I suppose I was the obvious choice as a stand-in. I liked the job. I liked doing it and I didn't like to refuse him. It's all full of the same old platitudes this. It sounds like I'm saying 'because I'm a fucking good fella'. I want to do something constructive in assisting myself and the members of my class. I couldn't see myself standing by and see someone else doing it.

So Ronnie became Mick's stand-in and it worked out amicably enough until 1968. By autumn of that year Mick's position had become untenable. Several issues impinged upon Mick's position. The most important single event was the unofficial overtime ban called by the PTA stewards and supported by the members of a mass meeting at the Liverpool stadium. The overtime ban had been called as part of a strategy in pursuit of a national wages claim (see page 172). The ban had much greater support amongst the stewards in the A shift. The stewards on this shift were advised to moderate their activities by the National Officer. They firmly told him what he could do with his advice. The B shift stewards were weakening and, as a result of a mass meeting called on an evening when the A shift was on nights and attended by predominantly B shift workers, the ban was called off. The elder statesman was in a flat spin.

Ronnie Walsh was on A shift as were Eddie Roberts and Gerry Flaherty. At a euphoric canteen meeting the lads on the shift overwhelmingly voted to continue with the ban. 'The lads on our shift were marvellous. To their everlasting credit they stuck by their stewards and we really had the Company going. But the organization let them down.' Management was exerting severe pressure against the A shift stewards, and Mick wasn't supporting them. Ronnie Walsh was moved off his job. His members got him reinstated. They refused to start work. They marched in unison right around the paint shop to the plant manager's office to complain ... to demand that Ronnie be put back on the paint mix where he could function as a steward. Ronnie got his job back but the spectre of the 'ball and chain' remained. The 'old days' weren't so long ago. Something had to be done. The organization had to be put back on its feet again. The two shifts had to come together. The lads had to be given a lead or all would be up. Mick obviously couldn't sort it out, so someone else would have to have a go. Eddie *had* to take the job on. They argued and they decided. Ronnie had had enough, and the lads were determined. They weren't going to vote Mick in again. Ronnie was no longer going to be a stand-in, he was going to be the steward. In the face of this Mick pulled out. He hadn't wanted the job and he'd hand it over. Eddie became the convenor. His task was to reintroduce 'forward thinking' into the Halewood organization.

Eddie Roberts was brought up in Selbourne Street. In the centre of Liverpool 8. Cosmopolitan, downtown Liverpool. The girls on the streets. Racketeering and Rachmanism. An old-established working-class area. Second and their generation 'coloured' Liverpudlians. An area with a strong sense of community – 'the cops had no chance of finding you if you got back on Selly.' Carol lived across the road. They married in their teens.

Eddie's father abandoned his mother. He was a 'fly fella'. The last time he and Eddie met they fought. That was while Eddie was still at school. Eddie was a clever lad. He won a scholarship to one of

Liverpool's elite grammar schools – the Institute. The only lad from the area. He had no friends there. His mates, the members of his gang, would meet him at the gates. He hated it at the Institute. 'They hated to see you smile there. I think Ford's must have been behind them.' He did his homework on the bus. He spent his evenings on the streets.

He left school when he was fifteen. He had to. He didn't mind but he would have liked to have tried his O levels. He had one or two jobs in quick succession.

When I left school I didn't know where I was going. I had no idea what I was going to do. I knew I had to get a job. The Labour sent me to this small factory. I was interviewed by the man in charge and he was pleased to get his hands on someone from the College. They gave me a job as a trainee. I was going to learn the ins and outs of the factory from top to bottom. I stayed there two days I think. The foreman told me that I was to start by sweeping up. I told him he could stick it. I wasn't sweeping up for anybody. So I left. If I'd stayed I'd probably have been the manager there now. Twenty-three quid a week . . . and the Company bike.

His next job was at a trouser factory. His mate Jimmy Hagan was an apprentice there and he got him a start. (Jimmy became convenor at the Standard Triumph factory in Liverpool). That lasted a day and a half. The foreman sent him to fetch a fella – 'Who are you then? – running messages for the foreman . . .' Bang. Eddie hit him in the mouth. The fight reconvened at the clock and the two of them, along with Jimmy Hagan, got their cards.

From the trouser factory Eddie and Jimmy moved to Dunlop's. Eddie's uncle worked there. He could have got him into an apprenticeship but Eddie wasn't interested. He wanted the money. He wanted to be on production. On piece work. His experience of Dunlop's was an eventful as that of his previous workplaces. But he stayed this time. He still got involved in fights. He is remembered as 'the lad with the big eye. He always had a big lip or a closed eye. He was always fighting, that lad.' Fighting on the street. Playing tricks in the factory. He got attached to a 'character'. An ex-professional boxer. He'd sit on the back of the bus after work alongside Clarkey who'd entertain the packed bus.

You'd be into town before you knew where you were. It's a long journey but you never used to notice it. He'd start up as soon as he sat down. Usually he'd pick on someone 'Hello, here he is . . . the Pope's best friend' and he'd carry on for the whole journey. Y'know everybody collapsed with laughter and this fella wishing the earth would swallow him up.

Jokes in the bus, jokes at work.

At the end of the shift we'd run for the clock. I don't know why we did but we always ran for the clock. It just meant we had to wait on the bus but we just had to clock the card. Well one day I run to the clock, grab for my coat and it's tied up in knots. It was Clarkey. He was a strong bastard and he'd really tied it up tight. I couldn't move it. So the next day I took some boxes of those very small tacks into work. I made a tiny hole in the pocket of Clarkey's coat, tipped the tacks in and then gave the coat a shake. The tacks spread all through the lining. When he came to pick it off the hook it was like a ton weight. Months later he'd come up to me and say, 'I leaned back against the chair last night and had a tack right in my spine ... you bastard.' He was a good skin, Clarkey.

Dunlop's, however, was an organized plant and at Dunlop's Eddie and Jimmy came into contact with the union. Almost the first thing they did was to work out the piece rates. They calculated that all the wages were wrong. They told the steward. He was a bit put out – 'You know you lads didn't ought to be calling me down here like this.' But he listened and they were right. For months the wrong rates had been paid. Eddie and Jimmy got about thirty bob back pay. 'We bought the steward a packet of fags. The other bastards got pounds. They didn't buy him anything.'

Eddie's contact with the union was increased when he became involved in a dispute. His department was running down and he was offered another job in another part of the factory – 'on the shoes'. It was a production job and he accepted it. It transpired that he was ineligible for the job and was offered a 'boy's job' instead. He refused and was threatened with the sack. He got no help from the steward so he took off, got the help of a steward he knew and eventually the convenor, Stan Pemberton.

That was the first time I'd met Stan. I was amazed. I'd never met anybody like him. 'What's this,' he said, 'they offered you a job and then when you arrived they put you on to something else. We'll see about this.' Y'know great big powerful figure marching off to see the foreman with me behind him. I got the job on the line. Then Johnny Jones became the steward and I started helping him out. I think that's when I first saw how important trade unions are. He was a real hero ... Stan Pemberton.

By the time Eddie arrived at Ford's he had a better idea where he was going. He had a pretty good idea what factories were about. He wasn't going to get pushed around ... he had always known how to defend himself with his fists, and at Dunlop's he'd learned the important defensive significance of an organized shop floor. He became established in the small parts section of the paint shop. He attended the first union meetings and became minutes secretary of the Branch – 'I was one of the few who were handy with a pen.' He was steward on his section with lots of support from the lads. He developed a close friendship with other stewards on his shift. He knew Billy Brodrick and Sammy Glasstone well, and he learned a lot from them. He also maintained his contact with Stan Pemberton and the stewards at Dunlop's (see below). It was these friendships and alliances that structured his trade union activism and his militancy. His ingrained cussedness and intelligence was enough to make him stand out against the Ford world. This opposition was nurtured and controlled by the fabric of social relationships within the shop steward organization at Halewood and the Liverpool Labour movement in general. These relationships helped him over crises and allowed him to develop into a sophisticated shop-floor activist.

Dear Eddie,

Many thanks for your letter which I received today. First of all let me say how pleased I am to hear that the seeds so ably planted by yourself and others are now beginning to 'shoot'. This is a harbinger of the tree and finally the 'fruit'. Be sure to nurture the shoot (plenty of attention and care).

Secondly, the membership already attained could be a power in the Region. The potential you indicate will certainly lead to one of the biggest branches in the country.

Thirdly, you can be sure that so far as our branch is concerned, unity of membership is a necessary prerequisite to membership advancement in industry. You can rely on Dunlop's Speke.

. . . You can depend upon my full support *in every quarter*: . . . But Eddie, *you* can make a job of this if you continue to put industrial matters first.

That's all for now young friend. Support you can depend upon from here. Use you obvious power wisely and put the membership first at all times. Good luck.

Yours sincerely,
Stan Pembo

The significance of these relationships can be illustrated by comparing Eddie Roberts with Les Carville (see pages 153–4). Like Eddie, Les had no family tradition of union activism. He left school and went into the army. He married and accepted that he had to settle down. He came to Ford's for the money and with some idea of getting

on. He had a baby girl and he wanted to buy a house. Like so many
.others he had a rude awakening. He was sent to work on the trim line.

This Company made me a trade unionist. The supervisor we had was worse
than you'd get in the army. Y'know a real 'stand to attention' type. I'm a
Roman Catholic and I always used to think the shop stewards were a load of
Commies. Y'know the sort of thing you read in the papers. But when you're a
part of it, it's a different thing altogether.

He was working with a 'good bunch of lads', he stood up to the
supervisor and became a steward. In fact Eddie suggested to him that
he should take the job on. He became extremely active, the torment of
supervision on the trim and a hero to the lads on his section. He went
to the TGWU summer school in Cirencester and in 1967 was talking of
going to Ruskin College 'to educate myself to help the members of my
class'.

Both he and Eddie were on the Joint Works Committee of the PTA.
Eddie was on the A shift, Les on the B shift. Both were young, and the
most militant stewards on their shifts. They differed temperamentally.
Eddie was much more assured, Les threshing around, tensed up, still
didn't know where he was going. He was also extremely isolated. He
had the support of his members on the section but had built up no
strong links with the other B shift stewards. Like Eddie he had made
enemies but had established no social network either within the plant
or outside. Unlike Eddie he had no political base. This made him
extremely vulnerable. It also retarded his political development. He
didn't know where he was going.

In 1967 he came up against the crunch. He committed a number of
censorable irregularities and the District Officer of the TGWU, Bill
Brodrick, demanded the withdrawal of his credentials as a steward. He
was no longer a steward. He asked to be moved off his section of the
trim into the final assembly department. He moved. He began to enjoy
the free time. He made virulent attacks upon the TGWU. He talked
about recruiting members into the NUVB. But he liked the free time.
His wife liked him being at home and she wanted him to become a
supervisor. Les was still threshing about, still isolated. He became a
supervisor on Richie Rowlands's section. And a particularly unpopular
one at that. Threats from Richie and from Billy McGuire. Near
physical violence. Les had joined the other side.

The assembly-line workers' relationship with the car plant is a
tenuous one. It has been described as a 'brittle bond'. A bond based on
the need for cash from which all moral committment is absent and

which can be easily broken. The militancy of car workers is based on this 'brittle bond'. This militancy creates problems for the activist, but it also finds expression through union activity. For this militancy to survive as a radical force within society it has to be linked with the socialist tradition of the past and projected towards the future political development of the working class. It has to be attached to ongoing radical working-class traditions. Les Carville's experience symbolizes the fragile basis of the assembly-line workers' radicalism. If isolated, it can go either way.

The case of Les contrasts clearly with that of Eddie. Through relationships with old activists as well as mates of his own age in the PTA plant, Eddie was able to develop the past experiences and traditions of the Liverpool working class in an entirely new setting. These relationships enabled him to transform the consciousness of a street gang activist into that of a class conscious industrial militant.[2] This stress upon social relationships is important as a corrective to prevalent psychological theories of leadership. Eddie and Les had quite different personalities and this is important. Equally important, however, is the social context within which these 'personalities' develop both an understanding of union activity and a base from which to project such activity. Eddie was able to build such a base both within the Ford factory and outside. By 1969 he had established himself with the Labour movement on Merseyside. Driving around Liverpool with him involved you in a catechism on Liverpool union activity. 'That's where John lives now ... Freddie lives there, I don't know whether you met him, he was at Ford's, he's a steward in English Electric now ... Jack lives around the corner, you met his brother once, big lad ... Frank used to live in this house ... there's Ronnie ...' Social networks such as these operate within most social situations and they achieve paramount importance within local Labour movements. They form the basis of the activist's political capital. Through contacts such as these the activist can bring to his own work situation the experiences of other workers in the area. The contacts are a source of information and support. They can be turned to for a strike fund collection, a sympathy strike or the black. The ability to call upon such information and support is an important part of a shop-floor activist's armoury. It is

2. There were costs. Carol: 'It's the job I think. It's taken his spirit. There's no fun in him anymore. When he was at Dunlop's he was always joking. He'd come home, and we'd go for a bevvy or to the pictures. Now he just sits – or talks union. It's a rat-race up there. And we've got older – bugger Ford's.

through such contacts that leaders emerge in factories and stamp their impression upon the local scene.

During the time that Eddie was convenor of the PTA he became thought of as a 'charismatic leader'. During the 1969 strike there was a strong tendency for the press on Merseyside to see the strike action of ten thousand workers at Halewood as a manifestation of one man's magnetic personality. The 'personality theory' apart from being a useful cornerstone to any witch-hunt and agitator scare, throws out of focus the important organizational background to the leader. This doesn't mean that Eddie Roberts was unimportant. That if there hadn't been an Eddie Roberts there would have been someone else just as good. Eddie Roberts, like all men, is a unique individual. But it would be a mistake to isolate his individuality from the social framework of his life. He had a significant influence upon the way the PTA committee developed in the 1960s. Particularly after 1968. But this significance cannot be detached from the *existence* of the committee throughout the sixties. It was established in him and him in it. The existence of the committee created organizational forces which supported his activity as a convenor. What he did do, was to personify and thereby develop a tendency that had been growing within the committee throughout the 1960s. The idea of 'progressive leadership'. His brilliance as a negotiator and tactician added a unique dimension to this tendency. His two years as a convenor illustrate the strengths and vulnerabilities of this approach.

Industrial relations

The work of Industrial Relations at Ford covers every aspect of staff and hourly personnel administration – we have an atmosphere which encourages the exploration of new ideas and the development of new practices to help carry out our responsibility for ensuring that the right human conditions at work are created and maintained.

Industrial Relations staff in Ford come from various academic and industrial backgrounds, but all share the ability to plan, implement and control.

From: *Graduates in Ford*; Ford Motor Company (recruitment pamphlet, 1971)

10 Strike 1969

The modern epics are written in newsprint. One such epic dominated the front pages of British newspapers in the February and March of 1969. The Ford workers were on strike. Until then few people in Britain were aware that the Ford Motor Company owned an estate in Liverpool. For them Ford was at Dagenham. By March they knew of Halewood. The struggles of workers in the Halewood plants throughout the 1960s were entirely local. They were based in and enclosed by the plants. In 1969 a history of domestic strife broke surface and culminated in the first national stoppage of Ford plants in Britain. The strike raised many important issues. In part it can be seen as a product of the 1960s. The clauses in the agreement which aimed at penalizing 'unconstitutional action' fit into a period dominated by conflict over job control. The resignation, during the strike, of Mark Young, the Trade Union Chairman from his post on the NJNC and of Les Kealey the TGWU National Officer on the NJNC from the union, under pressure from the lay membership, highlight the tension that had built up between the trade union bureaucracies and their rank and file during the 1950s and 1960s. The Company's insistence on 'penalty clauses' and its recourse to the High Court took place against a backcloth of a Royal Commission and a White Paper from the Labour government advocating control of the activities of shop stewards. All the ingredients of industrial relations in the 1960s were contained in the strike. The shop stewards at Halewood were a product of this period and the strike was the quintessence of the conflicts they had experienced in the plant during that time. It was their final stroke and it turned out to be a glorious one, for this strike, above all others and perhaps above all else, marked the *watershed* between the 1960s and the 1970s. It was, as the Halewood stewards never tired of saying, not a money strike but a strike of principle. It was a turning point for the Halewood committee, in that they won an open fight on the issues that had plagued them for the previous six years. It was also a *watershed* for the shop stewards generally within the TGWU, because it revealed for the first time what the new General Secretary, Jack Jones, meant by 'union democracy'. The TGWU of Jack Jones in the 1970s was to be quite different from the union dominated in the 1950s by the iron-handed austerity of Arthur Deakin. Jack Jones was to break away from this tradition in a way which Frank Cousins never attempted. The 1969 strike revealed the potentialities of this 'new approach', and it also hinted at its limitations.

The 1969 strike can also be seen as a turning-point for the British working class and the Labour movement as a whole. The struggle was extended to the High Court and the DEP. As it progressed, the Labour government became more and more involved and increasingly antagonistic towards the strikers and Jack Jones's shop stewards. It was the harbinger of a lost election and of the 1970s when strikes would be bigger and longer and take place under the close scrutiny of the State.

It is worth looking at this strike.

'If this one gets through. If they get away with this one it will all be up. We'll be back to Victorian times. The ball and chain won't be in it. We'll have lost everything ... the lot.' Jimmy was talking in Eddie's front room on Selbourne Street. He'd come around to ask Eddie to sort out his tax. He showed me a pay slip. 'Look a'da. Twenty-one bleeding quid an' da bastard Ramsey tells me I ern thirty quid a week. He's nor on.' Jimmy left muttering about the need for a revolution. He left a couple of bob for each of Eddie's kids and went for a walk around Liverpool 8. He meets other lads from Ford's. They have a few bevvies and talk. They talk a lot about the strike. About Ramsey, the penalty clauses, Victorian times. They've been on strike for a week. They'd be out for another three. And they'd win. They'd knock back the 'penalty clauses' and sort out the bureaucrats. They wouldn't get as large a pay increase as they wanted, but they'd go back into the plant united – victorious.

It's cold in Liverpool 8 in February, at half past six in the morning it's freezing – more often than not it's wet as well. Eddie was going to the plant to organize the picket. Standing at the bus stop at the end of Princes Avenue. Freezing, and the bus didn't come. 'Kenny said he'd give me a lift if I needed it. Trying to get Kenny up is murder though.' Bang, bang ... Kenny arrives at the door. Bare feet, pushing his shirt into his trousers. 'Sorry Ed ... I hate these mornings.' In the car and out along Aigburth to the plant. Once he's awake Kenny is happy. 'What a strike. Great ... One big fucking strike ... bam ... A beautiful clean strike. Everybody out ... no scabs. And we're going to win ... bom, bom, bom ... we're going to win this one.' At the plant

gates a few stewards in a huddle. One lad's come right across Liverpool
... on three buses. 'It makes me mad this. They think that just because
they're on strike they can have a lie in. They just don't want to come
and picket.' It's all part of the morning ritual. There are no scabs, no
one to stop going through the gates. There's no real need for pickets.
But just in case. The cops are there too. Just in case.

Half an hour is enough. Off to Garston for a bacon sandwich and a
cup of tea. 'Fuck,' – Kenny's got a flat tyre – 'those bastard kids on our
street. I'll strangle them.' Change the wheel and into the cafe. A warm
and a talk. 'What's the situation, Ed?' Into the Garston Office for a
chat with Billy Brodrick. A few phone calls. On to Transport House or
Islington for a Strike Committee meeting. Telephone London. A
statement for the press. The next meeting at the Stadium ... Social
Security payments, organize strike ... a leaflet. 'It's bloody hard work
this, striking.'

The strike started on 21 February. The first strike day was supposed
to be Monday 24th but the lads in the transmission plant at Halewood
jumped the gun and took the Friday off as well. Like most strikes it was
unofficial to begin with, but was made official by the AUEW on the
Tuesday and by the TGWU on the Wednesday. Many of the unions
on the NJNC refused their official support. The GMWU was one of
these. It lost two thousand members at Halewood as a result. It also
suffered damage to its Liverpool office, which was attacked during the
strike by many of those men who were surviving without strike pay.
Support for the strike varied from plant to plant and union to union.
The three plants on the Halewood estate were solidly behind the strike.
It was their pressure which guaranteed official support and the
eventual favourable settlement which brought the lads back to work on
20 March.

The Director of Labour Relations of the Ford Motor Company at
the time was Leslie Blakeman. Sixty-five, bald-headed with large, sad
eyes. An industrial relations professional. Educated at Wallasey
Grammar School, across the water from Liverpool, he worked in his
father's solicitor's office and as a purser before taking his first job in
'personnel' at the Littlewoods mail-order business in the city. He
crossed swords with Sammy Glasstone when he moved to the Royal
Ordnance factory during the war (see Chapter 3). He came to Ford's in
1952 via a job at an atomic energy establishment. During his travels he
met and married Joan Woodward who was to become Professor of
Industrial Sociology at Imperial College, London. In 1969 he was
preparing to retire to a job at the newly-formed Commission on

Industrial Relations. He was already easing out of his seat at Ford's in favour of his deputy, Bob Ramsey. Leslie Blakeman was the professional and the 1969 package deal was to be his last piece of professionalism at Ford's. Instead it drove him to distraction. It was his 'most worrying and disappointing experience' (*The Times*, 12 March 1969). By the end of it he was to remark wearily that 'the sooner this nightmare is over the better. It's a great pity it ever happened' (*Guardian*, 19 March 1969). A pity perhaps, but it happened. Why did it happen? In fact what did happen?

The strike started on 21 February, but a lot had happened before this. During 1968 the Ford Motor Company lost over a million hours of production in Britain as a result of strikes and overtime bans. This at a time when it was launching its major £225 million export programme. The wake of the 1967 agreement had been more violent than senior management had imagined possible. So much so in fact that they gave serious consideration to a new wage claim presented tentatively by the trade union side of the NJNC in the October of 1968. A time when the existing 1967 agreement had almost another full year to run. But both sides of the NJNC were under pressure from the shop floor. A coordinated unofficial overtime ban had been organized for a while at the Dagenham and Halewood estates. At Halewood the resurrected Joint Shop Stewards' Committee had sent definite and uncompromising instructions to the national officers. They wanted a straight 10 per cent wage increase. Another bob an hour for the lads on the line. For the first time it seemed possible that a national Ford Shop Stewards' Combine Committee could be established as a viable force to coordinate action on the shop floor. Eddie Roberts had always maintained some contact with stewards in the other Ford plants, this contact became regular when he became convenor.

It's the only way. Some of the lads y'know they live within the confines of the plant. They don't want to know what's going on outside. They think they've got enough on to do a good job in that plant. But if you take that blinkered approach it stops you doing a good job.

We were tearing ourselves apart in that plant in 1968. When I became convenor I knew that I had to get the plant together again. Pulling together. I worked at it and I think I can take some credit for it because we did bloody well start to pull the same way again. But I also knew that if we were going to get anywhere with this new pay claim – which could unite the plant, and was doing – it would have to be a *national* effort. Eventually it would have to become an *international* effort. I pressed for that and the lads went along with it.

The NJNC *knew* that it had to come up with something. So it set up a 'working party' to consider the situation and come up with the best solution. At that time the NJNC was a bit like a secret society. No one outside it really knew what went on in it. The stewards who had pushed for a new claim knew that it had been presented and they knew that some sort of 'working party' had been set up but that was all they knew. They had no idea what was being discussed. Some of them, who were on good terms with their national officer, might have been able to squeeze out a few scraps of information. Others were just given the elbow. Over the years the Dagenham convenors, the 'Armchair Generals', had built up their contacts, and it was they who got the first whiff of the issues being discussed by the working party. There was to be a package deal, a wage increase with lots and lots of strings: 'penalty clauses' and 'productivity clauses'. All modelled around Barbara Castle's White Paper, *In Place of Strife*, and DEP directives. They didn't like it. Nor did the stewards at Halewood and Swansea. But it wasn't yet out in the open. The working party was disbanded in haste and confusion, and on 17 January the Company presented its proposals to the NJNC. Three days later the trade union side of the committee could give 'no precise details' of the offer but were said to be 'generally in favour' of its acceptance. It still wasn't out in the open. It came out bit by bit in the weeks that followed. The proposals were discussed at plant meetings, trade union delegates' meetings, convenors' meetings. The answer was always the same – 'we just didn't want to know'. The stewards did in fact get somewhere. Representatives for all the Works Committees attended a meeting addressed by Mark Young (Chairman of the NJNC and EPTU National Officer). He was sufficiently convinced of their opposition to push the Company at the next meeting on 3 February. The Company was prepared to increase its offer but not to alter the basic format of the package. The Joint Working Party was reconvened on the 10th. Young, Birch, Kealey and Gallagher deliberated with the Company's management team and recommended acceptance of the package to the full NJNC which dutifully acceded on 11 February. The package was accepted and it was all tied up. It was, however, done without the support of the key members of the Working Party – Birch of the AUEW (who voted against in the final meeting) and Kealey of the TGWU (who abstained). Funny . . .

The stewards were amazed. In response to their outrage, Jim Conway – General Secretary of the AUEW – commented: 'These men are just convenors, and they have no negotiating rights whatsoever.

> The first working party meeting was last November. Later that month, the Company produced a confidential document which developed its ideas about the sort of package it was prepared to negotiate. There were no details about the size of the wage increases it felt it could afford, but it did set out ideas about the 'good behaviour' guarantees it felt it must demand. Copies of the document appeared soon after at the paint, trim and assembly plants at Dagenham. How they got there is a mystery which will probably remain unsolved.
>
> Alex Hendry in *The Times*, 22 February 1969

My own view is that the officials of the unions involved have accepted the agreement and that's that' (*The Times*, 18 February). Well, as it turned out, that wasn't that.

The weeks between 17 January (when the Company first presented its proposals to the NJNC) and 21 February (the first day of the strike) were amazing ones which almost defy belief. In comparison to these chaotic days the strike was a reasonably straightforward event.

The first problem was the 'package' itself. The Company's proposals to the NJNC were lengthy and complicated. They were monitored to the stewards by the national officers, most of whom had either not read them, not understood them or wished to conceal them. Whichever it was the fact remains that these officials *agreed* to the proposals when the people *affected* had only the slightest understanding of them. And what they did understand they disliked.

What were the Company's proposals? What *was* in the package? The main parts of the deal were eventually laid out on 20 February by the Company in an *Employee Information Sheet*. First there was the pay increase. The offer accepted by the NJNC was for a $7\frac{1}{2}$ per cent increase – something like thirty shillings (£1·50) a week for an assembly-line worker. In addition the Company offered its workers two other major concessions: a scheme to offset loss of earnings through lay-off and a new enlarged holiday bonus. The Income Security Plan offered employees with over six months' 'service' a guarantee of two-thirds of their basic wage for five days of lay-off. Those who had been with the Company for over two years became entitled to ten days' benefit. In addition to this the holiday bonus was to be increased from £5 to £25.[1]

1. The Company also accepted the principle of equal pay for women (pressed on the TU side by the stewards at the 20 January meeting) and three days' paid leave in the event of a bereavement.

This would have suited the lads. A pay increase, a holiday bonus and a bit of security. That sounded great. Ford management knew just how good it would sound to the lads on the floor. But that was only part of the package. The carrot, the sweetener, call it what you will – the pay-off. There were no strings attached to the $7\frac{1}{2}$ per cent, the lads were to have that as a right. They had to qualify for the lay-off pay and the holiday money though. They had to be very good boys. (Images of childhood ... fathers and teachers. 'Only if you behave ...') To qualify for these concessions, workers in a particular plant must not indulge in 'unconstitutional action'. If any workers in a plant undertook such action they would discredit all other workers in the plant. They would relinquish their entitlement for six months. Neither could they claim off the 'Income Security Plan' if they were laid off as a result of action taken by their fellow workmates in the Company. To quote from the memorandum produced by the Company's Labour Relations staff:

It is important to make clear in this document that when there is a lay-off consequential to disruptive action within the Company, of either a *constitutional* or *unconstitutional* kind, the Income Security 'lay-off' benefit will not be payable.[2]

So access to lay-off pay wasn't going to be easy. It became even more difficult when it was appreciated what the NJNC had in mind when it talked of 'unconstitutional action'. The same memorandum defines it explicitly. It begins by quoting from the 1955 agreement between the Company and the unions (the *Blue Book*, see Chapter 3):

the parties agree that, at each stage of the procedure set out in this agreement, every attempt will be made to resolve issues raised and that until such procedure has been carried through there shall be no stoppage of work or other unconstitutional action.

And went on to point out that:

Breaching of the agreement can take several forms and the following types of coercive or sympathetic action taken to further a complaint or grievance, or to influence a dispute, outside the agreed procedure would constitute a disqualification from the Income Security Plan:

  1. Withdrawal of labour;
  2. Overtime ban;
  3. Concerted restriction of work output, whether by quantity of work produced, quality of work produced or the range of work undertaken. (In the

2. Throughout, and in all subsequent quotes, the emphasis is in the original.

event of the penalty clause being invoked for this type of action the plant
convenor and the shop steward of the employees concerned will be notified
beforehand of the Company's intention to do so.)

Employees responsible for unconstitutional action and subject to loss of benefits
for six months will be notified in writing.

The Company was at pains to point out that the six-month
disqualification wouldn't be brought into effect on account of an
'individual misdemeanor'. There was a new disciplinary procedure in
the package to take care of that. The six-month disqualification only
applied to 'concerted' action by 'a group of people' who attempt to
'coerce management'. It was about management's right to manage and
its right not to have its decisions interfered with at the shop-floor level
by organized groups of workers. This was central to the whole package
deal. A Company spokesman pointed out that 'the clauses which
attempt to discourage unofficial action are the cornerstone of the
agreement' (*The Times*, 17 February). What was also at the core of the
deal, and its acceptance, was the way in which the management and
officials on the NJNC understood the position of shop stewards and
convenors within the plants and within the union. Two things are
important here. Firstly, management and national officers alike had
become a bit frightened. They were being told what to do by a bunch of
upstarts who held no official position in anything. They were being
heckled as they left their meetings. Crowds of rowdies shouting
slogans. Mark Young was called a 'bent bastard' to his face more times
than he cares to remember during those weeks. They were frightened
and they were annoyed. Management had the additional direct
problem of profits. They had to take a grip . . . to be 'holding the reins'
once again. To do this they had to break the power of the shop steward
and they could do this only by loosening his relationship with
his members. This strategy was bolstered by the belief that the shop
stewards didn't really represent anybody anyway . . . This is crucial. It
crops up continually throughout the strike and is the key to an
understanding of how the NJNC behaved in the weeks that led up to
the strike. They didn't think the stewards represented anybody but
themselves. The stewards were big mouths who were going to be
sorted out. Of this they were certain. Ford management in particular
was convinced that the membership would vote in favour of the
agreement and ignore a strike call. They were also convinced that once
the agreement was implemented it would destroy the militancy of shop
stewards' committees like the one at the PTA plant at Halewood.

To this end there were still more strings inside the package, the 'Disciplinary Actions and Appeals Procedure' being one of them. Again we are back in the classroom. The Company's memorandum reads:

The maintenance of good discipline operates at two distinct levels:
1. In the first case there is the normal day-to-day running of the section with the supervisor issuing instructions and, as a corollary to his commendations, or encouragement, verbal rebukes to make employees aware of shortcomings in their performance or conduct. This type of discipline is informal in the sense that it is not intended to be recorded for future reference on the employee's personal Record Card.
2. In the second case we are concerned with the employee who is formally disciplined for having done something which is in itself of a fairly serious nature or which, although less serious, cannot be treated informally due to the frequency with which the same employee has repeatedly been guilty of similar action.

The new procedure concerns itself with only the second of these and is guided by a concern 'to correct rather than punish' the offender. To aid this corrective process it lays out a series of legalistic principles whereby the supervisor can 'establish the facts' of the case.

Once the facts are established and it is clear that an offence has been committed the offender must be formally warned that he is now the subject of disciplinary proceedings and he must be given details of what it is that he is alleged to have done wrong and be shown the evidence against him. He must be invited to comment on the facts as established and advised to seek the assistance of his shop steward if he feels he cannot adequately do himself justice in his reply.

After this the supervisor may or may not recommend disciplinary action.

When disciplinary action is recommended and has received the necessary authorization, the employee is informed by the appropriate Supervisor of the action being taken against him. At this interview, where the employee is being notified of a management decision, the presence of a shop steward would not normally be required. However, at the discretion of the employee, his representative may be present as an observer but not as a participant. The reason for this is that a shop steward should not appear to be carrying any responsibility for the determination or award of penalties.

The action is then implemented immediately and written confirmation (except in the case of the verbal warning) is prepared and handed to the employee.

Should the culprit consider himself wronged he has the right of appeal.

If an appeal is lodged by the employee (or his representative) it receives full consideration, notwithstanding the fact that the disciplinary action will already have been implemented.

The pervasiveness of management's assumed right to manage is captured by this disciplinary procedure and others like it. It is based upon the premise that management has the right to run its establishment as it thinks fit, that the supervisor has the right to be obeyed. Only through these assumptions can 'disciplinary issues' be reduced to questions of fact, i.e. a man has 'committed an offence' or he hasn't. If the possibility of conflicting 'rights' is admitted, the problem of discipline and disciplinary procedures becomes both complex and invidious. Once it is admitted that the workers have 'rights' and that the supervisor may infringe these rights, the simple idea of a 'disciplinary procedure' becomes cockeyed. In fact it reveals itself for what it is is. Part of the armoury of the powerful.

To take an example. In a car plant many of the disputes likely to lead to indiscipline 'of a fairly serious nature' are related to the allocation of work and the workload – the 'blue-eye system' and speed-up. Acts of rebellion, refusals to obey, in such a situation involve the supervisor saying 'Do this' and the operator replying 'No – it's not right for you to ask me to do that'. The new disciplinary procedure allowed for no such conflict of principle. If you work for Ford you do as you're told. There can be no clearer statement of the general fact that to work in a factory means to work *on management's terms*. Some managers are better to work for than others, but the fact still holds. Workers are paid to obey. At Ford's the operative's only recourse in many instances is in an appeal to his workmates and his steward, and ultimately the strike. This, however, would be to indulge in unconstitutional action, which would disqualify the whole plant from the benefits of the package.

In discussing the issue of discipline and industrial relations, a manager at the Ford Motor Company said to me:

> I do think that a lot of our troubles involve disputes over *authority*. I don't think that there's much doubt about this. We've got a young workforce, better educated than ever before, working on boring, frustrating jobs. You don't get much sense of purpose out of working on the track. You don't feel inclined to take orders in that situation. I think we must start thinking in terms of a less authoritarian system.

There was no hint of such thinking in the Company's package deal. Each of the elements of the Company's proposals to the union supported each other. They were held together by a logic which derived from a resolve to re-establish managerial control of the shop floor. To prevent the re-emergence in the 1970s of another Dagenham of the 1950s. There was yet another part to it. One that rounded it all out and established general principles. It was known as the 'Enabling Agreement For the Continuous Improvement of Efficiency in Company Operations'. Incredibly it was never discussed openly throughout the whole period of negotiations and the ensuing dispute. It began with a preamble:

> The Company and the Trade Unions have always recognized that the efficiency of the Company determines its economic success and the benefits which all employees can enjoy.
>
> The purpose of this agreement is to set down the framework of principles within which the Company must operate and which, therefore, determines the contribution that employees are required to make towards improvements in efficiency; and to agree guidelines by which further improvements will be achieved.

It went on to spell out four main principles: continuity of employment; operating flexibility – 'the company's operations must be sufficiently flexible to respond to ... changes'; efficient utilization – 'employees will thus be involved in the need to meet, with ready acceptance, changing shift and overtime patterns'; and continuous improvement – 'the key principle'.

> In seeking these further improvements, plant management must interpret and apply the above principles so as to meet the specific requirements of each plant, whilst observing the normal consultative processes.

In relation to the rest of the package this 'Enabling Agreement' sounded decidedly ominous to the stewards at Halewood. The guarantee that 'normal consultative processes' would apply didn't help much.

> You know what tha' means. Tha' consultation. It means 'Hello – we're doing this today, that tomorrow, and you're all being laid off on Friday'. That's what 'consultation' means to Ford's. That's what they'd like to happen. They grant you the courtesy of *telling* you what they're going to do to you before they do it. You're not supposed to say 'Well we're nor having tha' for a start'.

The stewards' suspicions weren't put to rest by the fact that no one seemed to know anything about it. At the Ford Delegates' Conference of the EPTU Billy Dumbell – the plumbers' steward from the Halewood PTA – asked his national officer and NJNC member, about the Enabling Agreement:

He looked at me as if I was speaking a foreign language. He hadn't read it he said. I don't think he'd even heard of it. Then Mark Young told us all to belt up because we were just there to listen to him.

Then we told them. We said we wanted nothing to do with any of it. They could stick it. And the bastards went off and voted for it.

Finally as a *coup de grace* Leslie Blakeman's team added several clauses to the Agreement of 18 February. One read interestingly:

> If a dispute still exists when the procedure has been exhausted, then the trade unions individually or collectively will, before taking any industrial action, give a minimum of twenty-one days' notice in writing to the Company.

They had put the shackles on 'unconstitutional action'. Now they wanted a 'cooling-off period'.

The 1969 package deal was quite a package. It was received by politicians and the press with uncritical acclaim. The *Guardian* approved of the penal clauses thinking them 'a novel idea aimed at fortifying the agreement with an extra financial incentive' (13 March). Its Labour Correspondent, John Torode, thought the whole package 'first rate'. In an article on 19 February he labelled it a 'revolutionary pay and discipline deal'. On the 21st, however, in an article entitled 'Threat to Ford Deal by Shop Floor Guerrillas', he called the penal clauses 'meaningless' but asserted that 'on the surface the disciplinary provisions look sensible enough'. He went on to point out 'there is evidence that a number of other employers are looking excitedly at the Ford initiative'. So was the Department of Employment and Productivity. It had made it clear that the Company's $7\frac{1}{2}$ per cent pay increase 'will be allowed only if some form of disciplinary clauses are maintained' (*Guardian*, 17 February). In spite of all this. In spite of the vote for acceptance by the trade union side of the NJNC the agreement was never signed. Instead there was the strike.

At Halewood the shop-floor organization that was approaching disintegration in 1968 was a viable force again by 1969. It had re-established itself behind the national pay claim. Sectionalism *within* the plant had been transcended by an appeal to a solidarity which extended *beyond* the plant. The *Voice of Halewood* and the wage claim leaflets were used to bolster this solidarity (see page 261). The friction and disarray caused by the 1967 wages structure was left in the wake of a 10 per cent national pay claim. They were all going to take the Company on for a bob an hour. While there were still many grading grievances to be taken up, they were no longer the central concern of the stewards or the lads on the floor. Often they were taken up out of sheer cussedness. To have a dig at management, and the Company . . . and the grades.[3] But they also served to keep the stewards on their toes, while at the same time giving them a useful platform to organize around – 'They've had their pound of flesh now let's be sure that we're going to get ours.' The stewards knew that they had a fight on their hands.

We had no illusions whatsoever about what we were up against. We knew we had Ford's to beat and that was going to be hard enough. But then we've our officials on the NJNC as well *and* Barbara Castle and the whole bleeding Labour government. We knew this was going to be a tough one all right.

The news of 'penal clauses' that leaked out of the 'confidential discussions' of the autumn of 1968 confirmed their suspicions. This was going to be the big one. The 1967 agreement had put the stewards off package deals. They wanted a straight wage settlement with no strings. Yet the Company was insistent upon a package and the NJNC continued to talk in terms of one. The stewards wanted nothing to do with it. They wanted *no* package deal, let alone this one. They became increasingly aware that the package they were being handed was a particularly nasty one, and they wanted none of it. National meetings of all plant convenors confirmed this view. The package deal and the penal clauses mustn't be accepted. It had to be stopped. John Castle:

We knew what a Company like Ford could do with an agreement like that. You mark my words Huwie. You can imagine the tricks they'd be getting up to a week before the holiday break. And the lads would have that twenty pounds staring them in the face.

Frank Banton:

If we accepted those clauses it would be finished. They'd just break the militancy of the lads. The money grabbers would be scabbing and fighting the decent lads. It would be hopeless. The foremen would have a great time. They'd use it against us. It would be terrible.

The package deal had to be stopped. It wasn't going to be easy and the lads on the floor had to be prepared for a fight. They had to know what was involved. They *had* to be kept informed. Eddie remembers:

We knew this was going to be the tough one. But we knew that we had to win. We also knew that we could win if we could stick together. It was essential that we were all pointing in the same direction. Y'know none of us burying our heads

3. This seemed to have been a successful irritant. In 1971 the Company was very concerned to 'buy out' all further grading grievances.

in the sand thinking cash was just going to fall into our laps. Clichés I know but true nevertheless. We had to ensure that the lads on all the sections knew what was going on. We had regular 'report-back' meetings and produced a hell of a lot of leaflets. Y'know so that nobody could forget. Nobody did. Ford's made sure of that. The more the lads knew about the deal the less they wanted it. The lads were great. Great they were. They didn't waver once.

Whilst the negotiations carried on at national level, lads on the sections in the PTA at Halewood were organizing their own strike funds. Saving up for the strike. Ten bob a week to the steward. They were going on strike. On 26 January they met for their first mass meeting on the package. The stewards' recommendation of total rejection was carried unanimously. Armed with this support the TGWU stewards travelled to London on the 30th for the TGWU Ford Delegates' Conference. The conference existed to supplement the NJNC negotiations. Eighteen different unions were represented on the NJNC and each national officer communicated the details of the negotiations to a national conference of delegates from members of his own union at Ford's. Les Kealey, the TGWU national officer, was left in no doubt about the views of the stewards – 'We've told him straight. He could stick his package. He could go back in there and negotiate a straight pay claim.'

Les Kealey and the other national officers returned to the Company's headquarters in Regent Street on 3 February when the NJNC negotiated the 'final' settlement: the complete acceptance of Blakeman's package. While they were reconstituting 'working parties' and finalizing the clauses of the agreement the convenors of all the Ford plants were having their own meeting. Just along the road in fact. In the Regent Palace Hotel. They were meeting to consider what they should do given the situation in the NJNC and in the plants. As far as the NJNC was concerned they might not have been there. The official negotiations in Regent Street were conducted between the Company's IR team and the union officials. Each side was convinced of its own legitimacy; their right to come to an agreement which would bind the lads on the shop floor. They were unconcerned when the convenors overwhelmingly rejected the deal and served twenty-one days' strike notice on the Company, for they were sure that these men, as 'unofficial leaders', lacked support in the plants.

The Halewood convenors reported back to the joint stewards' committee on 7 February. This produced a further wage claim leaflet (see opposite). 'Halewood would not be found lagging behind should . . .

Wage Claim Leaflet

On Monday, 3 February, our union officials met the Company to progress our claim for a realistic wage increase, and lay-off pay without strings.

Our mandate was clear – we demanded a *minimum* pay increase of 10 per cent (1 shilling [5p]) per hour for all workers. We also wanted rejection of the Company's abortive 'package deal' proposals.

The Company's chief negotiators had made it known before this meeting that the unions could expect no improvement on their original offer. However, feeling has been running high throughout the Ford plants and this had been manifested in the decisions of numerous meetings of Ford workers who had made it plain that this time we are willing to fight and fight hard to obtain our fair share of the Company's improved profits. In the face of the obvious militancy amongst Ford workers, the Company's negotiators, despite their previous statement that they would not budge, made positive indications at Monday's meeting that they were prepared to make further concessions; these being:

1. An improved wage offer (no amount specified),
2. Increases in the proposed sick and lay-off payments,
3. Visible improvements in the Ford Pension Scheme, *and*
4. The principle of equal pay for women, provided progress could be made on the question of them accepting shift and overtime work commitments when required.

The Company would not, however, let go of their concept of a 'package deal', and remained adamant on the vexatious question of penal clauses. They only said that they would be prepared to look more closely to ensure what they might term a fair application of such penalties. On the same day a meeting of all Ford convenors took place, at which the views from all plants were examined. It was very clearly decided that if our union officials should prove unable to achieve through negotiation the very reasonable demands of Ford workers, then it will be necessary to take the Company on and recommend an all out stoppage to our members ... This then, fellow members, is the present position:

We will give the lead, the rest is up to you ...

Issued by the Ford Halewood Joint Shop Stewards' Committee 9 February 1969

Voice of Halewood – The official Organ of the Ford Halewood Joint Shop Stewards' Committees action become necessary.' From that point onwards the Halewood stewards were sure that they were going to be pushed to a strike and were pretty confident that the lads in the plants would support them.

> We just knew that. We knew that with the tradition we've got on Merseyside and the times we've had in that plant that the lads were never going to accept no penalty clauses. All the time you'd be meeting lads and they'd be saying 'we've got to stop the bastards on this one'. It was great y'know. We just knew they were going to come out. That we could rely on them. It was a good feeling.

The reliability of Halewood, the near certainty that the plants would 'go', was the central feature of the February weeks. Throughout that time the national officers were being lobbied by the representatives of the plants. The Dagenham convenors did little else. Jock McCrae (convenor Dagenham body plant):

> Me and Henry[4] went down to see Reg [Birch]. He wouldn't listen. He said 'Fuck off out of it. I know you. You're going to do this. You're going to do that. In the end your plants are working normally – you don't do fuck all.' He wouldn't listen. So we said 'Look Reg, we're not talking about our plants. All right . . . But Halewood is going to go. We're speaking for Halewood. It's only Halewood that's keeping this thing open. Now like it or not Halewood is going to stop. And the Halewood transmission plant can stop Dagenham in a week. *There's going to be a strike.*' That got through to him. For the first time I think he saw that a national stoppage was on the cards.

Birch was impressed. Impressed enough to vote against the deal on 11 February. So too was Kealey of the TGWU. After his dealings with Birch on the working party, he finally abstained at the meeting on the 11th. The February agreement went through without either of them. It certainly went through without Halewood. On 18 February the Joint Shop Stewards' Committee met and passed with unity and enthusiasm the resolution:

> That this Halewood Joint Shop Stewards' meeting recommends that a mass meeting of all Halewood workers takes place on Wednesday, 18 February 1969, and that the following recommendation from this committee is put to the workpeople:

> 'That in order to progress our claim for a realistic wage increase and the removal of the penalty clauses from the negotiated benefits, that a withdrawal of labour takes place on Friday, 21 February 1969 at 6.30 a.m., and that a recall meeting is called for two (2) weeks later, unless events dictate a recalled meeting sooner.'

4. Henry Friedman, convenor of the Dagenham River plant, and one of the tacticians in the Ford combine during the 1960s.

The meeting will be held at the Liverpool Stadium at 7.30 p.m. on Wednesday, 19 February 1969.

Ford management was getting worried. They had pushed a 'first class agreement' through the NJNC, and they wanted their plants to be working normally and the agreement implemented. It began to occur to them that it might not pass that easily and that the call for a strike might receive some support. They were convinced, however, that any support for the strike could only be based upon ignorance, that the vast majority of their employees would welcome the deal. In view of this Bob Ramsey, Leslie Blakeman's heir apparent, blooded himself with a letter to each of the Company's hourly-paid employees. 'Dear Employee' it began and went on to explain that the letter intended to clear up confusion and explain 'what the real situation is' (see page 265). It went on to explain to the employee that the agreement would lift his earnings from £28 to £30 per week, 'a figure well above the average for the whole of the Motor Industry'. The letter achieved anything but the desired effect at Halewood:

> They were ready to go anyway on my section and then they had this letter from Ramsey telling them they were the best paid in the industry and that they were 'confused' an tha'. Half of them were ready to take off. Start the strike a few days early. Anyway I persuaded them to 'stay in the ranks' and go to the Stadium and vote instead. They were down there, waving that bleeding letter from Ramsey.

They all went down there, down to the Liverpool Stadium, and voted to strike and to meet again a fortnight after the strike started – 'You need two weeks to call it a real strike.' They went back to the plant happy. Laughing. This was going to be *their* strike.

The management at Halewood was a bit disconcerted:

> They nearly fell through the floor when they knew we weren't scheduled to meet for a fortnight after the strike started. They were coming up to you all sheepish, 'Is it true ...' We told them that the next one would be another month.

The plant management knew that they had a stoppage on their hands. They were bending over backwards to placate the stewards:

> They were treating us like royalty. Nothing was too good for us. They'd got the wind up. They knew that Halewood was the place that was going to go and I suppose they thought that it would reflect on them in some way. I don't know. They were very docile anyway ... sheepish y'know.

They had also seen the effect that Ramsey's letter had had on the lads.

So much so that Mr A. G. Pearman, Industrial Relations Manager, Halewood Operations, issued a directive (ref. no. 50/205, 6493, emh) to all managers and supervisors:

Management is aware that the average earnings figure quoted in the Company letter to employees on 18 February 1969, has been the subject of strong reaction on the shop floor. The figure quoted is an accurate average of earnings across the Company and you should therefore make every effort to convince employees of the correctness of the Company statement.

It is also generally believed that the new increase of 9d. and 10½d. will still leave Ford employees at the bottom of the earnings league in the motor industry. This is an erroneous impression arrived at by comparison with maximum earnings in the Midlands. The true situation is that the new increase will assure our employees of a rate 10 per cent in advance of the average earnings in the motor industry and you should ensure by all possible means, that shop floor operators are aware of this fact.

The tangle that was to produce the Parity Campaign was evident in these weeks (as it had been in the previous two or three years). On 29 February 1969 the supervisors at the PTA plant in Halewood were caught up in the snare of wage differentials and comparisons. They had to 'make every effort to convince employees' that Ramsey's figures were right and that their own ideas about how much money they earned were quite wrong. Not an easy thing to do:

They stopped the line. Y'know they stopped it. That's bloody well unheard of in this place. *We* stop the line but their number one rule is 'the line never stops'. So that was funny for a start. Then the supervisors were calling all the lads on their area together. You can imagine it. A big circle of lads and the supervisor reading them this message from Pearman, it was bloody hilarious.

The atmosphere in the plant was euphoric. Almost carnival-like. The Company was on the run. Here was the Company breaking its own cardinal rule. The lads were going on strike and it just didn't know what to do – 'we must be on a winner'. Jack Jones:

Well we all gathered around the foreman see. I stood alongside him and all the lads were shouting and jeering. This went on for a bit so I held up my hands. Asked for a bit of quiet. And a bit of a clap. So we gave him a clap and he went red. He started to read this message from Pearman. He was stumbling along. Then he came up to a word he couldn't pronounce. I can't remember what it was, but I leaned over and helped him out. The lads cheered a bit.

The lads cheered a bit. They laughed, shouted, hooted and chanted throughout the plant. 'We are the Champions da da da da da . . .' They were a bit put out by the transmission lads getting away early on the

Ford Motor Company Limited
Halewood Operations

Halewood, Liverpool 24, England
Telephone: 051–486 3900
Telex: 62461
18 February 1969

Dear Employee,

You will have seen reports that a strike is threatened in opposition to the agreements reached with the Trade Unions last Tuesday. Many employees will be confused and wish to know what the real situation is and that is the purpose of this letter.

We have already received from the secretary of the trade union side of the NJNC formal notification of acceptance of the Company's offer on behalf of the trade unions. It is a first class agreement which includes substantial improvements conceded during negotiation and which does not take away any Trade Union rights. On the contrary it offers additional security and benefits for those who honour the procedure negotiated on their behalf as we believe the vast majority of our employees wish to do. It provides very precise time limits for the handling of grievances. The increases of 9d. and 10½d. per hour will raise average earnings from the present level of £28 to over £30 per week; a figure well above the average for the whole of the motor industry. The benefits will become effective on the agreed date provided the Department of Employment and Productivity share our view that the safeguards against unconstitutional action justify the cost of all the benefits.

There is no possibility of any improvement in the deal. The strike action that is being suggested can only hold back the substantial benefits of the whole package.

We are sure that in most cases our employees and their shop stewards are anxious to see the Company prosper because they know that it is only by satisfying our customers with delivery on time that we can obtain business to provide future security and improved benefits.

· We need your support to secure approval to the deal and our plants will be open for business as usual next Monday.

Yours sincerely,
R. J. Ramsey
Director of Labour Relations

Friday, but when they took off on the Friday tea-time they had no intention of coming back to the PTA and their bit of the assembly line for a while. Meanwhile in London things were stirring. The press was working itself up into a tirade and the NJNC into a flat spin.

R. W. Shakespeare declared that the 'Halewood strike is part of a plot by four shop stewards to bring Ford's twenty-three plants in Britain to a standstill' (*The Times*, 21 February). *The Times* had in fact already declared itself. It had thought Ramsey's letter a 'bold move', and in a leader on the same day declared itself unequivocally opposed to a strike which it called a 'Pointless sacrifice by the car workers' (*The Times*, 18 February). Revealingly it argued that the situation at Ford's had a 'surreal quality'. This quality derived not from the distance between discussions within the NJNC and the reality of the shop floor, but from the obstinacy of people who prefer 'the status quo to any change no matter how rational or beneficial'. *The Times* went on to give its explanation of this irrational opposition to change:

> When the Ford convenors talk of 'parity of wages with others in the motor industry' they are talking of the ransom money that their colleagues have been able, by applying pressure selectively, to squeeze out of the companies under a different system. They are also talking of the threat to their own power. The right to negotiate rates is power; the right to call men out on strike is power. If an agreement is made at company level the power of the local representatives is diminished. If the duly laid down negotiating procedure must be gone through before workers can come out on strike without risking a penalty, another element of this power is lost.
>
> Their power, therefore, rests on instability. But in any modern industry there is a premium on achieving stable conditions – which, on the labour side, means a reliable system of negotiating procedures resulting in binding agreements. This is in the interests of the employees – too often victims of the motor industry's notorious volatility. Who, then, are the convenors fighting for?

Certainly the issue was one of 'power'. But in locating the crisis of power around the heads of self-concerned convenors *The Times*, like the NJNC, revealed a deep-seated concept-blindness. It was inconceivable to them that the convenors had the best interests of their members at heart, and that the lads on the floor would follow them willingly in the face of an official directive from the national negotiating body. It was inconceivable that the lads on the shop floor could have the *right* to strike unofficially, and even more so that they *needed* that right. The world of *The Times* is a world where the established structures of power and law are endowed with a sanctity. Things are as they are because they are as they are and that makes them right. *The Times's* call for 'rational changes' and the rebukes it serves up for those who doggedly defend the status quo are a radical mask for a much more thorough-going conservatism. *The Times* is immediately repelled by any action which, even slightly, implies an attack upon the way things are run or the people who run those things. It understands such attacks as a self-interested concern for personal prestige, a criterion which is never applied to those who occupy the centres of power. In this respect *The Times* is not alone, for what applies to it applies equally or more to the other producers of newsprint.

While the press was abusing the convenors and the stewards, the trade union side of the NJNC was involved in its own version of musical chairs. The agreement still hadn't been signed. While each union had a seat on the NJNC, the committee itself could not automatically bind each of the constituent unions (or could it?). The agreement had to be authorized by each union in turn. It was an open secret that the national leadership of both the TGWU and the AUEW were unhappy about committing themselves to an Agreement that their national officers had not voted for and which their delegate conferences had overwhelmingly rejected.

In 1969 the leadership of both these unions was in the hands of men who differed remarkably in outlook and character from the 'union bosses' who had dominated the British trade union movement since the war. Jack Jones had all but taken over from Frank Cousins as General Secretary of the TGWU. The son of a union activist – he was christened James Larkin Jones – he worked on the Liverpool docks until he went to Spain to fight for the Republicans. He got wounded and returned to the Midlands where he was to be well known as an honest but tough and militant union organizer in the engineering industry. The 'ransom money' that *The Times* talked about in 1969 was the bread and butter of Jack Jones's job in the 1950s. The stewards at Halewood weren't disappointed when Jones took over:

> I'm not going starry eyed about anyone. I'm prepared to be disillusioned. Y'know I'm not going to be carrying a flag for anybody for the rest of my life, I'm not a 'Jones man' like some, but Jones *is* an improvement. He is concerned about the stewards and the lads on the floor. He's making some movement in the direction of listening to what the lads say *they* want, which is a hell of a lot different from what we've been used to. I think he's the best we could hope for at the moment.

Jones was the best that the stewards could hope for. When he took over as General Secretary it was with a background of shop-floor activity behind him, and with a genuine concern to introduce a greater potential for shop-floor decision-making within the structure of his union. Hugh Scanlon, Jones's opposite number in the AUEW, was in a remarkably similar position. Scanlon was an ex-member of the Communist Party who had succeeded the right-wing autocrat, Sir Leslie Carron. He had received solid left-wing support in his electoral defeat of John Boyd, the right-wing 'establishment' candidate. Like Jones, Scanlon came to the front on a wave of opposition to the old-style trade union leadership. He too was concerned to develop some form of rank and file democracy within his organization.

The situation at Ford's could not have pleased either man. It had too many signs of the unionism of the 1950s and 1960s. Apart from provoking an unofficial strike against the express recommendation of the national officers, the Ford NJNC contained other legacies of the past. Eighteen unions were represented on the committee, each with a single vote. The Amalgamated Society of Painters and Decorators, with under a hundred members at Ford, had a vote on the NJNC, as did the National Union of Blastfurnacemen. Although amalgamations had meant that the TGWU and the AUEW both had in effect two votes on the NJNC, this in no way reflected their membership strength within the Company. In 1969 the TGWU and the AUEW could claim between them about 33,000 members working for the Ford Motor Company. The other fourteen unions had about 12,000 (see Table 2). On resumption of work after the strike, a mass disaffection of members from the GMWU meant that the balance was tilted even more solidly in favour of the two large unions. Yet they could be overwhelmingly outvoted on the NJNC. On the shop floor, however, things were entirely different. Every convenor of the twenty-three Ford factories was either a TGWU or AUEW member. The overwhelming majority of the stewards were also from these unions. This contradiction – the membership and leadership in the plants dominated by members of the two unions; membership and leadership on the NJNC dominated by the other unions – increased the severity of the crisis.

Jones and Scanlon weren't too happy. Nor were many other officials and lay representatives within the TGWU and AUEW. Mass meetings across the country had indicated that the membership didn't want the package deal. Armed with these votes AUEW plant convenors lobbied the meeting of their national executive on 18 February, while TGWU convenors met with Kealey and Jack Jones in Transport House. Their protestations were not in vain. Neither of the unions intended to sign the Ford agreement. The AUEW's executive

Table 2 **Ford's unions** (1969)

Transport and General Workers' Union	17,500
Amalgamated Union of Engineering and Foundryworkers	15,000
General and Municipal Workers' Union	7,500
National Union of Vehicle Builders	2,750
Electrical and Plumbing Trades Union (ETU/PTU)	1,400
Amalgamated Society of Woodcutting Machinists	under 250
Amalgamated Society of Woodworkers	under 250
National Union of Sheet Metal Workers	under 250
United Patternmakers' Association	under 250
Amalgamated Society of Boilermakers	under 250
Power Group of TGWU	under 250
National Union of Blastfurnacemen	under 100
Amalgamated Union of Building Trade Workers	under 100
Amalgamated Society of Painters and Decorators	under 100
National Society of Metal Mechanics	under 100
Iron and Steel Trades Confederation	under 100

Estimated membership of the eighteen members of the Company's National Joint Negotiating Committee. Each has one vote. The AUEW and the ETU/PTU after recent amalgamations count as two unions.
From the *Sunday Times*, 2 March 1969.

proposal that negotiations be reopened with the Company was supported by the TGWU. The deal had, in a moment, become 'a dead letter' (Alex Hendry, *The Times*, 19 February). A dead letter that refused to die. The Company would not object to a meeting but it would not reopen the talks. Mark Young (EPTU and Chairman NJNC) was adamant:

> I will not be a party to capitulation to unofficial shop stewards and the undermining of an agreement. The AUEW decision is highly surprising. If the AUEW is successful in leading some of the others back to the negotiating table there will be some notable exceptions. It could mean the break-up of the Ford negotiating committee (quoted in *The Times*, 18 February).

The situation appeared stalemated. As Friday 21st approached, news from Halewood was awaited with expectation. Would the transmission plant go? It went. No production worker reported for work. The jugular plant was stopped and the whole estate was virtually certain to follow.

The TGWU and the AUEW still wanted to reopen negotiations. Les Kealey was away from London, and the responsibility for the

TGWU was handed over to Moss Evans, a Welshman from Birmingham and Merthyr.

> I was born in Merthyr in the Depression. My father was a collier. He had worked in the pits but he was unemployed from 1924 to 1937. There were six of us and he had his dole stopped, and we were on the Parish Relief.

He hasn't forgotten those days. He remembers going to ILP meetings in a basement in Cefn with his mam. He remembers the poverty and the suffering and his first job as a boy at BAC Guns in Dowlais. His dad had moved to Birmingham in search of work and after the war Moss moved there too. He got a job with Bakelite Limited and became an active shop steward. In 1956 he became a district officer of the TGWU.

> I don't know why I became an active unionist. Initially I think it was being Welsh. Nye Bevan you know. I remember during the war I used to buy *The Times* in order to read the verbatim account of Bevan's debates with Churchill. That made me a rebel. That and growing up in Merthyr. Then I remember I read a book called *Beer and Oysters* and then *The Ragged Trousered Philanthropists*. I was a convinced Socialist by that time.
>
> At Bakelite I served my active apprenticeship under a man called Jim Falkner. An active member of the Communist party. He was the shop convenor. I was a young lad. No experience. Jim helped me a lot. I was a young man representing older people and it was very comforting for me to have Jim to turn to.
>
> He wasn't too happy about me becoming a full-time officer, but he didn't discourage me. I think he was afraid that I'd end up like all the others.

Moss Evans was typical of the new type of trade union officer that had begun to emerge in the late 1950s and 1960s. The development of shop steward committees during that period meant that, in particular industries and areas, men were coming forward for full-time union positions with a long experience of shop floor 'unofficial' unionism behind them. Men whose political base lay not within the official lay committees of the union but rather on the shop floor with the rank and file. Sammy Glasstone and Bill Brodrick were just two examples of this phenomenon on Merseyside. They were examples of a widespread, if localized, tendency – the emergence of a radical wedge within the trade union bureaucracies. It is this radicalism that was beginning to change the nature of national bargaining in the late 1960s, and the nature of politics in the 1970s.

On Friday 21 February 1969 then, with the Halewood transmission plant stopped, Moss Evans was asked by Jack Jones to deputize for Les

Kealey at a meeting of the trade union side of the NJNC. He argued and convinced them that they had to reopen negotiations. By a vote of seven to three the meeting opted for further talks with Leslie Blakeman's team.

I got them to agree to that, but the TU side was split from top to bottom. Mark Young kept insisting that 'we are the NJNC ... we've already got the vote ... we've got an agreement and we're sticking to it'. Anyway the majority decided to come along with us. I contacted Blakeman. He didn't seem very keen but I said to him, 'Look. You've got a strike in Liverpool. We know that. Now we're not anxious to have a big strike and a long stoppage but that's what's going to happen unless we talk.' He said he'd have to consult his colleagues and that they'd need until Tuesday to consider the situation. So we arranged for a meeting of the NJNC on the Tuesday.

A further meeting was arranged then, after the date of the strike call. In preparation Blakeman pointed out that:

We certainly have no disposition to change the agreement. It should not be inferred that the meeting is likely to lead to any change. We will not offer more money, nor will we change the wildcat strike clause (*The Times*, 22 February).

and

We have gone as far as we can in giving benefits that we hope and expect the Department of Employment and Productivity will accept (*Guardian*, 22 February).

Mark Young was also preparing himself. In his view 'a strike would not now serve a useful purpose. It would defeat the purpose of the talks.'

As Chairman I would expect the men to be at work on Monday. Nothing has been decided yet in any way to undermine the agreement (*The Times*, 22 February).

Monday was the day of the strike. Hardly anyone arrived for work at Halewood, certainly no production workers did. The support for the strike was more patchy in the other plants. Swansea decided to wait on the national officials. Southampton and Basildon were out, but support was mixed at Dagenham. The Company was reported to be disappointed by the size of the stoppage at Halewood. 'If the Halewood plant stays out there can be little hope of production beyond Wednesday.'

The situation was entirely fluid. One thing was certain, Halewood was out and wasn't going back with the penalty clauses in the agreement. At Halewood the masses had picked up their bags and left. It wouldn't be an easy business to get them back in the plant. Politics … strategies … tactics. Telephones … the Halewood stewards … the Armchair Generals … the executives … the NJNC … strategies and tactics. The one known quantity … the Halewood lads out the gates. At home, decorating, watching the telly, having a lie in, doing the washing up. Waiting.

The NJNC met on the Tuesday as planned. Moss Evans was in Doncaster. Back in his proper job negotiating with ICI. The NJNC reaffirmed its support for the deal, with Les Kealey's vote in favour. They refused the Company's offer of a national ballot. Moss Evans was on Doncaster station, buying a newspaper.

> You could have knocked me over with a feather. I handed it over to Kealey. He thanked me very much for everything I'd done. I'd done a lot he said. Then he goes and votes for the bloody thing. When I saw the headlines I almost collapsed. I did though. It was a complete shock.

The NJNC had an agreement. The AUEW didn't agree. Its executive gave its official backing to the strike. The following day the Finance and General Purposes Committee of the TGWU followed suit. They had raised the stakes. With Halewood as their base they had lifted the strike onto another level. Swansea shut down. AUEW and TGWU members at Dagenham joined the strike. The Ford Motor Company was virtually at a standstill. Yet it kept its plants open. It insisted that it still had an agreement. An agreement which it intended to implement on 1 March. It opened its gates and at Dagenham several thousand members of the unions who had not made the strike official came in and were found work to do. It suited Ford's not to lay them off. They needed some workers to pay the new rates to on 1 March. So work was found for them to do.

Deadlock. At Halewood they knew that this was the big one. The watershed. The turning point. They knew the chips would be down on this one. And they were right. What they were also sure of was that the strike was for the lads. It was what their members wanted. It was *their* strike. The stewards were running it for them in between times, but it was *their* strike. When all the wheeling and dealing started, they kept reminding themselves of this. When Friedman and McCrae rang through to say that they were arriving at 1 p.m. Bernie Bradley insisted that 'they're not going to get a fucking platform. We'll talk to them but they're not coming up here messing our lads about.' Mick's return from the Finance and General Purposes Committee with the details of

Kealey's duplicity solidified his commitment to 'the lads on the floor'. The preservation of this commitment through a four-week official strike was not going to be easy. Already they were worried about being less than frank with the lads over the package. Bernie Bradley expressed this disquiet:

Let's face it, all we've had a chance to discuss is the Penalty Clauses. That's all the lads really knew about. I know its the most important thing but this is the lads' strike and we ought to have had a chance to discuss it in more detail. We've never mentioned the 'Enabling Agreement,' and we can't. If we throw that to them as well it will be chaos.

Letter to the Editor of the *Guardian*

Of one thing I am reasonably certain. If instead of calling an official strike, the two major unions had honoured the understanding reached by the sub-committee on 10 February all the Ford employees would be back at work.

Two things follow: (i) a modern enlightened agreement would have been implemented to the benefit of all concerned; (ii) the unions would have successfully asserted their authority over unauthorized calls for an unofficial strike by shop stewards, who by far exceeded their duty in so doing.

Les Cannon, General President, ETU
13 March 1969

The penal clauses *were* enough. The lads didn't need subtleties. Neither did they need it spelled out to them. They *knew* what those clauses could lead to. In effect that was what mattered. But this, together with the complexity of the 'agreement' and the way it was negotiated, meant that the stewards found themselves much more 'in the know' than the lads, much more so than usual. This worried them a bit. And the problem was not going to get any easier. For a start the strike was an official one.

That's the problem with an 'official strike'. In one way it's a good thing. On this one a national stoppage was essential and it needed official backing to empty all the plants. And it *does* give the lads some encouragement to know that they've got the whole organization behind them. I don't know why it is. Well strike pay helps of course . . . But it's more than that. It helps a bit with the wives as well I think if it's got the 'official' tag. But it means that a lot of things get taken out of your control. We can run the plant situation fine. But when you've a big official strike a lot of things are going to get done which you're not a party to. It's a difficult one . . .

To an extent they were able to cóntrol the situation. The autonomous strike by the three plants was a testament to their support amongst their members and added strength to their political armoury. Neither were they fools. They'd been coping with 'the bureaucrats' for a long time, and this strike had for them all the makings of a showdown. Of one thing they were certain. Kealey was finished. They wanted his job. As far as they were concerned he no longer existed. They had also had enough of the NJNC and Mark Young's chairmanship. Their strike had made a restructuring of the NJNC a likelihood. They intended to pressure this likelihood into an inevitability.

There was no doubt about that at all. No doubt at all. Kealey was going to go. We were *certain* of tha'. We told Jack Jones, we told everybody. We weren't having any further dealings with the bastard. *We* weren't reorganizing *him* or tha' fucking NJNC. It wasn't just Halewood either. We were probably shouting the odds louder than most but all the plants had had enough this time.

Kealey had to go. On 5 March he resigned his position in the union. He was suspended from further involvement in the Ford negotiations. Lots of things were said – his position became impossible and he resigned. After a lot of speculation in the press, Jack Jones gave his account of the affair:

The facts are that Kealey and I met a delegation of senior London Ford convenors. At that meeting the stewards made it clear that they were completely opposed to the penal clauses and other aspects of the agreement. They stated, correctly, that the union's official Ford Delegate Conference which had been held in January had unanimously adopted this view.

The General Secretary [i.e. Frank Cousins] and I have ... made it clear throughout that
  1. the Union's Executive are opposed to such penal clauses, and
  2. decisions of official lay delegate conferences could not be ignored by *any* officers of the union.
Letter to the Editor, *Sunday Times*, 16 March.

A few days later Mark Young resigned from his position as chairman of the NJNC. He thought the terms demanded by the TGWU and AUEW 'unreal'. He had been, he said:

... unhappy for some time about the way the trend was going ... My union believes this is a good agreement, and I reject the emotive attack on what the AUEW and the TGWU call the penal clauses. I think they are simply *quid pro quo* in the bargain. It's a bonus for good behaviour, and to attack them as penal clauses is very misleading and a distortion of what the agreement is about.

So Mark Young left, an unhappy man. The second part of a double victory for the stewards – 'We were really made up ... getting rid of those two bastards.' The way was clear for a restructuring of the NJNC after the strike. In this one respect – establishing the legitimacy of their positions and their right to be heard – the steward organization made a breakthrough in the 1969 strike. Jack Jones had put it on the line – lay delegate conferences *cannot* be ignored. The strike still had to be settled, however, and the longer it progressed the more and more powerful were the forces operating against the shop-floor workers. The stewards were operating under mounting pressure. 'It's hard work, striking.'

So too were Ford management. They hadn't expected the strike and it had come at a particularly bad time for the Company. Stocks of cars were low, as were stocks of British-made components in the Company's European establishments. Ford's badly needed a quick settlement.

Thursday, 27 February in the Garston Office. Thawing out, talking and waiting for the news – 'The Ford Motor Company has today taken legal action against the Transport Workers' Union and the Engineering Workers' Union' – 'What the fucking hell ...' The Company was seeking a writ to prevent these unions from changing the agreement. It was attempting to use the law to commit them to the NJNC agreement. Mr Justice Geoffrey Lane had granted the Company a temporary *ex parte* injunction against the unions, restraining them from taking further action until the hearing the following Monday. 'What the fucking hell ...' 'What does it mean?' For the first time they turned to me. 'Do you know what it means?' I was as amazed as they were. Trying to remember. 'Trade Unions and the Law.' Courses at University. Books I'd read. As far as I knew, the Company had no chance. But why were they doing it? The law was a bit hazy. Perhaps they knew something I didn't know. They're a big Company. They must have pretty good legal advice. Perhaps ... Why *were* they doing it?

The Industrial Relations staff at Warley were as amazed by the news as we were. What was going on? Leslie Blakeman, as it turned out, was leaving. This was his farewell. He had to get the agreement through. On Tuesday he was reported to be 'bemused':

I am just like Alice in Wonderland would have been. I am as confused and bewildered in this issue as any industrial relations man could be (*Guardian*, 26 February).

The professional was bowing out. Off to the CIR. But the reality of worker–union–management relations left his professionalism addled. He took legal advice. Thought he had a chance and acted quickly, decisively, desperately:

> In order to be effective a thing like this has to be done in hours rather than days. So I took the decision first and consulted afterwards (*Sunday Times*, 16 March).

At a time when Barbara Castle was attempting to introduce legislation that would bring the unions under 'the law', the Ford Motor Company and Leslie Blakeman decided to go it alone. It didn't come off.

After they had got over their initial astonishment the stewards' reaction was unequivocal. They weren't afraid of Ford's and they certainly weren't afraid of 'any old man in a white wig'. The reaction of the dockers in 1972 was seen here in embryo. They didn't have any illusions about 'the law'. They'd put up with it until it started to interfere in things they could do something about. Then they'd call halt. The strike was going on and the Company's recourse to the courts only heightened their resolve. Blakeman, however, remained convinced that the bulk of 'his' employees wanted to accept the deal and return to work. In reply to a joint statement by the TGWU/ AUEW leadership promising a return to work in exchange for the removal of the penal clauses and the cessation of legal action, he stated:

> The Company cannot accept the proposal that part of the package deal should be abandoned. The deal was agreed by the Company and by the trade union side of the National Joint Negotiating Committee and approved by the government as a package (*The Times*, 1 March).

He was convinced, he said, that many workers were on strike against their will. To entice them back he issued a threat. The qualifying period for the £20 holiday bonus would begin on 1 March. The agreed date for the implementation of the February agreement. A refusal to return to work would result in forfeiture of the bonus for the 1969 summer holidays. No one took any notice. While Blakeman still insisted that he had an agreement, the Company could now claim only its small van plant at Langley to be working at all 'normally'. More unions – including the NUVB – were making the strike official. At Halewood the situation had become even worse for the Company. The cars produced there are driven away on car transporters by drivers employed by Silcock and Collins. Their depot is alongside the Ford plants. The drivers are all in the TGWU, and their convenor, Wally

Nugent, is Chairman of the Liverpool road haulage branch. Wally has always kept close contact with the Ford stewards. He had met Mick Donnelly regularly while he was convenor of the PTA, and by 1969 he had become a very close friend of Eddie's. The drivers weren't too happy about delivering the cars during the strike but as Wally put it:

Y'know we try to coordinate our activities as much as we can but we couldn't really work a situation where we strike if they come out and they strike if we come out. They wouldn't be able to stop that plant for one of our issues. So what we do is to empty the car park. We deliver all the cars produced up to the time of the strike. And no more. We don't deliver anything that's come out of the plant during the strike.

The injunction changed things a lot. It converted a 'usual' situation into an 'original' one. The Court had constrained the TGWU and the AUEW from spreading the strike activity. It had frozen the situation. This very act, the formal implementation of a legal constraint, did more to change the situation than the national officials of the two unions could ever have dreamed up amongst themselves. At the Silcock and Collins plant, for example, the drivers went on strike for three days. Wally Nugent explains:

We called a mass meeting and Harold[5] came down to talk to the lads. I informed the lads of the situation. Of the injunction. And how it was that our unions officials were bound by a court order not to spread the strike. That was the situation see ... That's what the Court had done. So we couldn't be sure if Harold really meant what he was going to say to us or if he was just saying it because he had to. Because of the Court. So I put it to the lads that we'd been cut off from our officials and that the best thing we could do was to vote on the issue as we saw it ourselves. So we went on strike.

The introduction of a legal constraint, from above, at the request of the bosses, did little to calm the situation. It made the situation more complicated, and ensured that established lines of conflict became even more entrenched. The strike at Silcock and Collins was one of the more clear consequences of the Ford Motor Company's injunction. It serves to symbolize a much more general hardening of attitudes amongst the strikers, the stewards and the official union leadership.

As the March deadline passed, the High Court became, inexorably, the focus of attention. But Blakeman and the Ford Motor Company

5. Harold Verrinder, the road haulage District Officer of the TGWU on Merseyside. Another shop steward at Islington. A close friend of Wally and Eddie. The only TGWU officer in the North West with a union van. 'Britain's Biggest Union' on both sides. He called it 'the company car'.

had no chance. The writs, the agreement and the dispute gave Mr Justice Lane cause to sigh:

... and I sigh only because the whole matter is not a simple matter of law. It is complicated by what people will inevitably do regardless of what the law says. Unfortunately I am sitting as a judge, not as arbitrator. The thing is coloured by a relationship of management and labour.

Leslie Blakeman wasn't surprised by the judgement. His bluff, if it was a bluff, had been called. His gamble, which it certainly was, hadn't come off. Reluctantly he anticipated the return to the negotiating table.

As the strike progressed, the February agreement came under much closer scrutiny. Perhaps there was something in the stewards' case after all. The penal clauses had always appeared slightly suspicious, but the longer the strike lasted the more unequivocal were the statements of the union leaders. Even before the appeal to the High Court an important section of the national leadership within both the large unions were opposed to the agreement. The High Court action re-enforced this opposition. It also contributed to a systematic and detailed examination of the entire package. Things came to light that few people knew existed. On 3 March *The Times* reported:

Some union leaders not directly concerned with the negotiations said yesterday that they were 'horrified' when they discovered some of the changes proposed in the procedure for dealing with disputes.

According to one the 'speeded up' procedure might take three months to go through local stages and after that the unions would have to give twenty-one days' notice of a strike if there was no agreement.

There was still a feeling amongst labour correspondents that 'the Ford idea remains interesting' (*Guardian*, 3 March). Ford management might have been a bit impetuous, but there was still a lot the government could learn from its initiative. At the onset of the strike the opinion had been that the Company's move had been a courageous one, since it was 'attempting to establish discipline itself rather than appealing to the government for legislation' (*The Times*, 25 February). Its failure to make the February agreement stick led it to do just that. A member of Ford management was reported in *The Times* as saying:

This is the crunch, if this is any consolation. If ever a government needed to be impressed about the urgency of making unions honour agreements and keeping their members under control, then the time is now (28 February 1969).

This appeal to the state, coupled with the growing intransigence of the workers and their unions was to dominate the last weeks of the strike. The reconvened meeting of the NJNC that followed the High Court decision ended in great bitterness with a situation Mark Young described as 'complete deadlock'. Blakeman thought the situation 'deplorable'. Barbara Castle and the DEP were asked to intervene. The final stage had begun.

In Liverpool everyone was as resolute as ever. Money was getting short. Some of the lads were getting bored – 'What can you do with no money?' But there was no wavering. It had all become a bit routinized. There was no going back but the sparkle of the early days, the euphoria of leaving the plant behind, taking the Company on, had given way to a resolute doggedness. The routine of the strike had taken over. The occasional mass meeting lifted things. Unanimous votes. Resolutions of support. Laughs and jokes. Collectivity and solidarity. We're going to *win*. Between times it just went on. The members spread all over Merseyside. Watching telly. Taking the kids for walks. The stewards had their own routine. Checking on the social security payments. Helping out lads with problems. Organizing the strike pay. The large meeting hall at Transport House. Scene of the branch meeting. Tables around the four walls. Frank Banton and Gerry Flaherty organizing the money and the lists. Bob Henderson strolling up and down. Swinging his arms slowly from side to side in his worn sports coat. Occasionally clasping his hands in front of him. 'All right Bill . . . how's the wife . . .' 'Everything all right Frank? . . .' The lads in single file. Up the steps out along the corridor, through the main entrance and on to the pavement of Islington. 'The Strikers.' Patient, bored, reading the *Mirror* . . . a face, your mate. 'Fancy a bevvy after? . . . how many more in there?' 'Hello Ed . . . saw you on the box. You looked good.' 'About fucking time somebody said tha' ' 'Any info'?' . . . The five quid strike pay. A few bevvies. Off home.

The senior stewards are getting worn down. Eddie in particular. 'They always ask for him,' says John. 'The press, Granada, everyone. I don't know why it is, but they always want to speak to him.' Another steward put it like this:

There's a number of us who can do the job. In a day-to-day sort of way. But Eddie's got something about him. I don't exactly know what. Well . . . I couldn't stand up in front of the Stadium and talk naturally to the lads. Y'know. I'd be fumbling . . . making a speech sort of thing. He can just carry it off. He gets up there and tells them what the score is. They listen to him and they believe him.

As the strike went on Eddie began to look haggard. Bags under his eyes. Colour gone from his face. Physically and mentally tired. The press at his door day and night. The phone ringing permanently. Carol had an idea:

Y'know they'd just walk in here. We must have been daft because they'd come in and make a note of the telephone number off the phone. Then they'd ring up every day. And he always talks to them. He can't say no y'know. So we took the number off the phone and put a false one on. Some poor bugger in Liverpool's been getting hundreds of phone calls from the press and all sorts this last week.

But the press had to be dealt with:

You've got to deal with them. I know they distort what you say – especially some of them. There's some of them I *won't* talk to. But you've got to make some attempt to get the facts across because the lads will be reading the papers. That's the only contact the lads have with the strike outside the meetings.

That's why we go on Granada. I don't know whether we should but I *do* know that the lads like it. They like to see someone there giving their side of things.

The press, television, contact with the other plants, phone calls to London ... on the Inter-City. Meeting after meeting after meeting. And the picket in the morning.

But the strike was biting. They knew that. The dealers were short of cars. The Cologne plant had been stopped. The Company was beginning to talk about the consequences for the future. It was considering abandoning a £20 million investment plan for the Dagenham estate. It was, said Sid Harroway (Chairman, Ford Combine Committee and Deputy Convenor Dagenham Body Plant) 'a hoary old story' (*Guardian*, 1 March).

Earlier the Company had sent another letter to their employees. It was again signed 'R. J. Ramsey'. It told its readers that the 'penalty clauses' weren't penalty clauses but 'bonus clauses'. The strike, it claimed, was 'killing the goose that lays the golden egg'. The Company's reasonableness was contrasted with the insincerity of 'the trade unions' (see opposite). On the morning of the second Monday in March the letter in a Ford Motor Company envelope arrived at the homes of forty thousand Ford workers.

The wife came upstairs and said 'there's a letter here for you from Ford's'. I said to her 'You'd better open it love. It's for you tha'. Not for me. It's only addressed to me. They don't want me to read it.'

'That's right tha' y'know,' his mate said to me. 'They try to split your family. Turn your wife and kids against you. They'll do anything to get

Ford Motor Company Limited
Halewood Operations
8 March 1969

Halewood, Liverpool 24, England
Telephone: 051–486–3900
Telex 62461

Dear Employee,

Although the dispute between the company and two major trade unions has received a great deal of publicity over the past few days we feel that there is still a great deal of misunderstanding about the basic issues which are involved.

It therefore seems a sensible idea to set out for you once again – so that you can read it in the calm of your own home – what the company regards as the really crucial issues affecting all of us at this time.

As you know the 1967 wage agreement signed by all trade unions expires next July. Nevertheless the company agreed last October to begin discussion on a new wage agreement. These discussions resulted in a pay package proposal that offered an increase of $7\frac{1}{2}$ to 10 per cent as well as security against lay-off, extra holiday pay and so on.

A lot of discussion has surrounded the 'penalty' clause, but there was no penalty in this clause. It was in fact a bonus clause, because all it did was offer additional benefits to everybody who kept their word. Most of our employees live by this code. It is only the exception who doesn't and he would not get the benefits. It seems perfectly reasonable that if we were insuring people against strikes outside the company they would want to live up to agreements and so insure us against unconstitutional strikes in our plants which put our own people and people in other companies out of work.

The relief from unconstitutional strikes which it was designed to give was a necessary method of helping to defray the cost of the increase. It met the Government's objectives, which are to control inflation and consequently the prices of the things you buy. If agreed, it would also have helped to rebuild the waning confidence of customers abroad in the British motor industry's ability to deliver its vehicles on time.

Nothing in the agreement prevented any trade union from calling an official strike and we did, as you know, offer an improved and faster procedure for settling disputes.

We still believe that most of our employees look upon these arrangements as well worth having. Several of the unions shared this view as did the press and the public at large.

The arrangements were accepted by the trade union side of the NJNC in February. What we now know but didn't at the time was that the unions voted 7 to 5 in favour, which may seem a narrow majority, but it had always been the practice to accept majority decisions. There followed some unofficial action and we had another meeting of the NJNC when they reaffirmed the agreement – again by a majority vote. We then found ourselves in the extraordinary position of having an unofficial and an official strike and at the same time being told that the trade unions on the NJNC considered that we had an agreed arrangement that they expected the company to implement on 1 March. We then had to ask ourselves what we could do to solve the problem.

We took legal action to restrain two unions from resisting the NJNC agreement. The reason was that it seemed to us at this stage that this was the only way in which we could both honour what we believed to be the agreement on behalf of our employees and sustain the authority of the NJNC. We recognized, as we are sure you do, that without a properly constituted body to deal with on the union side we could soon find ourselves in a state of complete chaos.

The court action, as you know, was concluded on Thursday and the judge indicated that although we thought we had an effective agreement with the union side, this was not in fact so. The judge said the NJNC was only a negotiating body and that collective negotiations were not an agreement unless they were signed and accepted by each of the 19 unions concerned.

On Thursday, therefore, we said that the only practical way was to start all over again.

Some of you have been told recently that you are the forerunners in a fight against the Government's industrial relations White Paper. That is nonsense. Neither you nor we can possibly think that we can settle a political question that concerns every citizen by stopping production in one company. This is killing the goose that lays the golden egg.

It is difficult to understand why you and your family should be singled out to bear the brunt of a battle which puts your security at risk and should anyhow be settled by your MP.

We should at all costs avoid allowing side issues to creep into the negotiations, because the crux of the matter is: How do we produce a sizeable wage increase and justify it to everyone concerned.

The major concern in our relationship is to provide something that is good for everybody in Ford.

There are obviously very serious long-term issues involved here. We have customers all over the world who just will not wait for our cars, trucks and parts if we cannot deliver them. If you were told that you would have to wait months for a Ford, you would probably do what they are doing and buy something else. Buying something else not only affects the export business and the country's balance of payments, but in the long term it will affect your job, because the only way we can make wage awards is by manufacturing efficiently and delivering the goods on time.

Obviously, the company will do all that it can as fast as possible to get production started again so that we can have an agreement which will be accepted by you, the unions and the Government.

Quite simply we are looking for a workable agreement that will be observed, so that we do not have to keep stopping in our stride to deal with unconstitutional disputes, which ruin our production and waste your wages. We, and we are sure you agree, would like an agreement that would help regain the confidence of the world in British labour relations.

Last night we sat down with the unions and put forward proposals to wipe the slate clean and make a completely fresh start. Our suggestion was that on Monday there should simultaneously be a return to work and a withdrawal of the legal action, together with a renegotiation of the new pay deal.

We went to the meeting hoping that good sense and a will to start again would enable us to find a formula to allow normal working from Monday. Instead the trade unions demanded that we should increase our wage offer and drop the clauses which required people to a adhere to our procedure agreement. Naturally we did not regard this as a reasonable basis on which to start fresh negotiations.

It gave us no opportunity to find a meeting point and we have very regrettably had to report that fact to Mrs Barbara Castle's Department of Employment and Productivity.

Yours sincerely
R. J. Ramsey,
Director Labour Relations
Ford Motor Co. Ltd

that plant going again. Churning out profits ...' So prepared, the Company conjoined in talks with the DEP – and the unions. The stage was set for the final phase of the struggle.

Throughout the 1960s, but particularly during the years of the Labour government, the state increasingly involved itself directly in industrial affairs. George Brown's 'Statement of Intent', the Five Year Plan and the Prices and Incomes policies were all manifestations of a more general tendency. At the Ministry of Labour Ray Gunter implemented a firm line against unofficial activity by workers on the shop floor – 'the folk from whence (he) came'. The motor workers were identified as a special case and a special troubleshooter was set up to keep an eye on them. All this came to nought, Gunter left 'the bed of nails' which was re-christened the Department of Employment and Productivity. The major responsibility for labour relations was placed in the hands of Barbara Castle, Member of Parliament for Blackburn. Perhaps the workers would fare better at the hands of one of the Party's left-wing intellectuals than it had with a product of Valley Labourism. They had no chance. The main policy produced by the Labour government's DEP was contained in the white paper *In Place of Strife*. A document remarkably similar in emphasis to the Industrial Relations Act of the Tories which followed it. Barbara Castle wanted to control shop-floor union activity as much as Leslie Blakeman and Robert Ramsey. The 1969 package was deeply coloured by the thinking that had influenced Barbara Castle's White Paper. They were children of the same age. And affection for them set the tone of the talks at the DEP. While the talks were in progress the Minister of Employment informed the House of Commons that:

The package deal provided a pay increase well above $3\frac{1}{2}$ per cent – an average increase of 8 per cent. It was possible to approve it because it was part of a deal which ensured greater continuity of employment and greater productivity and these are the criteria which must be observed when assessing costs and savings of any such agreement.

The firm has offered to renegotiate either individual clauses or the whole package deal, following the resumption of work, and to do so urgently. But it is saying, and I think legitimate in saying, that it either has a new agreement, negotiated last month, or the current agreement, negotiated in 1967, and that this should be done constitutionally through constitutional negotiating machinery following a return to work. (Opposition cheers.)

The week of talks, monitored by Ministry officials, was not going well. On Friday 14 March, Ford laid off its remaining 4200 production workers. It was, in the words of a Company spokesman 'the first time this had happened since we began producing the model "A" at Trafford Park in 1911' (*The Times*, 15 March).[6] Some 38,000 of the 46,000 men and women who worked on the line for Ford had been on strike for three weeks. The time had come for Barbara Castle to intervene directly. Her officials at the DEP hadn't been able to break the deadlock. On the weekend of the 15 and 16 March, accompanied by her advisers, she met Blakeman and the national representatives of the TGWU, AUEW and EPTU. She had the support of a speech delivered by the Prime Minister, Harold Wilson, in his Huyton constituency, the previous evening. In his words the strike at Halewood was to be regarded 'as a mockery of all our efforts to build up employment on Merseyside'. He had already told a collection of businessmen in New York that strikes were to be the main problem faced by democracy in the 1970s. Barbara Castle was to protect democracy and the export drive. The strike had to be stopped, if possible with the retention of the penalty clauses.

The strike was stopped. The NJNC accepted an agreement on the Tuesday, and on Thursday 20 March the workers returned to their jobs on the line. The Company had not increased its wage offer. That aspect of the original 'agreement' stood, as did the disciplinary procedure and the 'Enabling Agreement'. What the Company had done was to concede on points of principle. There was to be no victimization of particular workers when they returned to work. The '21 days' strike-notice clause was removed from the agreement. That didn't seem a lot. What about the penalty clauses? Well the original penalty clauses were suspended, and a new Income Security Plan outlined. This retained the idea of 'the penalty' or 'the bonus' – but the stick it wielded was not a particularly hefty one. The Company agreed to

... pay ten shillings a week per worker into a holiday bonus fund. But the weekly payments for an entire plant would be forfeited if there was any militant action. However, the Company has agreed to place a £15 a year 'floor' under which no worker would fall because of unconstitutional action in which he was not directly involved. The full holiday bonus would be £25. This compromise was reached because the unions insisted that innocent men should not lose their full bonus payment merely because of trouble within their plant ...

The Company insisted on some collective element in the penalties in order that the moderates would have an incentive to keep militants in check ...

There is no union opposition to Ford's plan for a separate lay-off fund. Under

6. The Model 'A', of course, wasn't produced until 1927 and never at Trafford Park.

this, five shillings a week would be paid in for each employee in every week in which there had been no unconstitutional action within a plant.
Guardian, 18 March

Barbara Castle was pleased. In fact she said that she was 'delighted' that 'the protracted and costly dispute' was over and that 'the sooner the wheels get turning the better'. The wheels started to turn after the men had met at mass meetings.

The workers at Halewood, and their stewards, weren't too happy with the settlement. It looked as if Jack Jones had sold them out. Right down the river. They were annoyed that the increase hadn't been improved. They had come out for a shilling an hour and they had wanted to get it. The main thing they had been fighting against, however, was the penalty clauses and some semblance of them still remained. Had it all been for nothing? Eddie:

> We knew that we had to go back. We didn't like it all that much but we knew it was all over. The lads were pretty steamed up at the meeting and we told them we were going back but we weren't going with our tails between our legs. We were going back *united* into that plant. Y'know. Ford's may think they've won, that they've got their penalty clauses in but we know different. We knew that we'd given them a real fight. That they hadn't expected anything like the opposition they'd got and that we'd knocked back their penalty clauses. The ones they kept were pretty useless really and we were not having anything to do with them anyway. It was pretty clear y'know. We told the lads to forget about the lay-off pay and the holiday bonus. We were guaranteed £15 holiday bonus under the agreement and that was what we'd get. We didn't want to know about the ten bob a week for this and four bob a week for that. Ford's could stick it.

I was less confident, but they were convinced that they could handle the Income Security Plan, that it would make no difference to their position on the shop floor. And it didn't. The lads went back determined that they wanted nothing to do with Ford's handouts. The penalty turned out to be counter-productive. Rather than encourage 'constitutional behaviour' in Halewood it led to men indulging in any and every 'unconstitutional' practice to ensure that the plant was disqualified each week. Then they'd be told: 'There will be no funding this week.' Delegations to complain. 'It wasn't us, it was you.' The Income Security Plan never operated at Halewood.

The other concession that the strike had obtained was the promise of a reconstituted NJNC, and the stewards were adamant that they were going to get it changed their way. It took time (almost four months) but they met and got the support of Moss Evans and Reg Birch. Moss Evans had taken over Kealey's position and with the backing of the shop-floor committees and TGWU delegates he was prepared to take the TGWU out of the NJNC unless the committee's composition was radically altered. He had drawn up a proposal which would expand the TGWU and AUEW representation on the NJNC to five and four members respectively. The right-wing rump on the NJNC objected strongly and there followed months of the sort of acrimonious wrangling, that has always characterized right/left splits within the British Labour movement. But Evans was in a strong position, and he was also strongly committed to the idea of lay representation on the NJNC.

All we are, the national officials, is bloody professionals. We ought to be there to offer some help to the lay people if they need it. Nothing more. In this bloody job most officers want to maintain their autonomy, their autocracy really. If they're elected they claim that they *already* represent the members and have the right to speak for them. They think that they haven't got to listen to the stewards and the convenors. But it's the convenors who make sure that we do our bloody job.

The big problem in the trade union movement, and in the socialist society, is bureaucracy. The old structure on the NJNC was a perfect example of this. No bugger knew, really, what went on in there. The stewards and the convenors had to lobby all along the line. Picking up crumbs. I think the national negotiating body should be the convenors – with the national officers along in an advisory capacity, to represent the official union. And I think we'll get this at Ford's by 1974. Certainly after the amalgamation between us and the NUVB.

But there's a problem there as well. The convenors themselves may become bureaucratic. I say this because of the conversations I've had with shop stewards. They say that they come to work in their best suits, sit in their offices, too busy to see anyone. Or talk about what they are doing. So you need a national shop stewards' meeting to which the convenors on the NJNC will be accountable. I think we'll have all this at Ford's by 1974.

Moss Evans was a left-wing democrat, strongly committed to an idea of socialism which is hinged around an independent trade union movement and worker control of industry. He sees the future in terms of a gradual encroachment upon managerial prerogatives by the workers, a democratized trade union movement and a working class skilled enough in the techniques of modern industry to run it for themselves. A different man from Les Kealey. Living at a different time. He won out in 1969. Four convenors were elected onto the NJNC. Two of them – Eddie Roberts and Les Moore – were from Halewood. They had the company of Bill Brodrick who was elected at the same time. The union and the NJNC were opening up a bit. In that, the Ford workers had achieved something in 1969. It hadn't all been for nothing.

The late 1960s also saw a much greater coordination of Company activities on a European basis. Forward thinking has also been marked in the field of labour relations where in July 1967 a new wage structure was agreed by the Ford National Joint Negotiating Committee. Following a six months' evaluation of every employee's job a five-grade structure was introduced. The agreement included wage increases and productivity bargaining at all plants. The 1971 wage negotiations, following a nine-week strike, resulted in a new style two-year agreement and equal pay for women.

From *Graduates in Ford*, Ford Motor Company (recruitment pamphlet, 1971).

The Ford plant on Merseyside appears to have been suffering from a disturbing sickness since the ten-week strike over pay which ended just over two months ago. Labour relations have deteriorated to such an extent that a leading union negotiator, Mr Moss Evans, of the Transport and General Workers, expressed his disquiet publicly two days ago. Shop stewards at Halewood have complained repeatedly in recent weeks that the plant management has tightened its shop-floor discipline and was now 'playing everything according to the book'. The book in this instance is the *Blue Book*...

... in the normal course of events, procedures are interpreted to suit events and circumstances on the shop floor, but the Halewood stewards claim that since 8 April when work resumed at Halewood after the big pay strike, the management has insisted on observing the letter. The result has been disciplinary measures – including suspensions against shop stewards on eleven occasions ...

The Company denied having any devious scheme up its sleeve and insists that it merely expects employees and stewards to observe agreements. But it seems obvious that the Company has become meticulous about procedure since it agreed to pay a – by today's standards – modest increase in April. And the pressure is clearly on the Halewood shop stewards ... Inevitably, therefore, the Halewood workers have reached the conclusion that Ford's have decided to 'take on' the tightly-knit shop stewards' organization and are out to erode its strength. The 'purge' of the Dagenham plant in 1962, when several militants lost their jobs, is being recalled and stewards are wondering if Fords are trying to help history repeat itself. With a band of 'tame' shop stewards in its plants – so the argument runs – Fords would be in a position to change working arrangements, such as track speeds in the assembly shops.

Guardian 17 June 1971

11 Parity

Throughout 1969 whenever I met the stewards from Halewood, they would ask 'When are you going to finish that book?' 'We'll all be drawing our fucking pensions by the time that's in the shops.' Jack Jones was particularly sceptical: 'He'll *never* finish it. He's having us on, he's not writing a book at all.' On the defensive I'd reply that I was waiting for them to provide the last chapter. The Parity Campaign and the Ten Week Strike in 1971 did just that. But a book has already been written on this strike (Mathews, 1972). It sets out the details of the Campaign, so I shan't repeat them here. Rather I shall concentrate upon certain features of the Parity issue which cast light upon what has gone before and serve as pointers to the struggles faced by car workers in the future.

In 1969 the Ford workers came out best in an important skirmish with the Company. But it was only a skirmish. They returned to the plants, and although they ignored Ford's penalty clauses they couldn't ignore its line. They had won a foothold on the NJNC, through the presence of representatives from the plants, but this still left unanswered the question 'What now?'

The Halewood stewards had faced a crisis in 1968. As a consequence of the New Wages Structure a regular sequence of sectional walkouts punctuated the running of the PTA plant during that year. In the face of this upsurge many stewards were finding difficulty in offering any alternative to immersing themselves in the spontaneity of the mass. But they felt this to be a denial of leadership and they were provided with an alternative after Eddie's succession to the convenor's job. In a situation where no plant bargaining over the rate of pay or the work rate was permitted, the stewards found that their one alternative lay in the official union. They united the plant by pushing for a national pay increase through the formal union machinery, and this strategy continued after the 1969 settlement. The foothold on the NJNC was used to bolster another national demand. The demand for 'parity'.

The notion of 'parity' was no stranger to the car industry in the 1960s. While it burst into the public consciousness in 1971 it had been

Leyland Strike – The Facts

Unlike the Ford system, Leyland workers are paid on a piecework basis of a low flat rate supplemented by bonuses. This produces a multiplicity of differing rates. The present strike began on 18 May and is now in its fourth week. It began after talks had broken down on the rationalization of the piecework systems at the Leyland plants. The workers having found it increasingly difficult to maintain their level of earnings.

The union representatives have levelled a moderate and honest four point claim to management and requested quite naturally that their demands be confirmed by written agreement. This the management have categorically refused to do.

The claim is:

1 A demand for parity of earnings within the Leyland establishments which would yield a 200 per cent guaranteed bonus giving say a skilled man no less than £23 13s. 8d. for a 40-hour week.

2. A demand that indirect workers should receive no less than the 200 per cent bonus or average factory earnings whichever is the greater.

3. A demand for equal piecework earnings opportunity for female workers on their own rate.

4. A demand for a minimum wage of £18 10s. for new starters.

The strike is a direct result of management dishonesty and despite the earnest endeavours by the workers' representatives, no acceptable formula for a basis of resumption of work has been found.

The Department of Employment and Productivity have found nothing wrong with the unions' proposals, so the fight is clearly a direct conflict between the Leyland workers and the bosses of the Employers' Federation.

This dispute is receiving the same hostile press treatment that we Ford workers know so well ... Lord Stokes is allowed as much television coverage as he needs to attack the workers, attempting to demoralize them and bring them into disrepute. The lads have not been intimidated and remain solid behind their claim. There are nearly 9,000 out on strike which at this moment is unofficial. They badly need financial support if they are to win this struggle.

Let us as Ford workers and fellow car workers give them this generously and show the bosses everywhere that the Ford workers stand shoulder to shoulder with their Leyland colleagues and with trade unionists everywhere.

Issued by: the Ford Halewood Joint Shop Stewards' Committee, June 1969 an important issue for workers in the car plants for over ten years. It rested on the fact that the wage rates paid in some plants in the Midlands (where workers paid on piece rates had been able to push up the rate through strong shop-floor bargaining in periods of full employment) far exceeded those paid elsewhere in the industry. These differences led to an open conflict after the amalgamation that produced BLMC. In 1969 the workers at Lord Stokes's old Leyland factory struck for parity of wages within the new company. At Halewood the demands of the Leyland workers were seen as further support to the growing resolve amongst Ford workers to demand parity themselves. The stewards produced a leaflet explaining the nature of the conflict at BLMC (see p. 290) and organized a collection for the strikers.

The position of the Ford worker at Halewood and, say, the workers at the Morris plant at Cowley, in Oxford, differed in a number of important respects in the 1960s. The parity campaign arose out of these differences. Method of payment – time rates as opposed to piece rates – was one thing. Another was the conflict between the giant multinational capital of Ford (and General Motors) and the domestic, British capital of BLMC.

Both Ford and General Motors have increased the technological sophistication of their British factories rapidly since the last war. In 1969 Ford owned £5331 worth of capital for every worker employed in the British plants; at BLMC capital assets stood at £2254 per man. These different levels of fixed capital investment are reflected in the work rates at Ford and BLMC. If, for example, the total sales of the Ford Motor Company in 1969 were divided by the number of people the company employed, it would reveal that each person produced £8300 worth of vehicles for market. The corresponding figure at BLMC was £5000. *Ford Facts* stated that the amount of value-added in its plants (i.e. the total sales minus the cost of raw materials) compared 'very favourably' with their British competitors. The Trade Union Research Unit at Ruskin College, Oxford, estimated that each Ford employee added some £3500 to the value of the materials bought by Ford in 1968.[1] In a year each Ford worker in Britain produced a minimum of ten complete vehicles. His counterpart in BLMC produced only five.

Ford is an international producer. It owns capital, in the form of car plants, around the globe. To survive it must ensure that the rate of

1. *The Ford Wage Claim*, TGWU pamphlet, 1970.

return on this capital, the rate of profit, is maximized. The more capital-intensive the factory, the greater its technological sophistication, the higher the rate of output necessary for the continuance of that plant. The multinational producer is far more able than the purely domestic producer to manipulate particular local circumstances – such as a vulnerable work force – to its own advantage. By establishing work-rate standards in one place, like Cologne, the Company can make this rate reverberate throughout its other operations. This has meant that the American and Japanese car producers have consistently maintained a higher rate of profit on their European operations than have their European competitors. While in 1971 GM's return on its European assets stood at 10·5 per cent and Ford's at 6·5 per cent, all European producers (with the exception of Daimler-Benz and BMW) earned less than a 3 per cent return. BLMC's rate of return was only 2 per cent (Ensor, 1972). Ford is by far the most profitable of the British car producers and this fact became central to the campaign for parity.

The campaign got under way in the autumn of 1969. The stewards maintained their contacts with the stewards in other plants and with the national officers. Parity leaflets were produced regularly. There were stickers, badges and report-back meetings. The campaign was for 'parity', but at the beginning the Halewood stewards argued that the Company should be presented with a 'shopping list' of demands on which 'parity of earnings with the best rates paid in the industry' should be just one item. They wanted a complete renegotiation of the Blue Book. The stewards from the other plants weren't too keen. Eddie:

I remember Henry Friedman [convenor of the River plant at Dagenham] getting up and saying 'Eddie is a good socialist. He wants to improve the quality of life in the plants and I support him in that. But we're not having it.'

What did he mean?

Well Henry's line was that we could tie up all the things like line speeds, work allocation and tha' in the plants. Informally through the control we had established on the sections. What we wanted was for those controls to be formally recognized. Henry and the other Dagenham stewards thought this would complicate matters. Their line was – go for a straight pay increase that the lads can understand.

The Dagenham stewards won the day and they went for money. The brittle bond. Henry Friedman once said of money that 'a ten bob note is razor sharp'. It cuts both ways and in 1970 it cut the ground from under the stewards' feet.

They had the Company on toast in 1970 but the lads voted to accept Ramsey's offer (see Chapter 9). In part they lacked the confidence. To ask for so much. They took the four pounds. But by 1971 they were better prepared.[2] The TGWU got the Ruskin Unit to produce a detailed case for parity which was based upon the Company's profitability. This document (*The Ford Wage Claim*) didn't carry a deal of weight in negotiations at the NJNC. Such situations are dominated by power and not reason. Its effects were most strongly felt on the shop floor. Although not a propagandist document, *The Ford Wage Claim* strengthened the view that parity was a legitimate claim. It was in the ideological cement that it gave to the brittle bond that the document influenced the campaign for parity.[3]

The Company refused the demands of the union negotiators on the NJNC and made what they considered to be a reasonable offer of two pounds a week increase. The news of the offer spread through the Halewood plants. This time they didn't wait for the mass meetings. 'Two bleeding quid. You must be joking.' They stopped work and crowded out of the plants. They were out on an official strike that would last nine weeks. They would be outside the gates for ten.

2. So was the Company. Ford Europe had been experiencing a number of severe production problems with the new version of the Cortina. A strike offered the time to get these problems sorted out. They did not feel as vulnerable to a strike as they had a year earlier.

3. Although there were several important dimensions to the argument that took place at the NJNC meetings between Bob Ramsey of the Ford Motor Company (backed by the forty-seven officers who make up his Industrial Relations Department at Warley) and the trade unions (backed by John Hughes and Roy Moore at the TU Research Unit at Ruskin) two basic issues were involved. 1. The 'parity' concept. There was disagreement here over what 'parity' could and should mean, and over what should be compared with what. The Company compared its rate with national averages for the industry, and beyond, and concluded that Ford was a good payer. The best, rather than the worst in the industry. The unions compared the Ford rate with particular plants in the Midlands and argued that Ford was a bad payer, and that Ford workers had a right to be paid a rate comparable with 'the best in the industry'. 2. The 'ability to pay'. The Company argued that whatever the ins and outs of the comparison, it had no bearing on the way the Ford Motor Company was organized. It was paying as much as it could afford while remaining a viable company. The high level of capitalization – and the need for reinvestment – was used to justify the Company's rate of profit, while the unions used the profits to bolster their claim for a large wage increase. While it was important for the unions to pursue the Company's claims on profitability – pointing out the effect of depreciation allowances, development grants etc. – the argument breaks down at this point. What was fundamentally involved here (given the state of competition in the motor industry) was the distribution of Ford's income between wages and profits. A conflict between the rights of capital and labour. No magic formula can resolve this conflict.

The Claim for Parity –
A Report of Negotiations

This leaflet is to supplement and affirm the information given at the last report-bank meeting.

After much initial difficulty the newly constituted trade union side of the Ford National Joint Negotiating Committee sat down to meet the Company on the 25th September. This is the body responsible for negotiating your wages and working conditions and it has been reformed to include five convenors, two T & G, two AUEW, and one Foundryworkers' Union, also some district officials from the T & G, AUEW, NUVB and Municipal. It is expected that the additional knowledge of the new members and their close involvement with the shop floor will make the committee more effective and accountable to the democratic wishes of the workpeople.

At the last meeting on 25 September, the claim for parity of earnings with the 'Motor Manufacturing Industry' was put before the Company. Reference was made to the discussion which took place at the Department of Employment and Productivity in March this year, when it was made known to the Company that after the strike such a claim would be made on behalf of Ford workers by the Unions.

Just how poorly the Ford worker rates in comparison with others is illustrated by the following examples: for a 40-hour week –
Austin Longbridge, £32;
Rover Solihull, £27 18s.;
Morris Oxford, £32 3s. 4d.;
Pressed Steel Fisher, Castle Bromwich, £30;
Standard Coventry, £32;
Morris Engines, £32 8s.;
Pressed Steel Fisher, Common Lane, £34;
Maudly Motors Alcester, £31;
Jaguar, £32–£36;
Daimler £38;
Alvis £42;
Fisher Ludlow, £37, etc. etc.

THE FORD WORKER £21 1s. 8d.
AND THIS INCLUDES FOUR YEARS' SERVICE PAY.

It was pointed out to Management that most of these high earnings are achieved by various forms of payment-by-results system, which differ throughout the BLMC Combine. Therefore, the trade union side had sought a comparison more compatible with Ford's, and this was held to be the Rootes Agreement signed in June this year – which yields £34 18s. 8d. to workers there who work under agreements and conditions directly comparable with those at Ford's.

To substantiate the claim the following statistics were detailed, the point was also made that in a thirty-year period the Ford worker in dropping from being amongst the highest paid in the industry to the lowest, had simultaneously become the most highly efficient and productive and Ford's themselves had become the most profitable of all. . . .

e.g. 1	*Cars produced per man per month*	BLMC 0·41, Rootes 0·59, Vauxhall 0·68 *AND FORD 0·81*
e.g. 2	*Vehicles produced per operator employed*	BLMC 5·6, Rootes 8·9, Vauxhall 8·9 *AND FORD 11·7*
e.g. 3	*Trading profit per each £100 of sales*	BLMC £18 18s., Rootes £5 4s., Vauxhall £14 8s. *AND FORD £15 18s. TOP EACH TIME*

So you will see that Ford's lead the way in every field except the one most important to us . . . WAGES.

(Issued by: The Halewood Joint Shop Stewards' Committee)

Eddie was no longer convenor of the PTA at Halewood. In the summer of 1970, a job as District Officer of ACTS (the TGWU's clerical and supervisory section) became vacant and Bill Brodrick told Eddie that he thought he should put in for it.

I wasn't going fo bother but Bill said that it was obvious that I was going that way and that I'd be a fool to pass this chance over. And I thought if we've not built an organization here that can stand the loss of one man we've not done much.

And Selbourne Street was falling down. The middle of a city slum. Bad schools for the kids. Abandoned cars and litter in the streets. Eddie was seriously thinking about getting a job in Runcorn in order to qualify for one of the corporation's houses. The union offered him another way out and the chance to do the thing he most wanted to do.

There were advantages to the union job obviously. It's obviously better than a factory job. But I wouldn't have taken it on if I thought I couldn't do something, y'know. They've given me a free hand to organize any factory in the area. There's a lot of work for the union to do on Merseyside.

So Eddie had left. He had been told by Sammy Glasstone before the strike had started that he couldn't interfere, it wasn't anything to do with him any more. Eddie accepted that. The strike went on week after week. Picketing, meetings, social security. The same as 1969 but more of it. After eight weeks there was no sign of a breakthrough. It could go on forever. It didn't though, Jack Jones and Hughie Scanlon intervened again. They went over the head of Moss Evans and the NJNC and called a halt.

On Thursday 1 April 1971 the morning papers carried the news that a breakthrough had been made in the Ford strike. *The Times* reported that

an early end to the nine-week-old Ford stoppage is expected after a decision by the unions last night to recommend acceptance of a revolutionary American-style agreement, lasting two years but including a no-strike clause.

The Company had increased by one new pence an hour the pay offer it made during the fifth week of the strike. It gave the Ford workers an increase of around £4 per week. They were also to get an increase of £2 a week in December 1971 and a further £2 in the August of 1972. By this time, the *Sunday Times* estimated, the take-home pay of a Ford worker with a wife and two children would be around £27. Obviously the demand for parity had not been realized.

The 1971 Agreement also gave women workers equal pay. The Ford

Motor Company agreed to implement this reform earlier than the agreed date of March 1972. In addition to this, the Company conceded New Year's Day as a holiday. A concession which can only appear radical to someone ignorant of the absentee figures for the Halewood plants on that day. The agreement did no more than make a standard practice legitimate. Ford workers were now to be paid when they stayed in bed in the morning of New Year's Day. So the deal offered the workers little more than they had turned down four weeks earlier, with the promise of a bit more to come to cover inflation. In exchange for this, and the concessions on equal pay and New Year's Day, they had to promise not to present and strike for any 'economic demands' before 1973 ... and to raise no more grading grievances.

> The agreement specifies that there shall be no changes in occupational grading or wage structure during its life – it will run to 28 February 1973 'with no strikes or other action on economic claims before that date.' The unions will also have to pledge not to submit claims that would raise labour costs (*The Times*, 1 April 1971).

It was a 'revolutionary American-style agreement' and the decision on it was not to be made in the traditional way. There were to be no mass meetings. In 1969 the union side of the NJNC had turned down the Company's request for a ballot. But in 1971 Jack Jones and Hughie Scanlon got together with Stanley Gillen, the Chairman of Ford Europe, to arrange one. 'The ballot', said *The Times*, 'will take place tomorrow.' Already the Company had sent letters to its employees informing them of the agreed arrangements. The ballot would take place at the plants on the Friday 'allowing for a return to work on Monday' (*The Times*, 1 April).

Ford wanted to buy out short stoppages in the plants. The Company wanted to arrange a biannual face-to-face with the unions. A conflict that was predictable and could thereby be anticipated. The price it offered, after nine weeks of strike, was not a particularly high one. But it was accepted by Jones and Scanlon who in turn were able to weather a storm in the NJNC and get the support of a majority of the union negotiating team.

Their members received a letter from the Company informing them that a ballot would take place at their place of work between the hours of 11.00 a.m. and 5.00 p.m. on Friday 2 April. Their ballot forms told them simply that the union side of the NJNC was in favour of the agreement and asked them to indicate whether they accepted the agreement or not.

After nine weeks of strike you read something in the paper, or hear it on the news. Perhaps you go around to your mate's. You travel out to the plant. A few placards. 'No ballot – show of hands.' You look around. No one to talk to. 'Ah, fuck it.' Put your cross. Back home. In Liverpool most Ford workers never left their homes. Less than half of the 10,000 workers on the estate turned up to vote. Those who did, split 2514 to 2100 in favour of accepting the Company's offer. At Swansea there was a larger majority for acceptance (702–339) but there again over 40 per cent of the workers failed to register their feelings on the ballot paper. Under a headline which read 'Ford vote of 71 per cent for return to work' Paul Routledge wrote

> The nine-week-old Ford strike ... is as good as over ... The only difficulty facing the Company is whether the voting, which was unexpectedly low in some areas, including the militant plant at Halewood, on Merseyside, registered the true feeling of the shop floor (*The Times*, 3 April).

But as far as the stewards at Halewood were concerned the strike was anything but over. Of one thing they were sure, they had been 'sold out'. It had looked a bit that way in 1969 but this time they were certain. Jones and Scanlon had sold them down the river. The actual settlement was bad enough but the strings made it much worse: the two-year deal and, what was more, a rushed ballot. The mildest view was that Jones was in a difficult position, that the 16 per cent increase was as much as they could hope for in one go, but that 'to get the lads back in the plant by blowing them apart is bloody criminal'. Jones and Scanlon had sold out. They'd joined the bosses' side like those who'd gone before them.

It isn't surprising, given the British working class's history of struggle and defeat, that the idea of the 'sell-out' has become a part of its tradition. Workers who have taken on their bosses have frequently found themselves left by the trade union officials who have led them. Agreements have been signed, and strikes called off, when victories seemed possible, if not likely. Trade union officials have resigned their jobs to become managers or, since the war, to run the nationalized industries. In the face of such betrayals the idea of the 'bent' official has developed amongst rank and file union members. With this idea has gone the demand for a change of leadership, for the idea of the 'bent' official has focused attention upon the inadequacies of particular men, rather than the problems of particular organizations. It is important to say something to correct this emphasis. For while many union officials have been morally 'bent', there are probably an even greater number of honest, 'principled' men to compare with them. Jack Jones and Hugh Scanlon can be seen as such men. They represent some of the better aspects of the social democratic tradition in Britain. They believed in radical social change, they believed that the rank and file should have a significant say in the way their unions are run, and they believed that industry should, and could, be run by the workers. They, and not Harold Wilson, inherited the radical reformist tradition of the British working class. They were democratic socialists who came to the fore on a wave of working-class militancy. While their political beliefs led to quite marked changes within the TGWU and AUEW they could not transcend the fact that these organizations *were* trade unions. And that trade unionism both as an ideological form, and as a type of social organization, places severe limits upon the way in which a social movement can develop. In other words no matter how radical, or well intentioned, the men who become leaders of the trade unions are, their position within the union (and hence within capitalist society) creates severe problems for them if they try to put such intentions into practice. Without the backing of a vigorous socialist movement, capable of relating particular sectional struggles to each other, and extending struggles beyond the particular factory, the radical trade unionist finds himself in an insoluble dilemma. He fights by the rules of a system that he hardly approves of, within an organization that has proved itself manifestly incapable of changing those rules. Many trade union officers have yielded to the stress produced by this situation. Eddie Roberts saw this in 1970. After working in Transport House on Islington for a month or so, he found that his opinion of trade union officials had changed: 'They're not bent. I used to think they were but they're not. They're not bent. They're just tired that's all.' They're tired. Seeing no way out, they do a 9.00 to 5.00 job and try to forget about it. Eddie who was working around the clock – attending meetings all over the Region, all hours of the day – was chided for 'spoiling the job', 'rate-busting'.

'The bureaucrats' at Transport House are tired. They are 'bent' because they don't bother any more. They've got no fire in their bellies. While it is important to say these things it is important also to know why. For a while the slogan 'bent' may be a useful piece of rhetoric, it can lead to an inadequate political assessment of the situation. It is most important to locate the 'sell-out' and the 'bent' officer within the wider context of trade unionism itself. Moss Evans in his days as a shop steward shared the views of the Halewood stewards about union officials.

When I was a shop steward I wouldn't have the full-time officer on the job. I used to think that it was an affront to my ability. He'd always compromise. If we'd put in for tuppence we'd never get that tuppence. He'd always come out with a penny. He was a decent enough fella but we just didn't want him near the job. And of course the union officials were always used as a threat to us by management. 'I'm afraid I've no alternative but to report you to the full-time officers,' and then he'd be brought in to tell us that we were out of line. And that used to annoy me.

He too changed his views when he saw the job from the inside:

Once you've been a full-time official you realize that certain things are part of an agreement which the Executive have committed the union to and you are empowered to carry out.

You're obliged to follow it. It's out of your hands as it were. You know, it's the system I suppose. The system we work to. It's like everything else, you've got to give some order to it.

Now if I were to ring up Pat Lowry and tell him that he was in dispute before the procedure was exhausted he would say to me 'but there's another stage to the agreement'. Now supposing I was to say 'bugger that. We are going to have a stoppage because we're right and justice is on our side.' And I feel like saying that very often. Supposing I said that. I'd feel very unhappy if he said 'well, I'll have to have a word with Jack Jones' or 'I'll have to report you to your Executive'. Which is what he would say.

I don't know. As I say it's the system we work to. You've got to have some system . . . some regulative process . . . or you could end up making a lot of mistakes. I think we're getting somewhere. Christ its only 1971. There's years we haven't started yet.

Bureaucratic rules establish the nature of the trade union's relationship with the employer, and control the full-time official. The Pat Lowry example is a simple one which demonstrates a wider and more pervasive reality. The ending of the Ten Week Strike was but another manifestation of the fact that trade unions are so rooted in the fabric of capitalist society that the 'sell-out' of the rank and file is bound to recur in the history of trade union struggles.

In 1971, 50,000 Ford workers went on official strike, and almost half of these were members of the TGWU. An important group at Ford's but only 1 per cent of the union's total membership . . . working around the country, in sweet factories, on the docks, on farms and in the cabs of lorries. The Ford workers had received official union backing for their strikes in 1969 and 1971 because they had demanded to be heard within the union. They had pressured full-time officials and mandated their representatives on the lay committees of the union.

They had built up political support. That this support was forthcoming in 1970 and 1971 was also associated with the fact that a settlement at Ford's, obtained through an official strike, could set the pace in negotiations with other firms. In both those years, for example, the settlement at Ford's was followed by an almost identical agreement at Vauxhall, obtained without the cost of strike.

For these reasons Jack Jones and Hugh Scanlon gave their support to the Ford workers. But the longer the strike went on the more difficult it became for them to sustain it. The TGWU was running short of cash. It would soon have to sell off some of its assets. There were grumblings within the organization. 'What about us? ... They're earning twice as much as us. ...' And there was no sign of a weakening in the ranks of the Ford workers, nor of Ford's backing down. It could go on for a very long time. In this situation the union leader has a limited number of options. He can decide to sweat it out, accept the payment of more and more strike pay and hope that he can sell it to the other sections of his organization. Or he can escalate the conflict. Raise the stakes by drawing these other sections into the struggle. Such action presupposes preparation: that the other sections of the union's membership are aware of the issue involved, and are willing to struggle for it. It's very difficult to universalize a sectional pay demand. Although trade unionism lays stress upon the unity of workers, it is formed around the sectionalism of the working class. It tends to divide more than unite. A ten bob note can be razor sharp. Jack Jones and Hugh Scanlon couldn't escalate the struggle. It is doubtful whether such an idea entered their heads. For them, like their predecessors throughout this century, they had two options: sweat it out or settle. They decided to settle.

They settled with Gillen. But to settle is to call a halt. They had to sell the settlement to their membership. They had to ensure that the plants started up again, that their members returned to their jobs on the line. Their predicament raises in starkest form the contradictory pressures that are exerted upon a leader of a trade union. Jones had come to an agreement with Gillen. When asked on *Analysis*, a programme on Radio 4, whether the Agreement gave a strike-free guarantee to the Ford Motor Company, he replied that 'in the sense of an absolute agreement' there could be no such guarantee 'because we are dealing with people'. He went on:

all that a trade union leadership can do is bind itself in honour to try to observe the agreements it concludes with employers and this I believe in absolutely. In general the assurance we give to management is that we bind ourselves in honour – we will do our very best to see that the agreement is observed.

The notion of the 'honour-binding agreement' is one which has dominated the thinking of trade union leaders in Britain for as long as trade unions have been recognized. It unites right and left wings within the trade union movement. Jack Jones, in this respect, could be Arthur Deakin, who had said in 1954 that:

having entered into an agreement it is an obligation to see that it is carried out, not merely in the spirit but to the letter, until such times that adjustments are made by negotiation around the conference table.

The trade union official deals in shop-floor conflict. Through him, the conflict in the factories becomes routinized and manageable. But at the root of the agreements he makes with employers are the lives of his members who work on the factory floor. Without their support, the agreement (and by extension the union official) is useless. Deakin was able to enforce the acceptance of the agreements he made around the conference table with management. Since his time, however, members of his union have frequently broken the terms of the official union agreement. Jack Jones could not enforce agreements as Deakin had done. He was, and had to be, a different sort of General Secretary. The idea of participatory leadership found its strongest advocate in Jack Jones. After the 1970 settlement at Ford he wrote:

Not so long ago, agreements were made by a few officials. The stewards, representatives directly elected by the members, stood outside the negotiating building, to cheer or jeer, but never to take part. They could shout 'do your best', or 'don't let us down', but they were never inside to participate and judge for themselves. That has changed. The TGWU was the first to put lay representatives on the top negotiating body, men who have to live every day with the results of their negotiations. We insisted on reporting back to our members at every stage.

'This', he said, 'is democracy in action.' He went on to say what this implied for leadership:

To share authority in this way is not to 'abdicate leadership', but the role of the leader is changing, becoming much more demanding and intricate. He has to involve himself in making policy, discussing strategy and deciding tactics *with* the officials and stewards and not *for* them. He has to be prepared to put these collective views to the test of the vote of the members (*Sunday Times*, 22 February 1970).

Everything in the negotiating situation cuts across this approach. A frequent criticism made by managers of shop stewards is that 'they expect us to be able to make a decision but we can never get a straight answer from them. They've always got to go back to "the brothers".' There is severe conflict between corporate and representative images of trade unionism. This tension is experienced at all levels of negotiation and is particularly pronounced, and most subtle, at national level. More than one union leader has been admonished for not showing 'leadership'.

In 1970 when the workers at Swansea voted to support the NJNC's call for a strike, and acted on this vote by striking, while all the other plants returned to work, the *Sunday Times* abused them under a headline which read 'Swansea Tyrants'. This tyranny was possible because the trade union leaders had failed to lead (i.e. direct) the Swansea workers. On the same page as Jack Jones's article on 'Ford's: Shop Floor Democracy', the paper's leader-writer wrote: 'To defend the mavericks at Swansea as exponents of plant democracy is playing with words.' The message was clear: Jones and Scanlon ought to live up to their responsibilities and send them back to work. Both these union leaders felt vulnerable to such a charge in 1971. They wanted to end the strike and get everyone back inside the gates of the plants. Moss Evans explains:

> You've got to know how to end something. In 1970 we hadn't thought about ending anything. We thought that there was going to be a strike. And then only Swansea came out. Now it was right that they came out – and their action permitted us to keep the idea of parity as a negotiable item – but we were in danger of looking extremely foolish.
>
> Negotiations are a very funny game. To show a weakness when you're negotiating with management – even if under pressure from the membership – is just no good. Because you've got to back in there; back into the NJNC and start again next month. If you're made to look vulnerable once, you've had it next time around. Your position as a negotiator will have been undermined. And it's the membership that will lose.

The stewards at Halewood felt this in 1970 when their call for a strike was turned down. They had been shown to be vulnerable and this affected their position both within the plants and the NJNC. In the aftermath of the vote at the Stadium, PTA stewards were saying that 'you can have too much democracy. ... You've got to be able to guarantee the decision.' They overcame this, but the 1970 vote left its mark. Jack Jones and Hugh Scanlon were very aware of it when they negotiated with Gillen a year later. They had to know that the plants were going back. When attacked for intervening, at his union's national committee meeting at Eastbourne the following summer, Hugh Scanlon made the issue clear:

There comes a time, particularly after a strike has been on nine weeks and there seems not even a remote possibility of any meeting of the sides in the foreseeable future, when there are responsibilities on the president of the union that exceed the responsibilities of everyone else.

Jack Jones could have said the same thing about being General Secretary of the TGWU. The realities of trade union–employer relations exposed the limitations of, and the constraints placed upon, his idea of participation and democracy. When it comes to the crunch the General Secretary's word goes. One of the full-time officers in Liverpool, who supported the strike, was pleased by Jones's action because:

Jack Jones is acting like a General Secretary for the first time. The Ford lads have had a good run for their money. Now for the sake of the union they've got to go back.

So Jones and Scanlon called a halt. The ballot they called for was held, and on a low poll every plant voted to return to work. The strike was over – as an official strike. The lads had been blown apart. But at Liverpool the stewards decided that they hadn't finished yet.

If Jack Jones had come up here. Talked to the lads. Told them that it was all up, that the union couldn't afford any more strike pay. Y'know, put it to the lads. They might have said: 'All right Jack, that's fair enough, let's call it a day'. Or they might have gone on without strike pay. Y'know. But it wouldn't have turned them against Jones. What really made us mad was his agreeing, and then getting the Company to arrange a ballot for the lads to vote when there'd been *no* report-back meetings. Y'know everything about this strike and the way we've done things since 1969. Negotiations – leaflets – report-back meetings at the Stadium. Y'know *organized*. Everybody together, going in the same way. That ballot smashed all that. That's what we won't forgive Jones for.

They called mass meetings for the weekend. On the Saturday the men from the Swansea axle plant met and their vote reversed the decision made at the ballot. The Halewood transmission plant met on the same day and overwhelmingly accepted the resolution that the 'ballot and the offer are not good enough and we accept neither'. Their resolve to carry on with the strike was endorsed by a meeting of the PTA and MSB plants the following day. Halewood and Swansea were to go it alone again. Without Dagenham[4] and without the official support of their unions. Moss Evans explained to the press that:

The situation quite clearly is that we are honour bound to accept the decision of the ballot. The management offer was a good one. We have no dispute with Ford and our members who stay out tomorrow will be acting unofficially.

The unions may have been morally bound to the agreement with the Company and the decision of the ballot, but the stewards and many of their members weren't having it. They didn't like the position they were in, but they'd had mass meetings and the plants were not going to start. A Company spokesman described the situation as 'chaotic'. 'The strikers', he said, 'appear to see themselves as little gods. They're defying everybody. It's serious and we're worried' (*Guardian*, 6 April 1971).

The mass meeting cuts across the grain of our society. It is anathema to many people. Few things raise middle-class Britain to a greater show of moral outrage than workers packed into large hall, voting on important issues by a show of hands. In the first week of April 1971 the press directed this outrage at the stewards of the Halewood and Swansea plants. John Torode criticized them for attempting to 'sabotage the secret ballot by getting a "show of hands" majority for rejection in the emotional atmosphere of mass meetings'. Eric Jacobs described how the mass meeting was:

... one of the ways the militants had kept an appearance of complete solidarity throughout the strike ... it takes a hard man to raise his hand for a return to work against the grain of platform speeches, and with the Press and television naturally excluded (*Sunday Times*, 4 April).

It was left for Peter Jenkins, of the *Guardian*, to lay it firmly on the line.

Defenders of the trade unions – or rather their sympathetic critics, for it is becoming increasingly difficult to put up a reasoned defence – have been driven against the ropes by the latest activities of the Ford shop stewards at Halewood and Swansea. The verdict of the secret ballot has been over-ruled by the appeal court of the mass meeting. One form of democracy, the kind accepted in this country, has been countermanded by another form, democracy's perverted alter-ego – the rough plebiscite of the show of hands.

He went on to say that to try to defend such behaviour 'in the name of working people is an insult to the British working-class tradition' for

---

4. The stewards at Dagenham had in fact been able to call a mass meeting before the ballot. This voted to reject the deal, a vote which was overwhelmingly reversed at the ballot. The stewards accepted this second vote as binding.

the Halewood workers are accepting what a vocal group among them sees as a defeat much in the way that Everton supporters accept a defeat by Liverpool – by smashing their faces in; it's an old Merseyside tradition and one wouldn't build a political theory on it.

This innate 'roughness' of workers had, it seems, been given a free rein under the leadership of 'vocal' shop stewards. And the blame for this lay in the well-intentioned ideas of those who advocated 'shop-floor participation'. The TGWU's attempt to incorporate such 'participation' into its day-to-day activities 'makes an alarming cautionary tale'.

Their [Jones's and Scanlon's] admirable intentions resulted in some shop-floor representatives sitting in with the negotiators. But what happened. The real power was in the room next door where the shop stewards' committee ate Company sandwiches and drank Company beer. ... It was the self-appointed Politbureau of stewards which called the strike, within hours and in breach of an agreement with a month to run; and it was the duly constituted negotiators, reinforced by shop-floor representatives, who remained the shadow of power until, after nine weeks of bitter strike Mr Jones and Mr Scanlon reasserted authority and leadership over the heads of the discredited, elusive and – literally – irresponsible negotiating committee ('Ford and the Squalid Silence', *Guardian*, 6 April 1961).

There you have it, be nice to them and they take advantage. Give them a bit of responsibility and they abuse it, and drink your beer and eat your food into the bargain. Loosen the chain a little – no matter how well-intentioned you may be – and they'll bite your hand.

The middle classes, generally, have found themselves taxed by the existence of the workers. They need the workers, for without them who would be on the assembly lines making cars, freezers, infra-red grills and all the other things necessary for good living. But the workers also pose a threat to them. A threat tied up on their dependence – if power workers strike the grill won't work – and also in the fact that workers are below them in the social pile. The middle classes are afraid of 'falling on hard times', of falling into the working class, but even more afraid of the working class rising up to challenge their rightful place in the sun. In coping with this they have tended to interpret the working class through their own, specifically middle-class, images. They find the 'warmth' of working-class communities attractive. Homely workers are nice, it's when this 'warmth' comes on to the streets that it causes problems. For 'the workers' need leadership. Without this direction, they can fall into the wrong hands and be led astray. The miners on the picket-lines in 1972 had been so led, as had the power workers.

The more sophisticated upholders of 'democracy' recognize that a democratic society is no easy thing to organize. They see that an election every five years is not much use in itself and that it needs to be backed by lobbying, consultation, meetings in 'smoke-filled rooms', and the like. They are loath to extend the same principles of decision-making to the working class. This contradiction relates to the fact that the workers, because of their position in society, can justifiably make demands – redistribution of wealth and income, guaranteed employment, plentiful publicly-owned housing – which challenge the whole basis of the present social order. To extend 'democracy' to them in any meaningful way, carries with it the possibility that the balance of society might be changed. To escape this, and resolve the contradiction, the myth has been perpetuated that 'workers need firm leaders'; that workers are basically irrational and authoritarian and that for their sakes (for they often don't fully understand the implications of their demands) and everyone else's, they must be kept in check. Like Tolstoy's man on another's back, choking him, the upper echelons of our society will do everything to help the suffering of those beneath them save allow them to walk upright.

The mass meetings at Swansea and Halewood voted to stay on strike. The vote in these meetings contradicted the ballot. To explain this, critics have pointed to the 'emotionalism' of the mass meeting, to the fact that men are afraid to oppose the leadership in such a situation, that they are psychologically and physically intimidated. Mass meetings can be emotional. Some men can find themselves intimidated. Some leaders do flaunt their use of the platform. But none of these things are peculiar to workers or mass meetings. Neither are they to the point. In finishing a strike, workers have to decide to go back into a plant, and work on an assembly line on a vast shop floor, alongside hundreds of other men. Their survival in that situation is tied up with their relationship with those other men.

An executive who works in his own office may hold on to some notion of 'the team', but essentially he is in a position where he can rise and fall by his own efforts. That such men should think in individualistic terms – in terms of the sanctity of the individual and his precious right to decide things for himself – is not surprising. It would be surprising if the men who work alongside each other on the factory floor, where nothing they do *as an individual* affects the situation one bit, thought likewise. Mostly, in fact, they don't. They have some attachment to the collectivity and to collectivist modes of thought. In thinking of a package agreement they are inclined to ask 'how will this affect us?' The 'me' is in the 'us'. Thus while a 'secret' (i.e. private, isolated) ballot may have its uses in coming to a decision, to impose it at the end of a long strike, without mass meetings, was calculated to 'blow the lads apart'. For it denied them access to the collectivity, and thereby to themselves. It left them adrift. At the mass meetings men still voted to go back to work – something like a third of them wanted to go back, given the Jones–Scanlon settlement, the result of the ballot, and the Dagenham return. But a significant number changed their minds and voted to continue. To deny this, to argue against mass meetings in terms of their emotionalism, and the way in which they 'inhibit freedom of choice' is to fail to understand the reality of working peoples' lives. Moss Evans realized this. He knew that Jones and Scanlon had decided that the Ford lads had come to the end of the road. He understood why they had pushed the secret ballot clause through the NJNC. But he also knew that the secret ballot wasn't going to get the Halewood and Swansea plants producing cars again. More importantly he saw that the ballot could lead to severe splits within the workers' organization at Ford.

> I remember in 1970 I was asked about a ballot and I said that if the lads have mass meetings and say they want a ballot they can have a ballot. And I don't think anyone disagreed with me. If we had got together and devised it ourselves it would have been all right. But it all got a bit tainted by the Company thing.

'The Company thing', that fostered the idea of the sell-out. And this, together with the possible split between Swansea, Halewood and the rest, worried Moss Evans.

> If we're going to get anywhere at all, it's important for there to be unity between people at different levels and different locations. A split would only help the Company. I think there's a need for the Ford worker to have a reasonable relationship with Scanlon and Jones. Because they can do a lot for the motor workers in the future.

So, to heal the breach, Moss Evans travelled down to Swansea. On the Tuesday he spoke to 1600 of the 1900 men who work at the axle plant. The Windsor Cinema in Neath was packed – 'They played hell with me. Jesus Christ I thought they were going to put me in the dock.' He explained to them why he felt that they should go back. They listened and voted to return to work. By the time he reached Liverpool on the Wednesday, the stewards knew that it was the end of the road. Resigned, they recommended the mass meeting to follow Swansea and return to work. The end of the Ten Week Strike.

The return to work, then, was confused. This confusion made the stewards' organization, and the lads on the line, vulnerable. A vulnerability that was to prove fatal.

During the last weeks of the strike the stewards were hearing disturbing stories about meetings that were being held in the plant. Members of the technicians' union DATA were not on strike. While in the plant they were in a position to observe the regular meetings that the plant managers were having with their foremen in the North Canteen.

Real Nazi-type hate sessions they were y'know. It was unbelievable. They were all there, and they were really being encouraged to pour out all their frustrations and to direct them at the stewards and other activists. Y'know 'What are we going to do – we're going to smash them' sort of thing. Chants and shouts. And the management were assuring them that they would be backed up. They were really preparing for when the lads came through those gates again.

The stewards knew this but they could hardly believe it. They were sweating over the organization of the strike, and the call for a ballot and a return to work took them by surprise. Memories of the old days were beginning to fade. They were reminded soon enough.

From the outside Eddie and Wally Nugent could see it happening. Eddie couldn't interfere. Sammy had told him so and he accepted it. The stewards felt he should keep out of it as well.

I knew I couldn't do anything. There was a lot of talk that I had my finger in this and tha' but I didn't. I kept out of it. I don't think I would have organized the strike any different but I was sick about the way they went back. The lads had to be led back. Somebody had to get up on that stage and tell the lads what was going on in the plant; tell them about the foremen's meetings and tell them how we were going to take 'em on. But nobody did. They just weren't prepared for what was going to happen to them.

Wally thought that they ought to:

tell the lads that they were going to meet at Evans Medical before going to the plant. Meet there and march down the road and through the gates. Y'know – singing 'Hi Ho, Hi Ho, Its-off-to-work-we-go –' It's a hell of a thing tha' y'know. Taking the piss. Y'know as soon as the foreman tells you to do something if everybody starts whistling 'Bollocks -- la la la la la la.' Y'know what I mean? Well they can't go on. They can't survive in the face of tha'. And some of those lads can really take the piss.

But they just went back in and took a hammering. It makes me wonder y'know if they'd decided on a quiet life for a few years. I don't know.

They may have wanted a quiet life, what they got was the ball and chain. The old days all over again. Enforcing the rule. As it was written in the Blue Book. Power shifted from personnel to production manager. A new, planned 'firm line' was put into operation. The Halewood PTA was to be brought to heel. Stewards were to receive a full sixty-minute work allocation. They weren't to be allowed off their job without the express permission of the supervisor. The supervisors were to run the sections and the managers the plant. One of the stewards described the situation in the plants in a letter to *Socialist Worker* (26 June 1971):

> On the day the men returned this (new) policy came into operation.... 'Either do the job or get off the pay-roll' became the new Requirement to Operate.
> Day and night, local agreements on manning and conditions were ignored. Men were physically prevented from seeing their stewards.
> One foreman boasted: 'That's a jungle out there and I'm King of it.' The same one smashed every window in his department after complaints about the fumes and heat.

McCrone, a veteran of the battle at Dagenham in 1962, replaced Marvin Hughes as plant manager. It was to be the 'firm line' in earnest.

The first ten weeks produced ten strikes in the PTA. Senior stewards received formal warnings and suspensions. Bill Brodrick was hardly away from the plant. He accused Skinner, the site manager, of riding roughshod over the steward organization: breaking long established agreements within the plants. He must know that it would lead to a major confrontation.

Men, having been on strike for ten weeks, returned to work after the confusion of a ballot organized by the Company, found themselves in the middle of a struggle for which they were totally unprepared. They hadn't had a full week's wages for twenty weeks. The vulnerability of the stewards' organization increased as each week passed.

Turner has argued that workers in the car plants who have experienced periods of sustained conflict develop 'strike fatigue' – a sort of war weariness. Such was the case, he argues, at Dagenham in 1962. It would be reasonable to expect such weariness amongst the workers at Halewood in 1971. A long strike, a return to the speeded line, walkout after walkout, debts still unpaid and the summer holidays around the corner. In the second week of June their resolve was put to the test. John Dillon, the steward for the lads on the Magic Roundabout was sacked.

John had taken over from Bert Owen as steward for the wet deck section of the paint shop in 1968. He teamed up with Ronnie Walsh and Eddie Roberts.

He's a tough little character, John. Never afraid to have a go y'know. 'Where are they?' sort of thing. But if he was wrong he'd always admit it. He'd always admit it. You'd have an argument with him and he'd come back later and say 'You were right about that. I should have done....' He's a good lad, John.

John was blunt; forever at the point of things. A 'short arse'. He walked around with his chin sticking out. There was nothing phoney about John. He had the respect of the lads on his section and through the struggles of 1969 and the Parity Campaign had built up a strong alliance in the paint shop with Ronnie and George (Eddie's deputy).

The stewards' committee was shattered by the clamp-down that greeted the return to work. The severe imposition of the 'ball and chain' returned the stewards' organization to the early days of the 1960s – struggles were again localized, again they involved the issues of job control and the rights of the shop steward. Some stewards simply folded under the pressure. On the trim line, for example, Bob Costello was given a full sixty-minute work allocation. His union activity had to be fitted into a full operator's work load. And he was fifty by this time. It was physically beyond him. He asked to be taken off the line and was put on the brush, sweeping up. Other younger men, who had only heard the stories of the early struggles in the plant, found the direct experience of the 'ball and chain' too much for them. They simply didn't know how to cope. The struggles became centred on sections where the men, and their steward, had some idea of how to 'take on' the management offensive. The stewards on these sections were dealt with summarily. Warning after warning. Suspension after suspension. John Dillon was suspended on two occasions before the incident that led to his dismissal. These suspensions, like those inflicted upon other stewards, developed out of a conflict between what the lads on the line considered to be their rights and the rule of the Blue Book. Some of the lads on the wet deck got involved in an argument over manning with the supervisor. They wanted John to help them deal with the problem. Under the procedure the steward can only be involved in a dispute after a 'failure to agree' between the operator and his foreman has been formally recognized. This means that the steward can wait for two days after the dispute before he is called in. The lads wanted John 'now'. He came and was suspended.

On a number of sections, where particularly arduous or monotonous

First Steward Sacked

This morning John Dillon, Paint Shop A shift steward, was sacked. They sacked him for holding an 'unauthorized meeting on Wednesday 9 June'.

What we should remember now is that this is *only the thin end of the wedge*. They want to try to break up our solidarity that existed during the ten week strike and to dictate manning and line speeds. Once they have been able to sack one man, they will be able to sack anyone . . .

AN INJURY TO ONE IS AN INJURY TO ALL

The facts of the case

Thursday 8 April
The day we went back after the strike the management took three men off the job on the landing deck. Before the strike this had been an eight man job.

Monday 7 June
Management took another man off the job. The men sent for a steward who advised them to do the job to the best of their ability.

Tuesday 8 June
They were under constant pressure from supervisors with threats of the sack if they didn't do the job properly. Obviously this was impossible with only half the usual manpower.

Wednesday 9 June
One of the lads received a written warning for 'not doing the job properly'. The steward was sent for and he asked the foreman to rescind the warning. The foreman refused so the steward advised the men to try to do the job as best they could. *This the men did and have been doing since Monday*. The steward was then sent back to his own area. Later the GF, Mickey Mouse Williams, threatened the lads with the sack unless they guaranteed to do the job properly. This was the straw that broke the camel's back, and the lads stopped the job. They were refused the steward. The whole sealer deck came out in sympathy. Half an hour later everyone was laid off. But many of the lads decided not to leave the premises. The steward was on his way out of the plant when he was confronted by these lads who were very angry. They wanted to go to the paint shop to demand an explanation. The steward suggested they meet outside but they were determined to go to the

office so the steward went with them. He told Mr Lefreve that the men wanted to ask a few questions, but he replied that he would only speak to the steward. When the steward told the men this they barged into the office. Language was flying about and people got excited so the steward advised the men to go outside where they decided to meet again on Saturday at Transport House.

Friday 11 June
The steward was called to the plant to answer the Company's allegations of 'holding an unauthorized meeting' and behaving in 'a very abusive manner' in the paint shop office. The Company didn't have much of a case and they indicated they weren't going to press the charges. After talking to the unions the Company agreed to:
1. Rescind the written warning;
2. Lift all threats of sacking;
3. Have the man they took off on Monday standing by on the area in case the men got into difficulties;
4. To invite the district official, convenor and stewards from both shifts to observe the job with management.

Saturday 12 June
At the Transport House meeting the lads accepted the stewards' recommendation to return to work on Monday.

Monday 14 June
The man was put in the area as arranged at 9.15 a.m. John Dillon and convenor Bill McGuire were called to the Labour Relations Office and told by Mitchell, the LRO, and Andrews, paint shop manager, that the company had completed their investigations and were sacking John Dillon.

It has come to our notice that on Sunday 13 a meeting was held at the Adelphi Hotel chaired by Bob Ramsey, chief LRO for Ford Britain, with the foreman involved in the dispute, Connelly, who was star witness in allegations against John Dillon. Can we believe this was unconnected with Halewood management's sudden decision to sack John Dillon?

PTA Shop Stewards' Committee, 14 June 1971

jobs exist, the lads decide to share the work out by rotating the jobs. On the wet deck, the men alternated between using power-driven and hand-operated sanding equipment. This was against the rules, and the supervisor wanted it stopped. No more rotation of work. 'What do you think John?' John thought that the foreman was being stupid. He was suspended again and told in a letter that he was being punished for 'telling employees to disobey their supervisor who had instructed them in the way in which the job should be done, then telling them not to listen to the supervisor's advice'. The final incident took place on Wednesday 9 June and it involved a manning problem on the landing deck. The men on the landing deck used their physical strength to guide red-hot car bodies, slung in cradles, from an oven thirty feet above their heads, onto skips placed on a ground level conveyor. It's not an easy job and it can be dangerous. Up until April 1971 it had been work for eight men. These were reduced to five and and 7 June they were told that one more of them was being moved. From then on, only four men would work on the deck. They asked John. He didn't like it much but could only suggest that they 'give it a go'. They did it for two shifts. But the supervisor insisted they weren't doing the job properly. 'Well what does he expect. It's too much work for four of us.' On their third shift they were threatened that unless they did the job properly they would be sacked. Ah well, it might as well be for a sheep as a lamb. They stopped work and were making for the gates with the section behind them.

But the lads had had enough. They were fed up with being pushed around. 'Lets go in the office and sort the fuckers out.' They didn't want to leave the plant. They wanted to get something sorted out. John wasn't too sure. He had a good idea where this could all lead and he wasn't sure if he (and the stewards' committee) could handle it. But he asked the manager if he'd come on to the floor and talk to the lads. He wouldn't. So the lads went to talk to him. They invaded his office. Abused him, his supervisors and his Company. And left the plant.

It is clear that this incident involved a spontaneous outburst by these men against the speed-up and repression that they had experienced in the plant from the day they returned to work. It is also clear that the stewards' committee had lost its grip on the situation and was unable to give a lead in situations like this one. This default placed stewards like John Dillon in an almost impossible situation. Stuck between the lads (the masses) and the stewards' committee (the organization). What is also clear is that the violence that came to the fore in this dispute frightened Ford management. It represented a direct challenge to the tight grip that they wanted to keep on the Halewood plant. A direct challenge to them, what they stood for, their position in the factory and society. The 'firm line' had to hold. Bob Ramsey travelled up for a weekend meeting in the Adelphi Hotel. 'An example' – that was what was needed. Someone had to be made an example of. John Dillon was sacked on the Monday. It was, in the opinion of the *Financial Times*, 'an unusually severe step' (15 June).

A mass meeting of PTA workers during the Monday dinner break voted overwhelmingly to strike. Ford management, remembering 1962, might have expected this. What took them aback was the stoppage of the transmission and the body plants that followed a breakdown of negotiations on the Wednesday, and the call from the Combine Committee for a full national stoppage of all the Ford plants. The Ford workers were stronger in 1971 than they had been a decade earlier. The transmission plant was stopped and the axle plant seemed certain to follow. In the face of a further protracted halt in production Ramsey did a complete about-face. He accepted the union proposals that he had turned down only a few days before. John Dillon was to be reinstated, but not as a steward, and his activities in the plant would be subject to joint investigation.

The victory was an important one, although double-edged. The PTA stewards' committee was relieved that it was off the hook. They knew that they had to call a strike over the sacking but they weren't too sure of support from the other plants. When it came they were immensely relieved. On their return to the plant they found that 'they've called off their hounds'. The 'firm line' was eased, the 'ball and chain' put away again. The senior stewards decided to 'play it cool' for a while. They didn't push for John's reinstatement as a steward.

John was moved off the wet deck into the garage section. On the ground floor of the plant, the last stage in production where the car is checked, repaired and driven on to the park. Far away from the paint shop. He wasn't too happy. He wanted to know if the union still supported him. He wanted their moral backing. He visited Sammy Glasstone at Transport House and got the assurance that the union supported his actions; that as far as the TGWU was concerned he was all right. But he wasn't a steward, and the lads on the wet deck refused to vote for anyone else. They'd listen to Ronnie Walsh but no one else. Ronnie became *de facto* steward for the whole paint shop.

The Dillon sacking was an amazing time. It was incredible. It became apparent that the Company had set up a plan to trap us. Everywhere I went I could see Ramsey. Ramsey, Ramsey, Ramsey. One big net. I couldn't sleep. Ramsey everywhere pulling the strings. Manipulating the situation for a showdown.

I learned a lot from it though. A hell of a lot. I learned that you can never ease up. Once you've got them there, once you've pressured them into a corner you've got to keep them there. Because if you ease up once they'll get you. They'll walk all over you. They did that after the Ten Week strike. We nearly had our lot then.

The stewards' committee survived and, as we shall see, it established a working relationship with Ford in the 1970s. In that time, though, Ford was on the move, and as its global strategy developed so workers at Halewood were reminded of the vulnerability of their position within the Company; of that and the lessons of 1972. Because in ten years' time Ford, once again, would attempt to walk all over them.

The day is not far off when auto manufacturers will be producing the same line of product for sale everywhere in the world, with only the most minor variations amongst countries.

W. Bourke, Ford Executive, Vice President.

It is our goal to be in every single country there is, Iron Curtain countries, Russia, China. We at Ford Motor Company look at the world map without any boundaries. We don't consider ourselves basically an American company. We are a multinational company. And when we approach a government that does not like the US, we always say, 'Who do you like? Britain? Germany?' We carry a lot of flags. We export from every country.

Robert Stevenson, Ford Executive

12 Ford's Global Strategy

'Halewood workers strike over Ford discipline code.' A newspaper headline. The date: 12 May 1981. Ten years, in fact, after the end of the Parity strike. Ten years, yet the Liverpool plant still makes the same kind of news. In the House of Commons the debate had a familiar ring to it too, and it contrasted with the somewhat reserved tone of the *Financial Times* headline. There, Margaret Thatcher, the Tory Prime Minister launched into an attack upon the workers at Halewood (and those at British Leyland's Longbridge plant, for they were on strike too) who had brought the plants' assembly lines to a standstill. It was, she said, 'absolutely crazy'. Referring to them as 'these people' she asserted that they were 'putting some of their own jobs and those of others who supply them, in jeopardy. If we get increased unemployment because of the bad reputation of this country abroad,' she continued, 'they have only themselves to blame.'

It's a familiar story. So familiar in fact that it would be easy to conclude that little has changed since 1971. 'The lads' are still on the line, the same issues still stare them in the face and when they try to do something about it, their responses fall into a chasm of incomprehension. So, you may ask, what's new? To conclude that nothing was new, however, would be misleading. While certain things (those long enduring things like who is doing what to whom) haven't changed much, their *context* has altered dramatically, and in ways which we barely glimpsed, let alone anticipated, in 1971. For car workers, and for the rest of us.

In 1971, for example, wages paid to car workers in Britain stood at 26 per cent above the industrial average; in 1981 they fell 1 per cent *below* that average. In that same period the number of workers employed by the main car manufacturers fell from 304,000 to 196,000.[1] The effects of this have been dramatic. On Merseyside, British Leyland closed down its modern Speke No. 2 plant in 1979. The No. 1

---

1. See Labour Research Department, *Motors: End of the Road For Jobs*, London 1982.

plant followed three years later, and with it the end of 'Standard Triumph's' association with Liverpool. In Ellesmere Port, General Motors' Vauxhall plant remains but with a labour force halved since 1978. Today its operations have been reduced from a fully integrated production unit to one which assembles the Astra from kits imported from West Germany. There, eyes are turned to GM's projected assembly plant at Zaragoza in Spain, a plant which at full capacity could produce enough cars to fill GM's entire 1981 market share in Europe. If we add to this the closure of Girlings brakes, and the rundown of GM's AC Delco plant, employment in the vehicle industry on Merseyside has declined 37 per cent between 1971 and 1981. And in this experience, Merseyside has not been alone. Unemployment *doubled* in the West Midlands in 1980. Throughout that year, 1,000 jobs were lost each week, and the trend continued in 1981. In those two years 40,000 jobs were lost in the motor industry alone. And as the West Midlands economy collapsed so too did those regional outposts of vehicle production. In Scotland the Linwood plant closed on 22 May, 1981 – halfway through the People's March for Jobs – and 4,000 workers were added to the unemployment queue. A union official commented:

> There is nothing for them here now, or for their families. Some have not thought about what they are going to do, others are talking about emigrating and some will try to set up on their own. But £3,000 ... does not take you very far these days (*The Times*, 23 May).

A sentiment which was echoed by British Leyland workers, sacked at Bathgate a year later and by those put on the dole at Speke too.

Through all this (and apparently against all the odds) Ford stayed. That company with its estate at Halewood and new engine plant at Bridgend, to add to the axle plant at Swansea, entered the 1980s (for all the threats of imminent departure) as the *only* automobile company with significant production plant located in the regions. On Merseyside, Halewood (with its 14,000 jobs intact) stood out like an oasis in a manufacturing desert. There, where once labour turned over faster than the cards could be stamped, men waited on lists for a chance to get on the payroll:

> There's a queue a mile long – no ten miles long – to get into that place now. Henry's place is about the only 'good job' left in this town. Everything else is either shut down or shutting down. But Ford's is still there. I suppose its the only thing left to give us some hope really.

The British Car Market

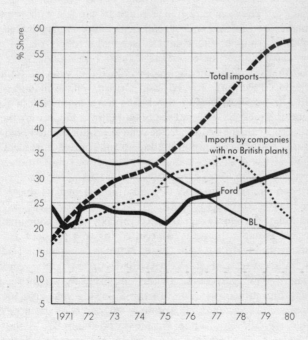

But what does this hope rest on? How secure is the future for car workers in Britain? To answer these questions we need to look closely at the pattern of these changes.

In 1970 the international vulnerability of British manufacturing was already clear, what was not so clear was the pace of change that would emerge over the next ten years. This process, hastened by Britain's membership of the EEC and by the 'oil crisis' of 1973, has been almost breathtaking in its scope, involving a dramatic restructuring of manufacture on a world scale. This has been most evident in the case of vehicle manufacture, and in this Ford has played a central part. An indication of the scale of the change can be obtained by looking at the British market for motor vehicles (see page 321). During the 1960s this was dominated by the British Motor Corporation whose 40 per cent market share was seen as 'traditional' and, to many people, unchangeable. The company had a range of models with respected brand names tied in to a widespread dealership. Amalgamated with Leyland and Triumph, the company seemed strongly placed in an industry whose output increased steadily to 1·92 million vehicles in 1972. But that was to be the high point. Since that year the trend has been steadily downward: for BL and British vehicle manufacturers generally. In 1980 just *half* of those cars were assembled in British plants and the industry's output dropped below a million for the first time since 1958. In 1981 commercial vehicle production fell below the 1949 figure. This is a collapse not a downturn! These events have been associated with a dramatic change in the level of competition in the British market, as *imported* cars took a bigger and bigger share. In this, 'foreign companies' (and the Japanese in particular) have been identified as a threat to British producers. However, a closer examination of the figures reveals the complexity of the issue involved. In 1980, for example, 'imports' accounted for 56·7 per cent of newly registered cars in Britain. Of those, 'foreign companies' (Datsun, Renault, Volkswagen, Fiat, Volvo) made up 23·34 per cent, the remaining 33·36 per cent being imports by British based manufacturers, principally Ford. In the following year, 459,365 new Ford cars were registered in Britain – 46 per cent of those were assembled abroad. Thus while Ford entered the 1980s as the clear market leader, its *production* in Britain dropped consistently throughout the 1970s.

'Imports' then are just one part of an increasingly complicated picture; perhaps in this case, they are more a symptom than a cause. During the 1970s, Ford developed the concept of a European production system around its 'Ford Europe' Company. As this concept unfolded (with the *continent* and not the state as the geographical unit of production) so too did particular plants become identified with single models. While Halewood once produced the Escort, Capri and the Thames van it now produces the Escort alone. All Capris and Granadas are imported into Britain from West Germany. In 1973 the Halewood branch of ACTSS (the white collar section of the TGWU) pointed to this tendency, and the vulnerability which Ford Europe created both for particular plants and for domestic components suppliers (see page 326). And this adds another dimension to the question of 'foreignness'.

Vehicle manufacture, as we have seen, involves the organization and assembly of a variety of intricate bits and pieces. These 'components' are produced in other plants often (in Britain) owned by other companies. Steel is one obvious example. It is often said that the fortunes of the country's steel and vehicle industries are closely linked. In the late 1970s however, at a time when BSC was closing plant after plant, Ford purchased just 40 per cent of its steel from British sources. Figures like those saw the 'sourcing' of components emerging as a sensitive political issue. When Ford established its new Escort, for example, it contracted its disc brakes for the car to Tevis, the German subsidiary of the US multinational ITT. As a consequence Girlings, until then the regular supplier of brakes for both the Escort and Cortina, cut the labour force at its Bromborough factory by 400. A year later the factory closed down. The Triumph Acclaim is assembled by BL at Cowley under licence from Honda. As such, the Italian government insisted that (with a Japanese component level of over 40 per cent) it wasn't 'British' and thereby had no privileged EEC entry into the Italian market. Political considerations such as these, together with pressures from within the NJNC, have kept Ford UK with something approaching 80 per cent of British components. But it was with wry smiles indeed that union officials listened to Ford Chairman Sam Toy complaining about Nissan in 1981. At that time Nissan's plans for a British plant were being widely discussed and Toy had expressed the view that a vital element in deciding whether the Japanese arrival would be of benefit to Britain was the level of European components – preferably British – to be used. As he put it: 'If I was in the component industry at the moment I would be terrified ... If Nissan comes to Europe it is in the interests of Britain that it comes to Britain – but on the right conditions' (*Financial Times*, 11 June 1981).

As one member of the NJNC put it:

They're crocodile tears really. Its only because we've continually made sourcing an issue that they've kept their percentage as high as it is. They've been forced to do it you might say. And it was painful for them.

And what goes for components goes for the plant too. Time was when British heavy engineering companies built the hardware (the presses, transfer machines and conveyors) that made up British body, transmission and assembly plants. That is no more. In 1978, the Vickers' Scotswood plant closed down in Newcastle. A giant plant in the heavy engineering sector, it had in the past provided car presses for all the major British-based car companies. It still produced presses (under licence from the German company Mueller) when it closed. Ford's new presses at Halewood were bought direct from Germany; so too were the robots.

The 'British' car when it isn't assembled abroad, therefore, is increasingly made up with 'foreign' components and assembled on 'foreign' equipment. So the picture isn't as simple as it seems. A Ford may be as 'foreign' as a Datsun. Certainly Volvo would make a case for being more 'British' than Ford, and even more so than GM. A fundamental change is taking place in the *system* of production therefore; a change developing alongside the increasing 'internationalization' of the market. This is the change we have to come to grips with if we want to work out what hope there is for British car workers in the 1980s.

Pick-up truck launch by Ford

Ford today launches in Britain a one-tonne pick-up truck built by its South African subsidiary. The Company expects to capture at least one third of the UK pick-up market which has been dominated by Japanese vehicles . . . Ford says 35 per cent by cost of the components are sourced from UK Ford plants . . . Ford will import about 6,000 of the South African pick-ups during the next 12 months.

Financial Times, 30 June 1982

In the late 1960s the locus of automobile production shifted from the region to the continent. 'Ford Europe' symbolized this and a similar strategy emerged in the Americas. There, plants moved out of Detroit – 'auto city' – to the rural areas of Ohio, California and the deep south and further into Mexico and the continent of Latin America. If Ford's Rouge Plant (with its integrated production system from iron ore to the car on wheels) was the symbol of Fordism at its height, the modern

The Capri

It is worth examining the Capri BW ('Body in White') and KD (Knock Down) achievements since the introduction of the first Ford of Europe common model in 1969.

	BW	KD
1969	66,749	13,540
1970	53,216	16,170
1971	36,061	5,935
1972	—	500

There has been no compensating increase in that Escort schedule at Halewood.

By far the most intensive area of activity in the application of Ford of Europe policies is the resourcing of component supplies from British vendors . . . Again it was the Halewood Capri, that first . . . commonized vehicle which proved to be the most graphic example of the trend.

	German suppliers	No. of components
1969	12	10
1973	121+	272+

West German Firms supplying Halewood with panels and sub-assemblies:

Vidal and Sohn	West Germany	Ext. front body panel
Koster and Sohn	West Germany	Plate assembly horn mounting
Grosshaus	West Germany	Bracket windshield wiper mounting
Flusch	West Germany	Fuel pipe clip
Sivers	West Germany	Reinforced mirror bracket
F. Herder	West Germany	Plate door rest
DAF	Holland	Panel windshield header
Le Phofil	France	Strainer door outer panel

At some time in the past these items have been produced at Halewood or supplied by British vendors . . . British firms who would normally supply Halewood on Capri PTA parts have lost part or all of their schedules on 249 different items to continental suppliers . . . on those items we selected for detailed examination . . . the British component was cheaper than that of the foreign competitor. We were appalled to find that 40 employees from Plessey's Cranham factory were made redundant when Ford re-sourced the car radio contract from Plessey (£9.70) to the West German firm of Blaupunkt (£11.50) . . . we later learned that Blaupunkt obtained the guts of the radio from Taiwan at a cost of approximately £5.00. When ACTSS approached the company to discuss what appeared to be a bad economic decision, we were told that it was not a suitable item for discussion.

From: Association of Clerical Technical and Supervisor Staff (ACTSS) Halewood Branch, *Report on Ford Motor Company*, 1973.

system contrasts in the way units are dispersed over a vast geographic expanse. While companies have always taken advantage of attractive locational sitings (the availability of grants, loans, cheap labour, etc.), the new system (orchestrated as it is by detailed computer control of component and unit production) gives them an added flexibility. To begin with, it lessens their dependence upon *particular* groups of workers. Ford got beaten in 1941 because all its eggs were in the basket of the Rouge. No longer is this true. Today, Ford's main assembly plants all replicate each other, and production can be switched with some ease from one to the other. Furthermore 'disaggregation' – as the process of breaking up the Rouge into smaller dispersed pieces has been called – allows the companies to take advantage of variations in labour markets across continents and around the world. With the stages of production split up in this way, processes requiring skilled labour can more easily be separated from those needing large numbers of untrained assembly-line workers. In these ways the new system gives added powers to the companies in their dealing on the factory floor and in the market place.

And the advantages of continental (and global) production don't end here. Ford's British and German companies (while registered as individual and independent entities) have a degree of mutual co-operation through Ford Europe, described by the company chairman Bob Lutz as 'absolute'. Based upon the same models and plants they purchase components through the umbrella company and this arrangement allows them to 'have all the benefits of size without the drawbacks' (*Financial Times*, 7 July 1981). Furthermore the nominal independence of Ford UK and Ford Werke (the German subsidiary) allows Ford to operate in 'two domestic markets instead of one', thereby accelerating the advantage it has over companies like BL, Renault and Fiat whose European operations are strongly based upon one 'home' market.

With the sinews of continental production established it was only differences between the European and US markets which contained the systems at this level. The oil crisis changed that too. As the 'small car' became established in the US market so too did the possibility of one range of car selling throughout the world. A range which in concept (low weight, highly simplified body shell, less chrome etc.) broke dramatically from the excessive styling developed by GM through Sloan in the twenties and thirties. A range which could also be produced globally. This is the concept which Ford termed 'project Erika' and which led up to the launch of the new Escort. GM had a similar project around their 'J' car, the Cavalier, while VW produced and sold the Golf in Europe, the USA and Latin America. These cars are 'world cars' in the sense that they. are both *produced* and *sold* globally. The model that is assembled and rolled off the lines at Halewood is the same as the one which is produced in Saarlouis in Germany. It is also produced at two plants in Michigan and in Japan by the Toyo Kogyo Company which produces Mazda cars and in which Ford has a 25 per cent interest.

To produce the new Escort Ford has pooled its worldwide resources on an impressive scale – a development made possible partly by the sheer geographical spread of the Ford empire and partly by the use of a trans-national computer network which since 1978 has linked design teams in America and Europe (*Sunday Times*, 28 September 1980).

Commenting on the project Philip Calwell, Ford Chairman, argued: 'It is no exaggeration to say that Ford and the auto industry as a whole are currently engaged in the most massive and profound industrial revolution in peace-time history.' While the extent to which this departure represents a radical break with the past can be exaggerated – Walter Hayes, Ford vice president of Public Affairs admitted that 'we invented the phrase "world car" . . . because we had to reinforce the faith of the US in the technical ability of our industry' (*Sunday Times*, 28 September 1980) – its publicity does serve as a pointer to the established trend within the motor industry towards global operations. The Escort, built in plants around the world – over a million models a year – also draws upon component suppliers globally. The cars assembled at the Wayne plant in Michigan will be made up of transaxles manufactured in Japan, shock absorber struts from Spain, rear brake assemblies from Brazil, British steering gears, Italian cylinder heads, hub and bearing clutch assemblies from France, door lift assemblies from Mexico, along with Taiwanese wiring and West German valve guide bushings. As with Ford, so too with GM. Its 'J' car project cost even more than the $3 billion Ford invested in Erika. GM, in the words of their president James MacDonald, were 'rolling $5 billion set of dice', with integrated production facilities in West Germany, Australia, Brazil, South Africa and Japan, the annual target for Cavalier production was set at two million units. The 'British' version of the model (the Cavalier) – made up with engines from Australia, transmission units from Japan and body panels from West Germany – is assembled at Luton from kits provided by its 'sister' Opel plant in West Germany.

And as the car manufacturers 'go global' so do their component suppliers. Commenting on the situations in the West Midlands, and the tendency for companies to merge and shift their production facilities abroad, Clifford Webb noted:

Ford and the other multinational motor groups are insisting that where possible key components are supplied from at least two countries to ensure that problems in one can be overcome by increasing supplies from the other. This could be met by selecting independent suppliers in different countries but, such are the volumes involved, there are significant cost-saving advantages to be gained by dealing with a single multinational component supplier (*The Times*, 16 December 1980).

This view was supported by Kenneth Gardner, finance director of Dunlop Holdings when speaking at the Fourth World Motor Conference in Geneva in 1982. The 'world car' he said:

... calls for component companies to meet two conditions. They must have sufficient capacity to meet the larger production runs, and they must have geographical flexibility to service the assemblers on a worldwide basis.

In this context the assessment by a correspondent of *The Times* was quietly understated:

Much of the discussion about the threat to the European car industry was centred on Japan ... far less has been said about ... the American companies active in Europe – GM and Ford – yet they are much more firmly established than the Japanese and likely to become even stronger in the next decade. GM and Ford have both come to realize that national boundaries are irrelevant when rising costs demand the biggest economies of scale (15 August 1980).

He went on to conclude that 'faced with Japanese efficiency on the one hand and the American world car on the other, BL, Fiat, Renault and the rest of the European manufacturers are in for a tough time. It is a situation that can lead only to more mergers, more government intervention and, possibly, some casualties.'

In 1980, informed opinion in the automotive sector reckoned that companies would need to produce over 2 million units a year to survive in the new context. At that time GM, Ford, Toyota and VW were the only companies in that league. Nissan, Peugeot – Citröen, and Renault with over a million and a half units were in there to be reckoned with. But in 1980, just half a million rolled off British Leyland's assembly lines. In a European industry with already more than enough plant and capacity to fill the market, the giant companies expanded their operations, investing more and more in order to increase their competitiveness, to survive and ultimately break their rivals. Here the contrast between the technical sophistication (the degree of planning

Ford Escort: European Sourcing of Components

Country	Components
Austria	radiator and heater hoses, tyres
Belgium	hood-in trim, seat pads, tyres, brakes tubes
Canada	glass, radios
Denmark	fan belts
France	seat pads, sealers, tyres, underbody coating, weather-strips, seat frames, heaters, brakes, master cylinders, ventilation units, hardware, steering shaft and joints. Front seat cushions, suspension bushes, hose clamps, alternators, clutch release bearings
Italy	defroster nozzles and grills, glass, hardware lamps.
Japan	WS washer pumps, cone and roller bearings, alternators, starters
Netherlands	paints, tyres, hardware
Norway	tyres, muffler flanges
Spain	radiator and heater hoses, air cleaners, wiring harness, batteries, fork clutch releases, mirrors
Sweden	hardware, exhaust down pipes, pressings, hose clamps
Switzerland	speedometer gears, underbody coatings
USA	wrench wheel nuts, glass, EGR valves
England, Germany	muffler ass'y, pipe ass'y, fuel tank filler
England	steering wheel
England, Germany	tube ass'y steering column, lock ass'y steering and ignition
England, France	heater ass'y
England, Germany	heater blower ass'y, heater control quadrant ass'y
England, Italy	nozzle windshield defroster
England, Germany	cable ass'y speedometer
Germany	cable ass'y battery to starter
England, Germany	turn signal switch ass'y, light wiper switch ass'y, headlamp ass'y bilux, lamp ass'y front turn signal
England, Italy	lamp ass'y turn signal side, rear lamp ass'y (inc. fog lamp), rear lamp ass'y

England, Germany	weatherstrip door opening, main wire ass'y, tyres, battery, windshield glass, back window glass, door window glass, constant velocity joints
France, Germany	transmission cases, clutch cases
England, Germany	rear wheel spindles
Germany	front wheel knuckle
England, Germany	front disc
England, France, Italy	cylinder head
England, Germany	distributor
USA	hydraulic tappet
England, Germany	rocker arm
England	oil pump
Germany	pistons
England	intake manifold
England, Germany	clutch
Germany	cylinder head gasket
England, Germany, Sweden	cylinder bolt
N. Ireland, Italy	carburettors
England	flywheel ring gear

Steel (body steel and forging barstock) from UK, Germany, Belgium, France, Italy, Austria (sheet) and Finland (bar).

The new world system

The first Brazilian cars built separately for Europe go on sale in Italy today. Fiat is launching a diesel version of its 127 saloon, the smallest diesel-engined car in operation. Built entirely in Brazil, the newcomer features the body of the Brazilian Fiat 147 which has been strengthened to cope with Latin American roads (*Financial Times*, 3 March, 1981).

It is a bitter paradox for Argentinian industrialists, farmers and, above all, workers that their country – one of the great bread baskets of the western hemisphere – cannot sustain a single tractor factory. Three manufacturers, Massey Ferguson, Fiat and John Deeve have already shut down in the course of 1980. The fourth, the Argentine subsidiary of Klockner–Hunbolt–Deutz, is due to close at the end of this year. In a pathetic last flicker of resistance . . . the Deutz Argentine workers have appealed to the Vatican to intervene (*Financial Times*, 4 December, 1980).

Volkswagen of Germany and American Motor Corporation, which is controlled by Renault of France, have entered into a deal with Chrysler Financial, the customer financing arm of the ailing US motor company. Each will pay an undisclosed fee according to the volume of business (*Financial Times*, 1 June, 1981).

After 77 years Goodyear Tire and Rubber company is ending production of conventional automobile tires in Akron, Ohio. The phase-out will result in the loss of about 730 production and salaried jobs . . . A new $180 million radial tire production plant at Lauton, Oklahoma will begin operations early next year . . . (and) within the next few months it will begin production at a $69 million radial tire expansion at its Gadsden, Alabama, plant (*Cleveland Plain Dealer*, 11 January, 1981).

A delegation from Iran National, the state car concern, recently visited the VW headquarters in Wolfsburg, but further negotiations are now being handled by one of VW's subsidiaries, VW Camihoes. This company, formerly Chrysler Motors do Brazil . . . is leading the talks with Tehran over the supply of machinery similar to that used for manufacturing the Colara model, part of the Chrysler do Brazil Dodge range of cars and trucks (*Financial Times*, 5 May, 1981).

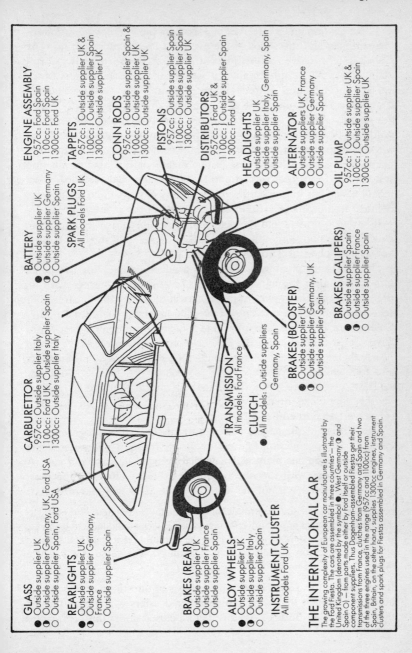

GLASS
● Outside supplier UK
●● Outside supplier Germany, UK, Ford USA
○ Outside supplier Spain, Ford USA

REARLIGHTS
●● Outside supplier UK
●● Outside supplier Germany, France
○ Outside supplier Spain

BRAKES (REAR)
●● Outside supplier UK
●● Outside supplier France
○ Outside supplier Spain

ALLOY WHEELS
● Outside supplier UK
●● Outside supplier Italy
○ Outside supplier Spain

INSTRUMENT CLUSTER
All models Ford UK

CARBURETTOR
957cc: Outside supplier Italy
1100cc: Ford UK, Outside supplier Spain
1300cc: Outside supplier Italy

BATTERY
● Outside supplier UK
●● Outside supplier Germany
○ Outside supplier Spain

SPARK PLUGS
All models Ford UK

ENGINE ASSEMBLY
957cc: Ford Spain
1100cc: Ford Spain
1300cc: Ford UK

TAPPETS
957cc: Outside supplier UK &
1100cc: Outside supplier Spain
1300cc: Outside supplier UK

CONN RODS
957cc: Outside supplier Spain &
1100cc: Outside supplier Spain
1300cc: Outside supplier UK

PISTONS
957cc: Outside supplier Spain
1100cc: Outside supplier Spain
1300cc: Outside supplier UK

DISTRIBUTORS
957cc: Ford UK &
1100cc: Outside supplier Spain
1300cc: Ford UK

HEADLIGHTS
● Outside supplier UK
●● Outside supplier Italy, Germany, Spain
○ Outside supplier Spain

ALTERNATOR
● Outside suppliers UK, France
●● Outside supplier Germany
○ Outside supplier Spain

OIL PUMP
957cc: Outside supplier UK & Spain
1100cc: Outside supplier Spain
1300cc: Outside supplier UK

TRANSMISSION
All models: Ford France

CLUTCH
All models: Outside suppliers Germany, Spain

BRAKES (BOOSTER)
● Outside supplier UK
●● Outside supplier Germany, UK
○ Outside supplier Spain

BRAKES (CALIPERS)
● Outside supplier Spain
●● Outside supplier France
○ Outside supplier Spain

THE INTERNATIONAL CAR

The growing complexity of European car manufacture is illustrated by the Ford Fiesta. The cars are assembled in three countries— the United Kingdom (denoted by the symbol ● West Germany ●● and Spain ○) — from parts made either by Ford itself or outside component suppliers. Thus Dagenham-assembled Fiestas get their transmissions from France, clutches from Germany and Spain and two of the three engines used in the range (957cc and 1100cc) from Spain, Britain, on the other hand, supplies 1300cc engines, instrument clusters and spark plugs for Fiestas assembled in Germany and Spain.

and organization on an international scale) of the *internal* operations of the company and the chaos of the overall system is most glaring. The global system is riven with this contradiction, and it reveals itself in many ways. At its most public it is seen in the competition which breaks out between European states (and their various regional committees) when one of the car companies announces plans to build a new plant. And as these new plants are brought on line so the productivity ratchet of speed-up and the threat of closure affects other workers in plants run by more vulnerable competitors or even in other plants in the same firm. This is the reality of the new production system, this too is the background to the last ten years at Ford. It's a reality which has impressed itself in a variety of ways upon the general political framework in Britain and upon life in the plants.

In order to understand the details of this reality it is useful to begin with the decision, announced by Ford in September 1977, to build a new engine plant in Bridgend in South Wales.

The Bridgend plant was set up to produce engines for the Erika project and after the announcement, Government ministers were, in the view of the *Guardian*, 'enjoying a rush of good will ... after their success in capturing Ford's new £180 million engine plant for Britain'. Celebrating this, the Labour prime minister commented that 'Ford have shown confidence in Britain. In return we must do all we can to justify that confidence by maintaining high productivity and reliability and good industrial relations' (10 September 1977). There's a lot being said here, even more when we add to it the reports that filtered through of the 'unprecedented level of state assistance' given to Ford (*Observer*, 11 September 1977).

The Bridgend plant was a key part of the Erika programme in Europe. The production figures for the new Escort necessitated the building of an engine plant with a capacity of 420,000 engines a year. A plant, on a par with the one in Cologne, and 'technically the most advanced in Europe if not the world'. As the *Sunday Times* observed:

production and quality control would be totally automated. So while its operators and, most importantly, its maintenance men would have to be highly skilled, the plant would be immune from the disruption that Ford had suffered at its *assembly* plants at Halewood and Dagenham. The question was: where should the plant be located? (9 October 1977)

In the search for a site, Ford, on the basis of questionnaires covering ninety-six subject headings, put together dossiers which they termed their 'Domesday Books'. All this behind closed doors until (priorities

Mr Masataka Okuma, executive vice president of the Nissan motor company is having quite a week. Last Thursday he was sitting in the strangers' gallery of the House of Commons, listening to one of Mrs Margaret Thatcher's ministers announce tentative plans to build a Datsun car plant in Britain. From there he went to Italy, where he presided over the establishment of the top executive committee of Nissan's fledgling joint venture with Alfa Romeo.

By Monday night he was in Nashville Tennessee, suffering from backache and skipping a celebrating dinner on the eve of a grand-breaking ceremony for the company's 300 million pick-up truck plant in Smyrna, a small town 15 miles south of Nashville. On Tuesday morning he was on a podium in a green and red striped marquee on the 850 acre plant site, which lies in rolling countryside alongside the Davy Crockett Motel struggling to make a formal speech above the hailing abuse of 1,000 construction workers, angry because Nissan had awarded the plant's main construction contract to a South Carolina company with an anti-union reputation.

Today Mr Okuma is in the more peaceful climate of his company's Los Angeles sales office winding up inquiries into the reasons for a tail off in Datsun's US sales of cars and trucks since August . . . Tomorrow he goes back home to Tokyo. (*Financial Times*, 5 February 1981)

established) 'word began to filter to the national governments of Europe that something big was afoot'.

Things then started to happen fast. As Tony Pender, 35-year-old commercial director of the Welsh Development Agency put it, the deal was:

exceptional for its size, and for the quite remarkably short space of time in which it crystalized ... There are other sites available in various stages of development in South Wales but the timing is such that it had to be immediately available (*Observer*, 11 September 1977).

Ford was on the move. It needed a new engine plant and its Domesday Books reckoned that Bridgend would fit the bill. Well sited near the Waterton interchange of the new M4 road link to London, it was also surrounded by a potentially compliant labour force. Henry Ford, it seems, had been impressed by his discussions with workers and union representatives at the Swansea factory (he is reported to have told his main board in Detroit that 'Wales has the most intelligent and articulate labour force in the world' – whether that was a plus or a minus for the Bridgend plant isn't clear) and, as Pender pointed out:

within a 15-mile radius there are ... something like 10 to 12,000 registered unemployed. The pool of labour available is used to working in heavy industry, with the traditional steel, coal-mining and metal trades pretty well represented (*Observer*, 11 September 1977).

This same pool had been tapped earlier by Sony, who had 'enjoyed a strike-free record; the Japanese [having] nothing but praise for the Welsh workforce'. (*The Times*, 12 September 1977). Thus encouraged, more talks ... with trade unionists, the Welsh TUC, wining and dining, talking ... assurances. Henry Ford had long since gone on record about the British worker. 'I could not in good conscience recommend to my board any new capital expenditure in Britain.' He'd said that in 1971. In 1977, the formal institutions of the British Labour movement were lined up to convince him otherwise. At lunch in Downing Street in August of that year, James Callaghan, (wearing any number of hats – MP for the constituency, prime minister, leader of the Labour Party, influence upon trade unionists) put it to Mr Ford: 'Henry, we are turning this country round. And you, if you choose, can help us do it.' He decided to help; but at a price.

The Bridgend plant involved a capital investment programme of £180 million. Ford had been around Europe and, at sites in Cork and West Berlin (where city officials were reported to be 'staggered' at the size of the support package made to Ford), the company had a clear idea of the kinds of financial backing that would be made available to the engine plant. Bridgend, located in a development area, attracted an immediate 20 per cent investment grant. However, Cork had the offer of a £50 million grant, together with the exemption of profits for taxation. Another Welsh site – at Miskin in a *special* development area – carried a 22½ per cent grant. But Ford didn't want to go to Miskin.

The Ford solution was to dispatch an ultimatum to the Department of Industry to the effect that they had until mid-day the next day to come up with an equivalent package for Bridgend. This led to a bizarre episode on Tower Bridge the following morning. The British acquiescence needed a ministerial signature. But Eric Varley was out of town. Hapless DOI officials were obliged to send the papers to Tower Bridge where Alan Williams, the junior minister was on an official visit to the Port of London Authority (*Sunday Times*, 9 October 1977).

A bit of chat, a bit of muscle. That's how deals are done. And this was but one part of this particular deal. On top of the investment grant and the road (which we all paid for) there was more. Under section 7 of the Tories' Industry Act of 1972, levels of discretionary, or selective, assistance are available to help create jobs in areas of high unemployment. This, without question, was what Ford was doing in Bridgend. So the assistance – or rather its estimate – climbed past the £75 million mark. This was the quoted figure at the time. The Department of Industry, the Welsh Development Agency and the Welsh Office, while 'bubbling with pride' over the decision (*The Times*, 12 September 1977) and stressing the importance of their own 'speed and effectiveness' (*Observer*, 11 September), were much more tight-lipped about proffering the actual details of the deal. Over a period of months, however, it became clear that of the £180 million associated with the Bridgend plant, the government supplied £115 million – £75 million to assist job creation and £40 million under the regional grants scheme. All this on top of the free road facilities, the site and factory with public utilities, the rail head into the plant, etc. A minimum cost of £46,500 a job. And that's assuming no adverse effects upon jobs in the Dagenham engine plant.

A good deal for Ford then, and one all the more remarkable when it is added to the arrangement Chrysler were able to make with this same government a year earlier. (In that deal the government put up £160 million to save the Linwood plant, and Chrysler argued that it was putting up an equivalent amount. In fact the company only provided £30 million to be called upon in the case of dire emergency and made up the balance with £90 million in private loans, negotiated by Chrysler UK with the backing of Detroit.) And more remarkable still when seen alongside the fact that it was just the first payment in a series of 'trenches' of capital investment made available by the government to support Ford's Erika programme in Britain. That programme involved the upgrading of the Halewood estate, for which purpose the government provided grants of £150 million. Terence Beckett, then the Company's chairman and chief executive, remarked that 'we don't want to have to borrow with interest rates as they have been. That is an expensive switchback to get on.' He went on to say that the company was 'not planning to provide any more jobs'. The *Financial Times* noted that while 'more than half the machine tools used in the programme would be supplied by British manufacturers ... the Company was buying all its heavy presses from overseas' (8 May 1978).

When examining the details of these deals, one thing that is clear is the toughness of the positions taken by the Company negotiators. This is to be expected. As Hugh Stephenson pointed out in *The Times*, reaction on decisions on plant locations:

displays an anachronistic conception of what large-scale integrated manufacturing industry with an international base is all about ... with an international company there is no necessary correlation between the best interests of the concern and the best interests of any particular country in which it operates. In making a decision like the Ford investment, the Company will obviously have done the normal calculations (12 September 1977).

And so they had – 'normal calculations' shrewdly assessed by two American economists as involving not only 'comparative wages, tariffs, taxes and transportation costs but also the political and labour relations climate'. All these are assessed in the 'Domesday Books' and:

it is this ability of the world managers to weigh all these factors and to coordinate decisions on pricing, financial flows, marketing, tax minimalization, research and development, and political intelligence on a global level that gives the global corporation its peculiar advantage and extraordinary power (Barnet and Müller, 1974, p. 41)

Power which, it needs be said, is often exercised with relish. During the Bridgend saga, for example, Ford had paid little attention to Spain. Late on in the decision-making process a team of managers made a 'courtesy call' on Madrid. A senior official at the Ministry of Industry remembered how 'they told us that we had just one week to submit our bid. In that time we not only had to match the German, British and Irish offers – which they told us – but we had to add an extra percentage to overcome the transport problem ... we couldn't have done it in the time.' As the *Sunday Times* commented 'at the highest levels ... the courtesies were observed. But below board level, Ford men did not always bother to conceal their muscle' (9 October 1977). At his level, sexual imagery abounds: local planners talk of 'lying there with our legs open'; company executives joke about how 'it was just about "you can have my daughter if we can have the plant" '. Perhaps these ways of talking, offensive as they are, aren't significant; maybe, however, they are an all too clear insight into the ideology of hard-headed toughness which dominates the men who run this industry. (Paul Roots, who took over from Ramsey as Industrial Relations director of Ford UK made it clear in his 'man of the moment' interview in *Personnel Management*[2] that the auto sector was the place

2. *Personnel Management*, May 1982, p. 16.

for him – 'any bloody fool could have good industrial relations in a chocolate biscuit factory full of women'.) Here their 'toughness' is brought to bear upon nation states in what seems to be a decisive manner.

In commenting upon the Bridgend decision, the *Observer* noted the government's 'overwhelming need to ensure that the plant did come to the UK', given the state of the UK economy and the fact that 'Ford's major new plant investments over the last decade had largely been made abroad' (11 September 1977). While Callaghan is reported to have played a rather low-key role in the whole affair, the Welsh Development Agency and Department of Trade – in the figure of Sir Peter Carey, the permanent under-secretary there – were considerably less detached. Throughout the deal Tony Pender in Cardiff was:

aware that they were looking UK-wide and we had the very strong impression that they were looking in England, particularly in the North East. As ever in these matters one is only aware indirectly that investigations are going on in other parts of the country or abroad (*Sunday Times*, 11 November 1977).

In the face of such uncertainty the 'speed and effectiveness' of government assistance held the key, and it was this which was celebrated by Carey at the press conference. No one seemed too concerned about the details, the pros and cons, the numbers. What was clear was that the operation had been a success; everything – in this wheeler-dealer world – has a cost, and in this case it had been high enough to bring home the bacon. Everyone was pleased. Especially Ford.

Bridgend had a lot of advantages for Ford. To begin with, the wage rates there were at least 50 per cent below the German rate and that would allow the company to produce engines at £200 each – £50 less than in Germany. Also the trades unions – most notably the Welsh TUC – were bending over backwards to be helpful. It wasn't an assembly plant so there was less prospect of it turning into another Halewood or Dagenham (the assembly and body plants on these sites counted for 82 per cent of all Ford UK's disputes in 1976), and this into a continuing pattern of investment decisions within the company. As a financial analyst noted in New York:

Assembly is labour intensive, heavily dependent upon workers on the line. The weakest point in any auto company production line is the assembly plant. It obviously made sense for Ford to concentrate assembly in a location where it was strongest *vis à vis* the workforce. In Saarlouis, for example, there was high unemployment and migrant workers constituted a large percentage of the workforce. They were dependent upon Ford for permission to stay and that

depended upon good behaviour. In addition, wild-cat strikes were illegal there
... To expand assembly in Germany and component operations in Britain
therefore offered Ford the chance of squeezing the maximum productivity from
the combined workforces of both countries. For Ford, cutting labour costs
doesn't involve following cheap labour around the world.[3]

In the seventies, Ford had followed this strategy quite closely. It had
expanded component manufacture on the Dagenham engine lines in
spark plugs and carburettors and seemed reasonably satisfied with output levels. As the *Financial Times* correspondent put it:

like many other companies it seems to have come to the conclusion that in
fairly highly skilled engineering industry, or alternatively in smaller factories,
Britain can compete with any country in Europe. Problems arise when trying to
run big production lines in large factories which require a low level of skill. (10
September 1977).

So there were reasons enough for Ford to come to Bridgend. To these
can be added the strong *political* reasons which made Britain an
important place for Ford to invest in 1977. As we have seen, the UK
represents a central market for Ford. In 1980, *The Times* described
Western Europe as 'the most highly concentrated and lucrative market
in the world' (10 September). Yet even in this context the British
market offered exceptional profits. Since the collapse of BL, the prices
in Britain had increasingly widened above those charged on the
continent, and by 1980 a 25 per cent difference was common (the
Metro sold for £2056 in Belgium and £3157 in the UK; Fiestas sold
for £2921 in Spain and £3255 in the UK). As Ford's sales in the
market increasingly became imported from its European plants so too
did the Company feel vulnerable to the (potential) threat of exclusion
to what has become its basic source of revenue. In 1979, Ford UK
made a profit of £386 million which was 70 per cent of the Company's
global profits in that year. Ford didn't want to rock this particular boat.
It knew too, that the Dagenham engine plant stood to lose 1,000 jobs
in the medium term as the Cortina engine range became rationalized.

From the Company's standpoint this rationalization is a logical step in the
process which had led to a completely common range of body shells between the
UK and Germany and which has already given common engines to the Fiesta,
Escort and Granada. But if that process meant a net reduction in the workforces
in Britain, Ford could expect to face a stormy time. Instead it has drawn the fire

3. Maryann N. Keller, 'Ford of Europe', Research Department, Kidder Peabody and
Co. Inc., 19 July 1978 pp. 16, 18. Quoted in 'The World Car: Shifting into Overdrive',
North American Congress on Latin America, Vol XIII No.4, July–August, 1979.

by the new project – established on a greenfield site where it has a better chance to establish manning levels to suit itself (*Financial Times*, 10 September 1977).

And so it proved. Three years later, the plant came on line after the Company had carefully recruited workers from plants like the stricken East Moors steelworks in Cardiff, which had closed down leaving its highly skilled 'elite' labour force available. A year after the start-up, Ron Todd, TGWU national official and leader of the trade union negotiating team at Ford was complaining:

I'm still arguing with the Company over rights for our members to visit the Bridgend plant. We've got everyone going round there, visitors ... the Japanese have just been round – from Nissan. Everyone's going round but not the people who work for the Company. The convenor of the Dagenham engine plant is particularly keen to visit the plant to see what is happening there but they simply refuse permission. 'No.' I can see what they're up to. They don't want any of the working practices established at Dagenham to be taken into the new plant. But they've taken such a hard-line attitude on this, we find it hard to understand. It's making it hard for us to find out what is taking place at Bridgend.

All in all then, a very good deal for Ford. A good basis for its next move for a new European assembly plant. Here it was the turn of the Portuguese, Austrian and French governments to be put against each other and, as always, the wheeling and dealing continued in dramatic style. In Lorraine, for example,

the Ford top brass descended in a flotilla of helicopters ... for talks with local businessmen and trade unionists. [They] let it quietly be known that they were worried about labour unrest in the area.

In Portugal, where the government was 'bending over backwards to give Ford wide-ranging assurances on tax relief as well as on the more delicate subject of labour relations', the constitution was seen as a problem. After the 1974 revolution the Portuguese labour code made it almost impossible to dismiss workers, and established statutory requirements for generous holidays and bonus entitlements. In the light of Ford's concern:

the Portuguese Government is believed to be considering a new labour code that will bring Portugal into line with the EEC (*Financial Times*, 28 February 1979).

As in Halewood, then in Valencia and Bordeaux and Bridgend, soon in Sines in Portugal, new workers learn about the ways of the Ford Motor Company. They learn about them directly and indirectly, as they work the line.

Low labour costs swing decision on engine plant

Ford places £180M bet on Britain

10/17

By Hazel Duffy,
Industrial Staff

... laghan and Mr P
Downing Street f
Mr Ford sou
from the Prim
was feasible t
goodwill undertake lo'
Ministers were ... in Britain,

By Diana Smith in Lisbon and
John Griffiths in London

FORD is to build a vehicle
assembly plant in Portugal
with a capacity of 200,000 units
a year, Mr Philip Caldwell,
chairman of Ford, and Sr
Francisco Pinto Balsemao, the
Portuguese Prime Minister,
announced yesterday.

The total investment will be
about $1bn (£581m). Some
5,000 jobs will be created.

Mr Caldwell, who delivered
the Ford letter of intent to Sr
Balsemao, said there were still
"several matters to resolve. I
do, however, hope and believe
that a final decision can be
reached before the end of the
year."

The factory would be buil
in Sines a new petrochemica
and industrial complex in the
south, which has a deep-wate
harbour. Ford's decision woul
fulfil a dream of attracting
major international concern t
the area, justifying Sines as
viable proposition rather tha
the multi-billion-dollar whit
elephant it has seemed t
many.

The Ford inv
sents th

Ford plans to build $1bn plant in Portugal

11/11/82

A triumph for Wales

By DAVID FREUD in Bridgend

10/1X/77

THE new Ford factory was
the talk of the day at
Bridgend yesterday. Mr.
Phillip Warren, an executive
director of the Welsh Development Agency which is providing
the site for the engine plant,
went as far as depicting Wales
as a flagship of British industrial effort.

"Coming within a year of
Hoover's announcement that it
was building a new factory in
Merthyr Tydfil it means two
major foreign manufacturers
have taken the plunge and
invested in the U.K.—disprov-
ing criticisms about "British
sickness," he proclaimed hap-
pily.

British sickness or not, South
Wales desperately needs the
jobs. The high cyclical level of
unemployment in Britain as a
whole is even worse in Wales—
because of a structural weakness
caused by the rundown of the
traditionally labour - intensive
steel and coal industries. Unemployment in Wales during
July was running at a rate of
8.8 per cent., compared with
6.7 per cent. nationally.

In Bridgend itself unemployment is well below the Welsh
average. In July it was 7.8 per
cent. in the overall community
area, which takes in nearby
towns like Maesteg with a large
number of unemployed. Bridgend itself, originally a market
and trading town on the flat
plain between the valleys and
the sea, is relatively pros-
perous. The two adjoining industrial estates—Bridgend and
Waterton—which lie to the east
of the town, offer employment

Bridgend.   *Freddie Mansfield*

to 6,650 people and include factories of 95 different companies.

The Ford site—178 acres on
the newer Waterton estate—
was strewn yesterday with
rubble and covered with
thistles and reeds. There are
sound reasons why Bridgend
has been so successful in building up industrial employment:
it gained the Ford project at
the expense of sites in Holland,
Belgium, France, Spain, West
Germany, and Ireland, as well
as three other Welsh sites.

Communications are superb.
The M4 motorway will run
alongside by the time the Ford
plant is ready. There is an
international airport at nearby
Rhoose, and a deep-sea port at
Port Talbot 13 miles to the
west. The site's accessibility reduces the problems of obtaining
labour. There are estimated to
be about 12,000 unemployed
people in a 15-mile radius.
People at the bottom of the
three valleys to the north, the
Ogwr, Llynfi and Garw, will be
a major source.

The development may mop
up some surplus labour in Cardiff, 18 miles to the east, where
the East Moors steelworks is
gradually being run down.
However, no one is quite sure
whether people will be willing
to commute the necessary distance. Engineering companies
already established are concerned that Ford's arrival could
accentuate shortages of skilled
labour which already exist. It
is thought that the development
will require about 250 skilled

men in the first stage alone.

Mr. Glyn Morris, director of
the Engineering Employers'
Association of South Wales,
said: "While I am delighted
from the point of view of Wales,
there is some anxiety whether
Ford will attract skilled labour
from other companies. However, if they do their fair share
of training there will be few
complaints."

Bridgend is unlike the other
industrial centres of South
Wales in one key respect, its
modernity. The factories on
the estate—which grew steadily
through the 1960s—are all new.
The housing estates surrounding the town are predominantly
post-war. Many were built in
the last 15 years. The contrast with the blackened grime
evident in areas of Port Talbot,
Cardiff, and Newport could not
be greater.

The Ford development pro-
vides a new dimension to Bridgend's steady growth. None of
the companies that have come
to the estates in the past—including the best-known, Sony—
have employed more than a few
hundred workers. Ford will
require 2,500 in the first stage,
and ancillary employment will
probably amount to another 800.

The announcement provides a
lesson on how to curb unemployment in the regions. Bridgend
is a natural growth point which
has been allowed to grow, even
though some of the labour force
will have to commute to the
factories. This looks like being
a better recipe for success than
bringing work all the way to the
people.

'What we have got to do is to disassociate ourselves completely from the British source.'

Henry Ford II, Ford Chairman, Manilla, 1971

FORD OF BRITAIN 1980:
SALES £2,920,000,000: PROFITS £204,000,000

'Of course we would not pull out of manufacturing in the UK because of the political ramifications. And it would decimate our market share. But the truth is that when future investment has to be made by Ford it will be bound to go to those areas where there is higher productivity and better labour relations.'

Sam Toy, Ford UK Chairman, London, 1981

Ford, as unofficials and shop stewards will tell you 'hasn't changed under the surface, it's still a hard, hard company. But it's grown a hell of a lot more sophisticated.' At Halewood, stewards point quickly to the structure of Company management, as a major change, and to the fact that, over the years, integration into Ford Europe has been accompanied by the detailed regulation of plant activities by senior Company personnel. Often this regulation is personal:

What has certainly happened is that the visitations to the plant by senior management from Germany or Detroit have become much more of a regular thing. These senior managers have a more regular presence in the factory. This has been part of a growing regulation and control over the smallest issue in the plant. Things such as a lay-off. If the plant is laid off, management at that level is involved.

Added to this personal involvement has gone a change in the balance of power within the managerial hierarchy of Ford UK. Production-line managers and the department of quality control were the key power-centres in Ford right through to the early 1970s. This was allied with a 'No-nonsense' approach to labour, an approach which was tried at Dagenham in the 40s and 50s, and brought to Halewood in the 1960s. It was an approach which produced the confrontation and penalty clauses in 1969. In the 1970s however – and after the damaging effects of the Dillon strike – Ford's approach altered.

In their regular reviews of performance within the Company, it became clear to the top decision-makers in Ford that the production problems experienced in the UK plants were of a different order from those in other European installations. In Germany, for example, the

Company's use of migrant labourers from Southern Europe for the most tedious assembly operations was a prime factor in its ability to organize production in the plants. So too the lasting affects of fascism upon independent forms of trade union organization in that country and also in Spain. The absence of these factors in Britain meant that the Company needed a more complex strategy. It was something which went against the grain but, as the first Henry Ford showed in 1941, ideologies can be bent to circumstances. His grandson realized that he needed to produce cars in Britain and that in those plants the problem of labour discipline (the ability and inclination of people to go their own way) was a matter of major importance, requiring detailed attention. To this end a department of industrial relations took on greater significance in Britain. Management review in this area was undertaken scrupulously in Detroit, and industrial relations managers pushed into key positions within the plants. In 1981, Ron Todd reflected:

> Industrial relations has changed a lot at Ford. Ten years ago the situation was such that the IR man advised the plant managers. Today the plant man is shifted more into the background and the IR man is in the centre. IR has come to the fore in the everyday operation of the plant. Right down to the foreman level: the foreman gets in touch with the IR man for his instructions. There's been a definite shift of emphasis.

It was a shift of emphasis which, in the 1970s, saw the Director of Industrial Relations (first Bob Ramsey and then Paul Roots) playing a central role in the development of the British Company. The effects of the shift can be illustrated in a number of ways, essentially, though, it involves a detailed attempt by the Company to accommodate the presence of trade unions; it involved an attempt to *capture* them. As he resigned from his position as Chairman of Ford UK in 1980, Terence Beckett reflected on the major changes that had taken place during his time in the job. One thing stood out, he said. In 1980 union officials and the Company were at one in their acceptance of 'the usefulness of the negotiating links that have been developed between Ford and the unions'. In his view 'an important transition' had taken place, from a time when 'the unions questioned our motives at Ford, to discussing the facts with us' (*Sunday Times*, 14 September 1980). An important transition indeed: how was it accomplished?

In 1969, the strike at Ford's made clear that an autocratic union leadership was unable to carry its members' support for a new contract. This failure persuaded senior executives of the need to alter its negotiating machinery in a way which allowed the NJNC to be clearly and firmly established as the fulcrum of negotiations within the Company. As one of the managers involved in these changes has noted:

> The Company's more liberally minded managers argued that Ford must come to terms with 'the challenge from below' and work with the newly selected leaders of the trade union side to develop a more business-like and trusting relationship. The presentation of the NJNC as an authoritative and joint union–management bargaining forum was regarded as the Company's top priority.[4]

This strategy was coordinated through the company's newly formed Labour Relations Committee. This committee, composed of senior executives and chaired by the Director of Labour Relations, was established with the view to 'consider and advise on major issues of labour relations strategy'. For the first time at Ford's, 'senior operational line and central staff managers accepted collective responsibility for all key decisions affecting the Company's relationship with the hourly paid workforce'. If they had a monster on their hands it was a monster they needed; they couldn't kill it so they would have to housetrain it.

This took a number of forms. The NJNC, opened up and democratized in 1969, was expanded further until, in 1978, the convenors of every plant were brought inside, as full members, sitting also upon the various sub-committees set up under its umbrella. This development is viewed with considerable pleasure by Ron Todd. For him it represents the key achievement of the 1970s:

> I remember when I was a deputy convenor at the Walthamstow plant, before they made any alterations in the NJNC, before there was proportional representation or any lay representation on that body. We used to stand outside the Piccadilly Hotel lobbying the full-time officials. We'd be waiting *outside*: waiting for crumbs of information. We've come a long way since then. The structure was fundamentally altered in 1969. After that we developed consultation facility for the convenors. They would be in an adjoining room during the negotiations which would be broken off to allow for consultation. That was another step forward. Now under the new representation agreement they sit in as of right. The convenors are part of the dialogue, speaking directly for the plant they represent, directly from their experience. You can only speak from your experience. If you're not in the plant you can't know about what's going on in it, what the people who work there are thinking. That's why it's important to have the convenors on the NJNC. It means that we now have a trade union side of fifty-four; people say it's a top-heavy body, but it's

4. Sander Meredeen in Friedman and Meredeen, 1980.

democratic, and if the alternative is going back to lobbying *outside* the building I'd go for a top-heavy body.

This is a significant account of important changes. What is understressed in it, perhaps, is the role played by the Company in the formulation of these new arrangements. For while Ford entered the reformed NJNC with some trepidation in 1969, by 1978 it had become a positive *initiator* of change. Les Moore who, as convenor of the MSB plant, had had direct experience of the NJNC in its various forms felt that by the mid-70s:

> The situation must have seemed untenable from the point of view of the Company. They were no longer bargaining with the trade unions as representatives of workers, but through them with the convenors' committee. Their best arguments, presented by highly professional negotiators, were being wasted on messengers. It would have seemed apparent that the answer to effective bargaining lay in breaking down the two-tier trade union negotiating and consultative structure and include both levels into the formal one. The convenors did not seem to realize the power of their secondary role and were pressing to be included, the officials were reluctant, but the Company insisted and in 1978, when all unions were satisfied with their levels of representation, the Ford NJNC was extended to include all convenors and additional lay representatives to satisfy the craft unions. The consultative arrangements were scrapped and so was any effective lobby.

What this comment points to is the systematic element present in the Company's attempt to get the union on board. It was an attempt to contain the Company–worker relationship within formalized Company–union procedures. As such the Company's commitment to the creation of a negotiating body which worked was a genuine one. The trick was to get it to work on your side and away from any form of 'campaigning' or 'rank and file-ist' trade unionism. The trick, really, was to get the NJNC and the institutions of collective bargaining to deliver the goods: completed, near-perfect cars off the line, regularly a thousand times a day. And to this end Ford, under Beckett, altered the framework of the relations between the Company and the union, both nationally and in the plants.

Nationally, the Company's senior executives were concerned to mend their fences after the bruising years between 1967 and 1972. They were concerned to convince leading union officials of their good faith, and of the Company's commitment to a manufacturing base in the UK. They wanted to be the good guys; and they wanted everyone to agree that there was a problem or productivity in the British plants – a common problem. To this end they were assisted by the report of the

Central Policy Review Staff on the future of the British Motor Industry. Published at the end of 1975 it professed a definitive counter-thrust to the Ryder Report on BL, produced under the earlier Labour administration. It predicted intense competition between the car companies in Western Europe and assessed that plants in Britain were ill-prepared for such a challenge. By way of some rather cursory comparisons (the key ones taken from Ford) the report illustrated the low level of labour productivity in Britain (overmanning, slower work-pace, poor maintenance, poor labour relations) and argued that the solution did not lie in increased investment. That alone would not be enough for, as they saw it, the basic problem was one of *attitudes* – of both management and labour – attitudes which had grown out of years of mistrust and conflict. The report argued that the weakness of British industry lay in face-to-face relationships and practices on the shop floor and concluded that:

It is on the shop floor that they must be corrected ... unless shop floor attitudes and practices are changed ... the British car industry will in the longer run go the way of the British motor cycle industry.[5]

This report was firmly cast in the thinking of the new IR approach at Ford. With common European models sourced at two or three 'technically identical' plants, Ford had for some time been comparing the output figures of its European installations. One shop steward at Halewood put it like this:

[along] with the Ford Europe concept has gone a growing standardization. The plant at Genk and at Saarlouis is the same as the one at Halewood. The Company uses the same parts in each plant and operates the same timings. And that means we're constantly having Saarlouis and Genk thrown at us.

And this is no exaggeration. In the 1970s the 'Cologne yardstick' was replaced with the 'European micrometer'. As the 'Ford Europe' plan unfolded so, too, did detailed plant-by-plant assessment of performances, of 'percentage off standard', become the order of the day. It was this approach which was supported by the CPRS report, and by a follow-up investigation organized by the Tripartite Committee of the Department of Industry under Eric Varley. The Committee (which included Terence Beckett as well as Jack Jones, Hugh Scanlon, Bob Wright and Moss Evans as well as a number of Ford shop stewards) investigated the operation of Ford's Genk plant and contrasted it with Halewood. On its publication the headline in the

5. Central Policy Review Staff, *The Future of the British Car Industry*, HMSO, 1975.

Financial Times read: 'Now Union Officials agree: Halewood less Efficient than Belgian plant'. Bob Wright agreed that 'there is no doubt that the Genk factory has a higher level of efficiency than the comparable plant at Halewood'. While the union officials were at pains to point out correctly that 'efficiency' is not simply a question of how hard people work, the door was opened for what that same newspaper described two years later as the 'torrent of statistics which Ford (has poured) onto the Halewood workers' heads to prove that they are the least productive in Europe'. In spite of the caveats, Ford had won the argument. It had got the union on board over the productivity issue. The visit to Genk also confirmed another of the Company's treasured principles – that continuous production was achieved more regularly in its European assembly plants. The committee made no bones about that: the workers in Genk did go on strike less often and this was a good thing. The report endorsed the view expressed by Paul Roots in *Ford News*:

> In car plants in other countries, when problems occur they carry on working while they are sorted out. When the foreman and the operator swear at each other, or the roof springs a leak, or a manager makes a decision which employees don't accept, people carry on making cars and earning wages while the people paid to sort out the differences get round the table (2 April 1976).

These two elements (productivity and continuity of production) were at the heart of Ford's IR offensive in the two plants in the 1970s. In their support, considerable revisions were made to the Ford code.

To begin with, the 'democratization' of the NJNC increasingly established a pattern where the plant convenors, as full-time negotiators on the Company's payroll, were in direct and more or less regular contact with both the national headquarters of Ford and the national centres of the Labour movement. *They* were members of the tripartite committee too, and they were at the heart of these discussions on the future of Ford and the British motor industry. Increasingly throughout the 1970s (at Ford and in other large companies) convenors became enmeshed in the national apparatus of their unions: they bridged the plant and head office. One consequence of this was that they were called upon to spend more and more time away from the plants; another (and at Ford this became more likely after the 1978 reform of the NJNC) was that they were expected to 'carry their plants' in support of commitments made nationally. All this had consequences for the internal operation of the plant committee. The enforced absence of convenors led to a second layer of 'full-time shop stewards' emerging in the factories. Ford recognized this, and became prepared to cede it as a general principle. The 'ball and chain' had no place in the armoury of the new IR strategist. While in the 1960s workers in particular sections struggled for the right of their shop steward to be released from the line to negotiate cases, these rights weren't generally questioned after 1972. Convenors' offices were established with telephones and filing cabinets: stewards had regular access to these offices and were generally allocated light duties and allowed a considerable degree of freedom of movement in the plants. Within these new arrangements stewards were encouraged to take on a variety of quasi-personnel and welfare functions – collections in the case of a death, arrangements for holidays, etc. Increasingly, too, there was a tendency for the section steward to become an administrator and not a negotiator, sometimes not even a spokesman. Under the new system the responsibility of the stewards lay in administering a system negotiated above their heads by senior shop stewards and full-time officials. In order to smooth this process, the Company (in response to regular criticisms of the procedure and its operation) had agreed in 1975 to a reform of the procedure by the introduction of a 'status quo' clause (if workers don't strike, management won't push the advantage while discussions are in process) and the removal of the national stage, shortening all discussion to meetings within the plant. In the event of a serious dispute emerging on the section, the operation of the new 'IR policy' meant the almost immediate involvement of the industrial relations staff and senior stewards. This was quite a change: and a carefully calculated one. It was done with all the thoroughness of the Ford approach. It was done on the basis of *the facts*. The company *had* to produce in Britain in order to retain the share of the British market. The comparatively low wages paid to the British workers, and the high prices in the British market meant that in the 1970s the management of Ford UK had an important degree of manoeuvrability. It invested this manoeuvrability in easing the pressure on 'manning levels' (those by common consent eased in this period) and winning the support of the trade unions. It represented one of the more elaborate pieces of 'industrial relations reform' attempted by a company in the 1970s, and it had a lot of implications for the pattern of relationships in the plant.

The stewards' committee on the PTA at Halewood remained quite stable during the 1970s. Eddie Roberts had gone and he was followed into an official's job by Gerry Flaherty and John Craig. It became a matter of pride for union activists that 'four union officials have come out of this branch'. In the body plant, Les Moore had been sacked for being absent without leave. Frank Banton and Ronnie Walsh had moved on, eventually to the plant at Speke and the dole. Most of the others remained. In 1982 Bill McGuire was still PTA convenor with more than ten years' service in the job and almost twenty years at Ford. Jack Jones had taken over as secretary of the branch. Richie Rolands was deputy convenor and also chairman of the joint shop stewards' committee. Here was a group of men who had been with Ford for a long time. A group who had gone through the 'ball and chain' years, and the years of speed-up; men who had sat out the 1969 strike, and had organized the Parity Campaign. A group who, in the early 1970s, felt they had been through something; who felt they knew the score, that they knew what trade unionism was about. They felt that they'd achieved something at Ford, that the organization had endured and this it was a strong one. To the new recruit they were a formidable bunch. The young men who went to work for Ford in 1975 noticed:

> The stewards were older guys. That's the first thing you noticed. They were all in their forties. They talked a lot about the old times, and they didn't work on the track. That's what we all noticed about them.

Another man, who worked on the trim lines put it like this:

> It was a bit like the Borgias. They had so much experience you couldn't tell them anything. If you went over with a complaint 'this is wrong, that's wrong' they always had all the answers. It was impossible to oppose them really. If you tried, they'd cut your head off. The impression they gave me was that they'd seen it all and they'd done all that could be done. If you opposed them you were 'anti-trade unionist'.

The changes here are important ones. They have to do with the passage of time, and with the way in which experience is distributed throughout an organization. In the 1960s the shop stewards' committee was built at Halewood as a product of struggles in the plant. The seventies were very different years. Growing numbers of the Halewood workforce were recruited after the 1969 strike. For stewards who had 'been through it all', a lot had changed. The new 'IR approach' conceded many of the things which the old Ford system had held dear; in particular it allowed for union representatives to be involved in questions of job allocation and timings. This fitted in with the computer control and the simplified model structure. Within this new production system the line speeds weren't increased illicitly during a shift, and models never appeared on the line out of sequence. It was less chaotic and more functionally austere. But the lines ran just as fast.

During this period I was living again in Liverpool and I talked to many people who worked at Ford as I met them on buses, in pubs or on WEA courses in Colquett Street. Quickly the conversation would turn to the situation in the plant. One man who had read this book said to me:

but there's one thing, you know. You get across a lot of things about the Ford system, but I don't think you get across the terrible sense of isolation you get when you're working on the lines. Particularly on the trim and final assembly lines. In the paint shop, or in the body plant even, there's more of a group feeling. I got that from the way you wrote about the paint shop. But on the trim lines you just feel so cut off from everything. And in that situation if you didn't have a steward who was there to stick up for you, to take your side, you were nowhere. You had nothing down for you there. But none of the leading shop stewards came from the trim lines. I think Gerry Flaherty was a trim steward when he was there, but most of the others were from the smaller areas – the paint shop, garage, material handlings. You know, the sections where you had a bit more space. On the trim you had no space. It's just you and the line. And you're alone really.

Alone as a number. Alone too with numbers being thrown at you. 'All the time we're outside the plant we get it from the media: "You can't produce cars as good as the Belgians; you're hopeless, you're going to close down, you don't deserve any better!" You *never* get away from it.' And always the constant reminder, as another factory closes, that there on the line alone you're one of the lucky ones. There is some evidence that by the middle 1970s those factors, in combination, were having a deep effect upon the pattern of life in the plants. Newspapers wrote of 'frustration and the fear of redundancy' resulting in 'careless workmanship' at the Halewood factory. In 1976, the Company sent a letter to the 11,500 employees 'from manager to sweeper'.

The letter which has the full backing of shop stewards, is the latest in a series from the management informing the workforce of the up-to-date situation at Halewood and attempting to allay fears of redundancy. A Ford spokesman said that they were trying to motivate people and get them back to the old Merseyside fighting spirit to produce the goods.

'The problem is that because of the state of industry generally morale is low, leading to a feeling of frustration and inevitably to this sort of problem,' he said. 'But we are saying there is not going to be any redundancy and we need the cars and can sell every one we produce.'

Previous letters and pep-talks to the men on the lines of a soccer manager's half-time chat to a losing team have resulted in improved production figures (*Daily Telegraph*, 11 November 1976).

The Ford system requires the steady, regular and persistent production of motor cars off assembly lines. In this it needs workers who will – above all else – do as they are told. Repeatedly line workers who reply to their supervisors with the words 'but I thought' have been told 'you're not paid to think . . .' The system requires obedience and for this it helps if workers feel a bit powerless; but it doesn't help for them to become so scared or disinterested that they don't care about the consequences any more. In the late 1970s at Halewood there is a suggestion that the Company verged on overkill with its statistical warfare. The comparisons went on unabated, and as one man put it:

They seem to think that if they pump us with all those figures it will make us work harder. But it can have the *opposite* effect as well; particularly given the jobs we have to do in that plant. 'What? produce more? But we're thick or we're stupid; we can't do any better . . . Think! You want me to think. But you've told me a hundred times I'm not paid to think!'

It was just a bit too much, especially if you suspected that it was a con anyway. After all the Company broke all profit levels in 1979 and that was after a strike and a wage increase they said they couldn't afford. So who's kidding who? In this vein production at Halewood continued – with interruptions – at around 700 or 750 units a day; less than the thousand the Company wanted, and a lot less than Genk and Saarlouis.

This was 'the Halewood problem', and it was this which contributed to another – more direct – dimension of Ford's plan for production. This involved quite fundamental changes in several of the work processes at Halewood, changes brought about by the introduction of computer control and more and more automation. While these changes took place throughout the 1970s, by far the most impressive single development was associated with the Erika project. The plans which took Ford to Bridgend also saw the retooling of the Halewood estate as the assembly location for the new Escort in Britain. Again Ford obtained the full cooperation of the trade unions who, at national level, were agreed that 'we can't turn our face against robots. That's the way production is going. And the Japanese are streets ahead as it is. We've got to accept robots.'

Ford don't like the term 'robot'. Halewood's manufacturing engineering manager, Derek Waeland, jokes: 'Ford engineers prefer the term "Universal Transfer Devices" – we are not quite ready to strike back at the Empire yet!"[6] This was in the autumn of 1980, when the doors of Halewood were opened to factory tours showing off the new technology. At Halewood ('the least productive plant in Europe' and the Escort plant where workers were paid the lowest wages) Ford introduced 'more UTDs than any other location in Ford of Europe and indeed any other car assembly plant in the UK'. At Halewood, the new machinery was concentrated in the body plant. Here thirty-nine robots were installed, all but two of them made in West Germany.

In the push to increase productivity and regulate production processes 'a major consideration was to reduce manufacturing complexity', and the robots facilitated this in a number of ways. To begin with they accelerated the movement toward 'multiple sourcing' within Ford. Derek Waeland again:

> The one big advantage of having this equipment at Halewood and at our sister plant at Saarlouis is that any development in process or reduction in cycle times can be instantly transferred from one plant to another simply by programming a chip in one plant taking it to the other and introducing in into the UTDs employed there.[7]

Within the plants themselves, automated processes had additional advantages. The robots were established in the areas which involved the sub-assembly of the body side and the under body. On these sections men had previously hand-welded the body on a roundabout or carousel; the parts being held together by jigs. To the Company these carousels 'were labour intensive and have always been the source of labour unrest'. Furthermore the organization of work meant that it was difficult, if not impossible, to trace defective work back to an individual welder: the situation was not amenable to 'accurate control'. So, as Derek Waeland put it: 'We haven't got control of the labour force, we can't force each man to put each weld in the right place. So we've tried to build in quality through the machines.' It is this which Harry Scarborough, a young researcher from the Technology Policy Unit at Aston University, identified as a 'new philosophy of production' at Ford's under the Erika programme:

> The new production is based on a high-speed, high throughput approach – the one robot underfloor line turns out assemblies at the *rate of 90 per hour*. The new philosophy is derived from a Japanese approach in which speedy and

6. Derek Waeland, on a Halewood Plant Tour, 1980.
7. *ibid*.

effective maintenance is vital, because buffer stocks between machines are kept to minimal levels – perhaps just half an hour's production. Ford hope to repair all 'normal' breakdowns within the space of 15–30 minutes or less.

The key to minimizing production down-time is through the use of extensive, distributed electronic control and fault-finding systems. Solid-state Programmable Controllers are widely used to control the machines and conveyors – as with the BL Metro plant – and are scanned continuously by four mini-computers in separate control rooms. The mini-computers give read-outs of faults and down-time to enable the electricians who monitor them to implement breakdown repairs within seconds of a problem occurring.

The robots and welding machines are themselves of modular construction for ease of repair and replacement – Ford claim that a complete robot could be removed and substituted by another with an identical programme in just one hour (Scarborough, 1980).

The 'new philosophy' was based upon an extension of the standardization of production procedures between the plants, which had been the hallmark of Ford Europe. It also involved the simplification of the body shell and the progressive elimination of key areas of 'labour unrest'.

Workers at Halewood were quick to note these changes:

Take the under body. On that body there used to be forty-eight men. They'd spot weld the under body together. Now seven men hand the parts into the machine, the windows close, press the button and away it goes. They used to be welders – they're *loaders* now.

They noticed too the effects upon control of the work process:

In the body plant there's no doubt that the new technology has had the effect of controlling labour more tightly. At one time you used to be able to bank up work. On the LCD (luggage compartment door) you could work at your own pace, bank work and finish early or take breaks. Now they've eliminated the stock on the floor and the labour produces to the pace of the machine. Another example would be the CO_2 booths. That was an enclosed booth with fourteen to sixteen men working on it. They ran the job their way at their pace. To management that was shocking, to us delightful . . . They couldn't control it so they eliminated the section.

It's a similar story but on a different scale in the PTA plant. There, automation has mainly affected the paint shop, but in a way which has (in conjunction with the simplification of the body shell and the use of new materials) eliminated the small parts section, and cut down dramatically upon the numbers of men employed in the spray booths.

Can I now take you through the body assembly process, starting with the body-side complex.

The body sides are made on two complexes – one for the lefthand and one for the righthand panels. The assembly sequence starts by placing the side panels with some small reinforcing into a loading transfer system. This transfer system automatically places the panels into the complex where they are mated with the inner wheel arch assembly and the covering reinforcement for the centre and front panels. This total assembly is then clamped onto two rotating shuttle jigs which alternatively enter a two-station multi-welder where thirty tack welds are placed.

The side assembly is then transferred to the ten-station UTD line – one for the righthand panel and one for the lefthand panel – where the accurate welding of such items as window and door openings takes place. The under body complex utilizes conventional multi-welders and UTDs to join the three sections – rear floor, centre floor and engine compartment together. The centre-floor assembly, made in a multi-welder, is fed to the centre- and rear-floor assembly and mated with the rear H frame on side- and cross- members. These are welded on a four-station rotating table by two floor-mounted Kuka UTDs. These together pass through another multi-welder making the centre- and rear-floor assembly complete. Another press-welder is used to make the front-floor assembly.

The engine compartment is made on an integrated transfer line by first assembling the fender aprons and front- and rear-engine cross-members. These are welded together by three floor-mounted Kuka UTDs and then transferred to a multi-welder where front body panel and lower dash panel are tacked into position. This assembly then passes to five more floor-mounted Kuka UTDs for the final welding of the engine compartment. The three main assemblies are then mounted together and enter the final press-welder which joins all three pieces together to make the under body complete.

Derek Waeland, Manufacturing Engineering Manager, Ford Halewood

It is on the trim and final assembly lines that 'job content' (that technical term for what you have to do and what else you *can* do to make it bearable) has altered least. Here too the computerized control systems made it all seem smoother (less 'cock-ups', no disputes over 'model mix'), but the jobs remained much the same. The same noise, the same repetition, the same isolation. For, as the the Ford Company's *News Release* made clear, with some obvious pride:

> More than four miles of production lines are needed for the final assembly of the new Escort, and at full volume one car will leave the assembly line every fifty-seven seconds.[8]

That was in 1980: the year that was to become the crunch year for the motor giants. In that year, the US market, long the sanctuary and monopoly of the Big Three American producers, faced up to the fact that the 'import penetration' achieved by the Japanese in 1968 was something more than a flash in the pan. They had achieved a major foothold in the US market, amounting (in 1980) to 22 per cent of all car sales. Ford (so slow to react to the danger signals) found its market share had dropped to an all-time low of 16 per cent. In the USA the Company lost $3.9 billion in the space of three years. In the face of this crisis Ford shut down plants, laid off workers and insisted, in the words of Don Peterson, its President, that 'winning significant improvements in productivity in America and Europe has to be a top priority'. Within this priority, Europe (where Ford still had a distinct edge over GM) emerged as being of critical importance. It was in Europe that the Japanese offensive would have to be fought hardest. And in this task 'Erika' took on even greater significance. It was going to *have* to pay off. Everything became secondary to this. Even the new IR approach.

A sense of the crisis at Ford, can be seen in the fact that the Company's European executives coined a new calendar: 'AJ' – After Japan. An 'AJ programme' to counteract the trend was launched in 1980: 'AJ2'. In that year Bill Hayden, head of Ford Europe, returned from a fact-finding visit to Japan, reportedly in a state of shock and with his view of the world in disarray. The Mazda plant which produces the Japanese version of the Escort was producing cars 30 per cent cheaper than they were being made in Europe. Up to that time, Hayden – and Ford executives generally – had associated Japanese expansionism with automation on the one hand and unprofitable dumping on the other. In 1980 he had changed his views: 'I have to say

8. Ford News Release, *Manufacturing the New Escort: Advanced Technology and Massive Investment For Halewood*, September 1980.

Ford is the classic example of a North American multinational where the overseas businesses are suffering because of mistakes made in the home market. A tactical decision taken in 1976 to provide the US with medium sized new models in the 1980s, reasonable enough at the time, proved disastrous. Ford has found itself two years behind . . . in supplying the kind of small, less thirsty cars customers are clamouring for . . . Ford's reputation is for producing carefully costed, basic and technically unadventurous cars – a mirror image of the Japanese variety – so it is not surprising that it is feeling the impact of the success of the Japanese, who can deliver a family car to the US or Europe for £700 less than Ford's economic price.

Financial Times, 12 November 1980.

quite frankly that I do not now believe [these accounts] . . . They are vastly more efficient than we are.' The Cologne yardstick moved up another degree as Hayden discovered that while it took 2·05 people to assemble a unit in the most efficient Saarlouis assembly plant, it took just 1·03 people at Toyota's Tsatsumi plant. The root of this efficiency was seen to lie in the 'ability and dedication of this workforce'; a dedication which gave the Japanese companies 'complete flexibility in terms of being able to work many more hours than their planning base'. In Japan the workers do as they are told, in the USSR too. The Company's document *The Challenge From Eastern European and Japanese Imports* spelled out the problem in detail and concluded of Japan:

The message is clear. They are not dumping surplus production at unprofitable prices. They are vastly more efficient than we are. Their high productivity enables them to manufacture and sell vehicles at competitive prices and quality levels throughout the world. Their profitability enables them to keep on expanding production output.

Given this the British operation had to come up to scratch. Halewood had to be run at close to full capacity. The message came from the top. The IR boys had better stop pussy-footing around and get some action. As Bill Hayden saw it: 'We need plain tough discipline' (*Financial Times*, 12 November 1980).

Ford has always been pretty tough on discipline. In 1969 they fought out a three-week strike in their attempt to introduce penalty clauses. They had an even larger strike on their hands in 1978 and at the end of that one had managed to expand further the package of financial disincentives associated with absenteeism, lateness and striking. The previous year – after the Dagenham plant was shaken by riots – a punitive system of lay-offs had been introduced. In November 1980 this philosophy expressed itself in a letter to all Ford employees. The letter referred to the 'appalling situation' in the plants, where unconstitutional stoppages – disputes which had prevented the company from building vehicles 'with the regularity necessary to enable us to compete with Japan' – had continued unabated. It explained how 'Ford is not fireproof. We have to become more efficient or we shall go under.' And went on to explain the nature of future working arrangements in the plant. This was the new disciplinary code. Under this, the rule was 'do as you're told'. If you break the rule, the supervisor will give you a reasonable length of time to reconsider (this became the 'ten-minute warning') and if you'd not seen the error of your ways you'd be sent home. Then – and here's the rub – someone else (your mate perhaps) would be given the same instruction – 'do this'. A further refusal, a further warning and then – lay-off. The whole plant shut down for two days. Furthermore, the company couldn't rule out the possibility 'at some future date of having to implement lay-offs in "innocent" plants immediately gainful employment ceases'. A nice letter to wake up to. To understand why it was sent, we need to look once more at the Erika project and the new car – the Escort.

The production of every new model of motor car has teething problems. So much is this the case that the *Sunday Times* in 1976 described something it termed the 'new car neurosis'. This 'neurosis' is associated with the potential disruption caused by a new car, with new parts, new jobs, new work allocations and timings. It can be a particularly acute experience in companies which take infinitely greater care in considering style-lines, trim and paint colour-charts than they do in considering the views, attitudes and feelings of the people who are to build the car. This, especially where the retooling involves massive new investment in new automated processes, and where workers feel that they have certain rights, that they shouldn't simply be told what to do, that problems should be discussed and negotiated over rather than decided by managerial fiat. All these came together in Halewood in 1980, as a management pressured by 'the J problem', squeezed by the technological difficulties presented by the new machinery and the standards established for the plant, tried to put a thousand Escorts into the park each day. One steward put it like this:

You can't automate *people*. This company will never understand that but you can't. You have to have people somewhere in the process and, with the new technology, that's placed Ford in a more and more difficult position. With the old technology, everything was duplicated. If a spot-welding gun broke down there was a replacement. But with the new automated processes and the robots there's no duplicates. So, if it goes wrong the plant is down, and it's been down often enough because this machinery has given them a lot more trouble than they'd expected. So they're under more pressure, and they're really in trouble if they've got problems with the labour as well.

The technical problems were quite acute ones. Patrick Wintour summarized the situation neatly when he wrote in the *New Statesman* that:

The initial stages of the new Escort seem to have had many more equipment breakdowns than normal on new models. Part of the difficulty has stemmed from the use of Italians and Germans to install the machines: by the time the workers wanted to explain problems the interpreters had gone. A variety of different installation contractors have been used and not a little buck passing has gone on. In addition, there was no proper trial period for the new model on the line. At Halewood – unlike Saarlouis – the new model was sent down the line intermittently, mixed with the old model. When full production started after the holidays, it was the first time that the workforce had dealt with a line full of the new cars (28 November 1980.)

So, back from the holidays, machines fouling up, new jobs, no time to discuss the timings – 'It can't be done', 'Do it' – no time to deal with problems of safety – 'It's too heavy', 'Do it' . . . 'Sod this'. In the month that followed the introduction of the Escort there were thirteen walkouts in the PTA and a further eighteen in the MSB. This was the 'Halewood problem' that Ford management reported to the press, and Paul Roots took to the NJNC in October.

Trade union officials who deal with Paul Roots contrast him with his predecessor Bob Ramsey. Ramsey was 'a gentleman – a nice man you'd say – he'd spend forty minutes explaining why it was he couldn't help you. With Roots you get to the bottom line a lot quicker. He just says " no". But at the end of the day its the same situation; the same answer. It's just a lot quicker with Roots.' And he was quick and to the point at the meeting. Halewood was out of control. The problem had lasted far too long. There had to be a new code of discipline. The trade union representatives demurred. Ron Todd:

It's a problem I have with Ford. My mind always goes back to the time when I worked on a Cincinatti mill at the Walthamstow plant, making aluminium manifolds to a two thou' tolerance. I was put on the job and I took a pride in it. If the tolerance was off I rejected it. Then the supervisor came along: 'Don't bother with that, don't bother with the rejects – we need them.' It was production that mattered; the God production; it mattered then and it's the same today. I said that day, 'Oh sod it.' And I've said that a lot since. I've been in this job as secretary for the trade union side, I've come up against this problem again and again. 'Halewood is off standard; Dagenham is off standard; there are too many disputes.' And I've said, 'Let's sit down and discuss the basis of these disputes; let's set up a committee which examines the broader aspects of the problem; let's do an analysis; let's identify the problem.' But the only committee they want really are ones which solve the immediate disputes; all they want is for the men to go back to work.

And that's what the Discipline Code was about. And we told Roots that there was no way that we, on the trade union side, were going to be Ford Motor Company policemen.

The meeting broke up and a special meeting of the NJNC was agreed for 10 November. On 5 November the details of the code dropped through letter boxes around the country. Todd again:

The code was never discussed. It was imposed over the head of the unions, throughout the Company. So it wasn't simply a Halewood problem – it was a problem of industrial relations within the Ford Motor Company. I said to Roots 'Don't you realize that if you send someone home and then ask someone else to do that person's job that – even if he violently disagrees with that man's behaviour – he won't do it, simply because he doesn't believe in it. You'll never bludgeon people into subjection.' I believe that we have to produce more in the plants, because we're killing ourselves the way we're going on, but we'll only do that through information and persuasion.

Roots replied, 'We don't need the trade unions.' And, for five months, Ford tried to run the plants in that way. One steward at Halewood explains how:

the disciplinary code was a major change. I believe it was their way of preparing the ground at a time when the Labour movement was vulnerable. It was another part of the AJ programme. It's a programme in which their aim is for absolute control ... The unions on the NJNC said they'd have nothing whatsoever to do with it – they washed their hands, as it were – but the company went ahead with it. Every Ford worker received a letter. The letter said that if a man is given an instruction there will be a lapse of 'a reasonable time' before he is suspended for the day. But 'reasonable time' has always been interpreted as 'ten minutes' in Halewood. And every time the ten-minute warning has been given the plant has been laid off. So to that extent the company has been promoting the shut down. When, previously, a dispute would involve one section and last an hour, now the whole plant is laid off for two days. But you can't tell how far the use of it has affected people. As soon as you've a problem, you're straight into 'Well if we don't get this sorted out I'll have to put the "ten minute" on'. That's how 'negotiations' are conducted now.

And it was in this context that production was carried out too; small sectional disputes were replaced by intermittent periods of two day lay-offs. In a company which, through the Blue Book and its negotiated procedures, had succeeded in formalizing whole areas of factory life bringing it under some rule or another, the new code had an incredibly arbitrary air about it. If a man was suspended for one day and then the plant laid off for two could he – the 'cause of the dispute' – return on the second day? What if the lay-off began on a Friday – did you lose two weeks attendance bonus? What was the rule?

That was the thing with the code. It wasn't in any agreement and it was very vague. So it just came down to power really: 'I know we don't say that but that's what we're doing – piss off.'

Les Moore, one time convenor of the MS&B plant, put together the details of one such piece of arbitrary decision-making in his old plant. The CO_2 booths form a central section of the plant. The area is known by the lads as 'the elephant house' dominated as it is by the large trunk-like tubes of the powerful extraction system necessary to prevent any deoxidizing of the welds. In this system air is extracted by vents on the lower walls of the booth and clean air blown in through the roof. In the summer it's nice to work there; in the winter it can be a bit like standing in a gale – especially on night shift. And toward the end of the night shift of 12 February, the men in the elephant house were a bit weary and, if not exactly frost-bitten, certainly feeling the cold. Les takes up the story:

The elephant-house workers asked for a temperature check at 11.45 p.m. and the result was acceptable ... At about 5.30 that morning ... another temperature check was called for and the results showed very little difference from the earlier check. While the examination was taking place the men in the booth were part working and part watching, as might be considered normal in such a situation. The feeling of being cold was general and they wanted to know what was going on.

The supervisor formed the opinion that work was not continuing normally at that moment and went out to phone his superiors, manager Booth and superintendent Anderson. Their decision – based on whatever the supervisor reported – was to apply the ten-minute rule. 'Instruct the men to return to their work or they would be suspended in ten minutes.' Meanwhile the men accepted the results of the temperature check but asked the steward if the strength of the blower could be reduced. This was not a problem merely the adjustment of a valve.

The supervisor returned to the booth with his instruction, the men had ten minutes to return to normal working or they were suspended. The steward told him that there was no problem. There was no stoppage of work, no protest. If they could have the blower pressure reduced everything would be fine. The supervisor went away ... He returned a few minutes later, the men considered conditions a little better but could they have it reduced a bit more. The supervisor said 'yes' and went away. This time he did not go to reduce the air pressure but phoned his superiors again. At this point the men were working, satisfied that their request was being attended to. From what the supervisor told the manager he was instructed to again inform the men they were again on ten minutes. Accompanied by the acting general foreman, the supervisor returned to the booth called the men together and told them he had no intention of reducing the air pressure as he considered conditions adequate, the men had the alternative of continuing to work or be suspended in ten minutes. (Moore, 1981).

Uproar. The foreman reckoned that he was being 'mucked about'. The men reckoned the same: it was they who had to work nine hours a night under the blowers, why couldn't he just listen to reason, if he'd just take the sixty seconds necessary to turn the valve there'd be no problem, what did *he* do all night anyway. In the end:

One man, trying to get some formality into the situation said: 'Mr — as my foreman, I am requesting you to please turn down the air pressure.' He refused and said that in his opinion the conditions were all right and they were all about to be suspended. The ten-minute ultimatum time was taken up by his confrontation and the men were duly suspended for the rest of that shift and the following one, and the rest of the plant laid off (Moore, 1981).

In this way output at Halewood stayed near the 700 mark, and the workers on the plant moved towards the strike in May 1981. The strike was sparked off by a dispute over work standards in the MSB plant. Men working on sub-assembly had been completing 55 rear cross-members in an hour. Under 'AJ' the number increased to 62. The day shift managed it for a shift but the men on the night shift thought the timings had to be wrong and that the Company was asking too much. 'Ten minutes.' The plant laid off. MSB and PTA. Ten thousand workers on the stones. As Nick Garett put it in the *Financial Times*:

When the Company introduced its new disciplinary code against unofficial stoppages last November it knew there was a strong possibility that it would spark a major dispute against the whole principle of the code. The dispute now appears to have started ... The Company and the unions always suspected that, if there were a battle over the code, it would almost certainly occur on Merseyside because of the plant's different labour history and because it was expected that the code would be used far more there than anywhere. And they have been proved right (16 May 1981).

During the dispute Paul Roots admitted that the code was a measure of 'desperation', but that the strike raised a serious question about the long-term viability of the Halewood operation. 'With this continuous loss of production one has to seriously consider whether to continue there' (*Financial Times*, 16 May). To the *Sunday Times* correspondent he said 'You cannot put your hand on your heart and say that there will be a Ford factory at Halewood for ever more' (17 May). As the strike bit, 'Ford union leaders [were] told privately that a prolonged stoppage could force the Company to accelerate its plans to reduce the workforce ... It could mean compulsory redundancies instead of voluntary departures and natural wastage.' In all, the Company was clear:

> We have to make a stand on this vital issue. The unions have side-stepped measures to discipline their members. We have no alternative but to go ahead on our own to try to bring some stability to our factories, particularly Halewood (*The Times*, 15 May).

For their part, the workers at Halewood and the official trade union structures were also agreed. The code had to go. Ron Todd: 'This is not just a Halewood problem. The issue is about the whole code itself.' Steve Broadhead, the MSB convenor, elaborated: 'This strike is indefinite until the Company treats our people in a civilized manner ... This dispute is not over the disciplining of four men. That just happened to be the thing that led to the suspensions. People are being laid off even though they are not involved in the dispute. We have got to the stage when we are not prepared to accept this any longer.' The lay-off. That's what incensed people. Still. Not Ford playing silly buggers; or the foreman being stupid. You expected all that. But the lay-off. 'Here you go – whatever the time – "on your bike".' *That's* what got people down. *That's* what produced the strike. They'd had enough of that.

Roots's response was to agree to a meeting with the unions, but to lay down clearly the terms of the debate. In doing so he makes many things clear about the Company's strategy as it has developed over the past ten years.

> We have examined not only the causes of the disputes, but the handling of them. We have devoted more time to this than anything else. The Company has strengthened the union position on the closed shop, shop steward training and employee communication but the end result has been nothing in relation to

observing agreements. The truth is that we have talked about this problem for thirty years. It is sad for me as I regard myself as a progressive personnel man. When we meet the unions next Tuesday in London we will once again address ourselves to this problem of people not obeying procedures.

British Leyland has had to close down factories, we have not. But we can't say we won't if things go on like this. We have to ask the unions to put their own house in order . . . we will have to have satisfaction on discipline before we reopen Halewood (*Sunday Times*, 17 May 1981).

So there would be talks. Talks over the code, but the core of the discussion would be about keeping the workers in the plants, on the lines producing the motors. In the end Ford backed off. Roots recognized that Todd wouldn't negotiate with 'a bludgeon over our heads' and at a reconvened meeting of the NJNC on 21 May withdrew the discipline code in return for a 'detailed commitment from union leaders to improve self-discipline on the shop floor'. Roots considered that the meeting had revealed 'a major breakthrough in trade union attitudes', and that the company had received 'a greater commitment from its unions than ever before'. Ron Todd agreed on the need to abide by procedures and increase production – but through persuasion (*Financial Times*, 22 May). As part of this persuasion Todd would himself send a personal letter to all Ford hourly-paid workers, drafted by 'a senior executive of the Company' and pointing to the need for 'self-control' in a context where 'the company and staff are beset by problems, chief amongst which are foreign competition, projected job losses, and the impact of new technology'. At the South Liverpool football ground there was a mass meeting of the strikers. They endorsed the recommendation to return to work. Richie Rolands, chairman of the joint shop stewards' committee thought that it was 'fair to say that we are pretty happy. The decision has taken the Halewood workforce back to the agreements they had before last November.'

The day before the lads returned to the lines Keith Harper ran an exclusive article in the *Guardian* based upon an internal management strategy review by Ford of Europe. The review, conducted six months earlier showed that:

the Company had decided on a project to introduce the new Escort at Valencia by August 1981 and that investment would amount to $30 million. Up to now Valencia has only produced the Fiesta. Coming so soon after it became known that Ford was to make some Escorts for European markets in Brazil from 1983, the move is an added worry to union leaders concerned about Halewood (*Guardian*, 25 May).

In a major speech in Manchester, Stanley Williams, director of manufacturing for Ford UK, laid it on the line:

> our analysis of world industry trends, projected on key economic indicators, and, more importantly relative union–company relationships leads us to the conclusion that survival of mass production assembly of motor vehicles in Britain is unlikely unless there is a total and fundamental change of attitude of all involved.

Ford Nederland, the Dutch arm of the Ford Motor Company, is to shut its Amsterdam truck assembly plant in September with the loss of 1,325 jobs.

The factory, which assembles the heavy trans-continental truck and the Transit light van, made a loss of F1 68 m (£13 m) last year and expects to lose a further F1 60 m in 1981.

The Amsterdam plant has been a thorn in Ford's side for several years, mainly because of its poor productivity. Absenteism is said by Ford management to have been averaging 25–28 per cent, far above the norm at UK and Continental plants.

Relocating its Transit production will present no problem to Ford since the principal manufacturing centres, Southampton and Genk in Belgium, are under-utilized.

Several of Ford's nine Continental plants could take up output of the Transcontinental but the UK must rank high in the list of possible relocation sites.

(*Financial Times*, 24 April 1981).

In pursuit of this change (in the UK and throughout its Western operations) Ford toyed with policies aimed at 'worker involvement'. At the Metuchen plant in New Jersey, line workers had been given the opportunity to drive the Escort prototype and as production got under way 'worker involvement groups' were organized to help solve problems and suggest improvements in the running of the plant. Inside the plant the walls were covered in Ford slogans – 'Build it as though you were going to buy it.' The *New York Times* represented the atmosphere as being one of 'enthusiasm with an undercurrent of fear ... earlier this year the company closed its Mahwah N. J. assembly plant, putting 3,700 employees out of work' (2 September 1980). Similar posters – 'See a gap there's a Jap' – and feelings existed at Halewood in the summer of 1981, as downtown Liverpool burned in the riots. Earlier, Steve Broadhead, convenor of the MSB plant, had described the thoughts of the workers he represented in this way: 'They see Ford making £386 million profit last year, but companies are

Merseyside and little is going into public service. The men feel they are being exploited' (*Financial Times*, 12 November 1980). And this feeling was little alleviated by the main thrust of Ford's AJ negotiations: the attack on manning levels, demarcation and all practices which interfered with flexible working.

With the union back on board, Ford squeezed an agreement on 'key efficiency improvements' out of the 1981–2 wage deal. (This deal was rejected overwhelmingly by workers in the Halewood plants, and the settlement is regularly spoken of in the town as 'a sell-out'.) So armed, the Company pressed on in pursuit of 'natural wastage' and with tighter discipline. In 1981, Bill Hayden was reported as being pleased with the 'quality we are getting from the plant', and with the 908 units average by the plant in July. But it had to be consistent; it had to be a thousand a day – regularly and with fewer workers.

A thousand a day. That's the story. That's life. *More Escorts*: more production, more commitment, more involvement. *More Escorts*: more door-handles, more windshields, more boot-locks, more output; a thousand a day, five thousand a week, millions and millions of Escorts. How many over the past ten years? Keep working, don't think about it. Think about the kids, and the house and the car ... Shankley's dead, governments come and go, we're still here. *More Escorts*: the Cologne yardstick, Saarlouis, Valencia ... now the Japanese. *More Escorts*: more production, more dollar bills ... more ... more...

MYTH ONE: 'Strikes in the motor industry are due to monotonous work and boredom'

Cars are mass produced by the same methods all over the world, so if doing work is the cause why doesn't every country have our strike record?

Paul Roots, Employee Relations Director, Ford Motor Company UK

13 'Do as You're Told': What Strategy for Labour?

The 1973 edition of *Working for Ford* began its conclusion with mention of Karl Marx and the speech he made in London in 1865 to the General Council of the International Working Men's Association. In his speech he dealt with the relationship between wages and profits and the role of working-class organizations. Towards the end of it he advised that the working class, in their struggles in the factories 'ought not to forget that they are dealing with effects, but not with the causes of those effects ... [that] they are applying palliatives but not curing the malady'. In short they ought to try to extend the struggle beyond the factory, and make demands other than purely trade union demands for better wages and the like. 'For trade unions work well as centres of resistance against the encroachment of capital. They fail partially from an injudicious use of their power. They fail generally from limiting themselves to a guerrilla war against the effects of the existing system, instead of simultaneously trying to change it, instead of using their organized forces as a lever for the emancipation of the working class, that is to say, the ultimate abolition of the wage system.'[1]

This judgement is a severe one, but perhaps apt. Certainly the century that followed these words produced a continuance of the 'guerrilla war' which occasionally left the factories and took to the streets, but in all these struggles the role of the trade unions has been to de-escalate rather than extend the struggle between labour and capital. The history of the workers in the British car plants since the war illustrates this clearly. In the 1960s these plants were dominated by skirmishes and a number of protracted confrontations between the workers and the employers. The car workers in this period were at the centre of the class struggle, yet the struggle never extended beyond the 'guerrilla war'. They struggled bravely and their resolve has frequently demanded admiration. Yet there was little evidence that they have been able to link their struggles positively with those of other workers.

1. K. Marx, 'Wages, Price and Profit', in Karl Marx and Frederick Engels, *Selected Works*, Vol. 2, Progress Publishers, 1969.

Neither did their battles produce radical political demands. In 1960 Dennis Butt wrote an article (Butt, 1960) based upon conversations he'd had with car workers and union officials in the Midlands. He found, for example, that they were basically uninterested in the problems created by the uncontrolled production of the motor car.

These men and their leaders are, of course, heavily preoccupied with problems of their daily livelihood and, never forgetting for a moment the gloomy record of this industry, their main concern is less for the unlimited demand for motor cars than for the possibility of another sudden surge into recession (Butt, 1960).

So it was in 1972. It was possible then to point to the way in which car workers on the lines in Britain had continued to screw on wheels, secure head-linings and install transmission units. How they have worked on the line and struggled to control it, fighting supervisor and the watch of the time-study men. And it was true. They had developed shop stewards' committees in the plants and combine committees to link them. They *had* taken on 'the bureaucrats' and they *had* taken on Ford. And they were still taking them on. It seemed clear then that if the history of the car workers showed anything at all about the 'new' working class it was that, faced with the complete absence of any meaningful political leadership, workers would not lapse into inactivity and acquiescence. They would, to quote Butt again, 'form their own organization – or use existing ones – and fight over the issues that stare them in the face'. And so they did; and they have continued to do that. In 1981, the Halewood workers kicked the Discipline Code into touch. Three years earlier, united with all Ford workers in Britain (and with considerable support and sympathy from other workers – in Britain and through Ford's European operations) they took on a recalcitrant management backed by a Labour government intent on preserving a 5 per cent pay norm. It was a gruelling two month struggle and during it John Bohana, a shop steward in the MSB plant at Halewood, kept a diary. In it he remembers that it was said 'after the 1971 strike that it would never happen again'. That strike had been so long, so protracted; so much had been taken on and, in the end, things had been so deflated. Yet:

it has happened, and many things were learnt in 1971 and applied almost immediately at the start of the strike. Many more stewards have played a full and active part in one way or another and many lay members have played a full part . . . The campaign leading up to the strike did not match the 1970/71 campaign, but I think, organizationally, it has improved (Bohana, 1979).

He ends his account fed up with the 'official line' that eased the pressure off the company and recommended the end of the strike, but confident of the potential for the workers at Ford to organize themselves, to struggle imaginatively and to win.

The 1978 strike was an important event. It saw the emergence of a new rank and file organization within the Ford plants. Based on the Langley van plant, disaffected with the way the 'convenor system' had linked contact between the plants directly through the official channels of the NJNC, it called itself the *workers*' combine committee. During the strike they collected funds distributed stickers and 'Fraud' badges parodying the 'Ford' logo; gave meetings and spread information. In Liverpool the *Big Flame* group sponsored a meeting at the AUEW offices in Mount Pleasant. The meeting was an important one as it combined a discussion of the Ford strike with an inquest into the closure of the BL plant at Speke and the failure of the trade union organization there to mount an effective challenge to the Company's decision. This was the paradox. Here in the same city, people tried to cope with the fact that – in the same industry – one group of workers had (when push came to shove) mildly accepted closure, while another appeared to be carrying forward the militancy associated with car workers in Britain in the 1960s. One unemployed BL worker was impressed by the talk given by the representative of the workers' combine. In this talk Alan Ayling had outlined, *in detail*, the situation in each of the Ford plants operating in Europe. Agreement had been made to ensure that none of the European assembly plants made up the production lost by the strike in the UK. Plant by plant the figures rolled out: details of Cortinas, Fiestas and Escorts; details of support from dockers, of Ford cars trapped on ships blocked on both sides of the channel ferrying backwards and forwards in the wind and spray. All this in support of the mass strike.

If we'd had an organization like that; if we'd known we had that sort of support throughout the Company it would have been a different story at Speke.

But, as another ex-steward pointed out, impressive as it sounded 'an official strike is one thing; an official closure is something else'. And this is an important point. The strength and imagination revealed by the Ford workers in 1978 was built upon a sense of their indispensability to Ford. There had been times in the past when they had felt less secure in this belief. After the 1969 strike, for example, the production system at Halewood was altered. 'Halewood' models were relocated within Ford Europe and rumour was rife that Halewood was to be reduced to a van plant. Such a plant would require just half the labour force employed in the PTA. Eddie Roberts was convenor at that time and he remembers how:

the lads were pretty scared really. They'd seen a lot of things happening and they really began to get worried about their jobs. I didn't give a shit, like. I don't want anything from anybody, particularly from these bastards. As far as I was concerned Henry Ford could go and stick his jobs up his arse. Well Henry came to the plant, see. A surprise visit. All I wanted to say to him was 'up you' sort of thing, but I couldn't. I couldn't because of the lads. The lads were worried and they expected me to do something for them. They expected me to attempt to make their jobs secure. So that's what I had to do. Me and Les Moore and Les Brookes went in there cap in hand to our Lord and Master and said 'Please, Mr. Ford, don't take our jobs off us.'

This exemplifies another aspect of the general fact that to work in a factory is to work on management's terms. Where management finds that its right to manage is being challenged within a factory, it is involved in a political struggle. Often this struggle takes the form of skirmishes on the shop floor, and at this level shop steward organizations can be extremely effective, and shop stewards can amass a considerable amount of political influence and personal prestige. Where the challenge to managerial authority seriously affects the profitability of the Company, however, the response of management is likely to be firmer. To lay men off or to close plants down permanently, ultimately involves political decisions, and it is at this level of struggle that the conflict between capital and labour becomes obviously biased against the worker. Capital is inherently flexible, machines can be written off, investment switched from one part of the world to another. Against the might of capital the power of the shop stewards' committee is negligible unless backed by a strong international organization.

During the crisis of moving work that followed the 1969 strike some semblance of national and international cooperation was achieved between the various shop stewards' committees. A system of blacking prevented dies from being moved beyond Dagenham and into Europe. But duplicate dies can be made and the microprocessors which programme the new robots can be carried in an executive's wallet. In the last decade and a half Ford and the other transnationals which operate in the vehicle industry have become more and more sophisticated in their operations and in their strategy for labour. To say this is not to overemphasize the power of capital. Ford, for all its sophistication and its power, *still* has to deal with workers, and their collective strength *can* at times give them an important edge. At Bridgend (for all the careful selection and the encouragement of a 'responsible' trade unionism closeted away from the rest) things have not measured up to the Company's pleas, and a radical shop steward organization is now firmly established in the plant. Also there is no doubt that the 1978 strike at Ford represented an impressive show of trade union strength and organization, which called into play an important degree of international and class solidarity. That strike broke the Labour government's 5 per cent pay norm and built upon wide-ranging support from workers in Britain and across Europe. But successes shouldn't be used to obscure the real problems posed to trade union organization by the global developments at Ford. For although the struggle continues, there is no mistaking the steady, inexorable movement by Ford to regulate the independence (the freedom of mind and action) of the people who work on the lines in its British plants. And in this process (accompanied as it has been by growing internationalization of the Company's production system), the problems of a purely trade union locus of action – of both the limited horizons of 'official trade unionism' and the 'factory consciousness' of the shop stewards' committee and the workers in the plant – has been increasingly exposed. Especially as the recession hits deeper and plant after plant closes down.

Last week a German ship carrying Fiestas was turned away from Harwich, so it was instructed by Ford to take its load to N. Ireland. There they were unloaded, and to obscure their origin, they were given new T registration plates, and driven in sixes onto the passenger car ferry.

Fortunately the seamen realized what was happening – traced the load – and now those six Fiestas are travelling twice daily to and from N. Ireland – apparently trapped for ever!

Ford Strike News, 1978.

In Liverpool in the late 1970s 'redundancies' and closures became everyday events – across a whole range of manufacturing industry: BL, BICC, Bird's Eye, Courtaulds, GEC, Lucas, Plessey, Meccano, Tate & Lyle. The story became the same everywhere: rundown and closure, redundancy – the sack. The *coup de grace* was Dunlop. Dunlop's was *the* trade union factory in the Liverpool area. Its TGWU branch had amongst its membership both the TGWU President and a member of the union's National Executive. Dunlop workers had been involved in the first one-day *European* strike across the range of Dunlop–Pirelli plants, and the Speke committee had hosted a European conference of Dunlop trade unionists in Liverpool in 1975. The 'Dunlop Way' had set the pattern at Ford's Halewood plant. But in 1979 the 'Dunlop Way' was 'out the door'. The workers fought a long campaign to resist the closure, but they lost, and the tyre plant closed, putting another 2,400 workers on the dole.

It was clear in 1972 that the shop stewards who negotiated with Ford were, by instinct and practice, no revolutionaries. While the majority of them would agree with the desirability – need even – for fundamental political changes in our society, few of them could imagine how this desire could transform their practice in the plant – at the point of production. 'Politics' was left to the political parties. Increasingly an antipathy to 'party politics', fuelled by reference to the practices of the Communist Party in the 1950s, became formulated in traditional 'Labourist' ways: emphasizing *not* the political nature of the workplace relations, but rather the separateness of work and politics, of trade union and party. These tendencies were encouraged by the developments Ford made in its bargaining arrangements. Increasingly throughout the 1970s, Ford has promoted a *corporate* system of collective bargaining, linking trade union representations at all levels into the Company's and (hopefully) sanitizing them from more general (class) relationships. In Liverpool, the shop stewards' committee (not known for its deep involvement in the wider activities of the local Labour movement) came to isolate itself more and more within the confines of the plant. Local trade unionists and politicians noted that the Halewood lads 'keep very much to themselves'. And, as one astute observer put it:

You see they've been out there at Halewood and they've been watching all these plants getting closed down. All around them well-organized plants have had a closure order put on them. And it's left them with a little bit of the psychology that they're a class apart. They're still out there: 14,000 members making good wages, a well-organized committee structure and so on. Why bother with the rest? But if Ford decides to do what Dunlop did, or BL did, I don't think they'd be in any better position to stop them.

This judgement is a telling one particularly when the *Financial Times* reckoned that every convenor of a motor vehicle plant in Britain should be preparing for the last sit-in. This article quoted a case of a shop steward:

who, [having] spent his working life in a factory near London, protested recently that employers no longer play by the rules. He and his fellow workers had been told that if they tightened their belts and rolled up their sleeves, their factory would make a profit and continue to provide jobs and prosperity for its catchment area. They did and the profits duly materialized. But not long afterwards the company announced that the factory would close. It was explained that the plant was in the wrong place for the market it was trying to serve. The work would be moved to mainland Europe. Probably for the first time it was brought home to this worker what the investment strategy of a multinational corporation means, and how powerless his trade union is to oppose it (*Financial Times*, 21 January 1981).

There can be no suggestion that the shop stewards at Ford have such a lack of awareness. For a decade and more they have been made aware of the movement of capital, of the logistics of model sourcing and of the threat involved in each new phase of investment and plant location. Within the working class, the Ford workers have experienced the 'new global system' in its most open form. This experience represents an enormous fund of knowledge. Their shop stewards *know* how multinationals operate. They are familiar with the language of 'transfer pricing', 'dual sourcing' and 'import controls', and they have no illusions about Ford. They know it's a hard company, and they know that if 'the bottom line' was right, Ford would pull out of Halewood and the UK without a second thought. The workers who have had Saarlouis, Genk and Valencia rammed down their throats for years know this too. They know that in the world of vehicle manufacture they are so many interchangeable parts. But in knowing this, they are also aware that Ford pays different wage rates across Europe; that German workers are paid twice as much with longer holidays and better social security and lay-off arrangements. While they have been told that wages are related to production and profit they know that every major wage increase gained from Ford (even in the most profitable years) has had to be fought for with the strike. It's not surprising if all this makes many of them a bit sceptical of Ford's statistics. As one steward put it: 'They're always taking our shop stewards across there – to Saarlouis – but you never get the Saarlouis stewards around Halewood. A lot of the practices in this plant are beneficial from a trade union point of view and Ford don't want them copied.' They point in particular to practices for safe working and in this they are supported by statistics: not Ford's but those of *Labour Research* and the *International Labour Organisation* which point to the fact that the rate of serious accidents and fatalities in the West German engineering industry is four times as high as in Britain.[2] All this they know, but it's a knowledge which doesn't necessarily solve the problem, posed by the European and global developments of

2. See, for example, *Labour Research*, 1979, pp. 35–6, *ILO Year Book* 1978.

Efficiency and Productivity

'We must become more efficient, we must be in a position to compete with the Germans and Japanese. Our *PRODUCTIVITY* is not as good as the Germans and is way behind the Japanese.' You have all heard that cry before I am sure, so let us have a look at what price these '*PRODUCTION*' figures over a twelve month period have come about. Let's look at how many accidents are '*PRODUCED*'.

Let's have a look for instance at the Press Shops. In Great Britain during twelve months there were 120 amputations in Press Shops, arms, legs, hands, feet. Frightening isn't it. One hundred and twenty limbs lying on the floor, just try and imagine it. But if you think that is bad just look at the '*PRODUCTION*' figures for Germany. They have roughly the same number of Press Shops as we in Britain. But in a twelve-month period they had a staggering 1200 amputations – incredible isn't it. They had reason to be delighted with that, because the year before, they had 2000 amputations. However, *nobody* can compete with the Japanese, whilst they have a few more Press Shops than Britain, their '*PRODUCTION*' figure for loss of limbs is SIX THOUSAND.

What a price, a price paid solely by the workers, in perhaps the hardest jobs no doubt, for you can hardly have your arm amputated whilst jamming it in the office desk – can you? So next time management starts quoting '*PRODUCTION*' figures for other countries, ask them to produce the accident figures as well. You could also ask them how many immigrant workers have lost their work visa because they happen to become a statistic in the accident book. And, finally, ask yourselves are you prepared to put life and limb at risk in the pursuit of efficiency!!!

From: *Halewood Worker* Christmas Edition, 1981.

Health and Safety and its Problems

Much of the automated machinery has had to be totally re-guarded because it did not meet UK legal requirements let alone satisfy the stewards. In the new unit replacing the carousel (or roundabout as it is better known here) the robot welders had to be totally enclosed because it was possible for maintenance to be carried out while the line was working. Ford's answer was to issue all electricians with a letter telling them not to work on moving machinery. The stewards were not satisfied and demanded that the area be enclosed and that an interlock guard be fitted. On another new machine, where three components are placed in a frame then welded, the operator merely stood back from the machine and pressed a button. The stewards argued that it was quite possible for someone to press the button while their hand was still in the machine and so a new mechanism was installed whereby the closing of the guard operates the machine so it is impossible for someone to have their hand inside when the welding units fire. However, this improved guarding has meant that the jobs are done marginally slower and that maintenance 'on the go' has not occurred. The Company are quick to point out that this makes Halewood less productive than Saarlouis or Valencia.

From Dave Eva, *Points of interest from visit to Ford, Halewood*, WEA Liverpool, Mimeo, 1981.

Factory's Robot Kills a Worker

An industrial robot has killed a worker who was trying to repair it, the first accident of its kind reported in Japan, which has the world's largest robot workforce.

Details of the accident, which occurred in July at a plant of Kawasaki heavy industries were revealed yesterday by the Labour Standards Bureau of Hyogo prefecture, western Japan. Kenji Urada, aged 37, a worker at the Akashi plant of the company, was trapped by the work arm of the robot which pinned him against a machine which cuts gears. He had entered a prohibited area around the robot to repair it, the Labour Standards Bureau said.

From: *Guardian*, 9 December 1981.

companies like Ford for British workers and the British (and international) Labour movement.

To begin with, there's the problem of international *organization*. Here Ford's (international) strategy for production and marketing contrasts with its insistence on dealing with 'industrial relations' on a purely national basis. Ron Todd sees the problem in this way:

> At the European level there's been a definite change in the management structure over the time that Ford got Europe integrated. But there's been no change in our own side. We have to develop our *own* international links – through AG metal, the UAW, etc. – and not as a structured one with the Company. We have no bargaining relationship with Ford Europe. I've argued with Paul Roots on this any number of times. A closure of the Amsterdam plant affects us. It affects us directly at Southampton, and more generally too. We should be involved in discussions on things like this. But he's not prepared to consider it. More and more Ford is operating with the idea of a world car. More and more the Ford UK is just part of a whole world operation under the Detroit board. The needs of Detroit are paramount and it could mean that any decision in Europe is controlled by this need. We need to have some control over the situation.
>
> It suits Ford to deal with the British unions, the German unions, the French unions . . . it suits them. They know that but they just waffle when you put it to them. But it's nonsense for them to tell us that it doesn't matter. A decision at Genk; a turn of the screw at Valencia; a decision on its supply of car heaters . . . it all affects us. And that's why there will have to be a closer knitting together of the union committees that exist. We all have common problems with this Company. And we're all coming to realize that.

The realization, however, has been slow to transform itself into coordinated trade union action, and Ford has remained resolute in its refusal to grant international 'bargaining links' to the unions represented in Ford Europe. In this context 'internationalism' has been furthered in a number of ways. The official meeting at Valencia in 1980 was one example. Another has been the variety of imaginative unofficial contacts which have been developed by groups and individuals over the past ten years. The workers' combine, for example, has cooperated with Counter Information Services and the Transnational Institute to organize European conferences at Copenhagen, Langley and Bordeaux; all aimed at promoting links between workers in Ford's European plants. The upsurge of workers' resistance in South Africa – in which the strike at the Ford plant played a critical role – saw representatives from the South African Labour Education Project speaking at Transport House in Islington to the TGWU Halewood branch. In the Philippines workers from a Ford

NO PROD DEAL

3. No Productivity Deal

On Friday, Ford's are going to offer us a productivity deal. We should have none of this. Already productivity at our plants is amongst the highest in the whole of British industry. Higher productivity will mean:

★ **Harder work and more accidents. Ford of Germany has twice the number of accidents per million man hours worked than we suffer in Ford of Britain.**

★ **Financial penalties for absence or lateness. Last year's productivity deal at Vauxhall meant that anyone who was late (because the bus was late, or the car wouldn't start, or the wife was sick) lost up to £5 of their wage pakcet.**

Inevitably this will mean less jobs - because Fords won't have a pool of experienced labour to cover for absenteeism PLUS it will mean that the mini-shift is here to stay. Anyone who misses the Friday mini-shift will be heavily penalised. We should be paid for the work we do, and the hours we work - and not made to pay for hours we don't work.

★ **Shorter meal breaks.**

Finally as we said last week - this year there will be NO MONEY in any productivity deal. Strikes over manning and conditions at Fords *plus* strikes in suppliers over wages will mean that we'll *never* hit production targets. And so we'd never get the bonus. It'll be like a donkey chasing a carrot fixed to its head!

Ford Strike News, November 1978

IS OUR CLAIM RESPONSIBLE?

Suddenly there's a lot of talk—from Callaghan, from Thatcher, from Fords and from many trade union leaders about 'responsible' claims. We know what they mean by this. They mean claims which will result in yet another cut in our standard of living.

Our claim IS responsible. It is *responsible* because the outcome of this claim affects not just our standard of living—but also that of our wives or husbands and children. And it will crucially affect the standard of living of thousands of other workers. If we win, so will nurses, local authority workers, other car workers—and so on.

Wage restraint has been one great con. We know there's plenty of wealth in this country—we know because we create it. It's just that the wealth isn't fairly shared around. So our struggle for a greater share of the wealth isn't a struggle just for ourselves. We Ford workers are no special case. All workers need more money and a shorter week. That's why we say our claim is responsible.

body plant, on strike in 1981, developed the slogan 'justice delayed is justice denied' and paraded with the 'Fraud' symbol. So, (in Britain, Europe, South Africa, the Philippines ...) there is a growing international *awareness* amongst Ford workers. What isn't clear is how this awareness will develop, both organizationally and *politically*. The fact that so many arguments and discussions amongst car workers (especially in Britain and the USA) switch between the poles of international solidarity and protectionist isolation is one illustration of this quandary – a quandary which derives from the tension that exists between internationally organized production and the national organization of labour and politics. In part this is revealed in the changing positions of Ford and BL workers in the 1970s.

In Port Elizabeth, the capital of the South African motor industry, both Ford and General Motors have been hit by a sympathy strike by their workers for men laid off at the Firestone tyre manufacturer. Some 1,500 workers at three Ford plants, and 175 workers from General Motors, downed tools after the dismissal of two Ford men who refused to fit Firestone tyres to a vehicle.

All the workers involved are members of the Motor Assembly and Components Workers' Union (Macwusa), a predominantly black union which, unlike Numarwosa, is not officially registered. The Ford and General Motors workers support the blacking of Firestone tyres until all the Firestone workers have been reinstated.

The South African motor industry has been hit by a series of disputes in the past 18 months, the last of which was a pay claim at Sigma, which manufactures Mazda, Peugeot and Citröen cars; after a short strike at the company's Pretoria plant the pay claim was settled.

The disputes have shown a considerable degree of coordination, with workers in Pretoria striking for similar pay rises to those won in Port Elizabeth.

Financial Times, 21 May 1981

In 1978 at the time of the Ford strike, British Leyland had been in the hands of Michael Edwardes for almost a year. Brought in as chairman of a company in crisis by a Labour government whose leader had, in the view of the *Economist*, given him 'the nod ... to play it tough. The government is known to want a solution of the Leyland problem wrapped up by early Spring' (14 January 1978). He wrapped it up as he closed the TR7 plant at Speke. He carried on – with the less muted backing of Thatcher and Joseph – and under his guidance 60,000 workers left the company in three years as thirteen factories were closed. Derek Robinson, the convenor of the Longbridge plant and chairman of the combine shop stewards, was sacked – ostensibly for opposing the 'plan'. Speed-up came to BL as the reduced labour force was threatened and cajoled into producing more and more cars. In a speech to the American Chamber of Commerce in London, Edwardes made plain that 'in the first five months of this year BL produced an estimated 170,000 cars – about 4 per cent more than in the same period in 1980 – with 30,000 fewer workers than a year ago'. (*The Times*, 18 June 1981). In the plants, observers point to a 'macho' style of management and to the increasing 'fear' of the people who work the lines: speed-up, sackings, closures.

In this process a curious paradox emerged. In 1977, before Edwardes's arrival, BL produced a document, termed a 'concept study', in which it identified the major problem it faced in the plants.

In Ford and Vauxhall, management are forced to use work-study techniques to determine the speeds and to establish manning levels after appropriate consultations. In Leyland cars, although practices vary from plant to plant, there is widespread opposition to work measurement and to the setting of manning levels at anything other than the 'Persian Market' principle.

Four years later the boot was on the other foot as the *weakness* of BL emerged as the key reference for all managers and workers in British car plants. In Liverpool, the dramatic and ruthless closure of the Speke No. 2 plant was seen as a decision of enormous significance: a *nationalized* firm under a *Labour* government – what chances with a US multinational under the Tories! And at Ford in 1980 (the year of record profits for the UK company) workers in all the plants voted to accept the Company's offer, in spite of the advice of their leaders to strike for more. In the wake of this decision, a group of workers and shop stewards at Halewood decided to develop a regular broadsheet called *Halewood Worker*. An earlier Christmas Special had proved a great success, and it continued in a witty, iconoclastic way to assist in the task of breaking down the isolation and the 'lack of communication' between workers in the plants. In 1981 it asked the question 'The pay deal: why did we accept it?'

On Thursday 5 February 1981, we felt the results of our decision to accept the wage and conditions agreement for 1981. The wage packet didn't actually bulge, in fact most people were absolutely shocked at the pathetic 'increase' in the rate. It is useless for individuals to claim 'I didn't vote for it' or 'I didn't attend the meeting'. The fact is locally and nationally we did accept – why?

In trying to work out an answer they approached thirty-six workers, each on separate sections. 'Why?' The answers were interesting. Aside from the occasional maverick response ('because we're a gang of bloody nutters') what emerged was the overwhelming reference to 'fear'. People talked of a 'sense of insecurity', of 'despair' and 'a lack of belief in our own strength', of 'stories about cutback', 'Maggie's policies' and, arching over everything else the 'fear of Ford' together with some colourful references to the threats used by Michael Edwardes in his dealings with the workers at BL and the possibility that Ford would follow suit.

Here is the paradox. In Britain a weak national company, owned by the state and backed by successive governments, creates the conditions for Ford (strong, multinational . . .) to tighten the screw. It's a paradox which springs from the fact that even across Western Europe the politics of different countries (the class relationships and state forms) take on particular distinct (even unique) elements. It is this which any company-based trade union organization (whether official or unofficial, 'rank and file' or 'bureaucratic') will find a problem. For while international links, contacts and organization grow of necessity within Ford, many of the problems faced by Ford workers in Britain (just now the problem of 'fear' and the politics that produce it) stem from beyond the company. Within the motor industry the need and the opportunity for such a development is more clear than anywhere else; clearer, too, than at any time in the past.

The significance of the motor trade to the economies of the western world cannot be overstated. In 1974 the publication *Eurofinance* estimated that the automative industry directly (in the manufacture of vehicles) and indirectly (component manufacture, distribution and repair, etc.) provided employment for twelve million workers in Western Europe. To this figure can be added the number of people whose work in the steel, rubber, plastics, communication and transport industries whose employment is dependent upon automobile production. In all, the survey suggested that 30 million workers – 23 per cent of the non-agricultural labour force of Western Europe – are in employment which is linked, by one route or another, to the fate of the motor industry. It is this which makes the restructuring of the industry being undertaken by the giant firms of such enormous destabilizing significance. In Britain, the TUC's investigations of job losses and redundancies in 1980 saw the vehicle industry accounting for 23·4 per cent of redundancies declared between October 1980 and February 1981. The report reckoned that for every three jobs lost in vehicle manufacture a further two were lost in component supply.

In the face of such an assault, the spontaneous reaction is to run for cover. And in Europe and the USA it is this spontaneity which has been reflected by the initial stance of the trade union organizations. Ten years ago there was talk of enlarging the area of the collective bargaining to encompass the broader aspects of working life. Since 1978 the pressures have been on to close it down to the bare essentials – money and hours – with the companies reluctant to talk about hours and increasingly intent upon cutting wages! The extent of the change is quite dramatic. The pay claim presented by the trade unions to Ford UK in 1973, contained the following paragraph:

Within this stronger emphasis on the human needs of the labour force, we should be not only programming a major reduction in actual working time, but also a joint programme to redesign jobs and work pressures and to break away wherever possible from short repetitive job cycles, which represent the most inhuman feature of the work pressures in the industry.

The paragraph was highlighted in heavy type, and while the objective was never coherently pressed in the unions' six-point claim, the contrast with the position which the national officers of the unions find themselves in today is enormous. 'With things as they are,' says Ron Todd, 'we've found that the points to do with the quality of life in the plants have tended to get forgotten. It's now a question of "jobs" rather than "what sort of jobs".' His face twists with regret as he says this. A regret genuinely felt, and one which rests on the facts as he sees them. 'Facts' which have been presented to trade union officials endlessly during this century and before. Some things don't change. Given the established nature of 'orthodox trade unionism' the facts are clear. At the moment the working class has its back against the wall and there's nothing to be done until the pressure eases up. As in the UK so in the USA. There, after the signing of the 1979 contract with General Motors, the *New York Times* commented that 'the early seventies' notion of making conditions on the assembly line more tolerable was not a matter of great importance' (23 September 1979). And, as one observer put it, 'The union is resigned to the fact that the corporation controls the workplace' and that the only strategy open is to 'take the money and run'. In the face of the growing crisis, the psychology of the UAW leadership was aptly summed up by the union's president Douglas Frazer. In his speech to the 1980 convention, he remarked that 'if you see a light at the end of the tunnel, it is probably an oncoming freight train' (*Progressive*, August 1980). So keep your head down, stick close to the wall; if a plant closes down, be thankful it's not where you work; if you're offered overtime don't complain, get the money when you can because in this industry you never know when the freight train will hit.

But is this the only feasible 'strategy for labour'? Is it even a viable one given the massive changes which are taking place in the motor industry and in manufacturing generally? Some would have us believe so. Eric Ogden for one. When Labour MP for the West Derby constituency in Liverpool (he switched to the SDP in 1982), he attended a press conference which had been called by the local officers of the TASS to publicize their pamphlet on the future of the motor industry on Merseyside. Ogden's contribution was based on the assumption that 'if the motor industry goes, then Merseyside is finished', and the clear solution – 'the lads must make more cars':

> The Escort is a world beater. If Ford could build 1,100 a day it would mean a further 500 jobs for component makers. At the moment we are going the same way as Scotland and as the TR7 plant at Speke. They said it couldn't happen but it did. The only way is for the lads on the shop floor to back the managements (*Ford News*, 12 June 1981).

'Do as you're told' – that's the solution. If you don't like it, there's plenty of others outside. The Germans can do it, so can you. The Japanese will finish us unless you do as you're told. Increasingly 'the Japanese threat'. Ever since 1980 when Ford launched its 'AJ' campaign, and when Bill Hayden informed the managers and workers of Ford Europe that in Japan:

> Everyone must do what they're supposed to do, when they are supposed to do it. Japanese discipline and worker dedication is such that this situation is maintained. All workers work together as a team and will cover for their colleagues as required (Ford Motor Company, 1980).

It works in Japan because the workers are dedicated. It works without pain or discomfort. It works because it's efficient and because people have the right attitudes. So the story goes. But maybe there's another side to this account.

In 1980 *Working for Ford* was published in Japan. It is interesting to read the comment it provoked from a Japanese car worker. Writing in a rank and file labour weekly he said:

> While reading through, I nodded with sympathy and sighed. Everything written was astonishingly like the experiences we had on the shop floor here in the Japanese plants ... If you have ever struggled on the shop floor, here in this book, you'll find the record of your own experience.

A remarkably different interpretation; certainly one absent in the AJ propaganda. The truth of this interpretation was captured in an account written by Satoshi Kamata of the six months he spent as a seasonal worker at a Toyota plant in 1972. Launching the book – *Factory of Despair: Diary of a Seasonal Worker* – in 1973 the author asked that:

when you visit the Toyota company and stand in front of the signboard at Toyota Hall, I want you to think of the sweat and labour of the assembly-line workers behind the rapidly changing numbers (quoted in Juako, 1981).

The sign, like the one at Ford's headquarters in Detroit, records the number of cars that roll off the assembly line. Kamata's account of his first days as Toyota employee number 8818636 is graphic:

Once the line starts moving at 6.00 a.m., transmissions to be assembled continue flowing exactly every minute and twenty seconds without stopping for five hours until 11.00 a.m. I should say not 'exactly' but 'cruelly'. When the line stops at 11.00 a.m., everybody throws off his gloves and immediately leaves his position. Marching off, the grease stuck to their hands, they rush to the toilet to empty bursting bladders. Then they run to the dining hall 100 metres away. The line starts moving again at 11.45. Since we have to arrange supplying parts sixteen minutes earlier, there is no time to really rest. The line stops at 2.15 p.m., stay thirty minutes for overtime. Went back to the dorm after walking for forty minutes hardly moving my legs, which were like lead. Utterly exhausted. Is this the life of a worker for the auto maker who boasts itself as No. 1 in Japan and No. 3 in the world?

It turned out that it was.

From the moment I step through the gate of the plant, and from the moment I show my ID card to the guard, I exist only as a number. It is as if leaving myself, my soul and mind, checked in at the gate, like leaving a coat.

And it got worse. Overtime, speed-up, alterations in the work and shift patterns, all in the space of six months; as workers, 'bound together by one steel belt – capital', worked the line for Toyota. On the last day he talked with a 'full-time worker'.

'It's your last day, isn't it?' 'Yeah I'm going to be released from the prison.' 'Well, we're lifers.'

'Lifers'. The word says a lot. Much of the publicity given to the 'Japanese factory system' stresses the commitment which comes from stable, life-time employment with the company. It rarely stresses the darker, more threatening side of this 'security'. Nor is it questioned in real detail. (Ford's AJ document, for example, discloses that the average age of the Toyota worker is 27, while workers in Ford UK average 40 years of age.) The company housing, and the sick-visiting foreman is a surer indicator of the nature of the system than the singing of company songs. So too the contrast between the wages and living conditions of 'lifers' with the temporary worker and those in the 'subcontract' sector of the Japanese economy. At Nissan in the 1960s, temporary workers were segregated at work and housed in 'barrack-styled huts with an allocation of approximately two square metres of space per man'. These workers were involved in an important confrontation with the Company in 1971. After one worker was sacked:

a 'Defence Committee' was formed among ex-school friends, young workers and activists (not union men) to begin agitating and leafleting for his reinstatement. Then in January 1971 the management of the Kyoto factory suddenly, and without notice, announced changes in the terms and conditions of work of the seasonal workers employed there. The changes amounted to an effective loss in wages of 4,000 to 6,000 yen ($11 to $14) per month, thus sparking off a revolt among them which soon fused with that over the dismissed worker and began to develop into a comprehensive attack on the enslaving nature of the work process and on the enterprise itself. While unrest at the factory was at its peak, a 'goon squad' of company and union men was got together to beat up the dissidents and intimidate them from further action. This group of thugs became known as the Nissan SS. Uniformed and some 300 in number they represent a refinement in repressive technique over earlier labour troubles in which goon squads or the regular police force have been called in *from outside* to act as strike breakers or to crush radical student movements.

What the eventual outcome will be of these struggles cannot be known. In the case of the seasonal workers Nissan decided that they were 'unstable' and 'lacking in feeling of belonging to the enterprise' and announced in March that they would be employed no longer (Halliday and McCormack, 1973, p. 185).

Of equal significance is the role of the trade unions within the Japanese factory. In the post-war period of reconstruction under McArthur, Japanese workers formed themselves into independent trade unions, often with militant leadership. These unions were broken up as successively the companies launched a 'second union' movement, aimed at establishing a system of 'in-house', company unionism. It is this structure which has maintained itself, and has become the envy of Ford. In the 1960s at Nissan, all the officers of the union (all the 'shop stewards') were foremen. At Hitachi in the early seventies, 60 per cent of the chairmen of departmental union committees at the Furasato works were foremen or superintendents. There, trade union activism

Another wave of struggle came in early 1973, from January through March. Then the presumably impossible happened! At the height of the struggle, assembly lines, which the company never stopped even in the case of fatal labour accidents, were finally brought to a halt!

The struggle began on 8 January. Upon reporting at the factory after the New Year holidays, seasonal workers were told that the factory would start operating on a 'two-nights-off-a-week' basis. The introduction of the new work-day system would mean a tremendous reduction in wages as well as intensification of labour, as mentioned above. But the seasonal workers, who would be affected most seriously by such a system, were not informed about it until it was actually put into practice. The enraged seasonal workers immediately took revenge. In the first day of their work, some intentionally made dozens of rejects, others refused to work and milled into the labour management office. Although it started on an individual basis, the struggle soon grew into a collective one. The means of organizing were the assembly-line conveyors that kept carrying rejects and leaflets until they were finally stopped for two full days when 300 seasonal workers went into a wild-cat strike and occupied plant offices.

Matuso Kei, 'Nissan Motor: Hell's Battlefield', *Solidarity Motor Bulletin* 3.

encouraged promotion and managers exercised a strong influence upon the election of union officers. As one union official put it: 'One always approaches the company first. One's got to make some kind of settlement, because sometimes the company might say: "no it would be very awkward if this chap was elected as an officer"' (see Dore, 1973). At Nissan today, the conduct of 'union elections' ensures a similar stability. Listen to this account by a worker at the company's Oppama plant:

When we vote, we are asked to gather around the supervisor's desk in a group of several at a time, and write out our voting slips right on the spot, on the desk in front of everybody. The desk is an ordinary office desk of about 1 metre in width. And standing beside the desk are the election administrators, I mean, the assistant manager and the shop steward, who watch closely to see if we write down the right name (quoted in Kiyoshi, 1980).

In this way elections of Nissan workers' union standing committee proceeded throughout the 1970s. On no occasion was a candidate opposed. On no occasion did the successful candidate get less than 99 per cent of the eligible votes. It is this situation which a US reporter tried to penetrate in 1982.

It is not easy to pierce the shell that surrounds Nissan. Workers are reluctant to talk openly for fear that their words will be used against them; those who do talk ask not to be identified. When I arranged a meeting with Tsutuma Higashi (not his real name), it is clear how pervasive this fear is. I follow him, ten paces behind, until we reach the privacy of his apartment, a two-room flat (the size of a one-car garage), where he lives with his wife and his infant son. The precautions are necessary, Higashi tells me, because he has been followed recently by a union member from the plant. He once spoke against a union proposal at a shop-floor meeting and he has since been branded a radical and subjected to periodic surveillance. 'There's a practice of "family" at Nissan,' Higashi says, 'and workers are forced to put on a good face. The definition of the "Nissan man" is one who is never late, never takes a day off and never complains. But the workers at Nissan don't depend on the company or the union – they depend on the workers, on their own strengths . . .' But it seems they don't trust people; they depend only on themselves. 'I really feel like I work in a desert, a shop-floor desert where all the workers are grains of sand – dry, unconnected. There's no sense of warmth; no humanity with the workers.'[3]

Here the account resonates with the conclusion reached by Kamata Satoshi:

How similar the labour in this auto plant to slave labour! How similar it is to Sisyphus! If it were punishment for some crime, what kind of crime was it? Should it be a crime for a worker to try to lead a normal life.

A 'normal life'; that's something that gets lost behind the stream of figures. More numbers, more production, more . . . but never the question 'Production for what?' Never to question the *purpose* of the whole mad escapade that pushes some people out of work while others – 'fortunate to be employed' – are worn out on speeded lines. That's what's behind the talk about 'competiveness' and 'AJ'.

In 1975, Moss Evans gave evidence to the House of Commons Expenditure Committee who were investigating the motor industry. He was asked for his views on 'workers' control' of the industry and gave this reply.

If I went to a meeting of workers who were out on strike for an increase in shift differential and suggested that workers' control was the solution to their problem, they would throw me in the canal.

3. John Junkerman, ' "We Are Driven": Life on the Fast Line at Datsun', *Mother Jones*, August 1982 p. 23. Similar accounts are provided by Martin Glaberman, 'US Auto Workers Visit Japan', in *AMPO Japan-Asia Quarterly Review*, Vol. 13, No. 1, 1981 and 'Japanese Auto Workers: A View From Below' in *Speaking Out* Vol. 1, No. 3, May 1982 PO Box 15365. Detroit, Michigan 48215, USA.

He obviously had a point, and in a way echoed the view of Leonard Woodcock who, when President of the UAW had criticized 'academics' for the 'elitist nonsense' they wrote about the workplace. 'If some company said to us tomorrow "OK, humanize the plant", we wouldn't know where to start.' And that is a fact. But when notions of 'humanization' and 'control' are stripped of their abstract quality workers on the lines in car plants know *exactly* where to start. Given the chance they work slower; they work back the line; they share out jobs; they mess around – all to create that bit more space, that bit of room to lead 'a normal life'. Yet it is precisely this space, (call it autonomy or independence; call it control or humanity) which the march of capitalist expansion seeks to regulate and ultimately deny. And it is this space which has – in the welter of numbers – been forced underground *politically*. The logic of Ford and of Nissan (compare these last quotations with accounts of Ford in the thirties in Chapter 1) has won the political battle: their numbers have overcome, politically at least, and the 'Japanese menace' is firmly established in the minds of car makers in Europe and the USA.

To say that car workers in Britain need an alternate policy for the British motor industry is an understatement. Ten years ago it was clear that while the workers and their shop stewards edged up against (challenged and made fun of) the prerogatives of management and capital in the plant, this had never been developed in a *systematic* way. While it was important to see power struggles in the factory as *political* struggles, they represented a politics that tended to operate within certain limits. In a way they had an enduring, almost endless quality; a refusal to accept, hedged by a reluctance to entertain the possibility of things being better. And certainly almost everything in their experience confirms that reluctance. After BL (when the state stepped in to save the company with the Edwardes regime!) it's hard to see nationalization as holding any solution – certainly not one which permits a 'normal life' at work. But equally it's hard to envisage a 'strategy of labour' in the motor industry which doesn't take issue with the question of 'public ownership' and what it would mean to bring the Ford company under wider control: under the control of the people.

Ford, and not the Japanese, destabilized the British motor industry and in its present form there can be no guarantee that the industry has a long-term future in Britain. Certainly the trade unions are able to exert no pressure (or influence even) upon these developments. In 1973 when George Henderson, national officer of the ACTSS raised questions of component-sourcing with the Company, Bob Ramsey made it clear that it was none of his business. Furthermore:

Mr Ramsey's refusal to accept this offer – on the grounds that they ran the Company and not ACTSS – was followed by him expressing annoyance at ACTSS's activities in collecting information about the Company's business. Mr. Ramsey [also] informed [George Henderson] that unless ACTSS members were prepared to stop their campaign immediately and hand back the confidential Company documents, Ford would consider withdrawing recognition and reducing the negotiating rights of ACTSS.

Eight years later (and in the middle of the AJ programme) Ron Todd still found that:

At every strategy meeting, we have something called 'future prospects'. I don't mind that, but it's just them telling us what's going to happen. I think it should be a two-way thing. We should widen the discussion. I told Roots: 'If I want to find out about our future I have to read the *Guardian* or the FT.' They don't want to open the discussion. They want the managing director to make his twice yearly presentations and leave it at that. Every attempt to broaden the discussion – on the sourcing of steel, on components, on the European stage – always comes from the initiative of the union.

And so it remains. 'Future prospects' are not our concern; they're best left in the hands of the powers that be. But if the last ten years have told us anything, it is that these 'powers' (linked still, and to an enormous degree, with the rights of private property) are not likely to make Britain a better place to live in. The opposite in fact. When I talked with shop stewards in the late 1960s about the prospects of a better society, one run on a more egalitarian basis, based upon need rather than greed – a socialist kind of society – this response was a common one:

If we thought about that we'd go crazy. I just can't afford to think about things like that. Sometimes I ask myself: 'Where are we going? What does all this add up to?' Then I'm in another meeting, or on a case. We leave it to people like you that. Ideas about a new society and that.

Well at the time 'people like me' hadn't come up with a lot, and it was clear even then that the solution didn't lie in any intellectual blueprint. Nor did it lie in 'better leaders' or the would-be 'condescending saviours' who people the higher reaches of the Labour movement. It lay – if it lay anywhere – in a conscious process of people thinking and acting upon that whole range of 'refusals' which made up the working class in struggle. There, perhaps, in learning from each other's struggles – past and present – in documenting and assessing them, lay the ground for an authentic strategy for labour.

In many ways this process has begun. The 1970s were, perhaps, less flamboyant years than the 1960s but certainly they had a solid quality. The 1978 strike at Ford was an achievement of real substance. In meetings throughout the country shop stewards explained their case. In Newcastle a meeting of engineering workers was deeply impressed by the account:

> What impressed me most was the way they talked about the nurses. They said that under this 5 per cent pay norm, if the Ford workers sacrificed and accepted the norm, there was no way other workers – lower paid workers – would benefit from that sacrifice. As they put it, they could only help other workers by breaking the norm. And they convinced most of the people there I reckon.

Here, in the level of organization and the willingness to spread the discussion and the argument lie the possibilities of another kind of politics. So, too, (and in a different way) the support given by dock workers to the call by Vauxhall workers to disrupt GM's plans to import its new model from Spain. In another way, the involvement of shop steward's committees from eleven car plants with the Institute of Workers' Control in the production of their *Workers' Enquiry into the Motor Industry* (CSE, 1978) was an important event too. Bringing together evidence of workers' experience of 'capitalist development' within the vehicle industry it stressed the need of a kind of accounting very different from the one practised by Ford. It pointed to the potentials of a planned industry and the need to question both the 'quality of life' in the plants and the kinds of products that were made in them. In this, the report echoed the views of one car worker, who after the closure of BL's plant in Speke remarked: 'I don't think we should be producing bleeding sports cars that nobody can afford anyway. The plant could produce something useful.'[3] It could still, and Ford's robots could perhaps be put to better use too. The men who work with them recognize that:

> They're marvellous machines. The people in Halewood and the area should be jumping up and down at the marvel of it – human ingenuity producing something like that. But instead it's a source of worry.

This paradox – human potential alongside worry, tedium and despair – is the paradox of our time. It is one which we need to urgently resolve for, in the UK at least, time is getting short.

The man on the engine dress has just fitted another gear box . . .

3 Quoted in *What Happened at Speke?* TGWU Liverpool, 1980.

References

ARNOLD, H. L., and FAURETE, F. L. (1915), *Ford Methods and the Ford Shops*, New York.

BARITZ, L. (1965), *The Servants of Power*, Science Editions.

BARNET, R. J. and MÜLLER, R. E. (1974), *Global Reach: The power of the Multinational Corporations*, Simon & Schuster.

BEYNON, H. (1968), 'A wildcat strike', *New Society*, September.

BOHANA, J. (1979), *Report on the Ford Motor Company Halewood Strike over Wages and Conditions Commencing September 21st 1978*, mimeo, Liverpool.

BUTT, D. (1960), 'Men and motors', *New Left Review*, no. 3.

CLIFF, T., and BARKER, C. (1966), *Incomes Policy, Legislation and Shop Stewards*, London Industrial Shop Stewards' Defence Committee.

COLE, G. D. H. (1936), *Conditions in Britain*, Clarendon Press.

DORE, R. (1973), *British Factory – Japanese Factory*, Allen & Unwin.

DRUCKER, P. F. (1950), *The New Society*, Harper & Row.

ENSOR, J. (1972), 'How Europe's car makers fare in the profit league', *Financial Times*, 13 September.

EXCELL, A. (1981), *The Politics of the Production Line: Autobiography of an Oxford Car Worker*, History Workshop Journal Pamphlet.

FINE, S. (1969), *Sit Down: The GM Strike of 1936–37*, Michigan University Press.

FORD, H. (1922), *My Life and Work*, New York.

FORD MOTOR COMPANY (1980), *The Challenge from Eastern Europe and Japanese* Imports, mimeo.

FRIEDMANN, H. and MEREDEEN, S. (1980), *The Dynamics of Industrial Conflict*, Croom Helm.

GALBRAITH, J. K. (1963), 'Was Ford a fraud?', in *The Liberal Hour*, Penguin.

GLAZER, B. G. and STRAUSS, A. L. (1968), *The Discovery of Grounded Theory: Strategies for Qualitative Research*, Weidenfeld & Nicholson.

GOODMAN, J. F. B., and SAMUEL, D. S. (1966), 'The motor industry in a development district', *British Journal of Industrial Relations*, vol. 4.

GOODRICH, C. L. (1920), *The Frontier of Control: a Study of British Workshop Politics*, Bell & Sons.

HALLIDAY, J. and MCCORMACK, G. (1973), *Japanese Imperialism Today*, Penguin.

HINTON, J. (1973), *The First Shop Steward Movement*, Allen & Unwin.

KIYOSHI, YAMAMOTO (1980), 'Labour–Management Relations in Nissan Motor Company Ltd (Datsun)', *Annals of the Institute of Social Science*, vol. 21.

LEE, J. R. (1916), 'The So-Called Profit Sharing System in the Ford Plant', *Annals of the American Academy of Political Science*, vol. LXV, May.

LEONARD, J. N. (1932), *The Tragedy of Henry Ford*, New York.

MARQUIS, S. S. (1923), *Henry Ford: An Interpretation*, New York.

MATHEWS, J. (1972), *The Ford Strike*, Panther.

MOORE, L. (1981), *The Dynamics of a Dispute: How Ford Regulate Industrial Relations with the Ten-Minute Rule*, mimeo, Liverpool.

MURPHY, J. T. (1972), *Preparing for Power*, Pluto Press.

NEVINS, A. (1954), *Ford: The Times, The Man, The Company*, Scribner.

NEVINS, A., and HILL, F. E. (1962), *Ford: Decline and Rebirth, 1933–1962*, New York.

NORTH, D. T. B. and BUCKINGHAM, G. L. (1969), *Productivity, Agreements and Wage Systems*, Gower Press.

RAE, J. B. (ed.) (1969), *Henry Ford*, Prentice Hall.

SARTRE, J.-P. (1969), *The Communists and Peace*, Hamish Hamilton.

SCARBOROUGH, H. (1980), *Working For Ford: Robots*, mimeo, University of Aston.

SEIDLER, E. (1976), *Let's Call It Fiesta: The Autobiography of Ford's Project Bobcat*, Patrick Stephens.

SINCLAIR, U. (1938), *The Flivver King*, Chivers.

SLOAN, A. P. (1963), *My Years with General Motors*, Doubleday.

SOKOLOV, R. A. (1967), 'The treatment of disability', *Journal of Occupational Medicine*, February.

STANTON, E. (1967), 'Inside the Ford defeat', in *What Happened at Fords*, *Solidarity* Pamphlet no. 26.

SWARD, K. (1948), *The Legend of Henry Ford*, New York.

THE CAMERON REPORT (1957), *Report of a Court of Inquiry*, Cmnd, 131, HMSO.

THE JACK REPORT (1963), *Report of a Court of Inquiry*, Cmnd, 1949, HMSO.

THOMPSON, E. P. (1968), *The Making of the English Working Class*, Penguin, 2nd edn 1970.

TOPHAM, T. (1964), 'Shop stewards and workers control', *New Left Review*, no. 25.

TURNER, H. A., CLACK, G. and ROBERTS, T. G. (1967), *Labour Relations in the Motor Industry*, Allen & Unwin.

WEINSTEIN, J. (1968), *The Corporate Ideal in the Liberal State*, Beacon Press.

WELLER, K. (1964), 'The defeat at Fords: some lessons', *Solidarity*, vol. 3, no. 8.

Appendix 1

The Ford Motor Company in Britain and Europe

The Company has two main centres of production in Britain – at Dagenham and Halewood – supported by a range of component plants.

The Dagenham estate (London)

This is a large complex which centres around a body and an assembly plant producing two main models: Fiesta and Sierra.

MSB: Metal Stamping and Body plant. Here the parts of the body are pressed from sheet steel and welded together.

PTA: Paint Trim and Assembly plant. Car bodies from the MSB plant are painted, fitted with interior trim and assembled with engines, wheels and transmission units.

Three other plants at Dagenham produce engines, wheels and trim. The Dagenham foundry produces iron castings for the engines.

The Halewood estate (Liverpool)

Again there is a PTA and MSB plant which produce one main model: the Escort. A trim manufacturing plant is attached to the PTA and a transmission plant produces a range of transmission units.

These main manufacturing operations are replicated in Europe by "sister" plants at Cologne and Saarlouis (in West Germany), Genk (Belgium) and Almusafes (Spain).

In addition to these six major estates, Ford also owns a range of other operations. Component production has tended to be separated from the major centres. Axles are produced in Swansea, engines in

Bridgend, automatic transmissions in Bordeaux, and castings in Leamington.

The Company also produces agricultural tractors (at Antwerp and Basildon) and a range of commercial vehicles (at Langley and Woolwich).

The UK company has its administrative headquarters at Warley, near Brentwood in Essex. This also serves as the headquarters of Ford Europe.

Appendix 2

A Bibliographic Note

Since 1973 a number of important publications have been produced which relate to both Ford and the changing circumstances of the British motor industry. In this regard the British socialist and trade union movement has made an important contribution. Counter Information Services has brought out two 'anti-Reports' on the motor industry: *British Leyland: The Beginning of the End?* and *Ford*, both available from 9 Poland Street, London WI. In London the *Red Notes* group has brought out two lengthy documentary pamphlets: *Workers' Struggle and the Development of Ford in Britain*, and *Fighting the Layoffs at Ford*. Both available from Box 15, 2a St Paul's Road, London NI. The 'Ford Workers Group' ('The Combine') produces a regular bulletin on the situation at Ford and this can be obtained from Room 265, 27 Clerkenwell Close, London ECI. The Institute of Workers' Control conducted its own inquiry into the motor industry, *A Workers' Enquiry into the Motor Industry*, published in 1978 by the Conference of Socialist Economists and available from them at: 55 Mount Pleasant, London WCIX OAE. The Labour Research Department has brought out a series of reports on the motor industry, most recently: *Motors – End of the Road for Jobs*, available from LRD Publications Ltd, 78 Blackfriars Road, London SEI 8HF. The trade union AUEW (TASS) has brought out two reports: *A Policy for the British Motor Industry* (1976) and *Merseyside Motor Industry: End of an Era?* This second publication was helped by the Merseyside Socialist Research Group who also published *Merseyside in Crisis* (1980) available from 23 Glover Street, Birkenhead, Merseyside.

In contrast with an industry like mining, the motor industry suffers in the number of detailed accounts based upon the experiences and activities of its workers. The tape-recorded account of Arthur Excell's experiences at Cowley (*The Politics of the Production Line*, available from History Workshop Journal, PO Box 69, Oxford, OX2 7XA) is hopefully the beginning of a series of such accounts and the prospect of a 'workers' history' of the British motor industry. The diary of the 1978 strike kept by John Bohana (see p. 371) and the documentation by Les Moore of the Disciplinary Code in practice (p. 361–2) are invaluable accounts. Others like them should be encouraged and published. Other "insider accounts' have appeared in print. Journalist Edward Seidler produced a blow by blow account of the decisions which led up to the launching of the Fiesta: *Let's Call it Fiesta: The Autobiography of Ford's Operation Bobcat*, Patrick Stephens, 1976. Elsewhere, ex-Warley manager, Sander Meredeen, and ex-Dagenham convener, Henry Friedman, offer their revealing interpretations of the sewing machinists strike and the industrial relations system at Ford, *The Dynamics of Industrial Conflict*, Croom Helm, 1980.

Acknowledgements

For permission to use copyright material, acknowledgement is made to the following:

For extracts from *Ford: Decline and Rebirth* 1933–1962 by Allan Nevins and Frank F. Hill to Charles Scribner's Sons, copyright 1962, 1963 Columbia University; for the extract from 'Ford's Partner' from *Business Week* to McGraw-Hill Book Co.; for the extract from *Labour Relations in the Motor Industry* by H. A. Turner, G. Clack and T. G. Roberts to George Allen & Unwin Ltd.

Subject Index

Name Index

MORE ABOUT PENGUINS, PELICANS
AND PUFFINS

For further information about books available from Penguins please write to Dept EP, Penguin Books Ltd, Harmondsworth, Middlesex UB7 0DA.

In the U.S.A.: For a complete list of books available from Penguins in the United States write to Dept DG, Penguin Books, 299 Murray Hill Parkway, East Rutherford, New Jersey 07073.

In Canada: For a complete list of books available from Penguins in Canada write to Penguin Books Canada Ltd, 2801 John Street, Markham, Ontario L3R 1B4.

In Australia: For a complete list of books available from Penguins in Australia write to the Marketing Department, Penguin Books Australia Ltd, P.O. Box 257, Ringwood, Victoria 3134.

In New Zealand: For a complete list of books available from Penguins in New Zealand write to the Marketing Department, Penguin Books (N.Z.) Ltd, Private Bag, Takapuna, Auckland 9.

In India: For a complete list of books available from Penguins in India write to Penguin Overseas Ltd, 706 Eros Apartments, 56 Nehru Place, New Delhi 110019.

THE IMPOVERISHMENT OF BRITAIN
Peter Townsend

Since the early post-war years social conditions in Britain have deteriorated and poverty is increasing on a mass scale. This is the central argument of Peter Townsend's controversial book and is, he believes, the central problem of domestic politics.

The author begins by tracing the development of the problem – the growth of unemployment, the deprivation of racial minorities, unequal health provision and the erosion of public services. Next, he considers some of the major causes – the growth of multi-national corporations and international finance, monetarism and anti-social planning of the economy, authoritarian management of the state and expanding arms expenditure.

From this powerful analysis, he draws out the kind of policies which are required to create a radically alternative Britain.

TOWARDS 2000
Raymond Williams

What sort of world will we have in 2000 A.D.?

Mass unemployment and nuclear war are two of the crises which may darken an uncertain future. Here, the radical thinker Raymond Williams, examines our current predicament and points the way forward. Taking his essay on Britain in the sixties as a starting point, Williams reassesses and extends the arguments of *The Long Revolution* (a book which set the guidelines for the socialist debate). In discussing the major changes within British society, he raises proposals for fresh political structures which take account of true equality and revitalized socialism.

'The nearest thing the British New Left has to a sage' – *Observer*

A CHOICE OF
PELICANS AND PEREGRINES

☐ *A Radical Reader* **Christopher Hampton** £9.95

With extracts from the writings of Wycliff, Shakespeare, Bacon, Milton, Swift, Blake, Byron, Dickens and Marx, among many others, this major new anthology spans five hundred years of radical protest from the Peasants' Revolt to the First World War.

☐ *Computer Power and Human Reason*
Joseph Weizenbaum £2.95

Internationally acclaimed by scientists and humanists alike: 'This is the best book I have read on the impact of computers on society, and on technology and on man's image of himself' – *Psychology Today*

☐ *Astrology* **H. J. Eysenck and D. K. B. Nias** £2.50

Is astrology science or superstition? Two well-known analytical psychologists discuss the latest research and findings in a book that – for adherents of either side – will be an adventure.

☐ *The Germans* **Gordon A. Craig** £2.95

'This elegant and enticing work . . . dwells not on the familiar facts of German history but on some often neglected fundamental facets of German life and culture' – *The New York Times Book Review*

☐ *Mind in Science* **Richard L. Gregory** £7.95

Integrating and discussing ancient myth and philosophy, the rise of Western science, the developments of psychology and technology, and recent scientific discoveries, Gregory illuminates the nature of Mind. 'Few recent books can rival . . . its scope or its engaging enthusiasm' – *The Times Literary Supplement*

☐ *Who Cares about English Usage?* **David Crystal** £1.95

Including cartoons and quizzes to stimulate the mind, this is a highly entertaining guide to English usage by David Crystal, deviser of the popular Radio 4 programme, *Speak Out*.

A CHOICE OF
PELICANS AND PEREGRINES

☐ **Know Your Own Mind**
   James Green and David Lewis   £1.95

How do you *know* if you have a talent for solving problems, or creative work, or learning languages . . . ? This book contains nine assessments to help you build your own profile, discover your potential – and act on it.

☐ **The Mathematical Experience**
   Philip J. Davis and Reuben Hersh   £6.95

Not since *Gödel, Escher, Bach* has such an entertaining book been written on the relationship of mathematics to the arts and sciences. 'It deserves to be read by everyone . . . an instant classic' – *New Scientist*

☐ **The Tangled Wing** **Melvin Konner**   £4.95

How far are our emotions and actions affected by our biology? This new study has been acclaimed by *The Times Higher Education Supplement* as 'a pleasure to read . . . an outstanding work of scholarship'.

☐ **The World Turned Upside Down** **Christopher Hill**   £4.50

A portrait of radical groups and ideas during the English Revolution. 'Christopher Hill has that supreme gift of being able to show us the seventeenth-century world from the inside' – Arthur Marwick in *New Society*

☐ **Exploring the Earth and the Cosmos**
   Isaac Asimov   £3.95

From dinosaurs to black holes and space probes, this exhilarating book (and superb reference-source) guides us through the facts, figures, people and discoveries that have shaped our changing view of the earth and the cosmos.

☐ **Hen's Teeth and Horse's Toes**
   Stephen Jay Gould   £3.95

Essays on natural history by the author of *Ever Since Darwin*. 'He has the rare gift of communicating excitement . . . he challenges one furiously to think' – *Nature*

A CHOICE OF
PELICANS AND PEREGRINES